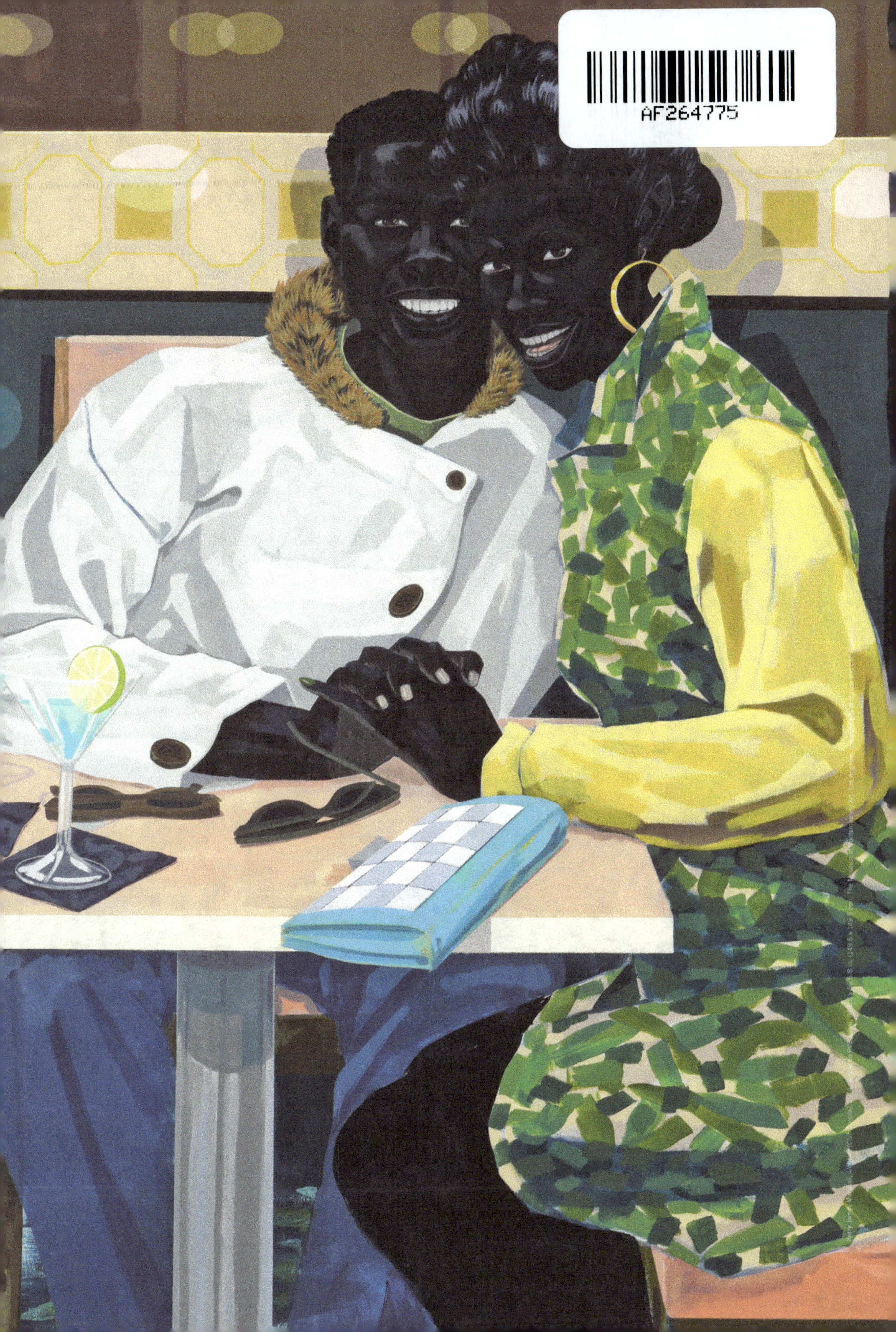
AF264775

AW 17/18

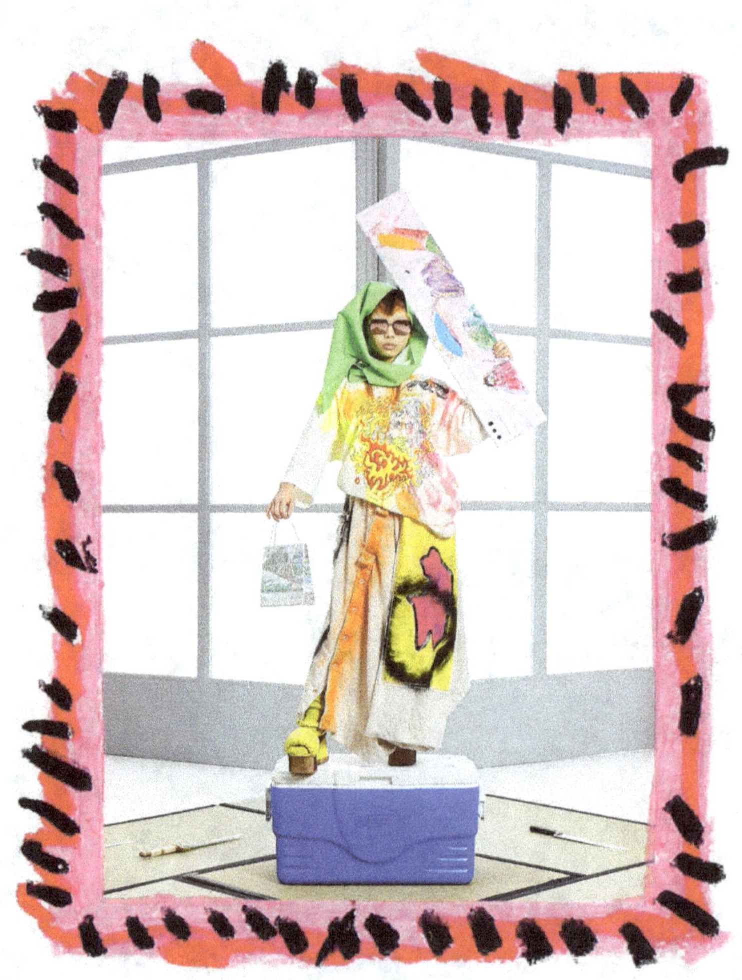

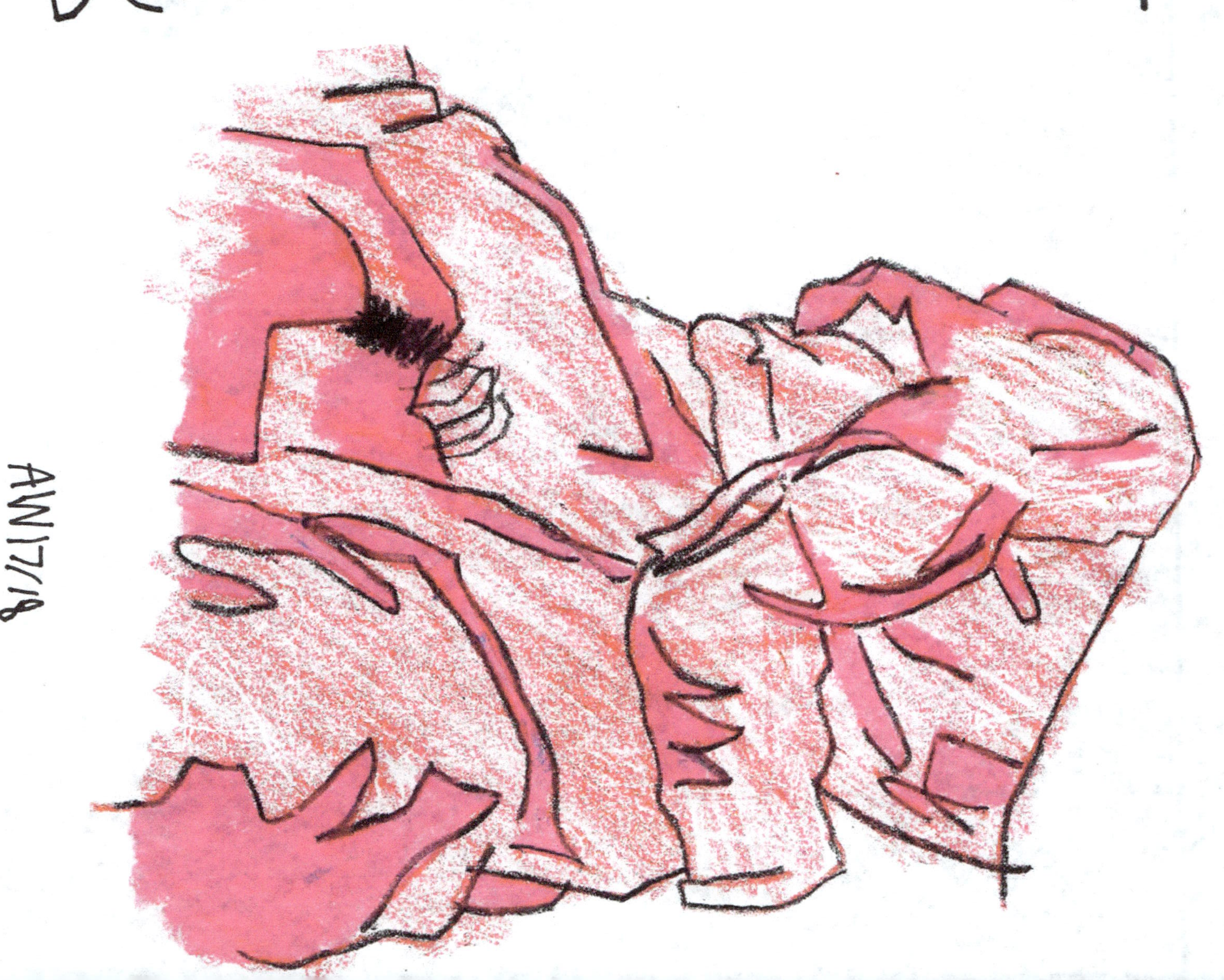
AW17/18

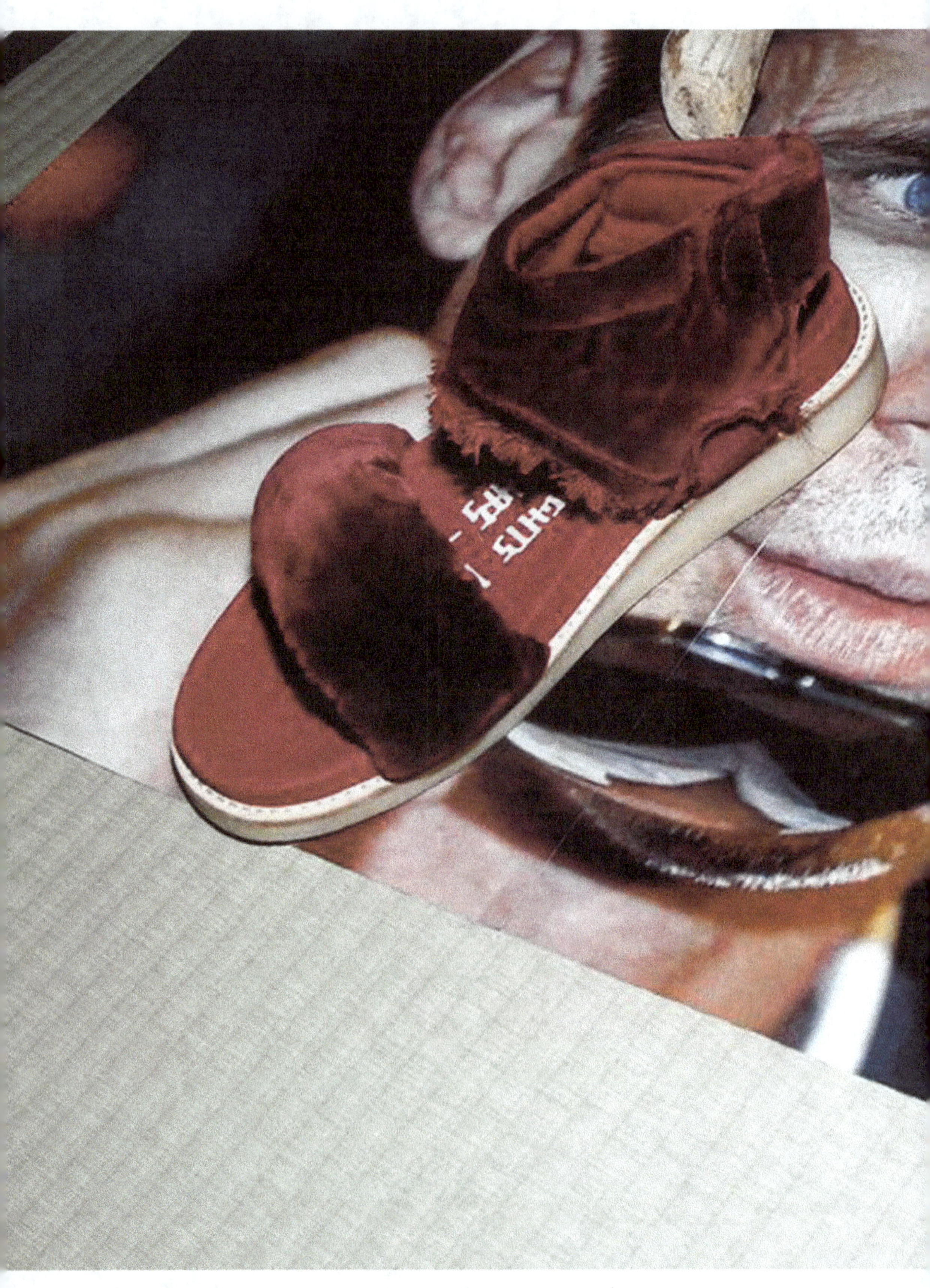

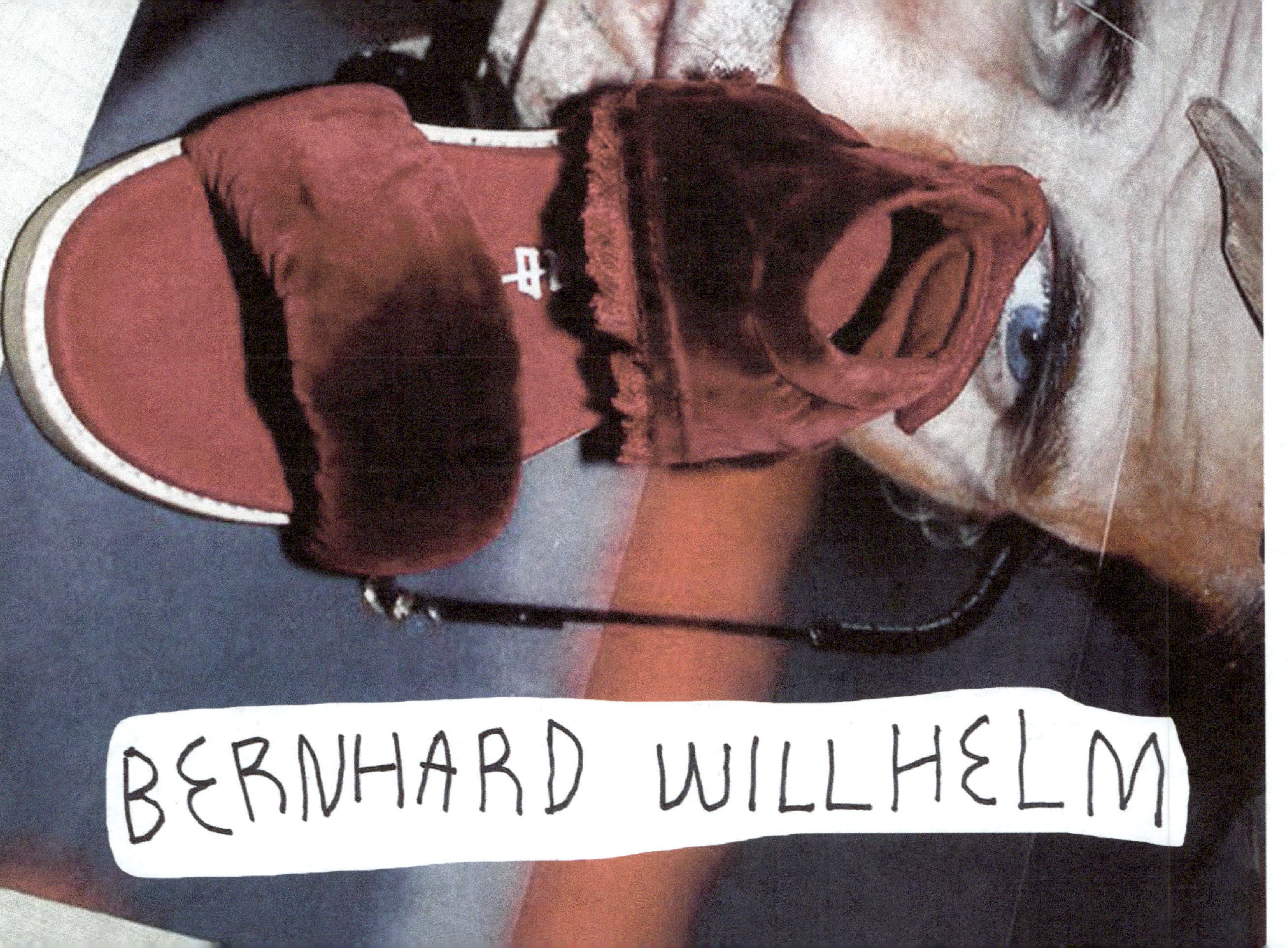
BERNHARD WILLHELM

ZANEROBE
RISE COLLECTION ZANEROBE.COM
register for your online code: znrb.co/znrbissue

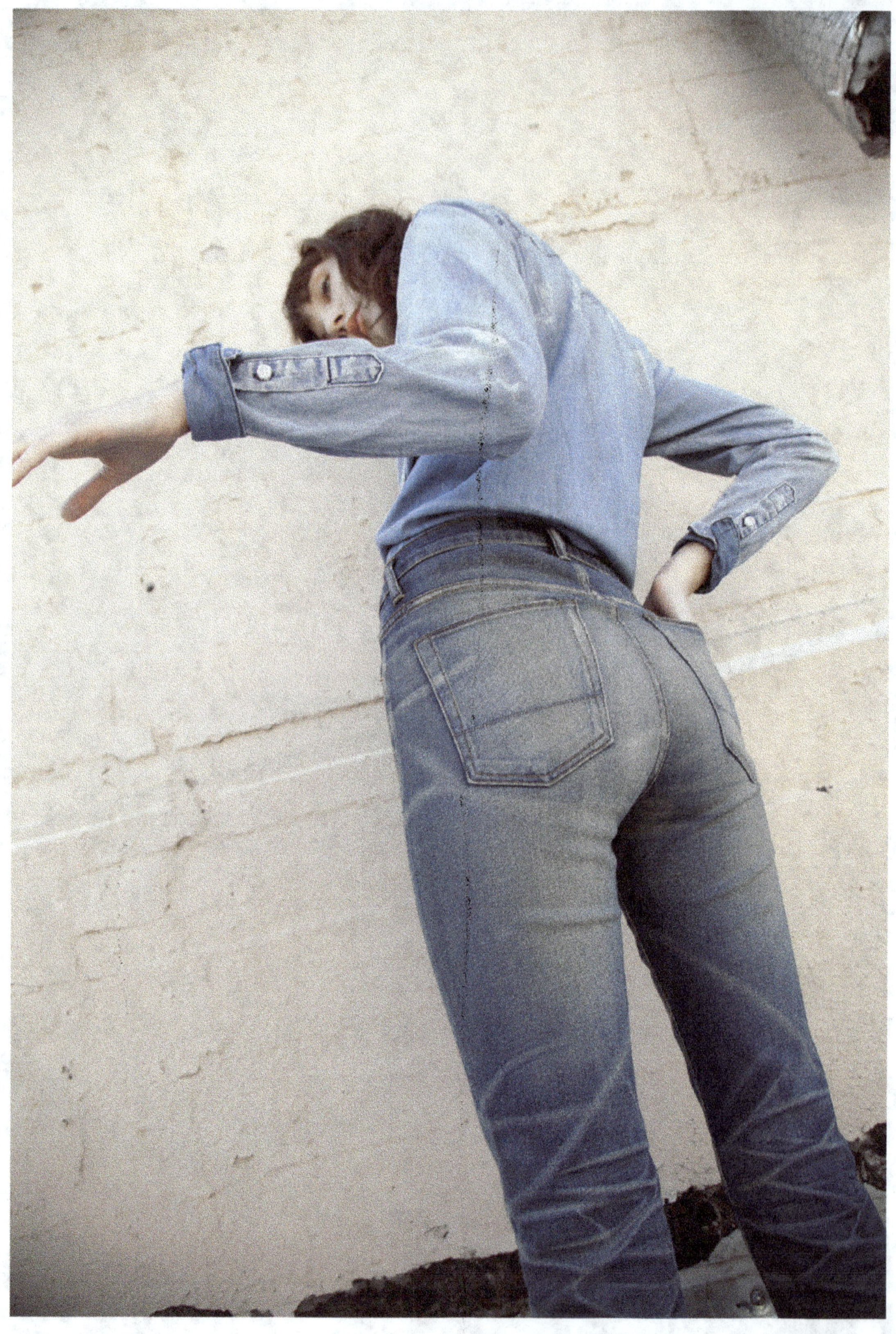

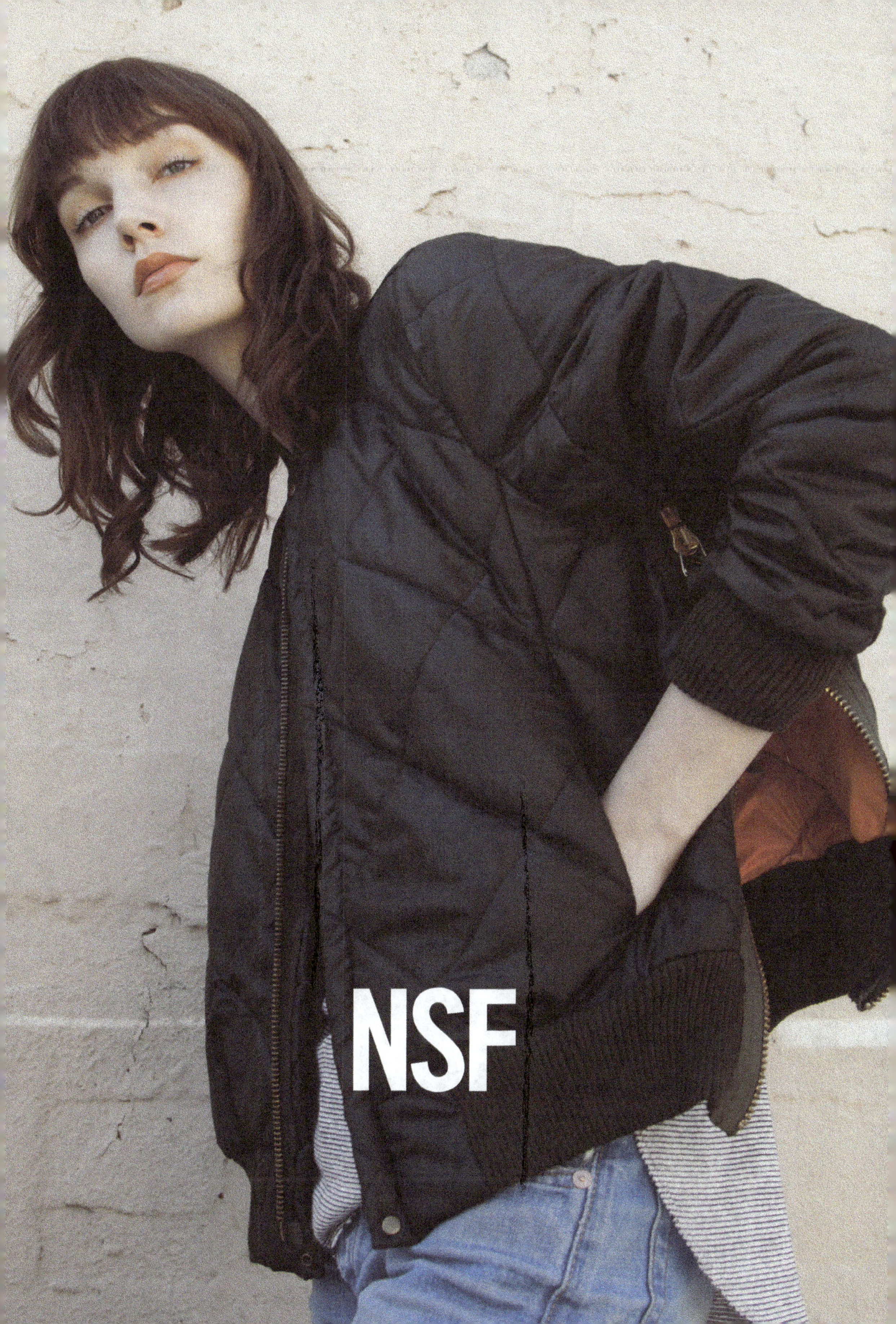

NSF

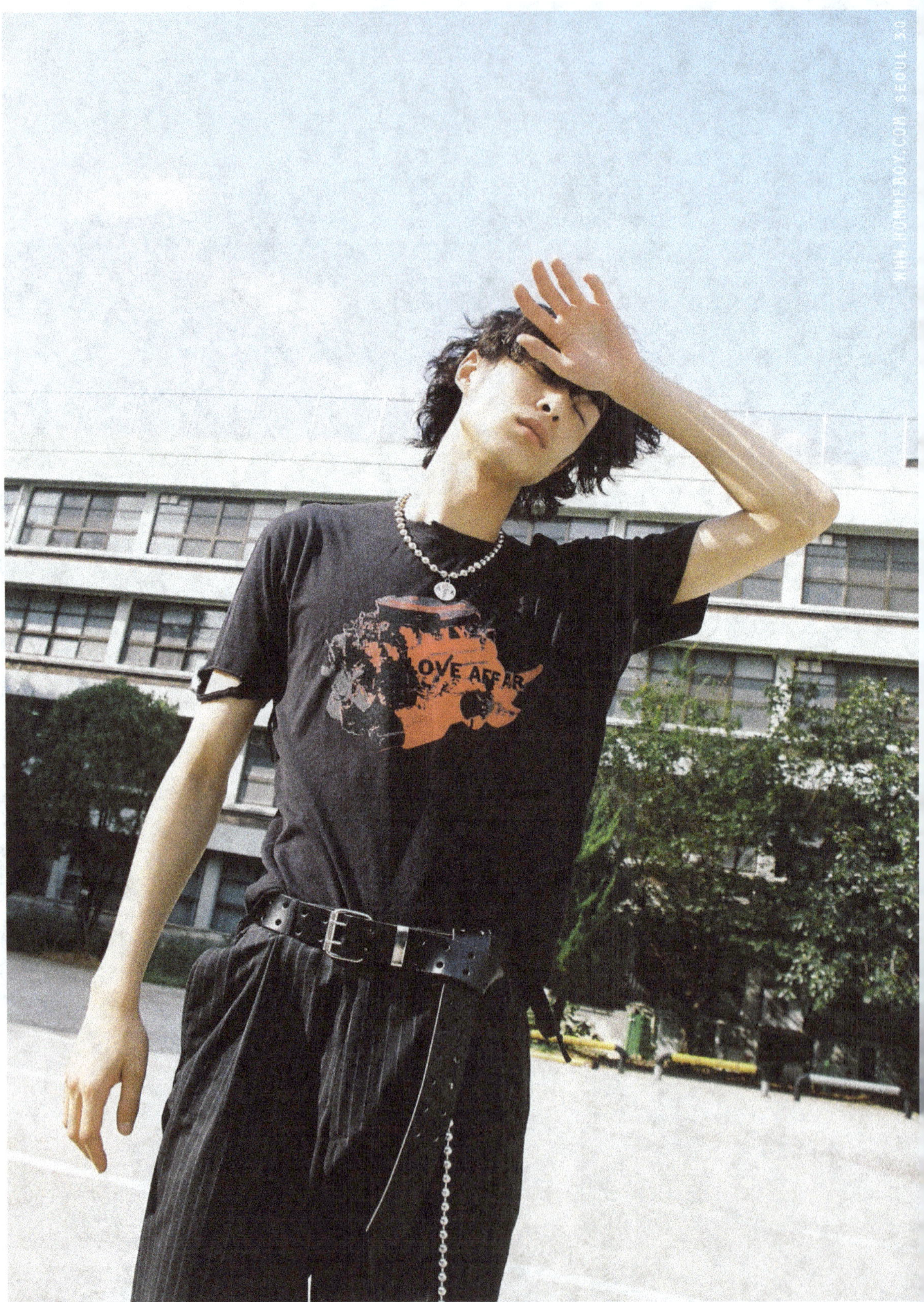

WWW.HOMME-BOY.COM SEOUL 3.0
LOVE AFFAIR

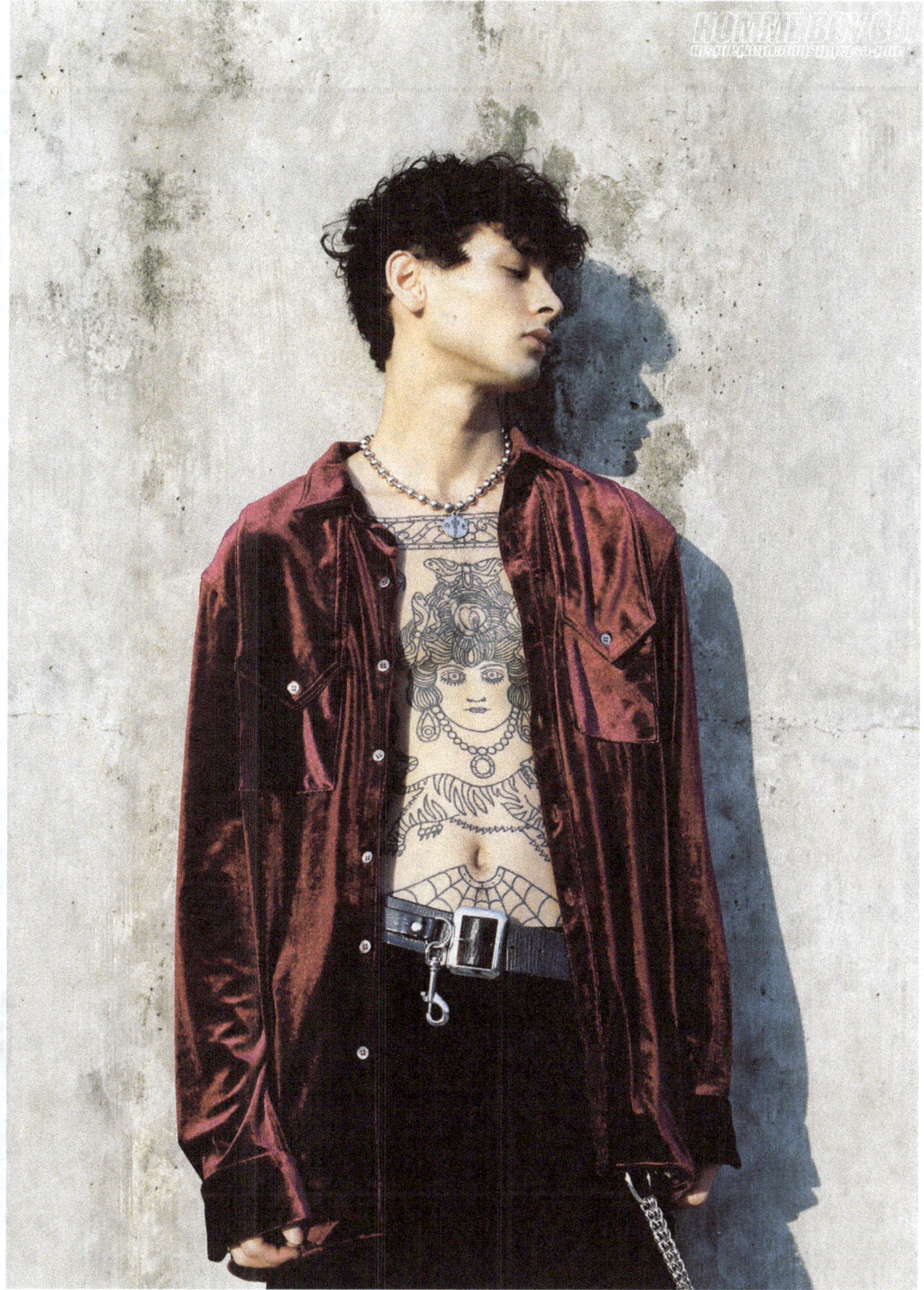
HOMMEBOY CO.

R.SWIADER

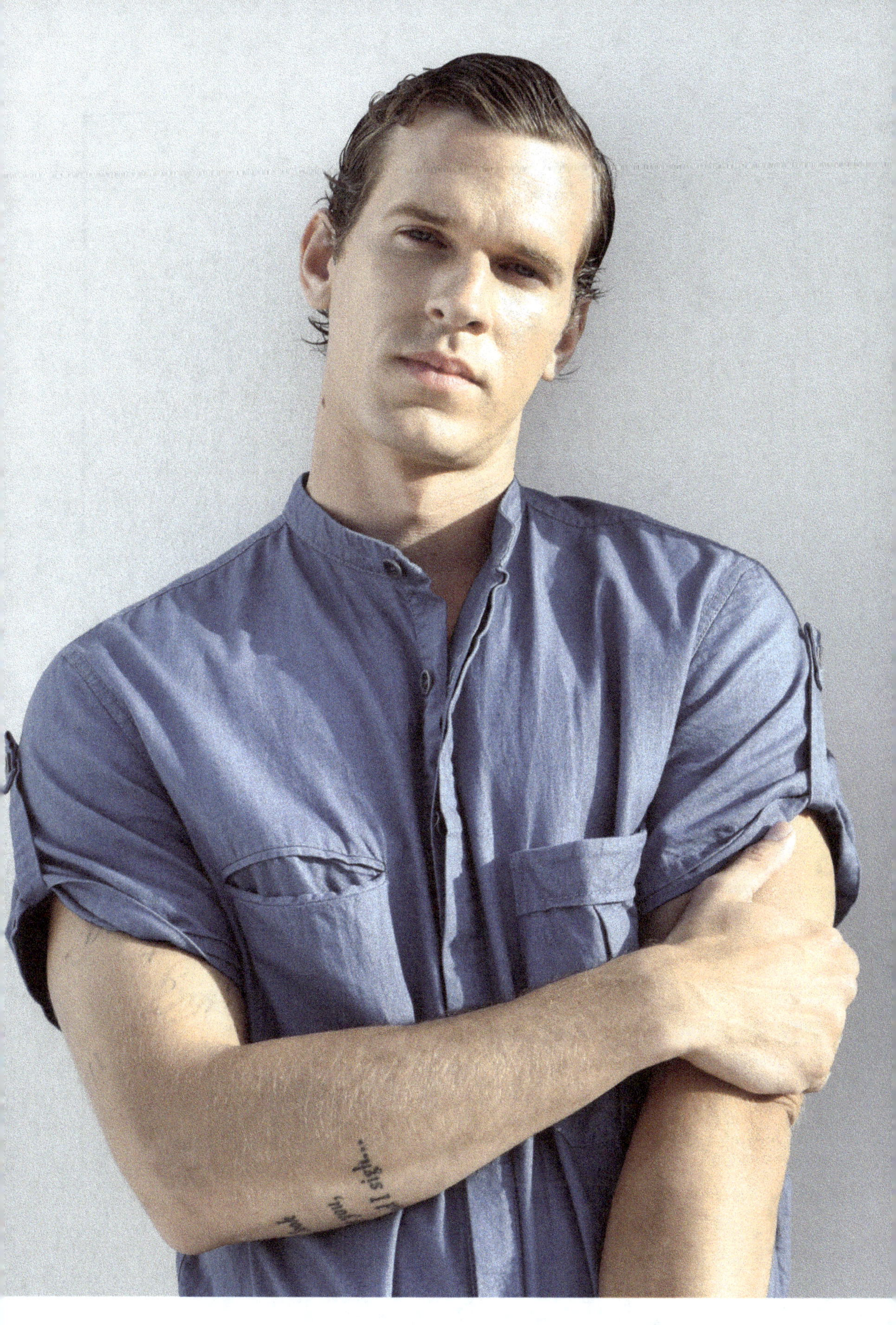

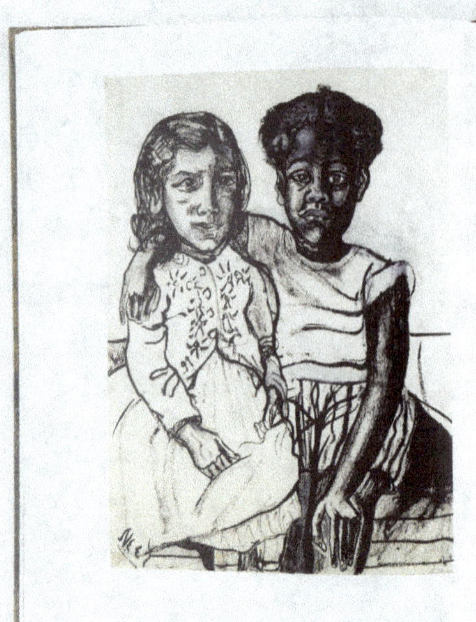

ALICE NEEL, UPTOWN

Book by

Hilton Als

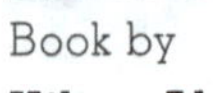

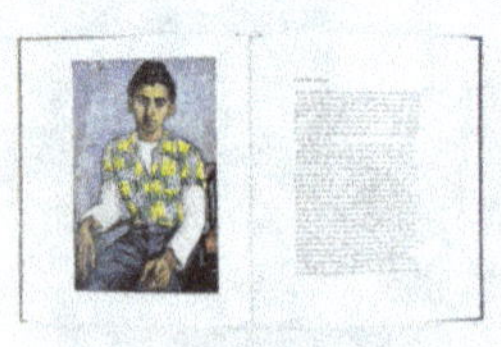

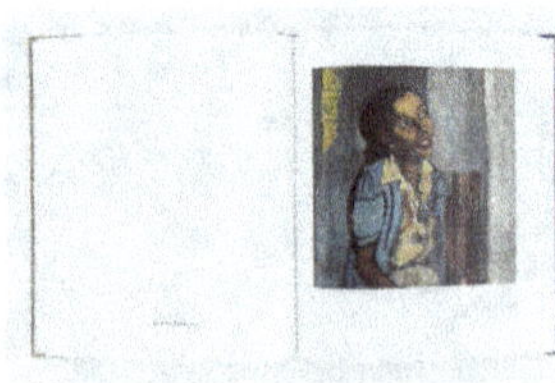

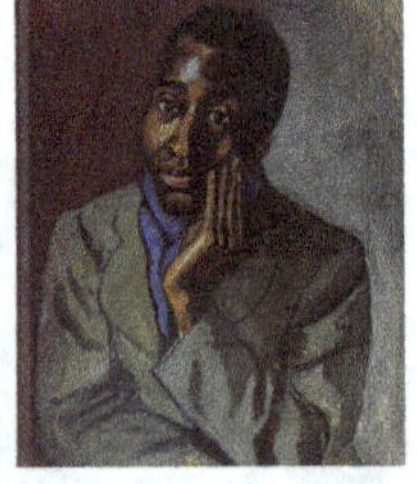

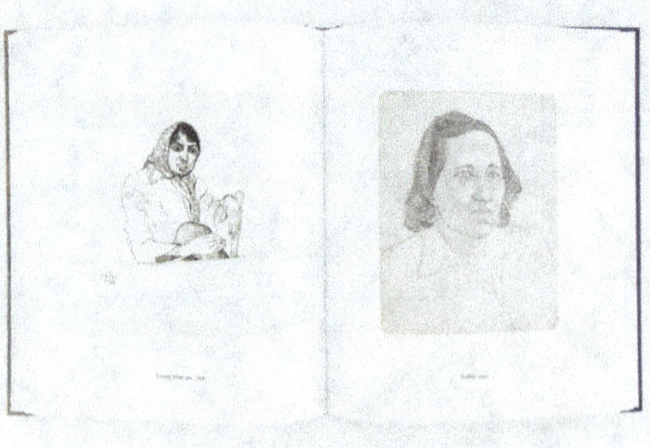

Fascinated by the diversity of mid-20th-century New York, renowned painter Alice Neels created portraits of people from all walks of life, including among her subjects a great number of African Americans, Latinos, Asians and other persons of color too often neglected in Western art. These portraits were candid, intimate, often humorous and by nature engaging with the political and social climate of her times. When author Hilton Als set out to gather Neel's most poignant portraits of American minorities in his book *Alice Neel, Uptown*, it was in his words "an attempt to honor not only what Neel saw, but the generosity of her seeing." *Alice Neel, Uptown* features both well-known figures such as playwright, actress and author Alice Childress; sociologist Horace R. Clayton Jr.; and community activist Mercedes Arroyo, as well as anonymous individuals like children, families, a taxi driver, a ballet dancer, a nurse and a boy who ran errands for Neels. Als pairs each portrait with a history of its sitter, as well as his own extensive insight into Neels' work. (David Zwirner Books)

LACAUSA
LACAUSACLOTHING.COM

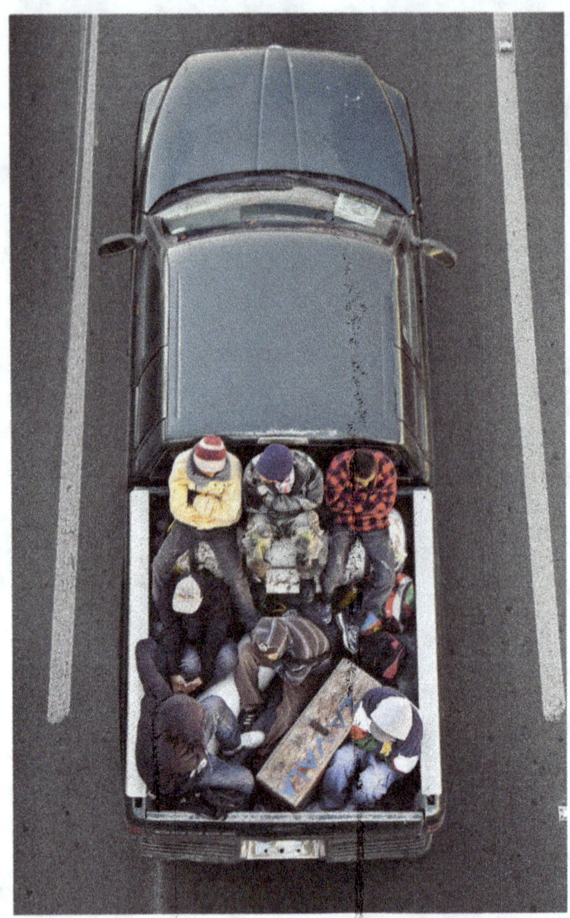

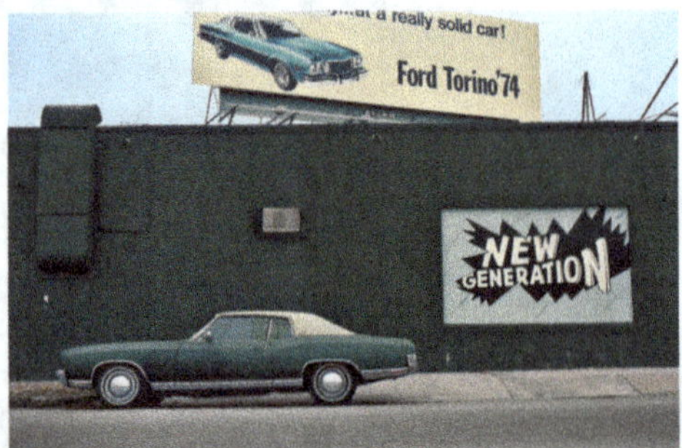

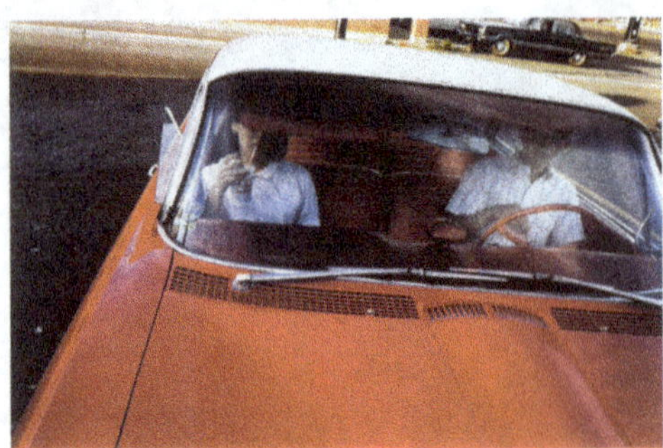

LEFT - Alejandro Cartagena, *Car Poolers #12*, The Carpoolers series, 2011-2012; **ABOVE** - William Eggleston, *Untitled*, *Los Alamos* Series, 1965-1974

AUTO-PHOTO: CARS & PHOTOGRAPHY, 1900 TO NOW

Book by

Xavier Barral

In a collection of over 500 works by 100 historical and contemporary artists, *Auto-Photo: Cars and Photography, 1900 to Now* documents the ongoing fascination of photographers with the form, impact and meaning surrounding the automobile. The invention of the automobile altered our landscapes, expanded our geographical horizons and drastically modified our appreciations of space and time. As well as exploring these paradigm shifts, photographers captured the automobile's formal qualities, function and design, and the geometrics of city roads and rural highways. Contributors and renowned photographers include Robert Adams, Brassaï, Langdon Clay, Robert Doisneau, William Eggleston, Walker Evans, Robert Frank, Lee Friedlander, Anthony Hernandez, Joel Meyerowitz, Daido Moriyama, Catherine Opie, Martin Parr, Ed Ruscha, Malick Sidibé and Stephen Shore. Other projects in *Auto Photo* shed fresh perspective on the automobile, such as a series of car models created by Alain Bublex for the Foundation Cartier show, as well as a comparative history of auto design and photography, scholarly essays and artist quotes. (Fondation Cartier Pour L'Art Contemporain/ Editions Xavier Barral)

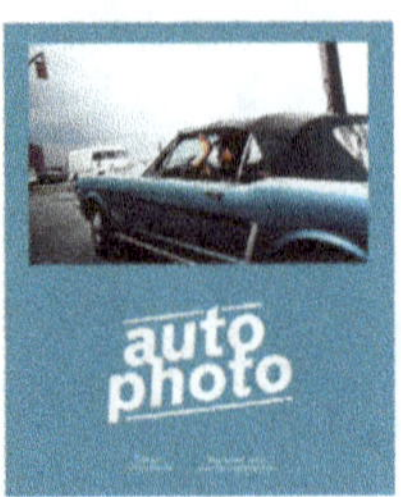

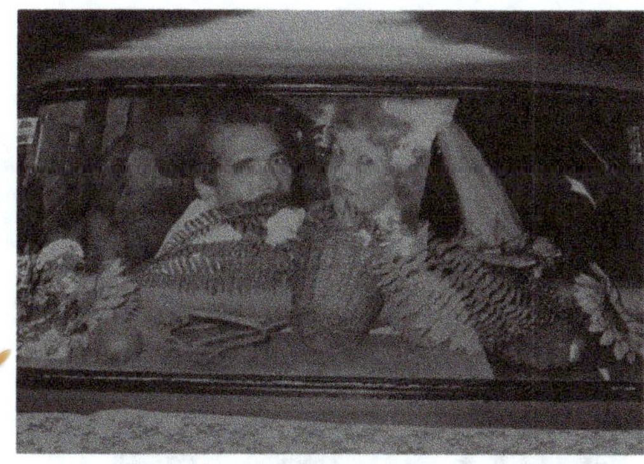
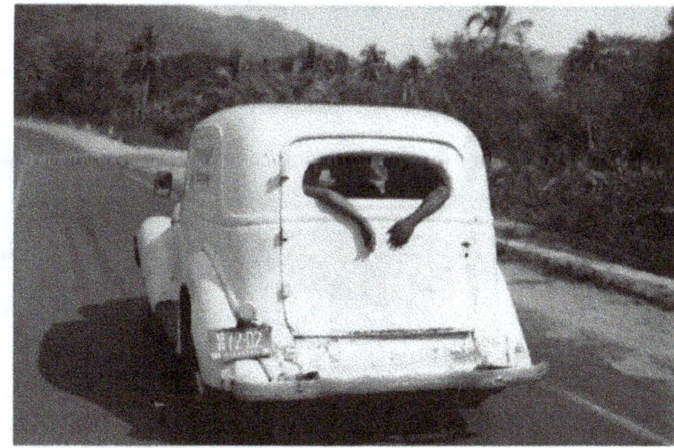

LEFT - Rosângela Rennó, *Groupe 1, Cerimônia do Adeus* series *[Farewell Ceremony]*, 1997-2003;
RIGHT - Bernard Plossu, *On the Acapulco Road, Mexico, Le Voyage Mexicain* series, 1966

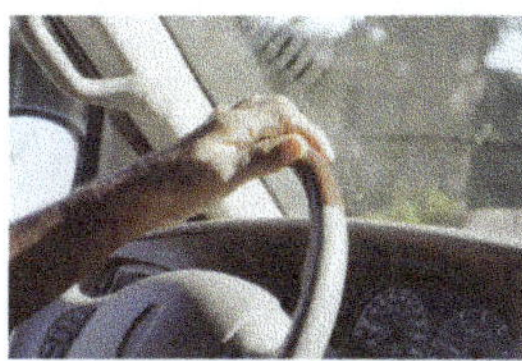
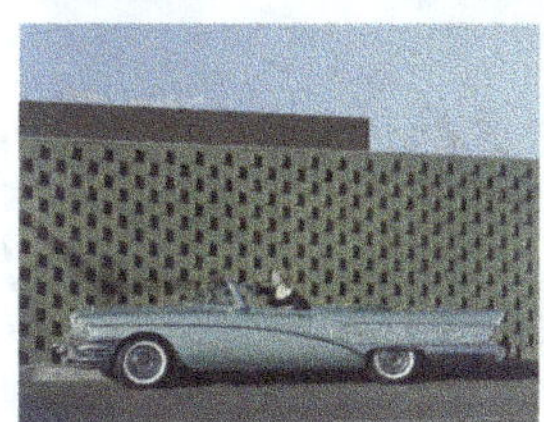
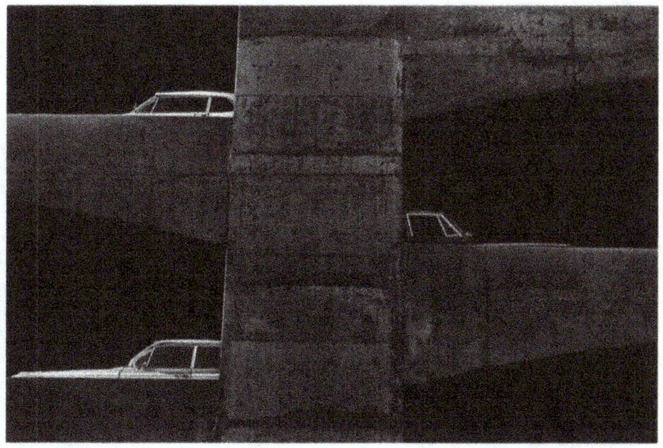

CLOCKWISE FROM TOP LEFT - Juergen Teller, *OJ Simpson n°5*, 2005; Ray Metzker, *Philadelphia*, 1963;
Luciano Rigolini, *Tribute to Giorgio de Chirico*, 2017, appropriation (unknown photographer, 1958)

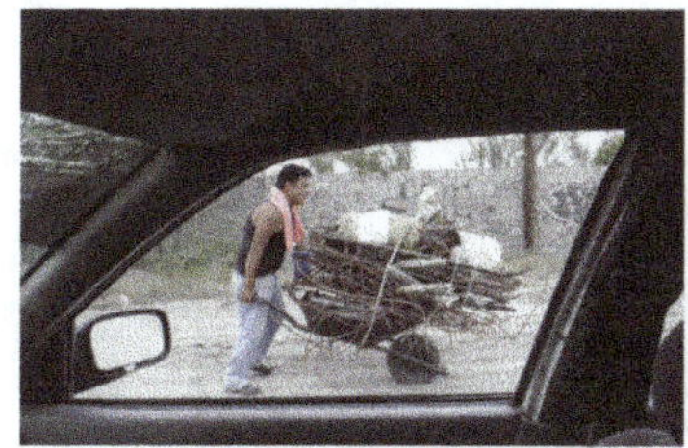
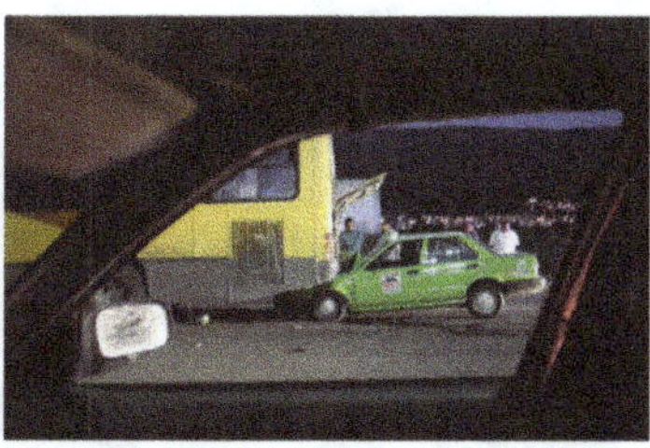
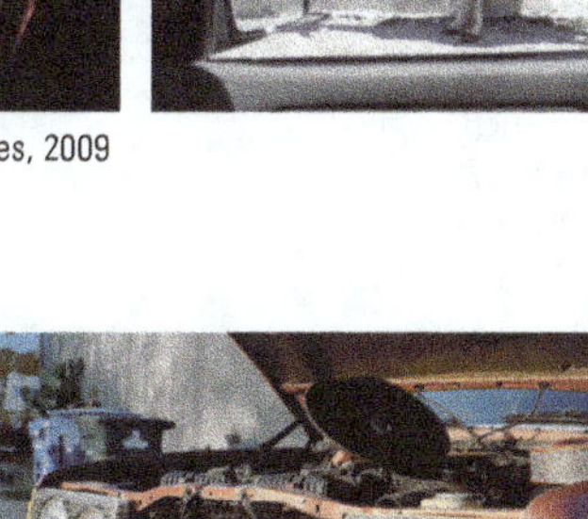

Óscar Fernando Gómez, *Windows* series, 2009

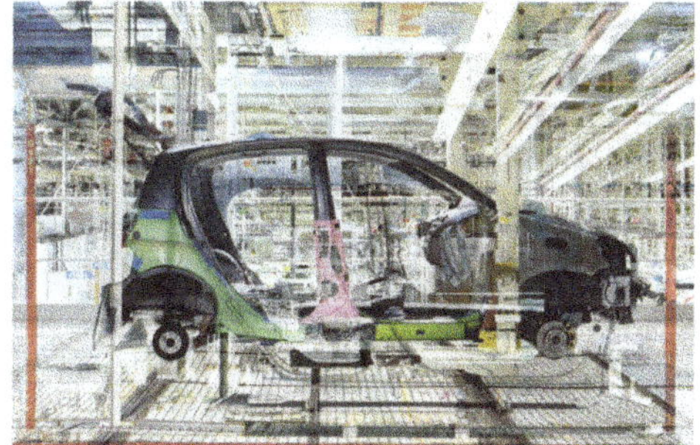
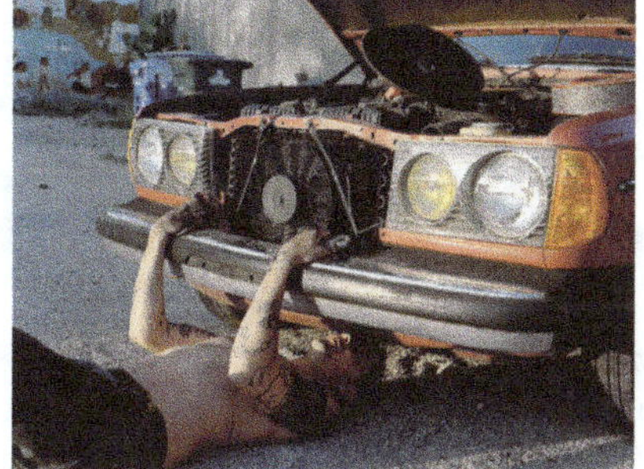

LEFT - Stéphane Couturier, *Toyota n°8, Melting Point* series, 2005; RIGHT - Justine Kurland, *280 Coup*, 2012

LIKE ART

Book by
Glenn O'Brien

"'Like Art' was the title of my *Artforum* column that ran from 1985 to 1990, but it was also my philosophy of advertising. Advertising was like art, and more and more art was like advertising. Ideally the only difference would be the logo. Advertising could take up the former causes of art—philosophy, beauty, mystery, empire. We were clearly living in a time of extremist hypocrisy where various forms of creative work descried one another. Price-gouging painters looked down on lowly craftsmen and entertainment journeymen. Millionaire rock stars adopted a quasi-communist stance, emphasizing the anti-commercial aspect of their work."— Glenn O'Brien

Influential writer, editor and creative director Glenn O'Brien built his life on a shrewd understanding of art as well as advertising. Beginning with his appointment by Andy Warhol as editor of *Interview*, O'Brien went on to become a social fixture in downtown Manhattan for the remainder of his life, wearing many hats including that of his *Artforum* column on advertising, which ran from 1984-90. Here, O'Brien covered a broad range of topics with perceptive gusto, including advertising in Japan, the Buy American campaign, Burger King, tobacco and alcohol ads, condoms, Max Headroom, computer games, the interplay of advertising and art, etc. Published just one month after his death, O'Brien's book *Like Art* compiles all of his *Artforum* articles, as well as a preface by Jeffrey Deitch, an introduction by O'Brien himself and previously unpublished dialogue on consumer culture. (Karma)

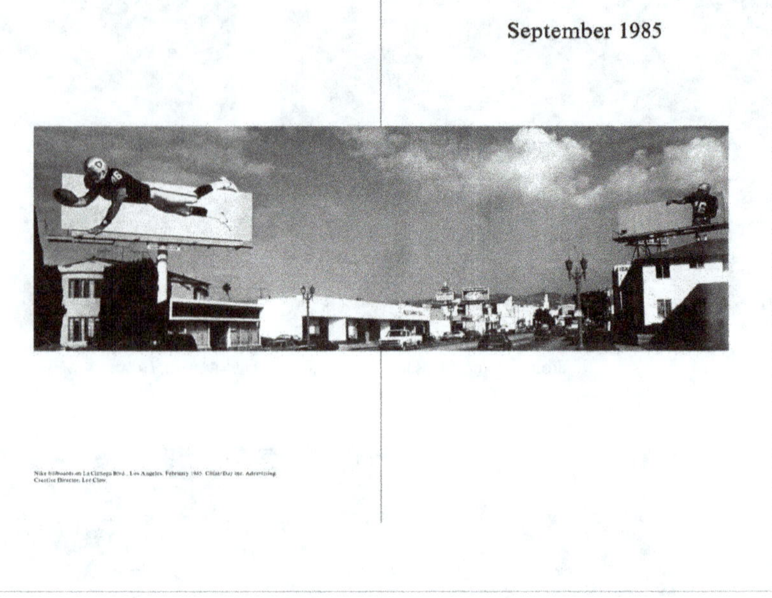

Nike billboards on La Cienega Blvd., Los Angeles, February 1985. Chiat/Day Inc. Advertising. Creative Director, Lee Clow.

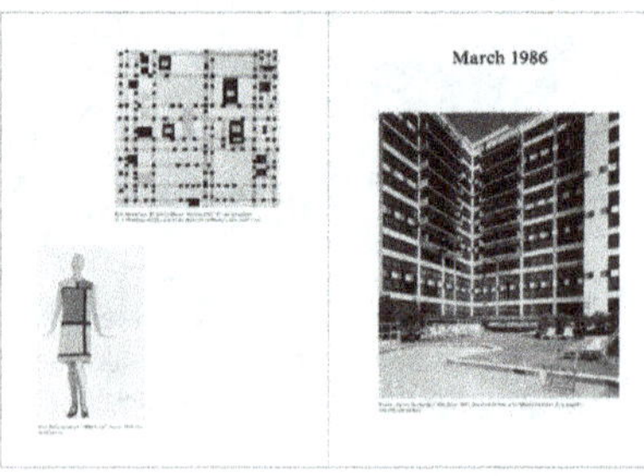

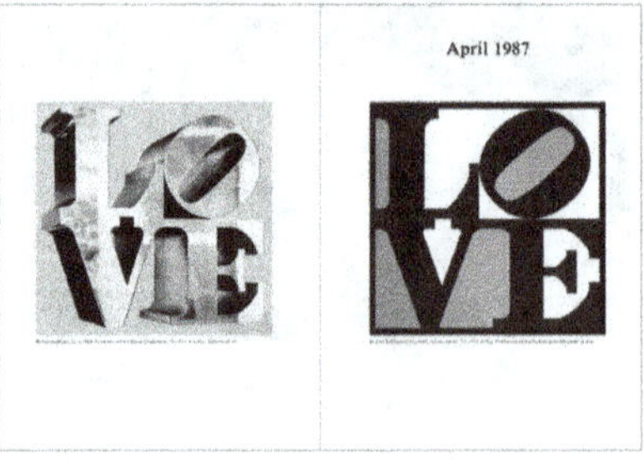

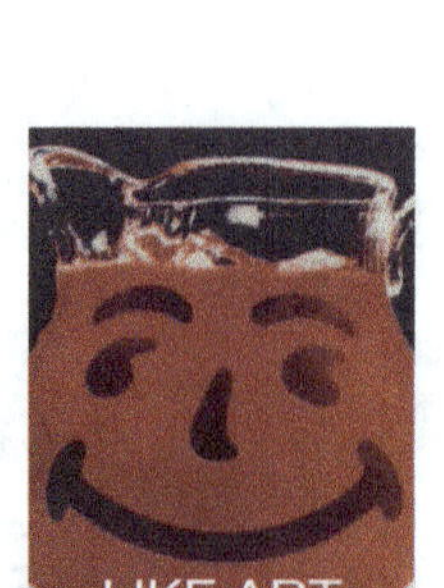

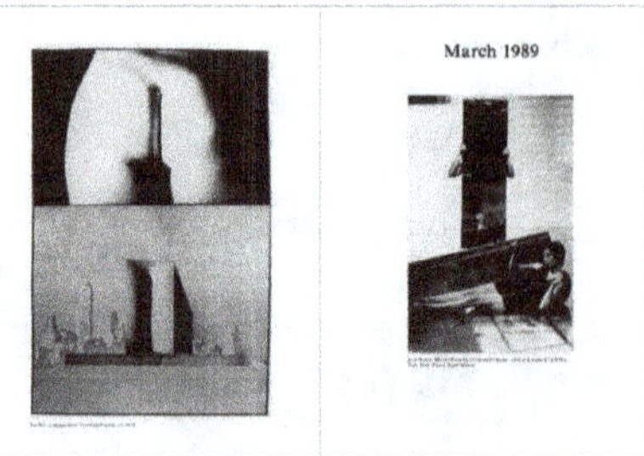

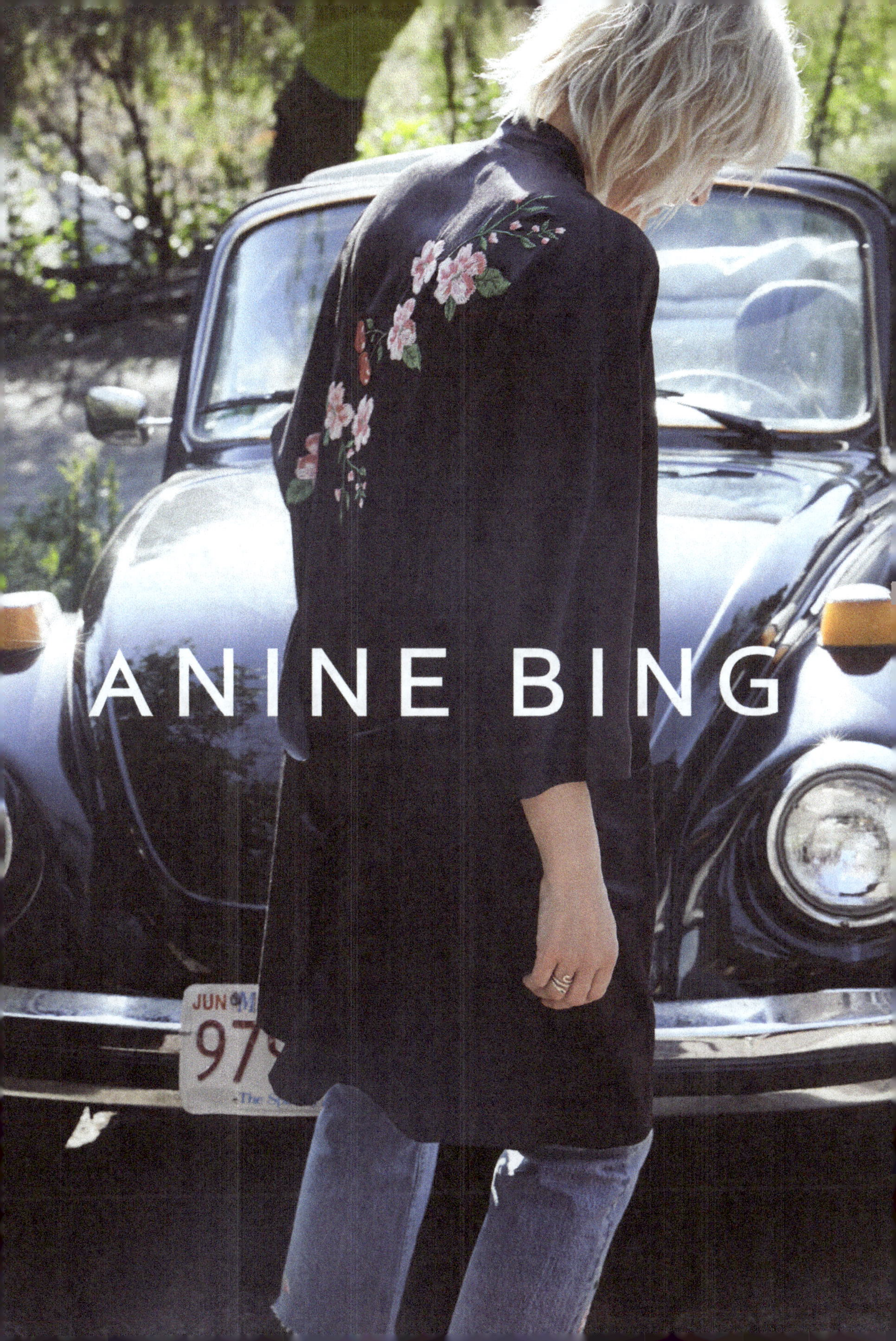
ANINE BING

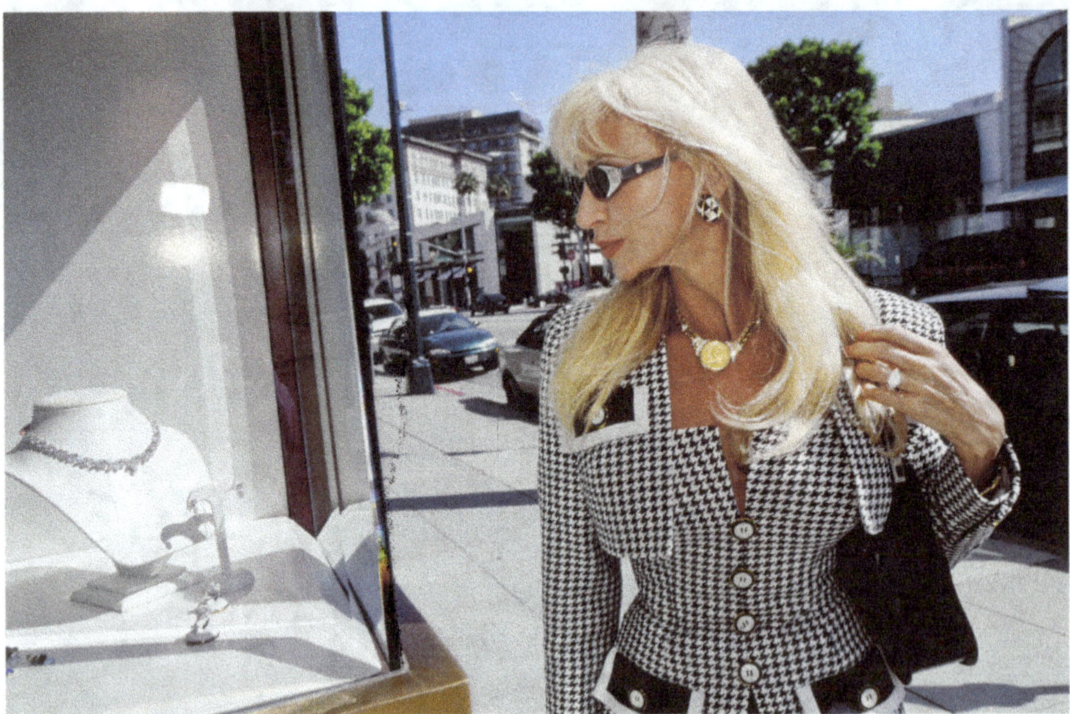

CLOCKWISE FROM ABOVE - A woman browses on Rodeo Drive, Beverly Hills, 2000. Outside of New York City, Rodeo Drive is the highest-rent commercial district in the United States; Suzanne Rogers, 40, in her home in Toronto, 2010. Rogers's style stems from a childhood fascination with the Edwardian-era candy-factory heiress Truly Scrumptious from the film "Chitty Chitty Bang Bang," whom she considers "the epitome of elegance"; Lil Jon, 33, sporting a diamond and platinum grill that reportedly cost $50,000, at the 2004 Soul Train Awards, Los Angeles.

GENERATION WEALTH

Book by
Lauren Greenfield

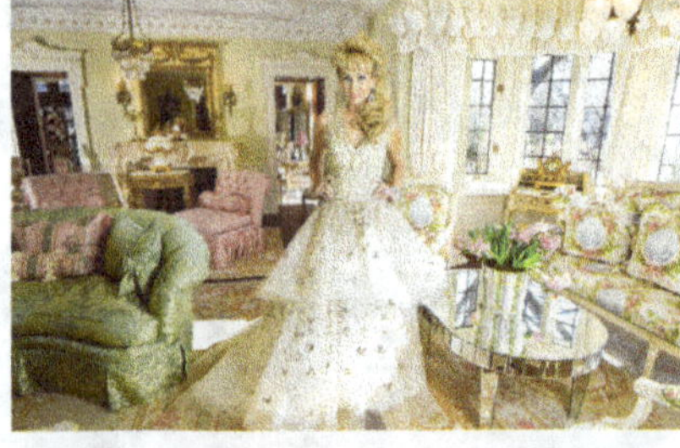

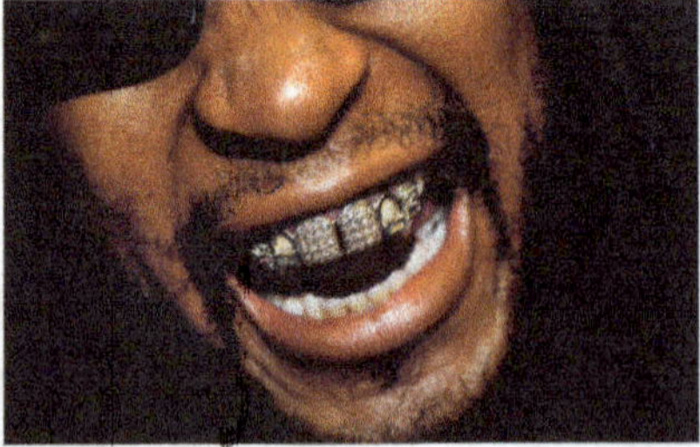

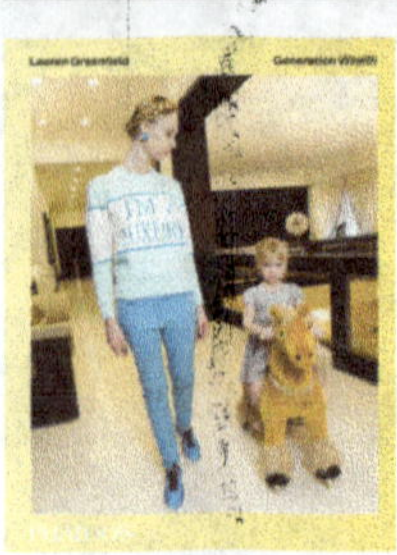

Generation Wealth, the most recent photobook from Emmy Award-winning filmmaker and photographer Lauren Greenfield, is not about actual wealth but the illusion of it. A renowned chronicler of consumerism and cultures, Greenfield examines the perception of wealth over the last 25 years as a consequence of a global boom-and-bust economy as well as pervasive pop-culture influences. Taken in major consumer hubs such as Los Angeles, Moscow, Dubai and China, Greenfield's photographs document how consumers attempt to bridge the gap between what they want and what they can actually afford, in an attempt to simulate the life they desire. "The work is really about aspiring to wealth and the influence of affluence and about our values more than what we actually have," says Greenfield. *Generation Wealth* archives Greenfield's third collaboration with the Annenberg Space for Photography, an exhibit featuring 195 photographs and 42 interviews as well as multimedia projections and short films. (Phaidon)

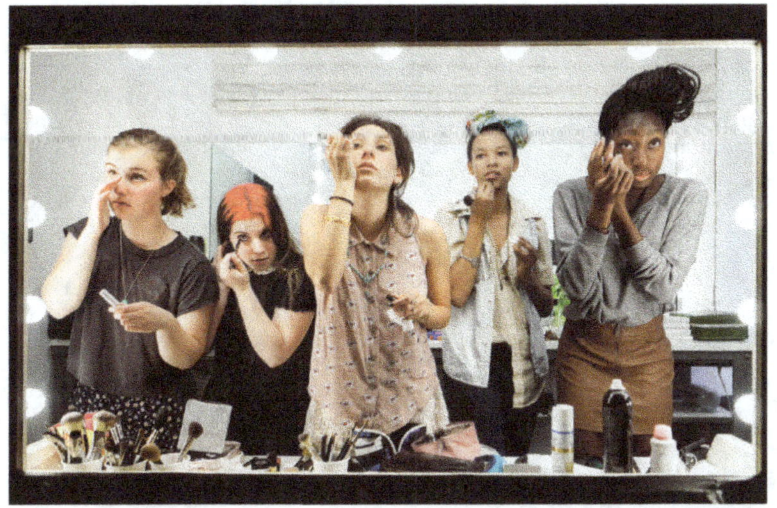

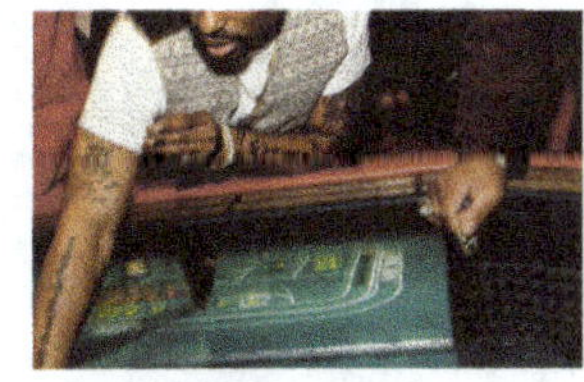

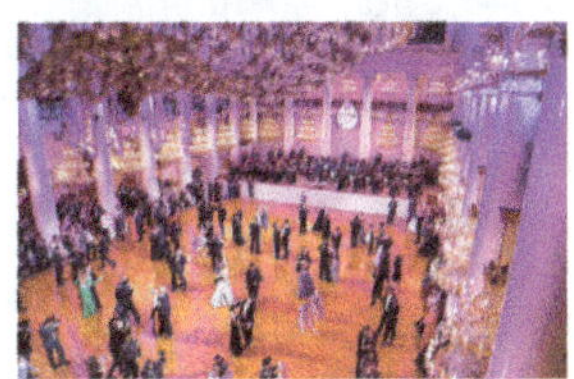

CLOCKWISE FROM ABOVE - High school seniors (from left) Lili, 17, Nicole, 18, Lauren, 18, Luna, 18, and Sam, 17, put on their makeup in front of a two-way mirror for the Greenfield's "Beauty CUL-Ture" documentary, Los Angeles, 2011; Tupac plays craps in Las Vegas, losing $10,000 in minutes, Luxor Hotel, 1995; A choreographed waltz, the main event at Tatler's Debutante Ball, in the Pillar Hall at the Palace of Unions, Moscow, 2014. During the Soviet era, the hall was used for displaying bodies of deceased leaders, including Lenin and Stalin, before their state funerals; Xue Qiwen, 43, in her Shanghai apartment, decorated with furniture from her favorite brand, Versace, 2005. In 1994 Xue started a company that sells industrial cable and has since run four more. She is a member of three golf clubs, each costing approximately $100,000 to join; Playmates at the Playboy Mansion's grotto, Holmby Hills, Los Angeles, 2000. In 1971 Playboy founder Hugh Hefner bought the 29-room house, built in 1927. Among its features are a screening room with a built-in pipe organ, a game room and a zoo and aviary; Jamie, 14, and a friend in the backyard of her Malibu beach ranch, Blue Heaven, where a golf cart is used for transportation, 1992. Jamie's father, Jerry Weintraub, promoted concerts for acts such as Elvis Presley and Led Zeppelin and produced many films, including "Nashville" and the "Ocean's Eleven" series

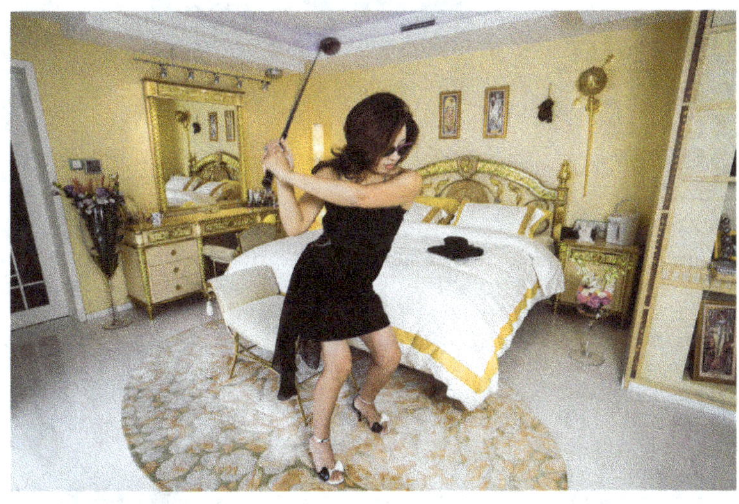

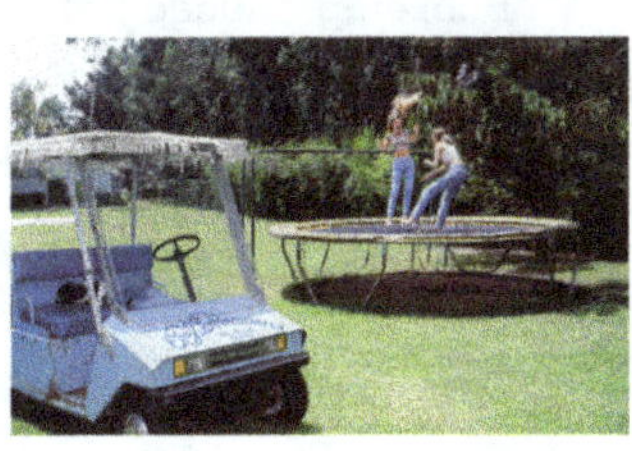

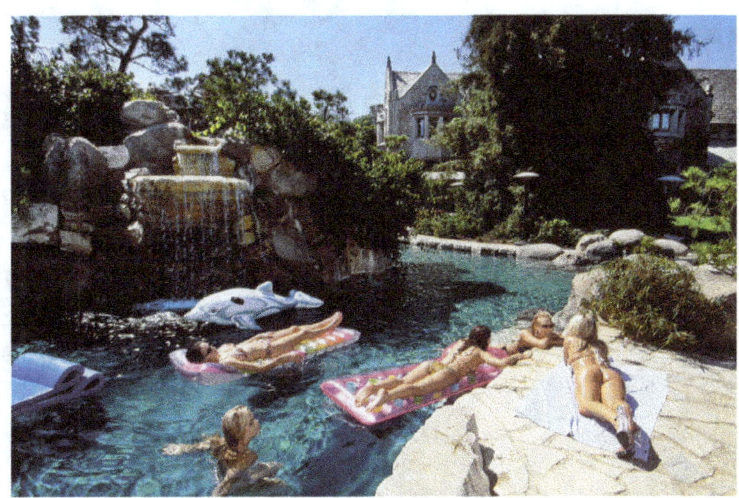

I'M NOT YOUR MAN

Album by
Marika Hackman

English singer-song-writer and instrumentalist Marika Hackman has been making waves since she and Cara Delevingne briefly formed a band as teenagers. Backed by her former schoolmate, folk artist Johnny Flynn, Hackman signed to Transgressive in 2012 and has opened for the likes of Laura Marling. *I'm Not Your Man*, Hackman's second and latest album, delves

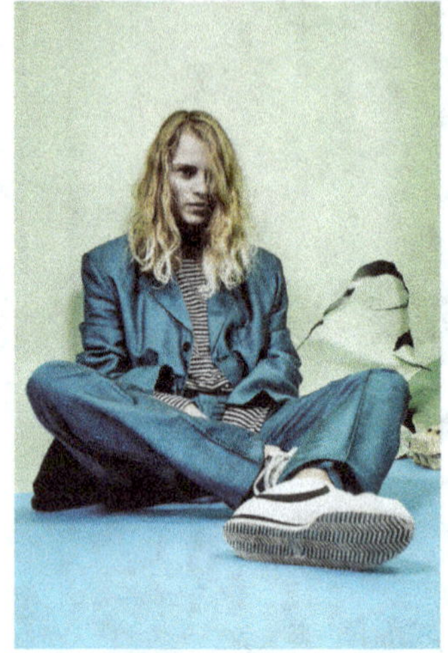

into issues of sexual identity, millennial ennui, social media and being young in the creative industry. And it's meeting with rave reviews. The album is Hackman's third project with award-winning producer Charlie Andrew, in addition to her EP and debut album. "The record's all about female relationships,

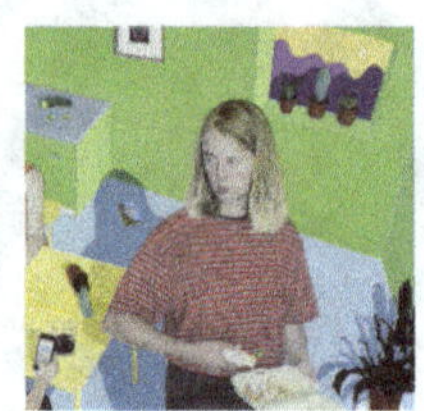

romance and break-downs," says Hackman, "but there's also a dim worldview going on. *I'm Not Your Man* can either mean 'I'm not your man, I'm your woman,' or it can mean 'I'm not a part of this.'" (Sub Pop)

BEST OF CRIME ROCK

Album by
Chain and the Gang

American musician, singer, author and talk show host Ian Svenonius came to attention in 1990 with his highly influential punk band, Nation of Ulysses. Svenonius went on to lead the likewise significant band The Make-Up, originally Weird War, as well as other lesser-known side projects. This summer's *Best of Crime Rock* is a collection of newly-recorded hits from Chain and the Gang—Sveononius' latest project formed in 2006 with bassist Anan Nasty, guitarist Francy Graham and drummer Mark Cisneros.

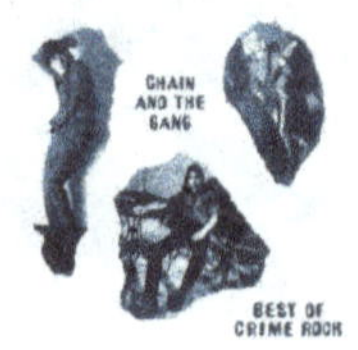

The album includes two brand new songs, and possesses a raw passion and arrow-sharp accuracy that hits at the heart of Chain and the Gang's ethos. In their own words, "Chain and

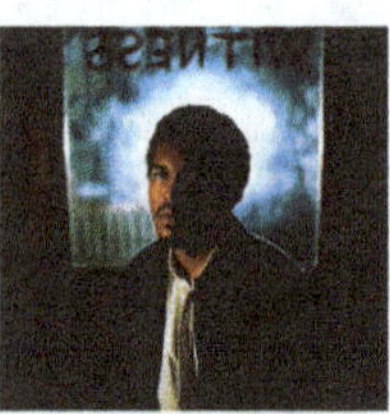

the Gang don't care about grades, likes, traffic or hits… They want total destruction of the insipid rock 'n' roll status quo and the foul system it purports to offer relief from—but in fact keeps afloat." (In The Red Records)

WITNESS

Album by
Benjamin Booker

New Orleans song-writer Benjamin Booker showcases ambitious talent in his second album, *Witness*, delving deep into his love for eccentric soul, R&B and blues. *Witness* draws on a variety of influences—from William Onyeabor's '70s African psych-rock

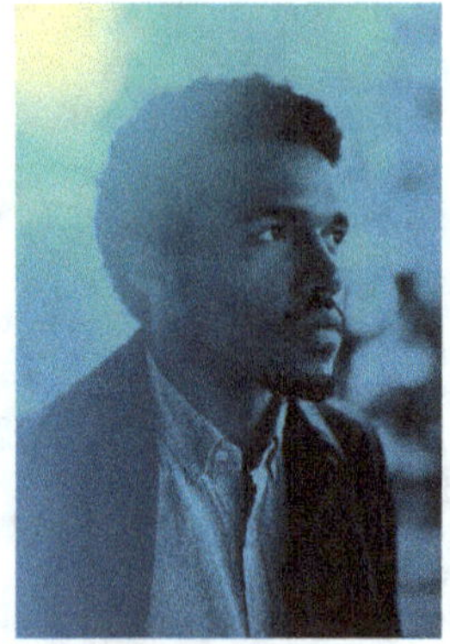

to Freddie Gibbs and Pusha T—while still invoking the garage-punk intensity that marked his eponymous 2014 debut. The title track is Booker's most pithy song to date and features guest vocals of Mavis Staples. As noted by NPR, "[Booker] — who's favored a sound like the blues, soul and rock 'n' roll mixed with gasoline and a lit cigarette—leans into more explicitly gospel territory here, letting his strepitous guitar take a backseat to an upright-piano melody and choral harmonies." All 10 of the album's tracks were penned by

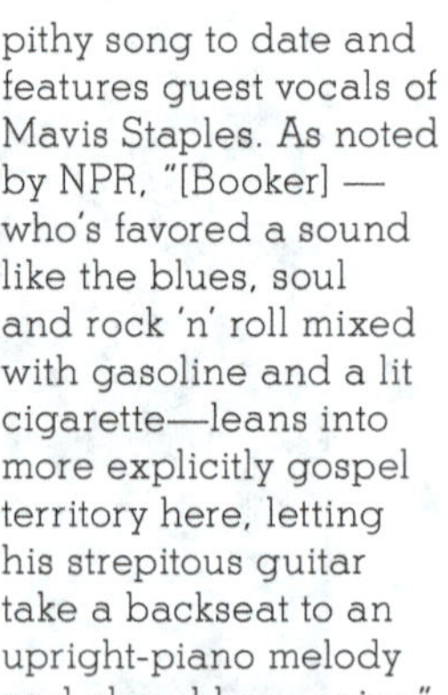

Booker, produced by Sam Cohen (Kevin Morby) and mixed by Shawn Everett (Julian Casablancas, Alabama Shakes). (ATO Records)

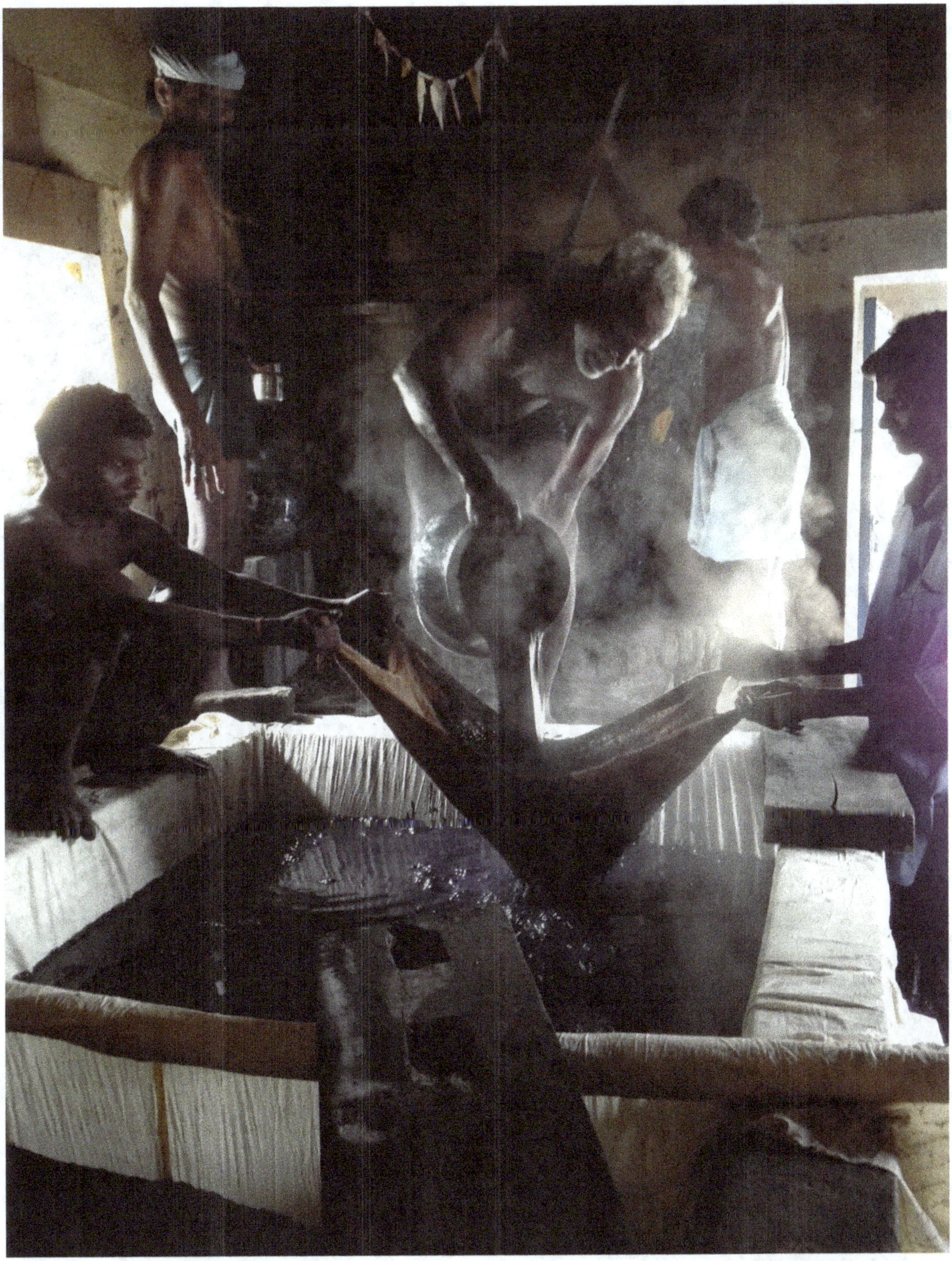

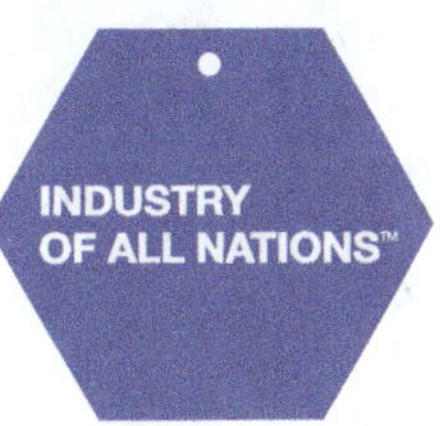

it's not what we do but how we do it.

BEDOUINE

Album by
Bedouine

Born in Aleppo, Syria, and raised in Saudi Arabia, Azniv Korkejian took the stage name Bedouine as a nod to the Bedouin tribes who live in Middle Eastern and North African deserts, travelling place to place by camel. Korkejian is a life-long nomad herself who immigrated to the United States with her family, living in Boston, Houston and throughout the South before moving to Los Angeles, where she spontaneously began writing music. It was never her plan to be a performer—Korkejian works in Hollywood editing dialogue and music. But sitting in her room above Sunset Boulevard with "a guitar in my lap and red wine or bourbon at my side," she wrote and performed for herself until it felt inevitable to start recording. Bedouine's self-titled debut layers her striking, soft voice over folk-inspired, finger-picked guitar.

What's your story of getting started as a musician? My first instrument was piano at age five. I played trumpet in school for a few years. I didn't really get into guitar until my twenties, which was around the time started writing songs. It wasn't until I moved to Kentucky and Georgia that my taste in music and songwriting evolved. But Los Angeles is what inspired the desire to be better. The distance between good and great is short but dense. When you hear someone great, it's a real kick in the groin. All of a sudden you're wont to throw away your whole approach and scrape the lining of your guts to see what you're capable of. That's what moving to LA ignited in me.

How would you describe your music? Nods to '60s folk and '70s country/country-funk, with the vocal dynamics of bossa nova, which is to say little to none.

How did you decide that this is what you were going to do? I rarely consider the notion that I have something to say, I just keep returning to it. I joke with my friends that it's something to do, that we all just need something to do.

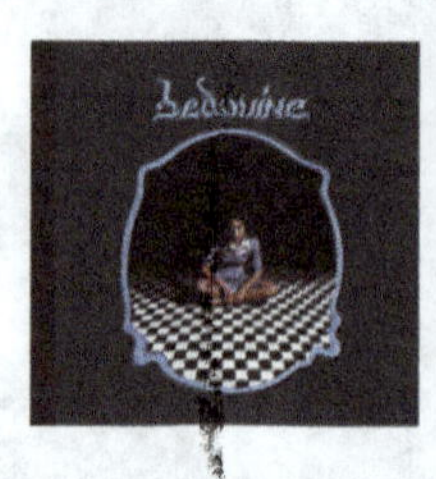

> **"THE DISTANCE BETWEEN GOOD AND GREAT IS SHORT BUT DENSE. WHEN YOU HEAR SOMEONE GREAT, IT'S A REAL KICK IN THE GROIN. ALL OF A SUDDEN YOU'RE WONT TO THROW AWAY YOUR WHOLE APPROACH AND SCRAPE THE LINING OF YOUR GUTS TO SEE WHAT YOU'RE CAPABLE OF."**
>
> **— BEDOUINE**

It's like a dog that starts chewing your things if it doesn't get enough exercise. If we don't let what's inside out somehow, we'll want to bite the walls or give up and stay in bed. So it's not one big decision. It's small, continual decisions; a propensity that builds momentum that may or may not lead to recognition. It's hard to imagine that something you volunteer yourself for can sustain you, but I guess that's the goal, so that you can get deeper and more devoted to it.

How does it feel to have finished your album? New. It's a very unfamiliar feeling, like

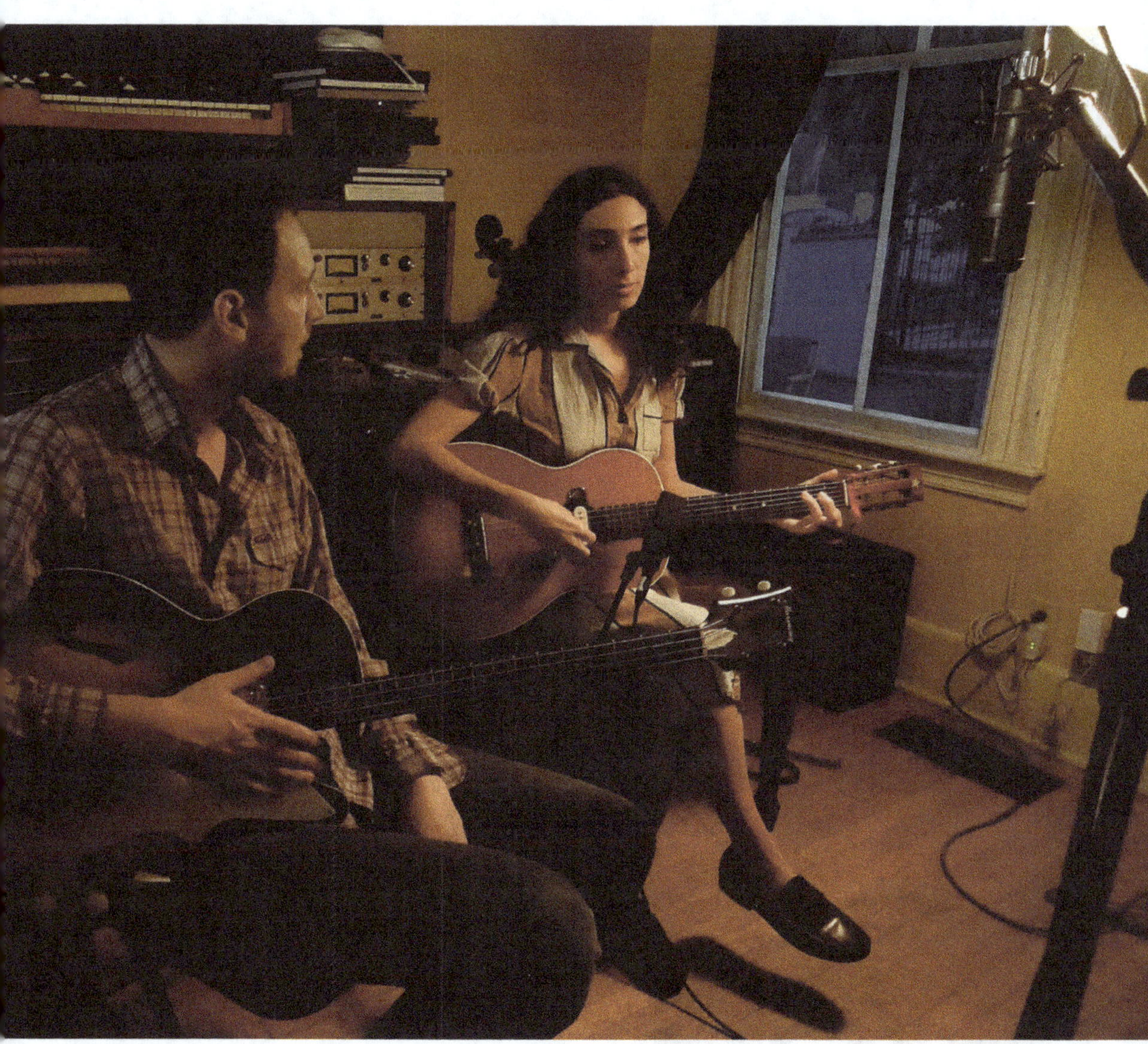

when you arrive to a place to stay overnight and in the morning step outside to see its exterior for the first time. While I was writing and recording, I hardly considered I had to step outside of the thing and look at its exterior.

What was the process like? I lived in a studio apartment overlooking a busy section of Sunset when I started writing what would eventually become the record. I'd sit tight at my table by the window, guitar in my lap and red wine or bourbon at my side. The writing started pouring out of me, one after another for months, inspired by Sibylle Baier's *Colour Green*.

I decided what was left to do was get ahold of a small tape machine and do what I had been doing all along but with a recorder in front of me. If I didn't start compartmentalizing, there would be too much floating around in my head or various devices.

When I sat down with Gus Seyffert to ask him about it, we recorded "Solitary Daughter" on a whim. We kept the first take, and he added some tasteful finishing touches. We seemed to have an understanding that it was something we would continue to do since it was so fruitful. The whole thing was so, dare I say, organic.

Can you tell us about your song "Summer Cold," which seeks to recreate the sounds of your grandmother's street in Aleppo? I wrote "Summer Cold" after repeatedly reading that the US was funneling arms to rebel groups in Syria. The weapons reportedly ended up in the hands of prominent terrorist groups, which had scattered themselves throughout the opposition movement. No matter your stance on regime change, that was a short-sighted, counter-productive solution that further aggravated an incredi-

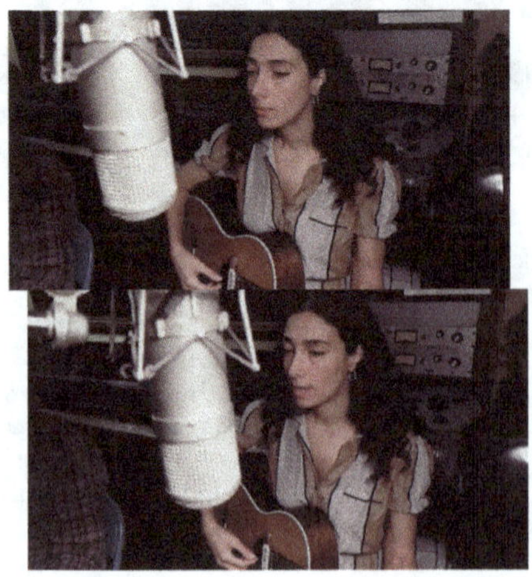

Regarding the soundscape, one of my fondest memories of Aleppo is waking up in my grandmothers

coffee or tea; donkeys pulling carts; storefronts rolling up their gates amidst the busy traffic on either side of a residential street. I recall it often, so it occurred to me to recreate it and I did, in the washy fog of an old memory. It's become an access point to a place I can't return to in the foreseeable future.

What are you working on now? I'm also a music editor for TV and film. It's pilot season for us, and I'm in the middle of one with a hilar-

"IF WE DON'T LET WHAT'S INSIDE OUT SOMEHOW, WE'LL WANT TO BITE THE WALLS OR GIVE UP AND STAY IN BED... IT'S HARD TO IMAGINE THAT SOMETHING YOU VOLUNTEER YOURSELF FOR CAN SUSTAIN YOU, BUT I GUESS THAT'S THE GOAL."

— BEDOUINE

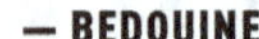

ious cast and crew. I'm really enjoying it.

bly tense situation. This song grapples with trying to understand how blindly pouring weapons into a country would alleviate devastation.

apartment to the sounds of the street below. It was a perfect collage: dice in a backgammon board; porcelain accents of

abigail spencer
LARSEN & LUND
CAPSULE COLLECTION

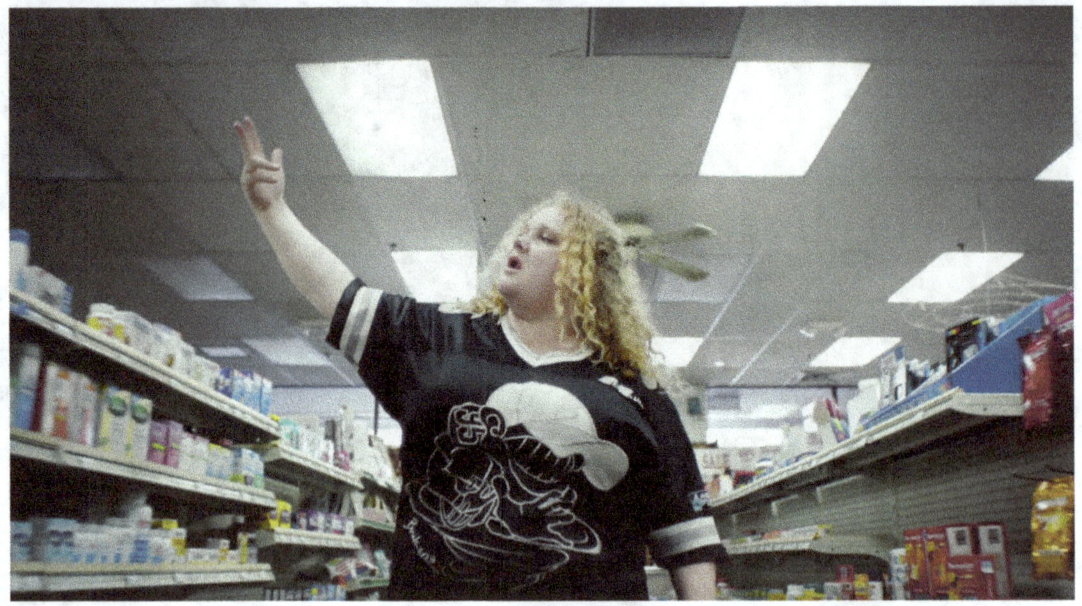

PATTI CAKE$

Film by
Geremy Jasper

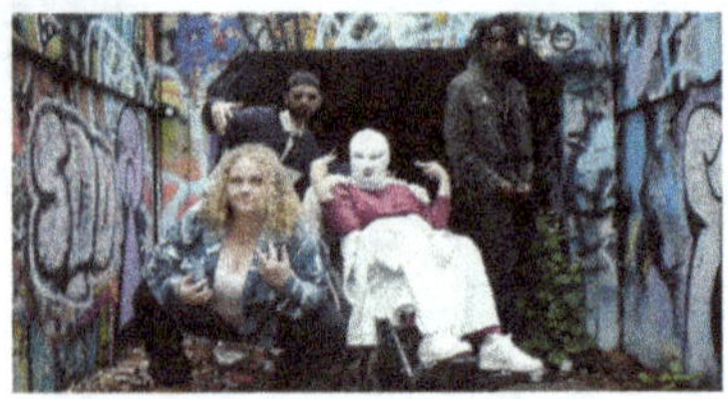

Danielle Macdonald stars as an unlikely rapper turned idiosyncratic hip-hop legend in this coming of age story from acclaimed commercial and music video director Geremy Jasper. Set in the gritty strip-mall suburbia of New Jersey, *Patti Cake$* chronicles an underdog's quest for fame and glory with humor, enthusiasm and unforgettable beats. The film is Jasper's first feature and screened in Sundance's 2017 U.S. Dramatic Competition, after which Macdonald was greeted with a standing ovation for her remarkable performance. (Fox Searchlight Pictures)

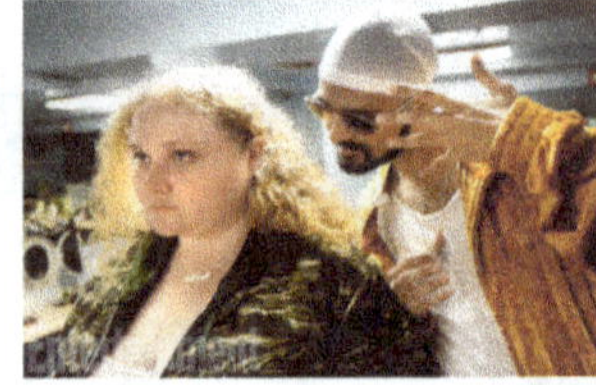

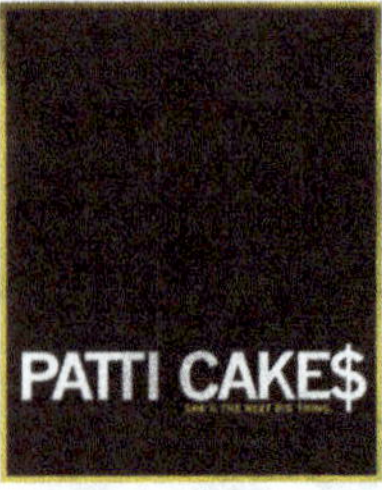

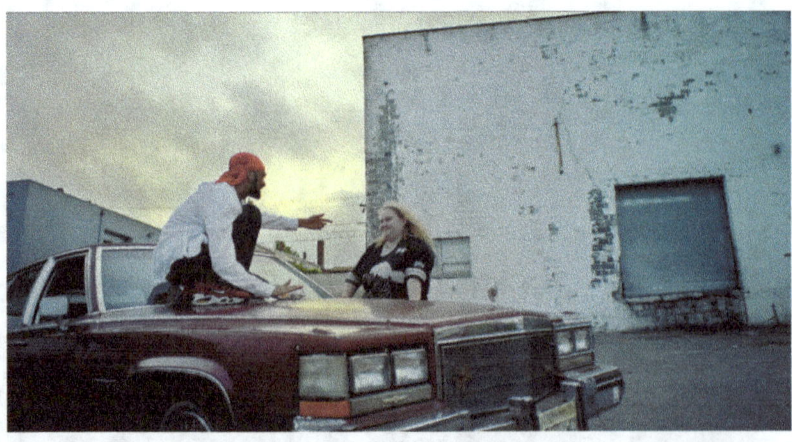

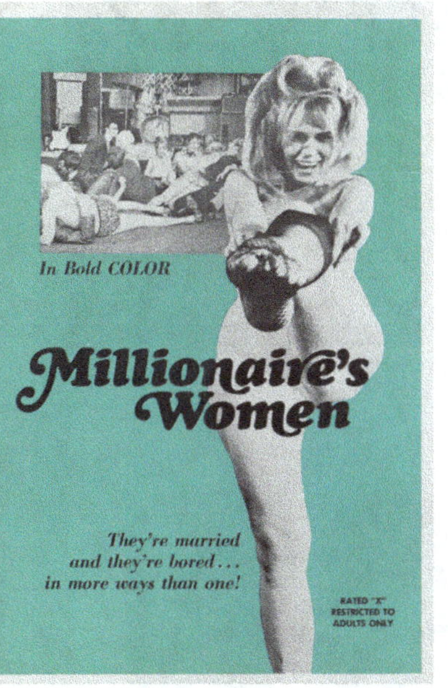

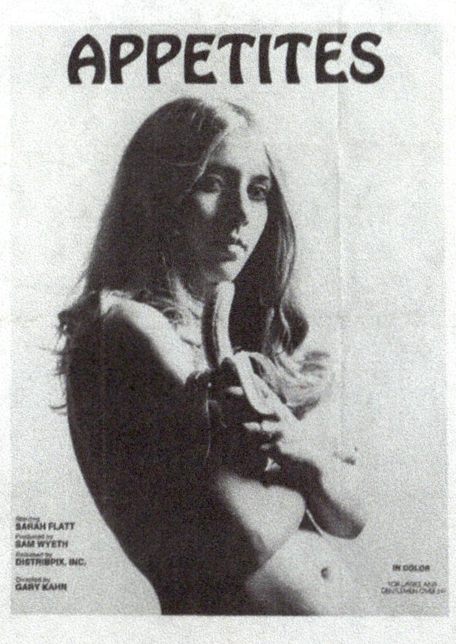

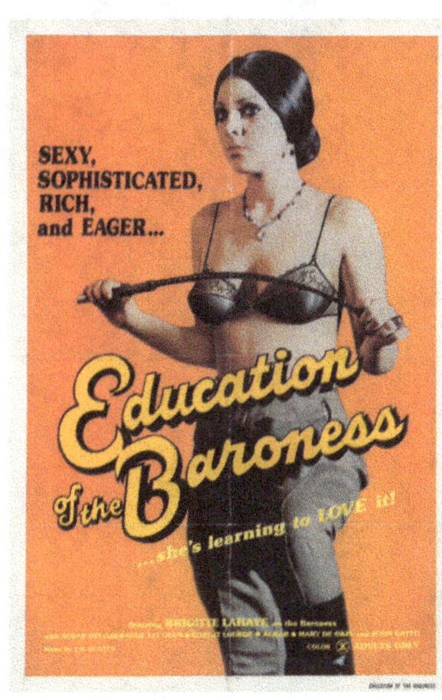

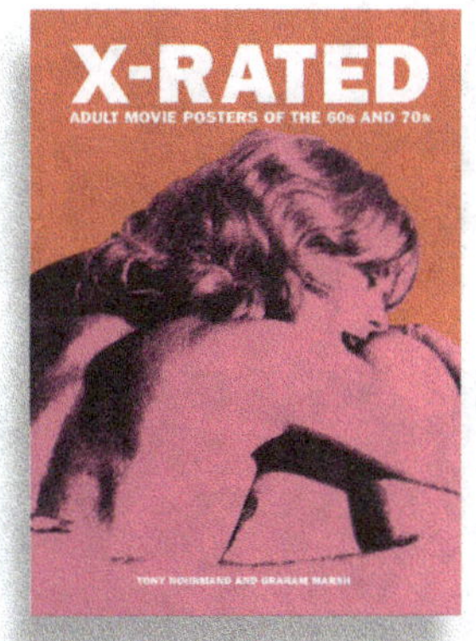

X-rated: Adult Movie Posters of the 60s and 70s

$49.95 Reel Art Press

Featuring over 350 orgasmic posters from the Golden Age of the X-rated movie.

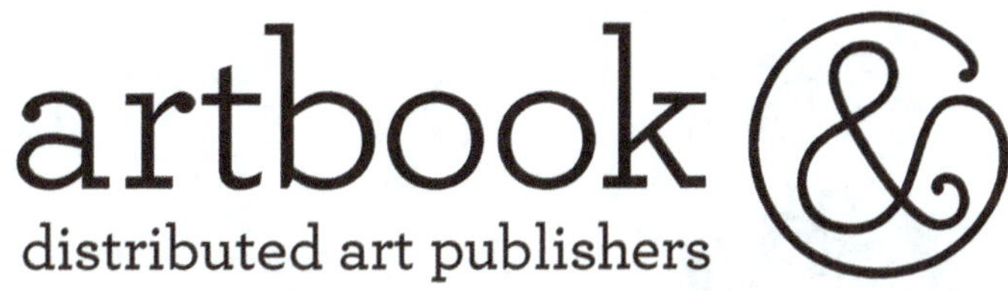

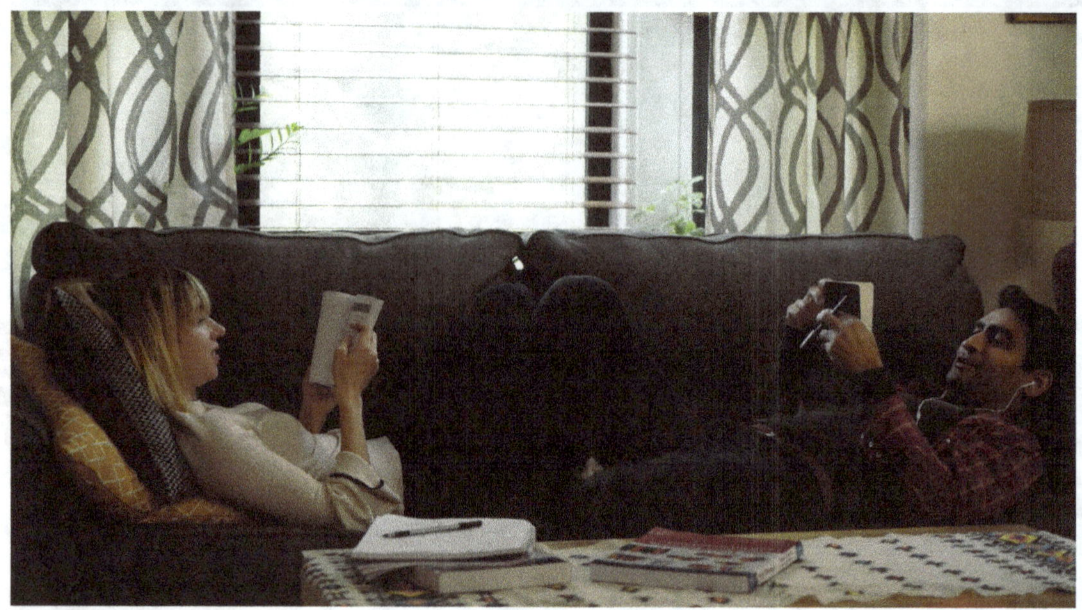

THE BIG SICK

Film by

Michael Showalter

From director Michael Showalter and producers Judd Apatow and Barry Mendel, *The Big Sick* is based on the real courtship of actor and comedian Kumail Nanjiani and writer and producer Emily V. Gordon. Kumail plays himself, a Pakistan-born aspiring comedian who connects with grad student Emily (played by Zoe Kazan) after one of his standup performances. When their one-night develops into a serious relationship, Kumail finds himself caught between love and the expectations of his traditional Muslim parents. To further complicate matters, Emily is beset with a mystery illness, compelling Kumail to navigate the crisis with her parents, Beth (Holly Hunter) and Terry (Ray Romano), while coping with the ongoing tug-of-war between his family and his heart. (Amazon Studios / Lionsgate)

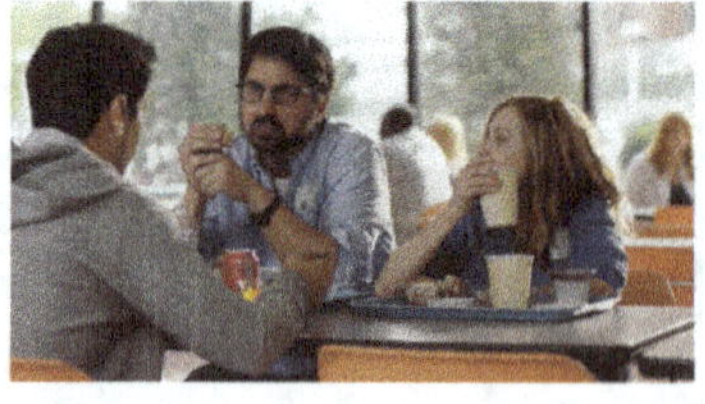

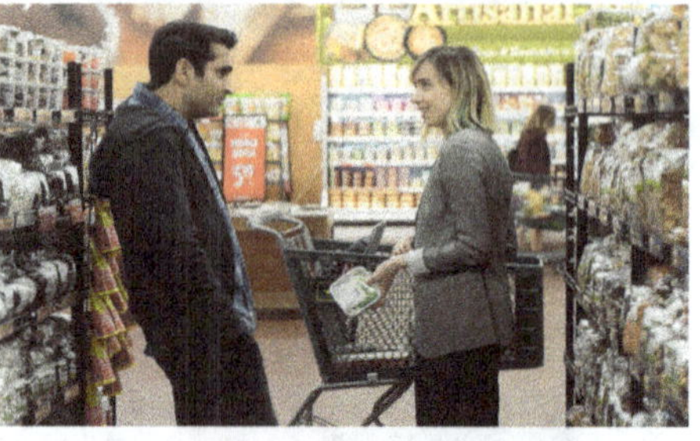

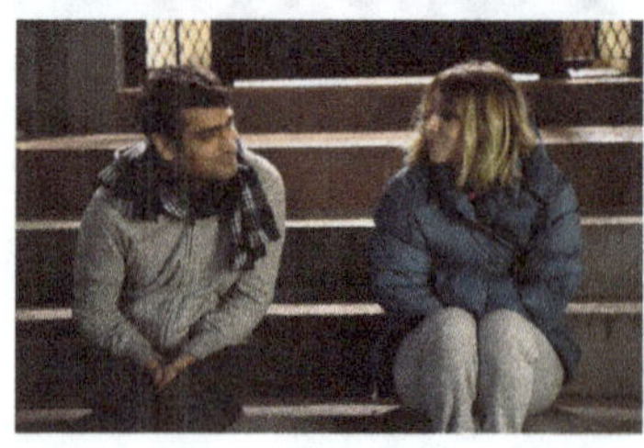

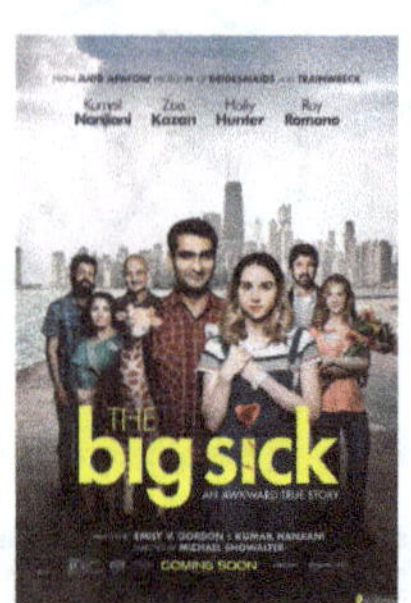

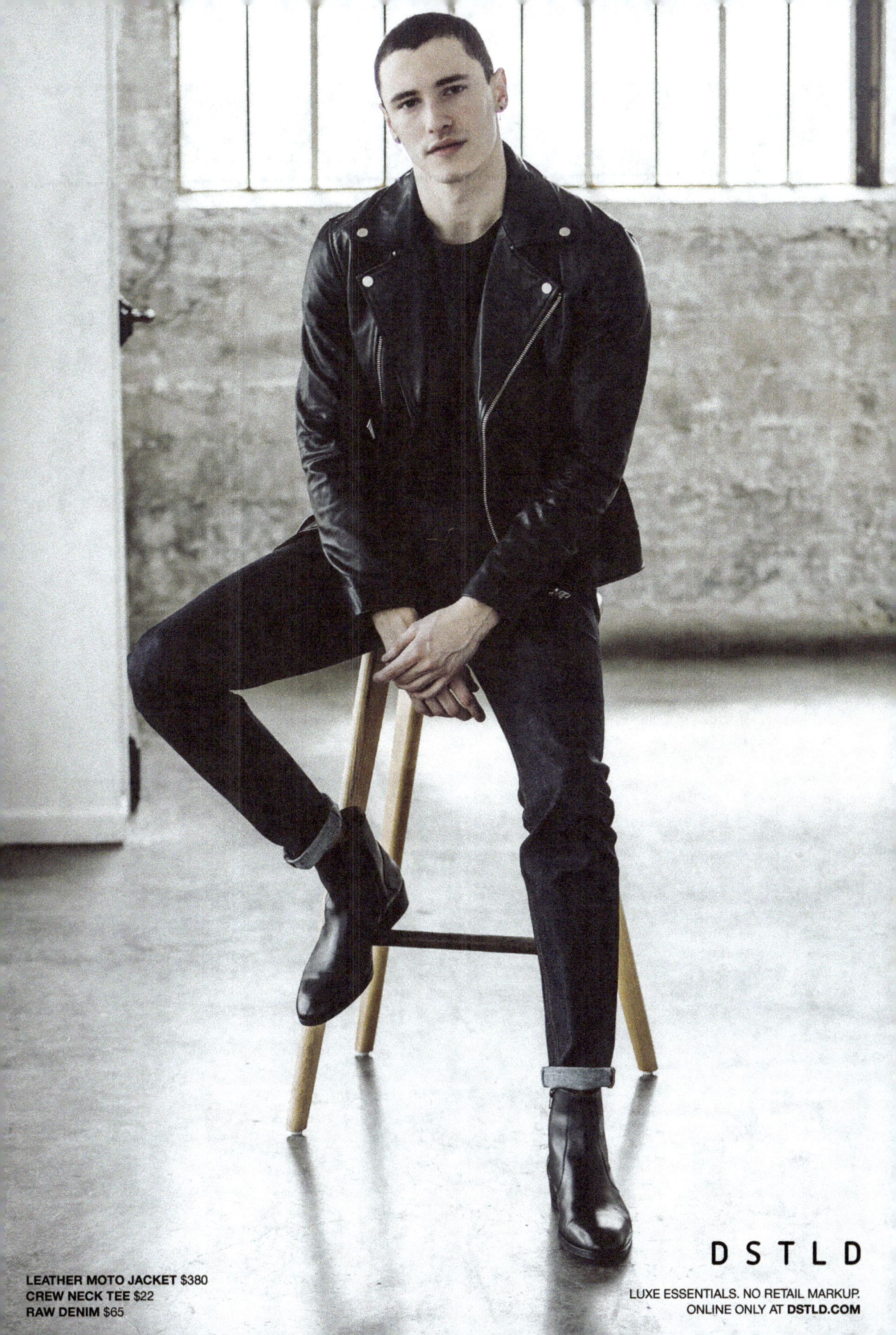
LEATHER MOTO JACKET $380
CREW NECK TEE $22
RAW DENIM $65

DSTLD

LUXE ESSENTIALS. NO RETAIL MARKUP.
ONLINE ONLY AT DSTLD.COM

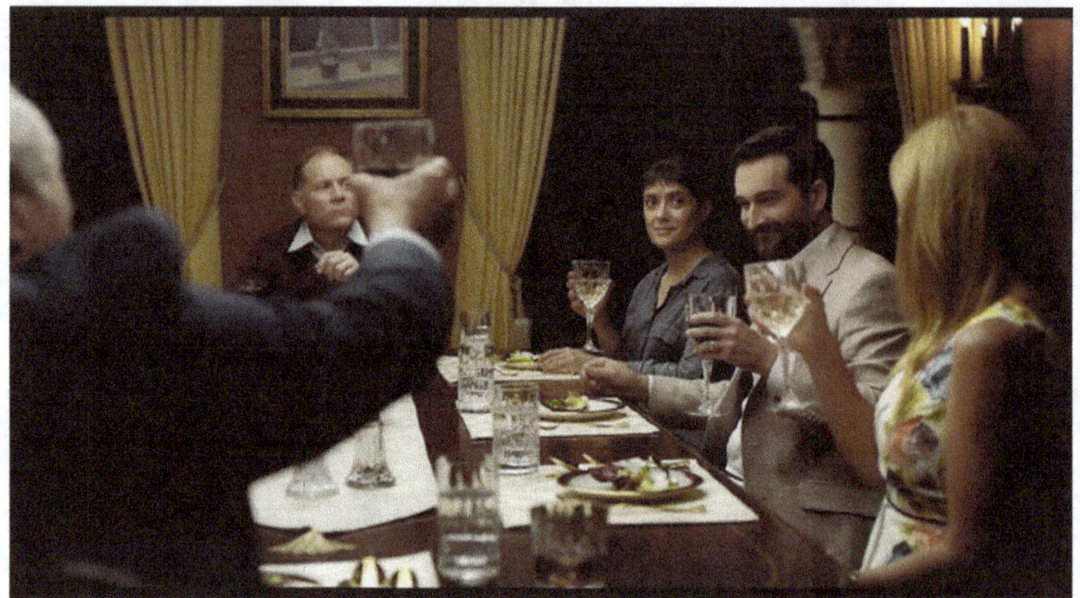

BEATRIZ AT DINNER

Film by
Miguel Arteta

Salma Hayek plays opposite John Lithgow in *Beatriz at Dinner*, the newest film from the award-winning minds of director Miguel Arteta and screenwriter Mike White. Hayek portrays Beatriz, an immigrant from a poor town in Mexico who has built a life as a health practitioner and whose path crosses with the self-made billionaire Doug (Lithgow) at a swanky dinner party in the hills of Los Angeles.

Exploring the widening gulf between the world's haves and have-nots, *Beatriz at Dinner* offers shrewd insight into contemporary controversies, from economic polarities to the necessities of human kindness. The film garnered praise following its premiere at this year's Sundance Film Festival in Utah and went on to launch the following Sundance festival in London. (Film Nation Entertainment / Roadside Attractions)

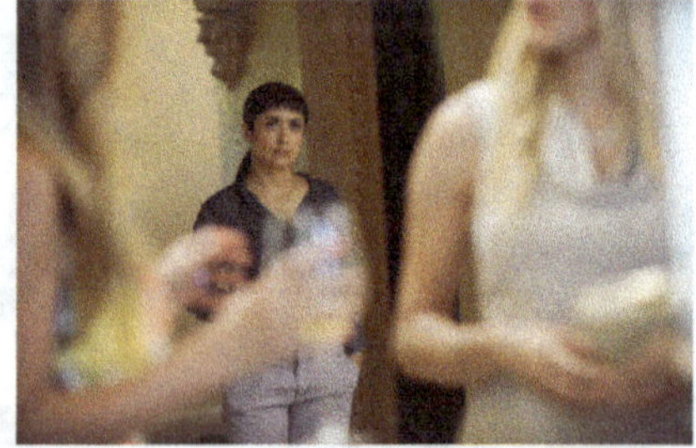

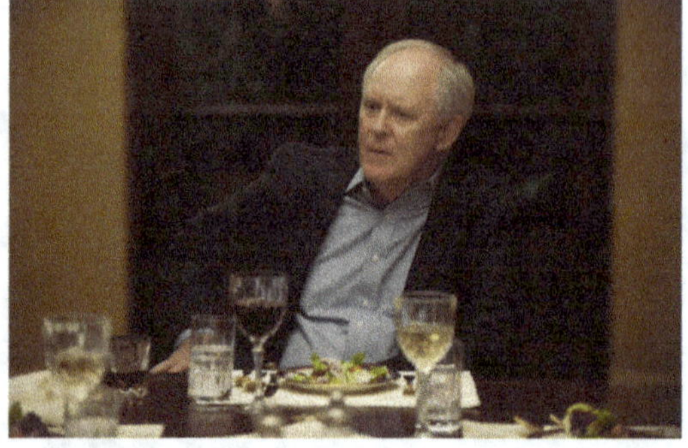

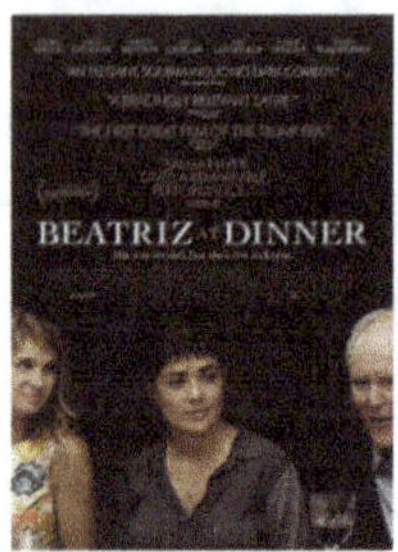

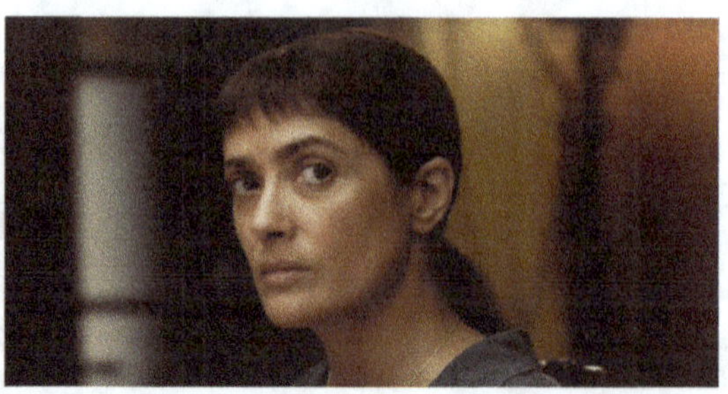

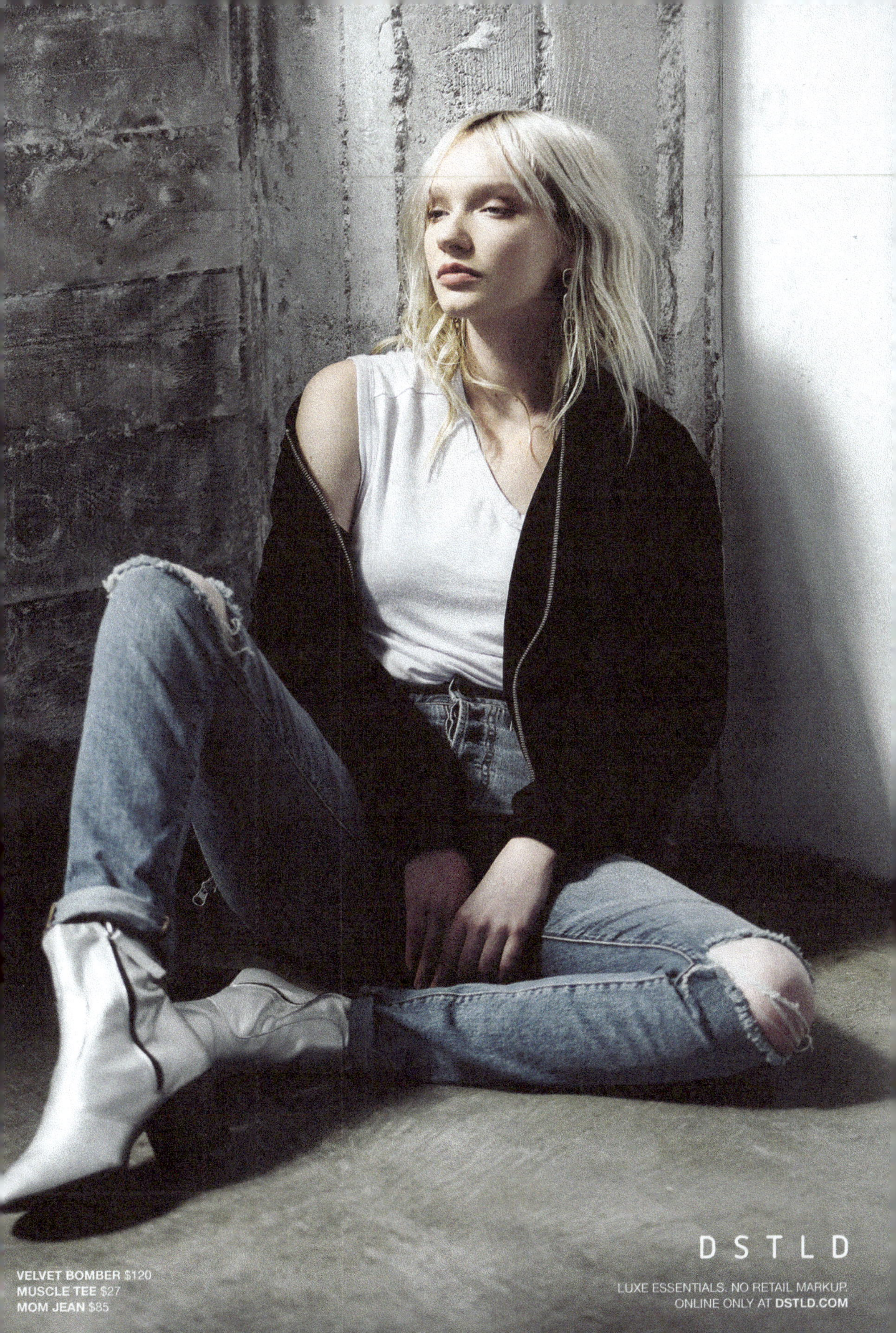

VELVET BOMBER $120
MUSCLE TEE $27
MOM JEAN $85
DSTLD
LUXE ESSENTIALS. NO RETAIL MARKUP.
ONLINE ONLY AT DSTLD.COM

JODIE COMER

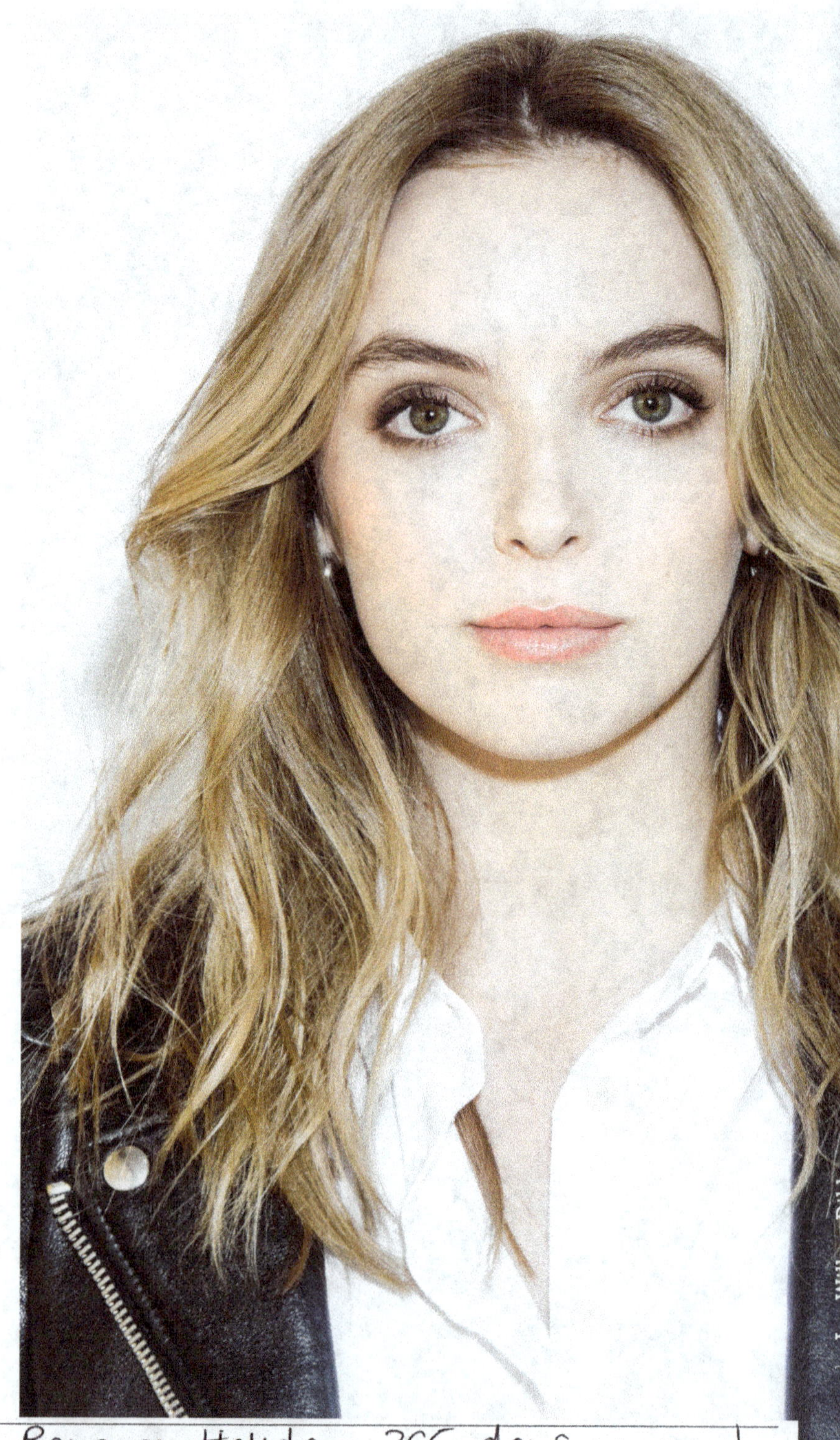

Hailing from Liverpool, England, actor Jodie Comer leads the cast of Starz' TV series The White Princess, *as the young Princess Elizabeth. She is also known for her roles in the BBC's miniseries* Thirteen *and the British comedy series* My Mad Fat Diary.

Birthplace: Liverpool, England

Education: School of Rock

Your idea of heaven: Being on holiday 365 days a year!

Turn-offs: Bad names, littering, delayed trains.

What was your first break? *Thirteen* for BBC Three, which was my first gig.

How would you describe your specialty or type? Well, I've been told I cry a lot, so maybe a crier would be my type. I don't know, people often pick up that I play characters that maybe don't seem

YOUR IDEA OF HEAVEN: Being on Holiday 365 days a year!

strong on the outside but they have an inner steel.

What do you think about the need for instant gratification? I mean, chocolate springs to mind when you say that. I think all in moderation. When it comes

little bit, but I think it's amazing, especially because I miss family a lot when I'm away. I like that I can have my mum and dad's and brother's face in the palm of my hand when I'm a long way from home.

What challenges do you feel the world is facing today? God,

 Book: *The Last Act of Love*. Music: Glass Animals. Film: I watched a film on the airplane coming here, *The Edge of Seventeen*. It really took me by surprise, I was laughing and crying on the flight. ▰

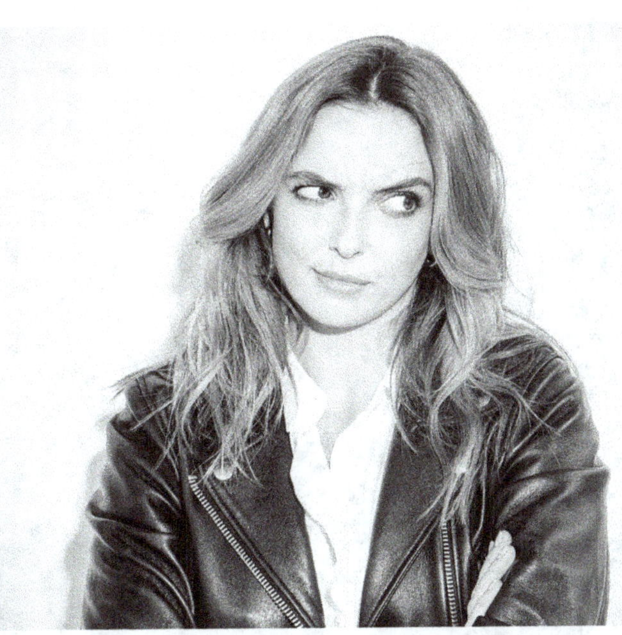

> "TECHNOLOGY DOES TERRFY ME A LITTLE BIT, BUT I THINK IT'S AMAZING, ESPECIALLY BECAUSE I MISS FAMILY A LOT WHEN I'M AWAY. I LIKE THAT I CAN HAVE MY MUM AND DAD'S AND BROTHER'S FACE IN THE PALM OF MY HAND WHEN I'M A LONG WAY FROM HOME."
>
> — JODIE COMER

to acting, I don't really believe in it. I think patience is something I'm still trying to master.

How do you feel about how interconnected the world is becoming? Technology does terrify me a

there is so much. I think we all just need to kind of connect with each other more on a personal level. I hate going to a restaurant and you see two people at a table, and they are both on their phones. I think we need to communicate in person more.

JODIE COMER
English actor Jodie Comer is known for her lead role in the Starz' TV series *The White Princess*, as well as starring in BBC's *Thirteen* (2016) and British series *My Mad Fat Diary* (2013–15).

WHAT WILL YOUR MOM SAY WHEN SHE SEES THIS? *When you go on holiday for 365 days, take me with you!*

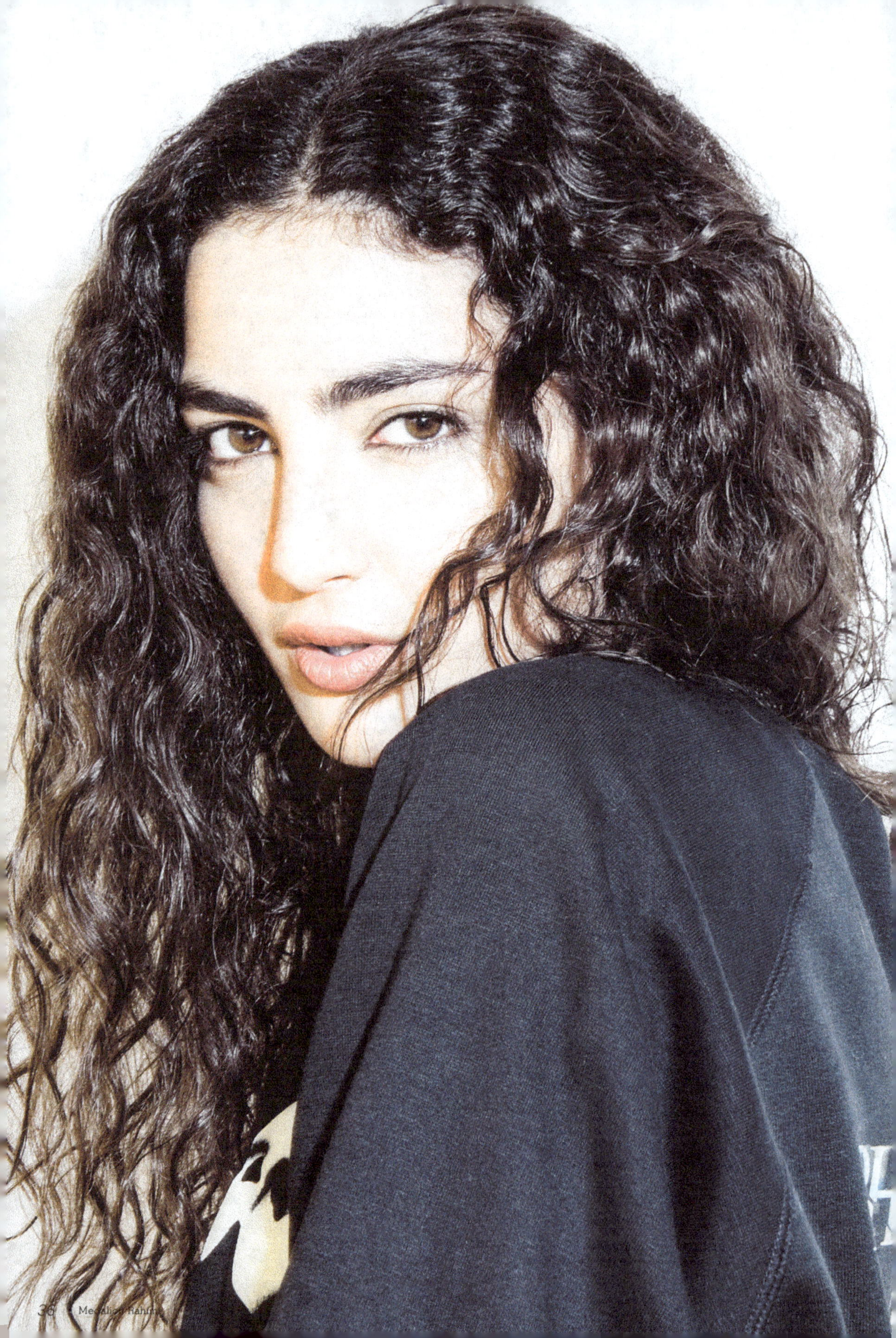

Medalion Rahimi

MEDALION RAHIMI

First-generation Iranian American Medalion Rahimi recently starred in Ry Russo-Young's film Before I Fall, *opposite Zoey Deutch, and appears in Shonda Rhimes' new American drama series* Still Star-Crossed. *She is also known her role as Princess Zara Al-Salim in ABC's* The Catch *and an appearance in the hit comedy show* New Girl.

Birthplace: Los Angeles, CA

Ambitions: WORLD PEACE... (and domination?)

First Break: My first big break was probably *Criminal Minds,* when I played a secretary. I didn't have an agent at the time, so I had just gotten the audition through a casting director who I met myself. And then I booked it, so it was really great.

Favorite way to communicate: Facetime, so I can see your face.

Inspiration: Nature, art, good books.

Car or diploma? A diploma. 100%

What's your story of getting started as an actor? I've always loved the performing arts. I took dance and music classes and enrolled in the local summer theater camp growing up. I did school plays in high school and decided, against some discouragement, to pursue acting. After graduating from UCLA's theater school, I went on an audition and a casting director noticed that I didn't have an agent. She offered to set me up with one, and when I met with the agent she told me that if I booked the role, she would definitely sign me. Lucky for me, I got the part!

What have you been in? I have been in *NCIS* and *New Girl.* Those were mostly just co-star, guest stars roles. I was in *The Catch,* which was probably the one I have been most known for, playing Princess Zara Al-Salim, and, most recently *Before I Fall.*

How do you feel about this career? It's a whirlwind. You never know what's going to happen tomorrow, and I

> **"PEOPLE SAY, YOU PLAY YOUR OPPOSITES REALLY WELL, SO I HAVE BEEN CAST AS A LITTLE BIT OF A MEAN GIRL OR THE CATTY ONE OR THE VILLAIN."**
>
> **— MEDALION RAHIMI**

think that's exciting. At the same time, it can be a little stressful, but it's so rewarding, and that's what keeps me going. For me, acting is cathartic. You really learn a lot about yourself and your emotions, as well as how to communicate openly and effectively with others. It is also a vessel for important stories to be told and can bring awareness to a lot of issues.

How did you decide

"I NEVER REALLY THOUGHT ACTING COULD BE A SERIOUS CAREER. GROWING UP IN A MIDDLE-EASTERN HOUSEHOLD, YOU HEAR, 'OH, YOU ARE GOING TO GO TO LAW SCHOOL, YOU ARE GOING TO GO TO MEDICAL SCHOOL.'"

— MEDALION RAHIMI

AMBITIONS: WORLD PEACE ... (and domination?)

Stateside T-Shirt

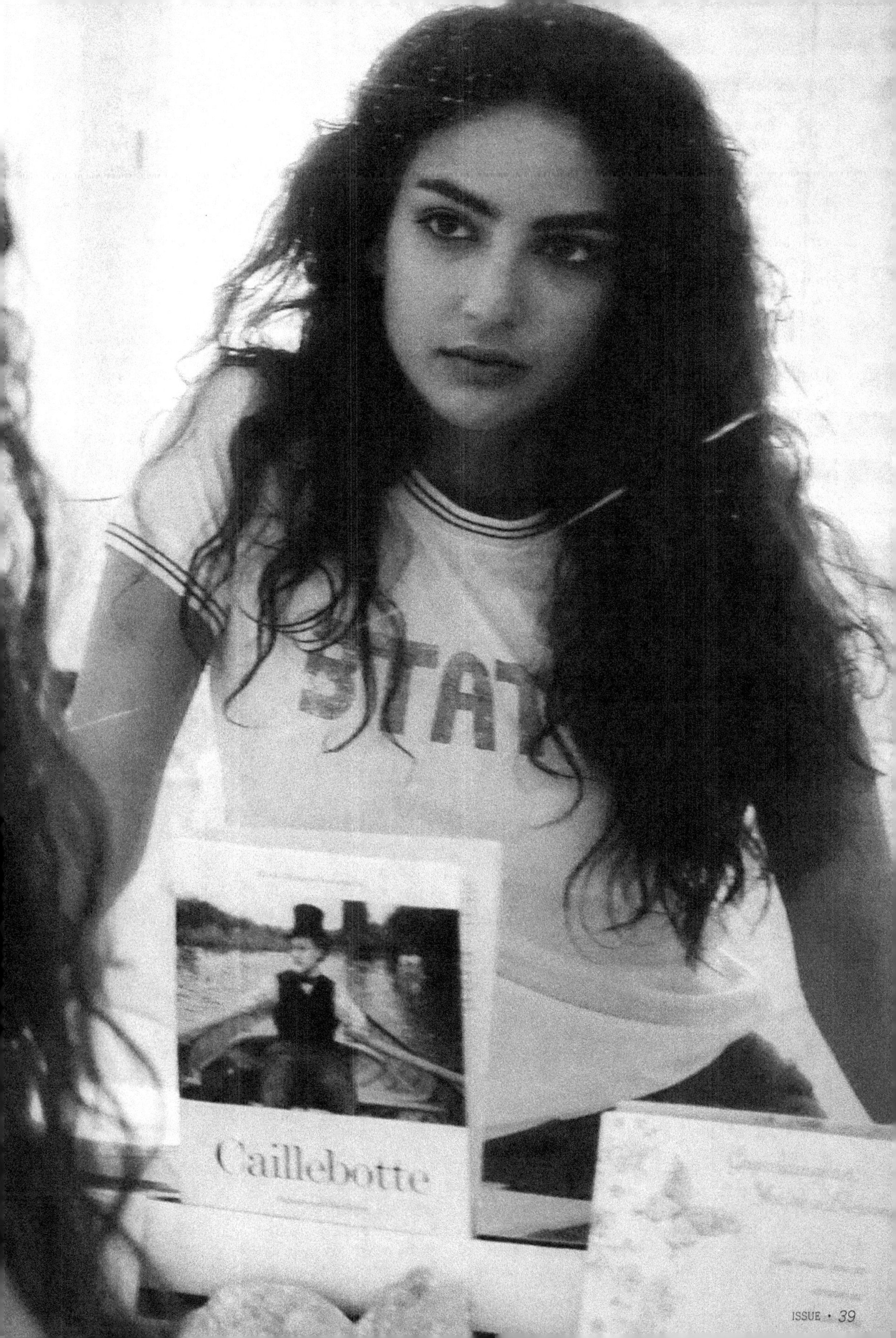

STATE
Caillebotte

to become an actor? It was really high school when I started doing plays. I never really thought acting could be a serious career. I wanted to become a journalist or doctor. Also, growing up in a middle-eastern household, you hear, "Oh, you are going to go to law school, you are going to go to medical school." We really had a wonderful high school director who inspired us and motivated us, and I just felt like myself the most when I was performing as someone else.

How would you describe your specialty or type? I have been lucky enough to play a few different people. People say, "you play your opposites really well," so I have been cast as a little bit of a mean girl or the catty one or the villain. And lately it's been a princess which is, I think, the best type-cast.

Who is your favorite actor you look up to? I love Meryl Streep, her career, the longevity of it. She is just so tal-

ented and totally loses herself everytime she performs. And I love Tilda Swinton. I love her androgyny. She is a chameleon.

What will be your ideal job? I would really love to do sci-fi action films where I could get some prosthetics and just kick ass.

Do you consider yourself to be lucky? I consider myself to be very lucky and fortunate, yes.

What advantages do you have? Probably just being someone of flavor. I think we need a lot more diversity in film and television. Luckily the industry is really embracing that right now, and so I am just going to ride that wave.

How do you feel about how interconnected the world is becoming? I think media plays a great role in interconnectedness for people around the

world. But I also think that technology can put a shield up.

What does the future look like to you? That's a good question. It's hard to say right now considering our current political climate, but I think the future looks bright.

How do you feel about having children? I would love kids. It's a scary thought. But if I was in the right place, I would definitely bring some

kids into this wonderful world.

What challenges do you feel the world is facing today? The world goes on a chart that goes up and down. It's progressing, and then it's regressing, and I think we are at a regression right now. But I think in a few years we will progress.

What is your favorite book, film and music right now? My favorite book: currently I am

reading a series of plays written by women about women. One of them was *Overtones* by Alice Gurstenburg. I really loved that play. I am about to read *Wide Sargasso Sea* by Jean Rhys. Movie: I loved *Moonlight*. Music: I really love Frank Ocean's new song, "Chanel."

What's next for you? I'm a regular on an upcoming Shonda Rhimes show *Still Star-Crossed* airing May 29th on ABC. It picks up where the play Romeo & Juliet

left off. I play Princess Isabella, Prince Escalus' strong-willed sister.

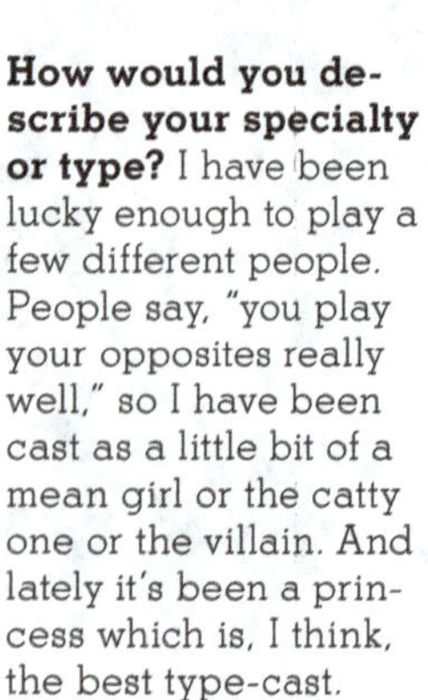

> ## "I WOULD REALLY LOVE TO DO SCI-FI ACTION FILMS WHERE I COULD GET SOME PROSTHETICS AND JUST KICK ASS."
> — MEDALION RAHIMI

MEDALION RAHIMI
An LA-born actor and first-generation Iranian American, Medalion Rahimi stars as Elody in the mystery-drama *Before I Fall* (2017) and in Shonda Rhimes' ABC series *Still Star-Crossed* (2017). Rahimi has also appeared in the shows *New Girl* (2011–) and *The Catch* (2016–17).

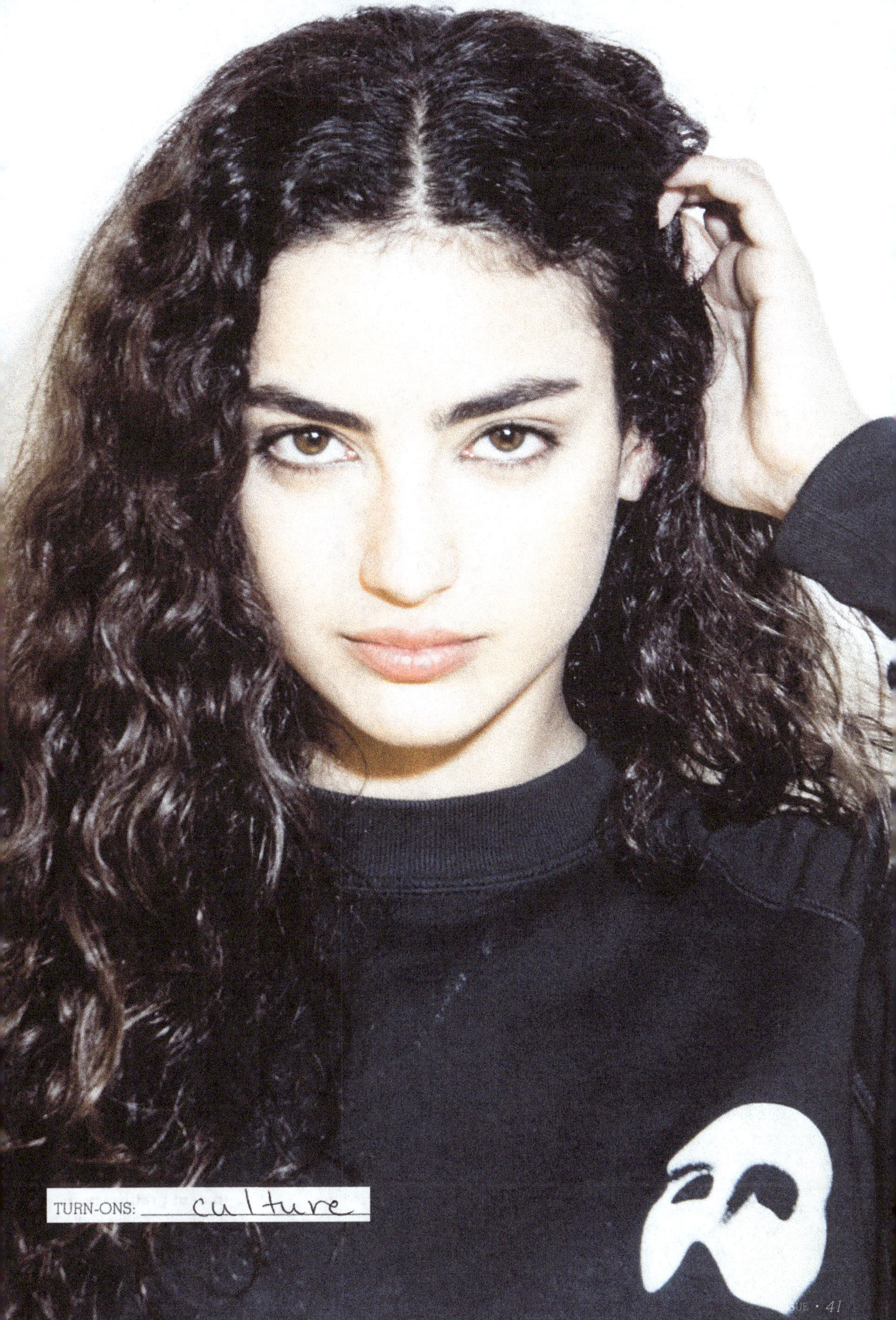

TURN-ONS: culture

MADELINE BREWER

Actor Madeline Brewer just finished her notable performance in Hulu's series The Handmaid's Tale, *a re-telling of Margaret Atwood's classic dystopian novel, starring Elizabeth Moss. Brewer had her first big break in the first season of the Netflix hit series* Orange Is the New Black *as Tricia Miller,* a drug-addicted 19-year-old. She has also appeared in Black Mirror and the web series Hemlock Grove.

> "**ORANGE WAS MY FIRST AUDITION FOR TV OR FILM EVER. I AUDITIONED AND THEN I CALLED MY MOM AFTERWARD AND I CRIED FOR 20 MINUTES, AND I TOLD HER I WAS NEVER GOING TO AUDITION FOR ANYTHING EVER AGAIN."**
>
> — MADELINE BREWER

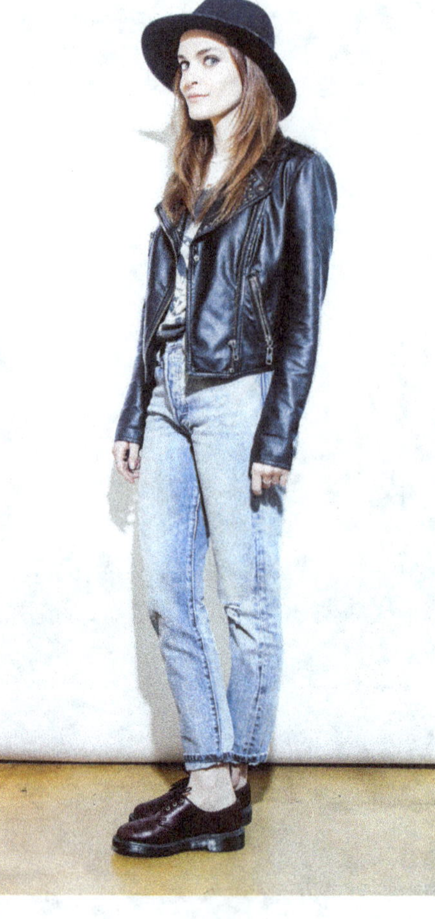

Favorite band: Pixies, Amy Winehouse, Beatles, Bibi Bourelly, Liz Phair

Education: AMDA

Birthplace: Pitman, New Jersey.

First break: *Orange is the New Black.*

How do you feel about this career? It's ridiculous, but it's a lot of fun. It takes a toll on your psyche sometimes, but I meet a lot of cool people.

How did you decide to become an actor? I did my first play when I was 7. I always wanted to do this. I wanted to do theater, but after I got the role on *Orange*, I thought, "This whole TV and film thing is a lot of fun."

Who is your favorite actor you look up to? There are so many: Amy Adams, Charlize Theron, Laura Dern, Reese Witherspoon, Naomi Watts, Cate Blanchett, Janelle Monáe, Lupita N'yongo.

Do you consider yourself to be lucky? Absolutely. *Orange* was my first audition for TV or film ever. I auditioned and then I called my mom afterward and cried for 20 minutes. I told her I was never going to audition for anything ever again. By the luck of the draw I got it, and it kind of started this whole thing.

What advantages do you have? I grew up upper middle class. I had parents who could send me to theater school and who were supportive of me. I have a good support system and all of the advantages that come with being a thin white woman in the acting industry.

What do you think about the need for instant gratification? It makes people lazy and impatient, but it's just the nature of our

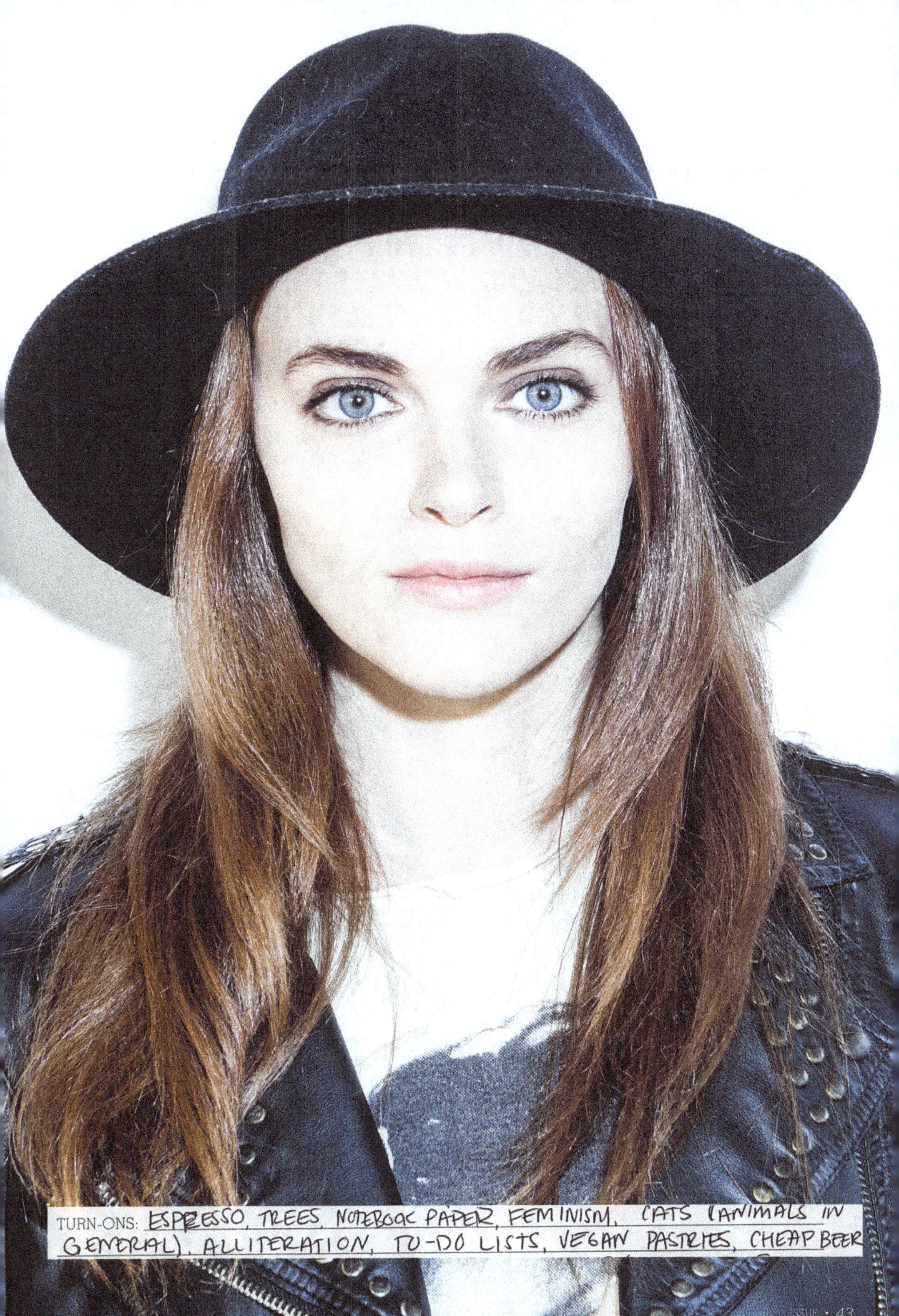

TURN-ONS: ESPRESSO, TREES, NOTEBOOK PAPER, FEMINISM, CATS (ANIMALS IN GENERAL) ALLITERATION, TO-DO LISTS, VEGAN PASTRIES, CHEAP BEER

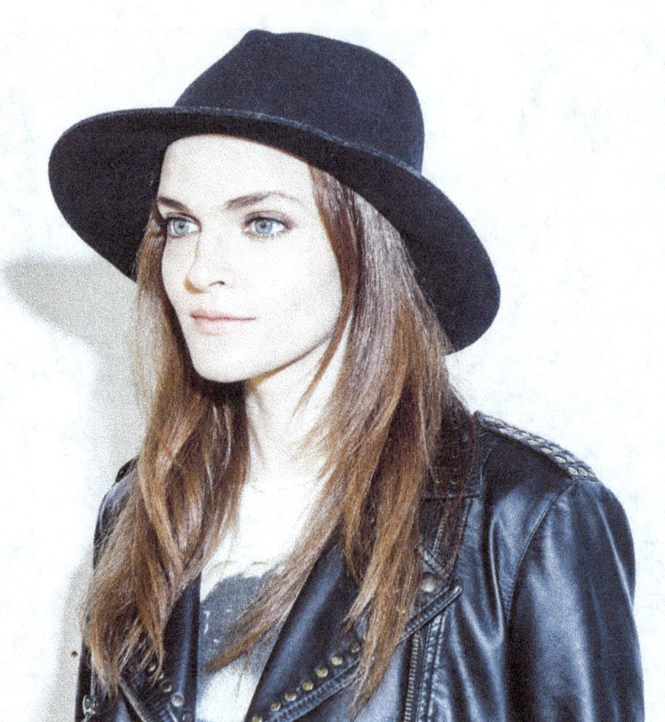

ADDITIONAL COMMENTS:

CARING IS COOL.

LOVE AND LIGHT!!!

MADELINE BREWER
Born and raised in
Pitman, New Jersey,
Madeline Brewer
stars in Hulu's series
The Handmaid's Tale
(2017). She first came
to attention for her
role in the hit Netflix
series *Orange Is the
New Black* (2013–17)
and has acted in
other shows including
Black Mirror (2011–
16) and *Hemlock
Grove* (2015).

society nowadays. It also makes people, I think, work a little harder for it. There are two sides to it.

What does the future look like to you? I've been reading a lot of Margaret Atwood so it's pretty dim. I have high hopes for the future because you have to, otherwise you will just fall into a dark hole and cry yourself to sleep every night. There are a lot of young people becom-

my own children. But motherhood is proba-bly cool—my mom was good at it.

What challenges do you feel the world is facing today? In summation, there is just such a lack of empathy in the world today. We don't care about our fellow human. Every individual only cares about their little bub-ble—which don't get me wrong, I care about mine too. There is a much bigger picture

right now? I'm reading *Oryx and Crake* by Margaret Atwood right now, which is part of a trilogy. It's haunting and scary and fascinat-ing. Movie: my favorite movie is *The Shining*. I recently saw *Get Out* which was just fantastic and topical. TV: I've been watching *Big Lit-tle Lies* which is great. And music: I don't have a nice car so the things I listen to in my car are on CD. Right now I've been listening to Alabama Shakes.

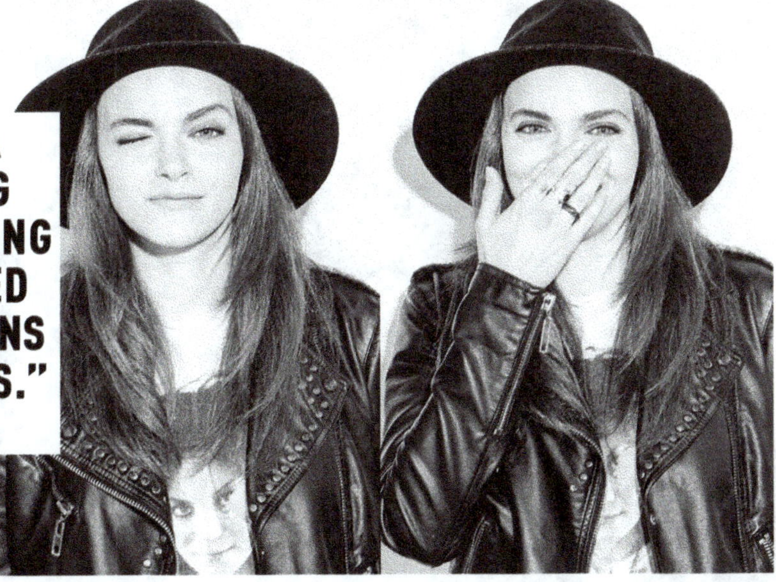

> ## "THERE ARE A LOT OF YOUNG PEOPLE BECOMING MORE INVOLVED IN WHAT HAPPENS TO THEIR LIVES."
>
> **— MADELINE BREWER**

ing more involved in what happens to their lives and having more of an interest and a say in what happens to them. It is so important that we are not just sitting idly by and watching the world happen in front of us.

How do you feel about having chil-dren? Good for people who do it. I don't want to do that. I want to adopt someday, but I don't ever want to have

that people so often forget, and people get left behind because of that.

What are you most grateful for? My family is the greatest thing that's ever happened to me. I have the best family in the whole world. They're my biggest supporters and the funniest, most intel-ligent people I know.

What is your favorite book, film, and music

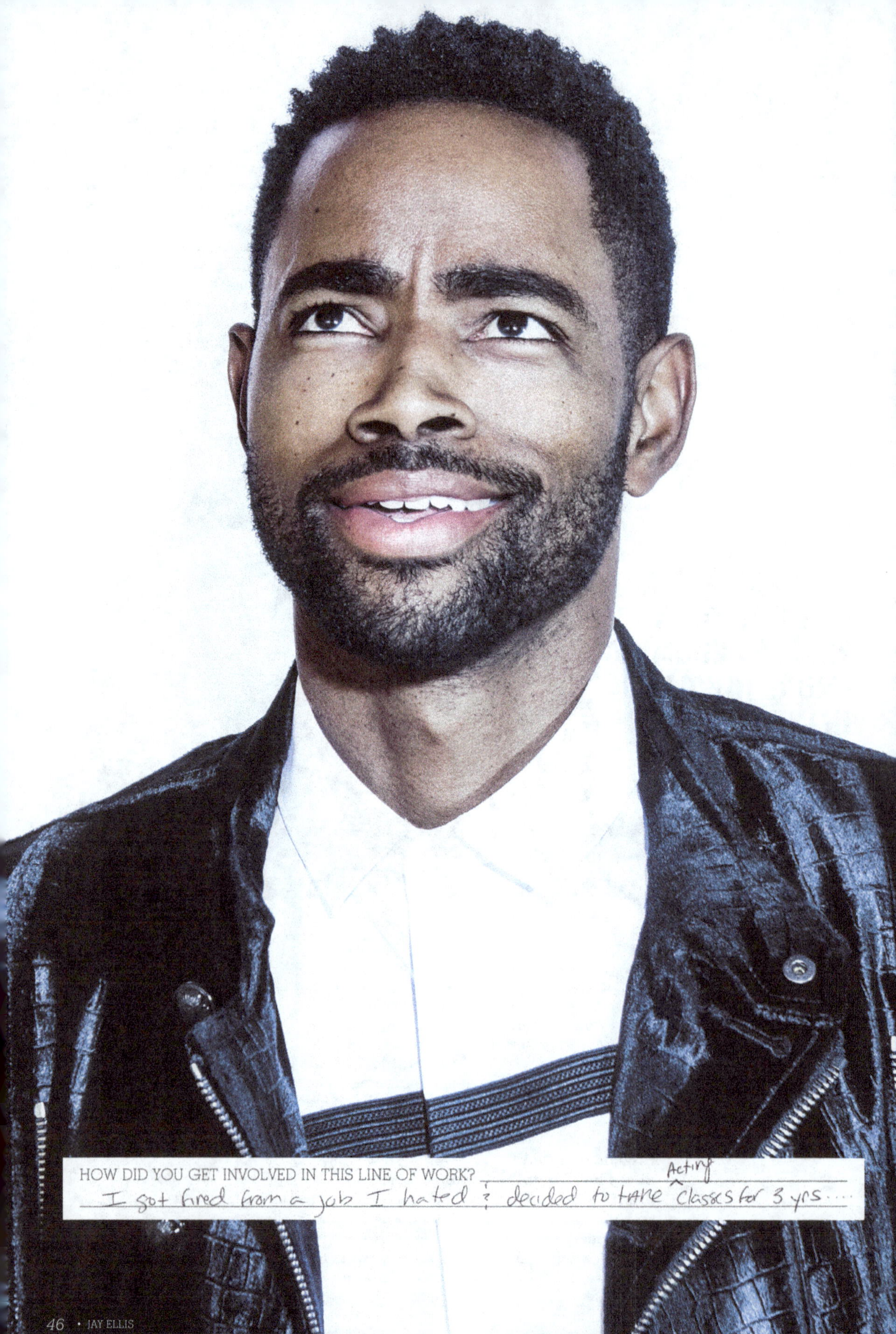

HOW DID YOU GET INVOLVED IN THIS LINE OF WORK?
I got fired from a job I hated & decided to take acting classes for 3 yrs....

JAY ELLIS

Born in Fort Sumter, South Carolina, Jay Ellis is a television and film actor currently starring as Lawrence opposite comedian Issa Rae on HBO's hit show Insecure. *His is a familiar face following appearances in Netflix'* Grace and Frankie *and episodes of* The Game *and* Grey's Anatomy.

Birthplace: Sumter, South Carolina.

Favorite food: Sushi, pizza, brownies.

Favorite band: Jay Z, Kendrick Lamar, Wale, M83.

Your passion: Learning, people, changing the conversation around young black men, telling great stories.

Where are you from? The world. My dad was in the Air Force. I was born in South Carolina, lived in three countries, five states, L.A... I actually don't know where I'm from. I'm just a citizen of the planet.

What was your first break? I did a movie called *Movie 43* that Elizabeth Banks directed, playing a basketball player in the 1950s. Then, after that, a TV show called *The Game*.

What have you been in? *Grey's Anatomy, The Game, Insecure, Grace and Frankie, NCIS...* I was in my house this morning if that counts.

How do you feel about this career? I'm good with this career so far. I feel like I have a lot of places to grow and a lot to see and a lot to experience.

How did you decide to become an actor? I got fired from a job and realized I always wanted to be an actor my entire life, but it just took a long time for me to get there. I didn't want to go back into what I was doing, so I got in the acting class and did it for like two years and then voilà.

How would you describe your specialty or type? I don't know. I'm a goofball by nature. I love comedy. I love drama. I love

> ## "I THINK I HAVE MY IDEAL JOB. HOPEFULLY *INSECURE* STAYS ON FOR 20 MORE SEASONS AND MY CHARACTER WOULD BE LIKE 55 OR 60 BY THEN AND RETIRE AND JUST RIDE OFF INTO THE SUNSET."
>
> **— JAY ELLIS**

everything. I should probably figure that out, actually.

Who is your favorite actor you look up to? Oh man! There are so many. Will Smith, Brad Pitt, Denzel, Daniel Day Lewis, George Clooney. There are so many, it's not fair.

What would your ideal job be? *Insecure.* I think I have my ideal job. Hopefully it stays on for 20 more seasons and my character would be like 55 or 60 by then and retire and just ride off into the sunset.

What advantages do you have? I don't know if I have any advantages. I think we're all alike trying to figure it out, stay one step ahead and not get left behind, but I like to think that I work hard and have good work ethic. I don't know, that's for other people to decide. I research quite a bit. I watch a lot of TV, probably far too much. I'm probably single-handedly keeping a few networks afloat.

What did you do before? Oh my God. I made smoothies. I sold women's shoes. I sold jeans. I worked in retail for a long time. I was a bartender. I worked the front door at a club.

How do you feel about how interconnected the world is becoming? It's a mix. I kind of love it because it allows you to be connected with so many people in so many different places at one time. On my way here this morning, I was talking to a friend of mine who lives in London thanks to WhatsApp. That probably wouldn't have been able to happen so cheaply or easily 20 years ago. But at the same time, we do need to put our phones down and just have human interaction every now and again because it's kind of cool talking to you.

How do you feel about having children? I love kids—as in *your* kids who go back home to you. No, I love kids, actually. I would love to have kids.

What challenges do you feel the world is facing today? I think we're finding ourselves in this weird place where we are probably as divided as we've ever been. It seems to be something that's happening across multiple countries, which leads to tension and turmoil, obviously

> # "I WATCH A LOT OF TV, PROBABLY FAR TOO MUCH. I'M PROBABLY SINGLE-HAND-EDLY KEEPING A FEW NETWORKS AFLOAT."
>
> — JAY ELLIS

within a country but also when it comes to international policies. I think one of our biggest challenges is just communication and finding ways to treat each other better and hear each other and love each other for who we are.

What are you most grateful for? My family.

What is your favorite way to communicate? Text message for sure, and I'm the dude who

said we should put our phones down. I realize that.

What is your favorite book, film and music right now? I'm reading a book about directing called *Directors Tell the Story*. My favorite film: I just watched *Glengarry Glen Ross* last night, so I'll just say that. Music: Kendrick Lamar, *DAMN*. Amazing. I think every single song was in the Billboard 100 last week. 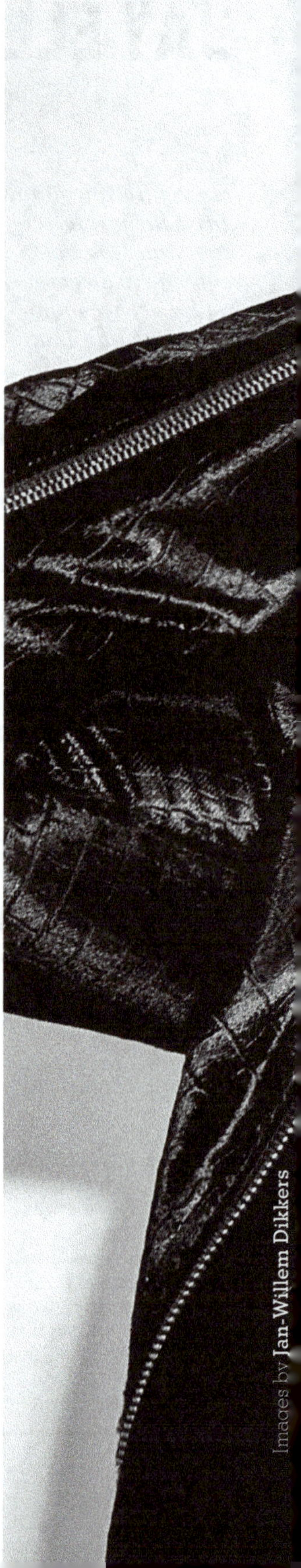

JAY ELLIS
Jay Ellis is an actor, philanthropist and entrepreneur best known for his roles in HBO's *Insecure* (2016–), *Grace and Frankie* (2015–) and *The Game* (2006–15).

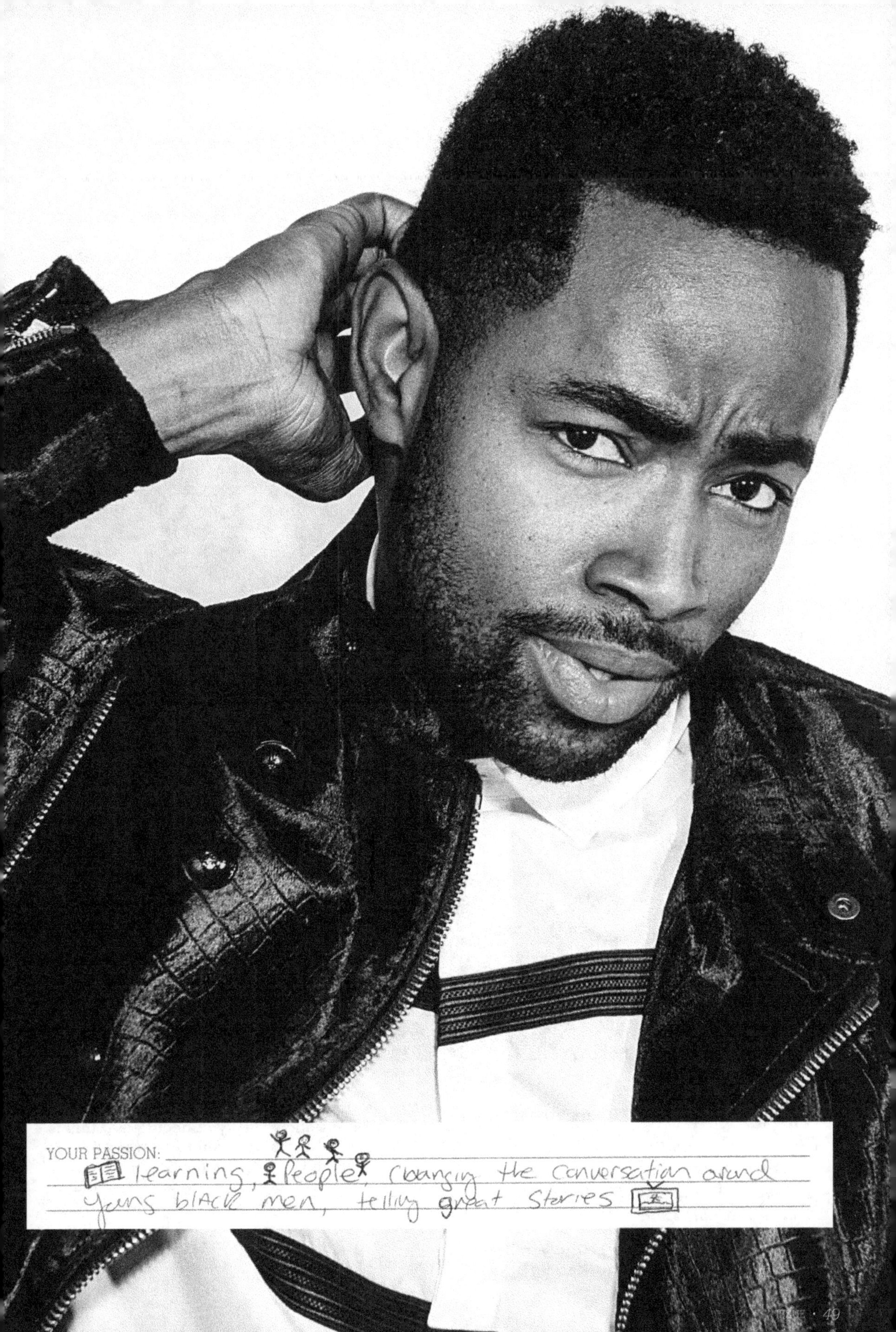

YOUR PASSION: learning, people, changing the conversation around young black men, telling great stories

KAREN ELSON

In Double Roses, *Manchester-born musician, super-model and mother-of-two Karen Elson delves into the personal and confronts the vicissitudes of her life. Elson's second album comes seven years after her critically acclaimed debut record* The Ghost Who Walks, *produced by Elson's then-husband Jack White.* Double Roses *was recorded in Los Angeles, at the world-renowned United Studios (neé Ocean Way) in Hollywood, with producer Jonathan Wilson (Jackson Browne, Father John Misty, Conor Oberst). Collaborators on the album include Patrick Carney of The Black Keys, Pat Sansone of Wilco, Father John Misty, Laura Marling and other prolific musicians. As part of a House Arrest video for* ISSUE, *Elson spoke about her influences, the making of* Double Roses *and what she plans to do next.*

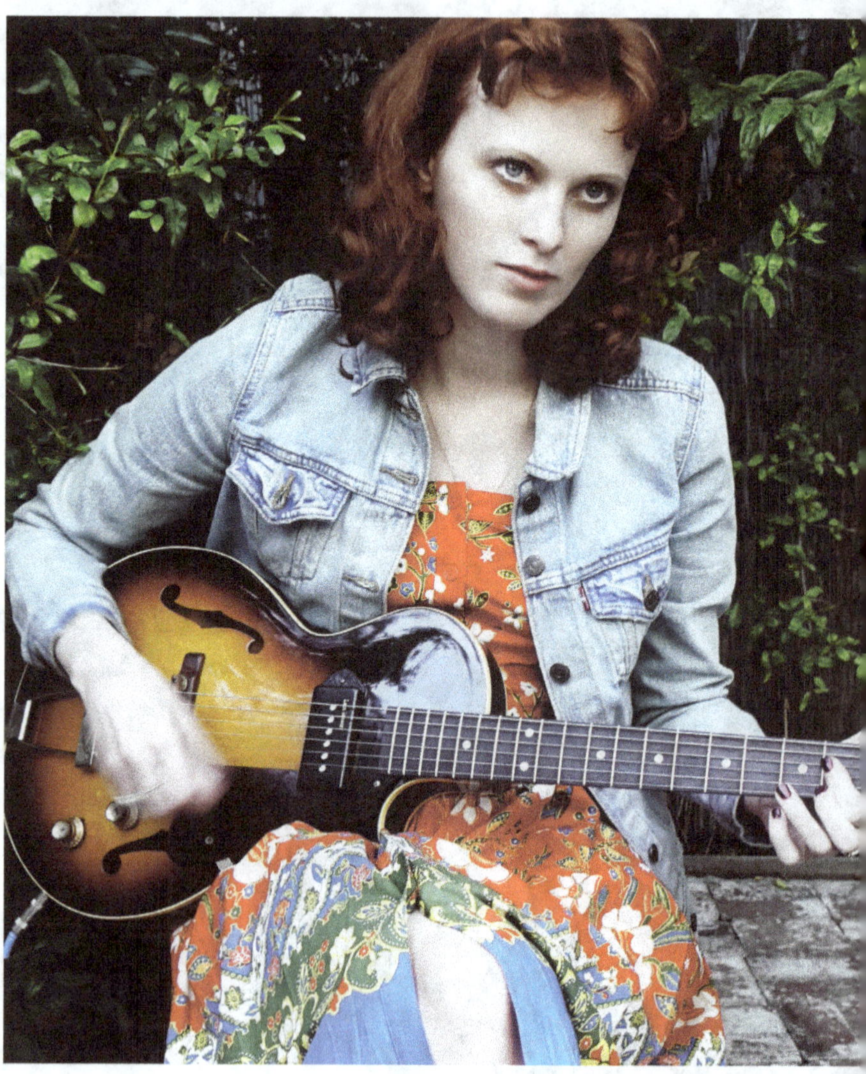

Where are you from?
Manchester, England

When did you start making music?
Around 13 years old

Who did you listen to growing up? So many terrible bands, but then when I was 13 I got into The Stone Roses, PJ Harvey, Nick Cave, Velvet Underground, and that was a turning point for me. Until that point though, it was boy bands. Not ashamed.

Who is your music influenced by today? Morrissey, Robert Smith and Hope Sandoval.

How and when did you decide that this is what you were going to do? Well I decided that when I was young, but it took me a long time to figure out how to get there. I love music so much. I love

KAREN ELSON
Karen Elson is a British supermodel, musician and advocate for children and women's rights. She recently released her second album in seven years, entitled *Double Roses*. She is also a founding member of the New York City political cabaret troupe known as the Citizens Band, which has incorporated actors and musicians such as Zoe Kravitz, Rain Phoenix and Nina Persson.

WIM WENDERS
Considered by many to be an auteur director, Wim Wenders is a German filmmaker, playwright, author, and photographer. His work exemplifies the New German Cinema era of the late 1960s. Wenders' narrative drama *Paris, Texas* (1984) scored him a BAFTA Award for Best Direction and a Palme d'Or at the 1984 Cannes Film Festival.

SAM SHEPARD
Sam Shepard is an American playwright, actor, author, screenwriter and director. One of his forty-four written plays, *Buried Child*, won the Pulitzer Prize for Drama in 1979. He is known for including surrealist, poetic and absurdist elements in his work, as well as depicting the nomadic outsiders of American society.

writing music, I love singing and I love listening to music. I'm such a fan that when it came time for me to start making music, I was quite shy about it for a while because I had such unrealistic expectations for myself. I never want to be mediocre in anything. I never want to do anything "okay." I want to do it good. So I had to learn how to be good-ish. Maybe I'm still not there, but I'm still going to try.

out your first album? I had a bit more experience. I didn't really know what I was doing walking into the first record recording. I wrote the songs and recorded them, but this time around I felt a lot more sure of myself and determined to make the record.

Who would you most like to collaborate with and why? Morrissey, Hope Sandoval and Robert Smith. Definitely. I want to be in a

Hold Still. Beautiful book. I guess because I've been on tour with Ryan Adams, I've been listening to a lot of his music at the moment. I've heard his music for years, but it's been nice to delve into it a little deeper, and I really like his new record. Film-wise, I seem to watch the same shit all over again. I watched *Wings of Desire* by Wim Wenders the other night. It's such a beautiful film.

"I WANT TO BE IN A ROMANTIC GOTH BAND SO BADLY. THAT WILL BE THE NEXT RECORD."

— KAREN ELSON

What was the inspiration for the name *Double Roses*? It's a Sam Shepard poem I fell in love with. I really like his plays. He wrote *Paris, Texas* that Wim Wenders directed. There's just something so stark and melancholy and romantic and lovesick that I really respond to.

How does it feel to have finished the album? It had been years to get the record made, so it was a huge sense of relief. Massive, in fact.

What was different this time around as opposed to putting

romantic goth band so badly. That will be the next record.

What are your interests and passions outside of music? I'm a mother with two gorgeous kids. That definitely keeps me busy, and I love being with them. I'm a crazy cat lady. I've got four cats, and I'm obsessed with them. I collect vintage clothing and old books. I like taking pictures and keeping myself busy.

What's your favorite book, film, and music right now? I just finished reading Sally Mann's autobiography

What's next for you? I want to make another record soon. I don't want to wait too long. This record took almost seven years to make, so I need to not give myself any slacking time. I've got to keep writing songs because that's what I love. After I finish touring, I'll get back into writing mode and figure that out. ◾

RUTH KEARNEY

Irish actor Ruth Kearney has a leading role as London in the Netflix original comedy series Flaked, *opposite Will Arnett. Her past roles include the BBC sci-fi drama* Primeval, *FOX's The* Neapolitan Novels, Elena Ferrante

Your idea of heaven: Being on a beautiful tropical island with friends and family and lots of Mezcal.

What was your first break? I don't feel like little too self-centric.

How did you decide to become an actor? When I was younger, me and my sisters used to put on these plays and films. My eldest sister was the director, the writer and the casting director. She used

What would your ideal job be? I always wanted to be a vet or work with animals in some way. I think if I wasn't acting something like that would be amazing.

What advantages do you have? Well, I'm an

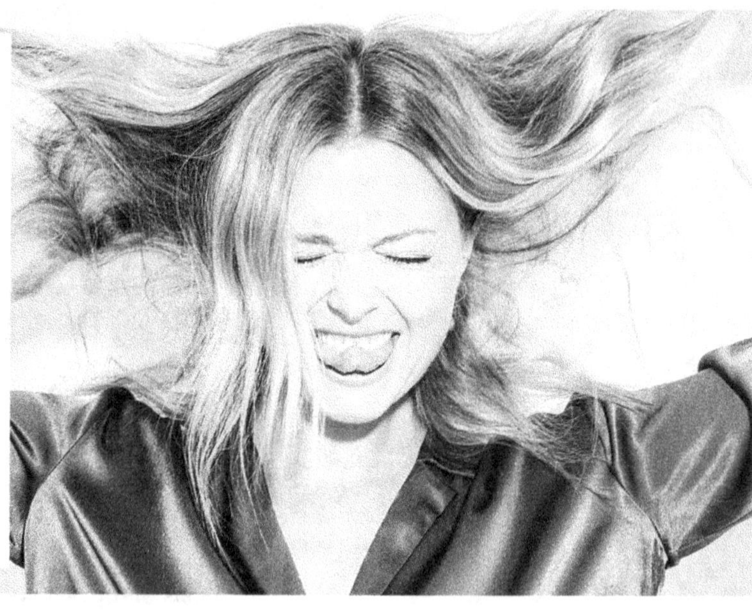

Following and dog walking—it's harder than you think!

Birthplace: Dublin, Ireland

Education: Degree in Classical Studies from Trinity College Dublin

Last Book Read: *The*

I've had my first break yet, but my first job, at a kind of drama school, was a very high-brow piece where I was part of a team stopping dinosaurs from entering into the modern world.

How do you feel about this career? It's a tough career, but I can't really imagine doing anything else. It can be great fun and really challenging, but at times I do worry it's a

to make me audition, and I remember standing out in my hallway waiting to go in, really nervous. I guess it just all started from there.

Who is your favorite actor you look up to? There's a lot of actors that I look up to. I recently watched Natalie Portman in *Jackie*, and I thought she was amazing. She carried the whole film just on the close-up of her face.

Irish dancing champion, so…

What did you do before this career? Lots of different things. I worked a lot as a waitress. I think the most recent job I had was a dog-walker. Which is far more stressful than you'd imagine.

Would you rather have a car or a diploma? A diploma. Because it brings you

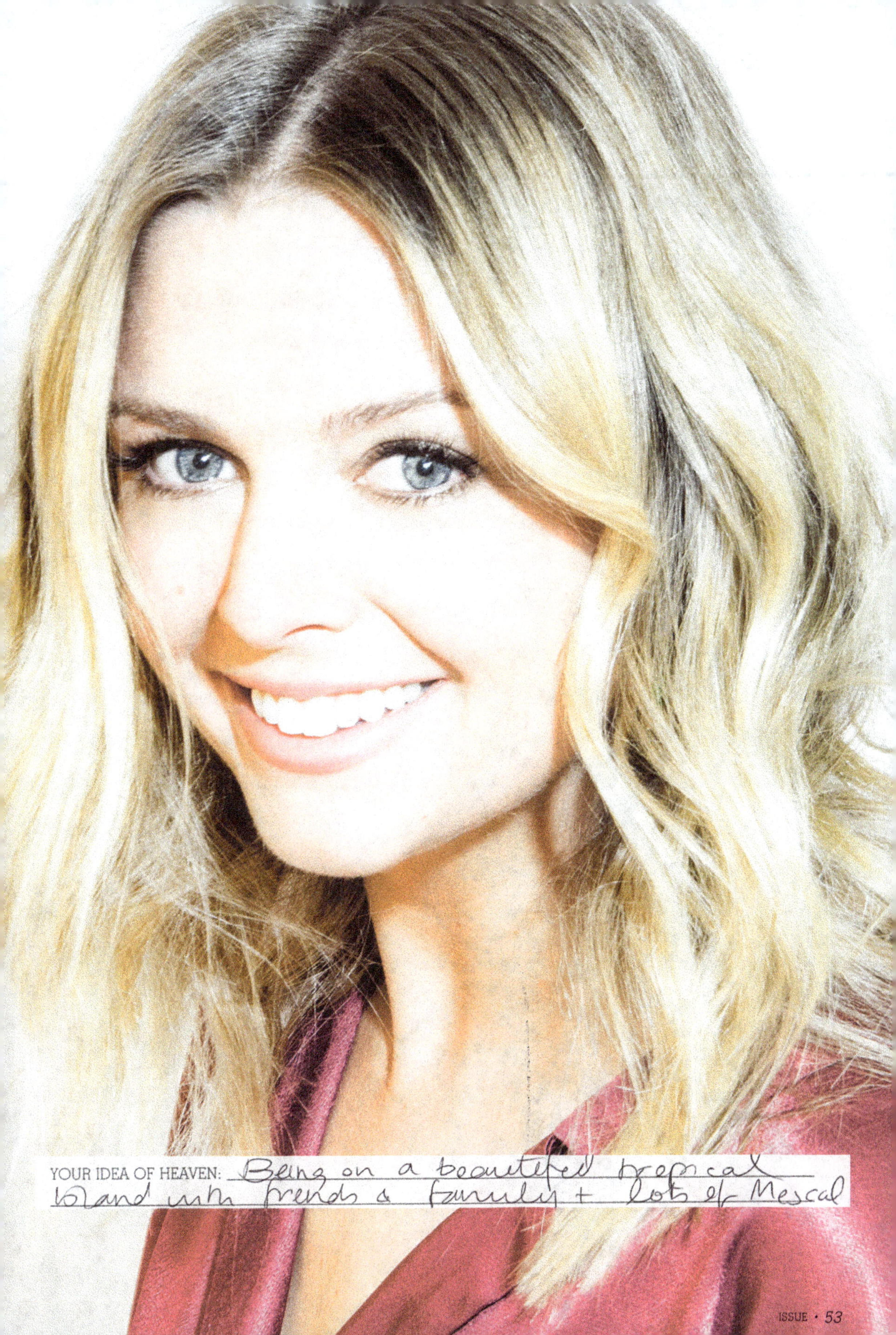

YOUR IDEA OF HEAVEN: Being on a beautiful tropical
island with friends & family + lots of Mescal

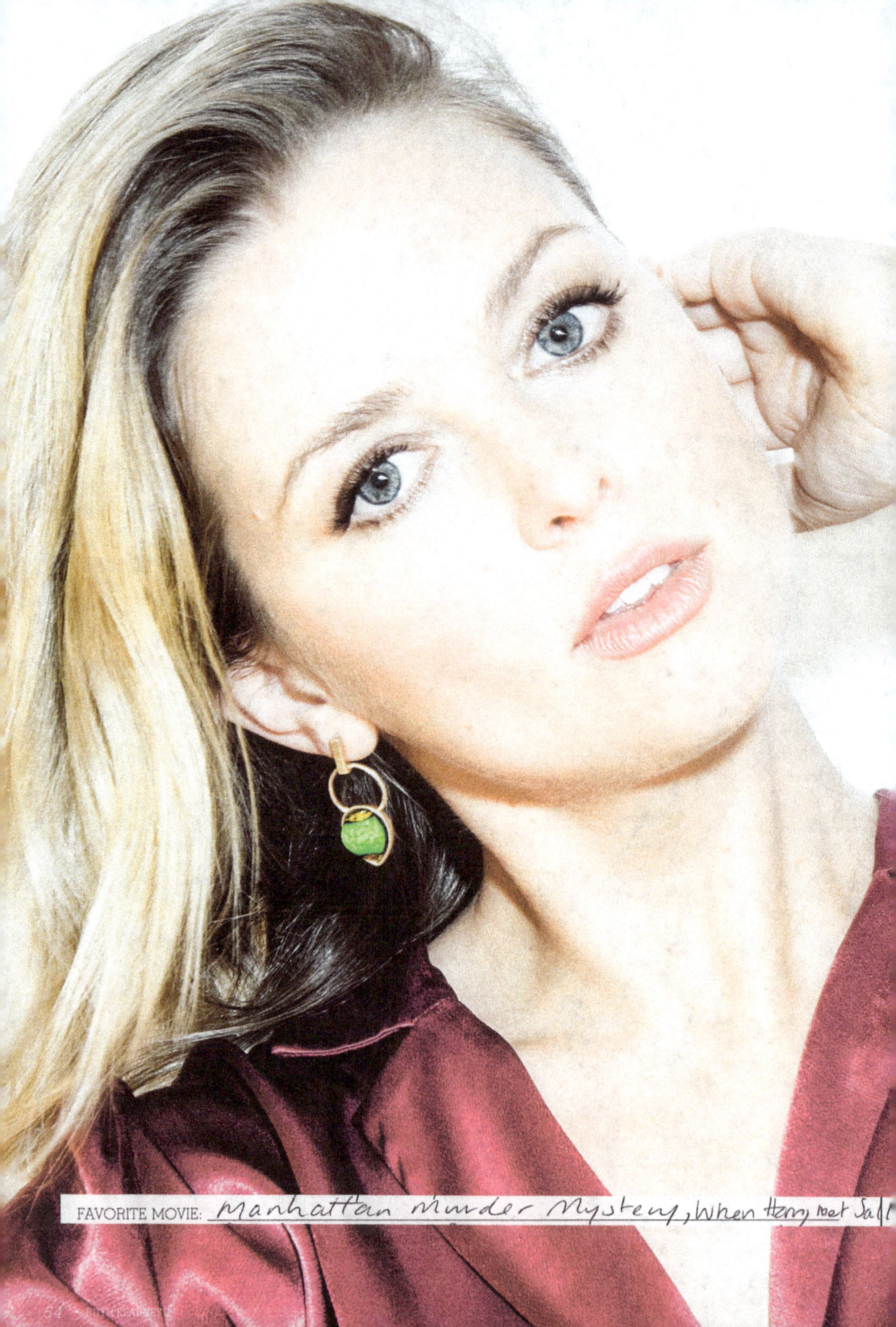

FAVORITE MOVIE: Manhattan Murder Mystery, When Harry met Sal[ly]

knowledge, and knowledge is power.

What does the future look like to you? Unknown and exciting.

ly intrigued to see it. I thought it was brilliantly done and amazingly acted. 🖼

"MY FIRST JOB, AT A KIND OF DRAMA SCHOOL, WAS A VERY HIGH-BROW PIECE WHERE I WAS PART OF A TEAM STOPPING DINOSAURS FROM ENTERING INTO THE MODERN WORLD."

— RUTH KEARNEY

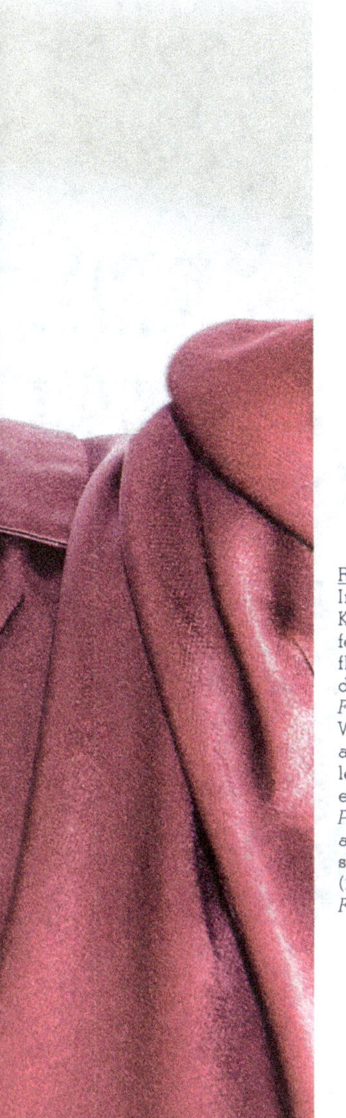

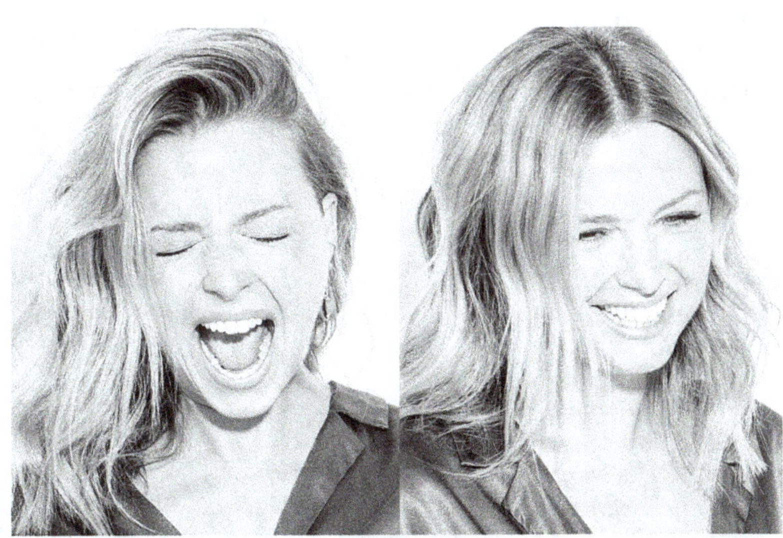

RUTH KEARNEY
Irish actress Ruth Kearney stars as the female lead in Netflix's Venice-based dramedy series *Flaked* opposite Will Arnett. Ruth is also known for her lead role in the science-fiction tv show *Primevil* (2007–11) and appearances in shows such as *Tyrant* (2014–16) and *The Following* (2013–15).

What is your favorite book, film, or music right now? I'm loving Christine and The Queens' album, and I recently saw Anderson Paak perform. The most recent book was Elena Ferrante's *My Brilliant Friend* and that series which is just so good. I hear it's being made into an HBO special, which I'm not surprised about. The most recent film I saw was *Get Out*. It had so much hype behind it, so I was really intrigued to see it.

VITUS SOLASHANKA: NEW CITIZENS

by **Clare Shearer**

"MANY TELL OF THE WAR BEFORE THEIR DOORSTEP BUT ALSO TELL OF PERSECUTION, INJUSTICE, DISCRIMINATION AGAINST WOMEN AND NO OPPORTUNITIES, TRAINING OR JOBS. SOME HAD EXPERIENCED DEATH DIRECTLY TO THEIR RELATIVES OR FRIENDS."
— VITUS SALOSHANKA

This spring in Frankfurt, Germany, large-scale portraits of refugees drape over the faces of multi-story buildings, old and new, as part of a public art project by photographer Vitus Solashanka called **New Citizens**. *His subjects come from Syria, Afghanistan, Iraq, Iran and Eritrea and have fled their countries to seek asylum and a new life in Europe. The show's title and intimate, close-up photographs are optimistic, boldly welcoming new faces into the fold of German society, but the reality leans toward ironic: Solashanka's subjects are not yet citizens. Many are still unsure of their fate in Germany or elsewhere. They are currently housed in a camp on the outskirts of Frankfurt in a series of mobile homes, where some have lived in limbo for over a year and a half.*

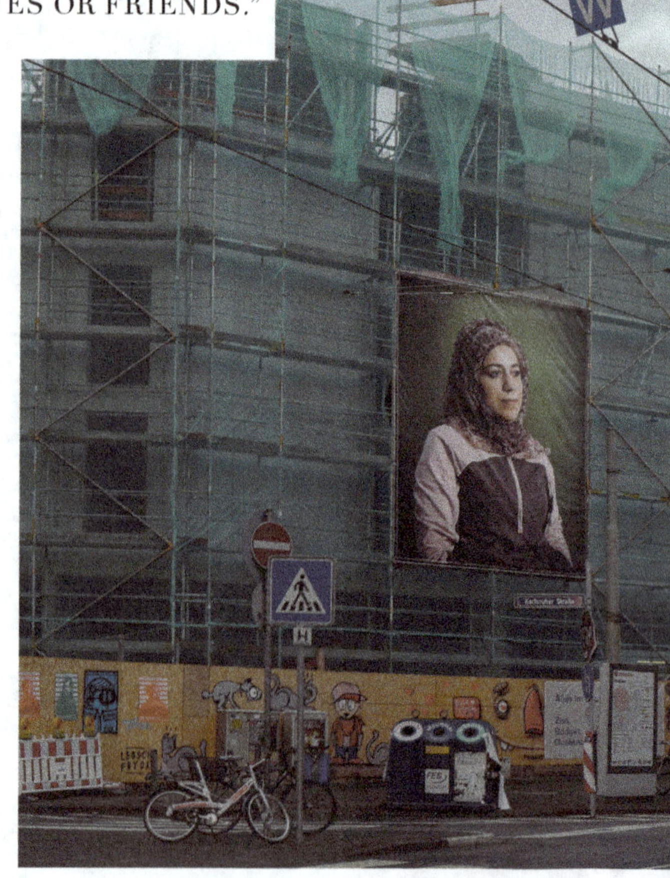

"Abeer" Ecke Mannheimer Str. / Karlsruher Str., Frankfurt

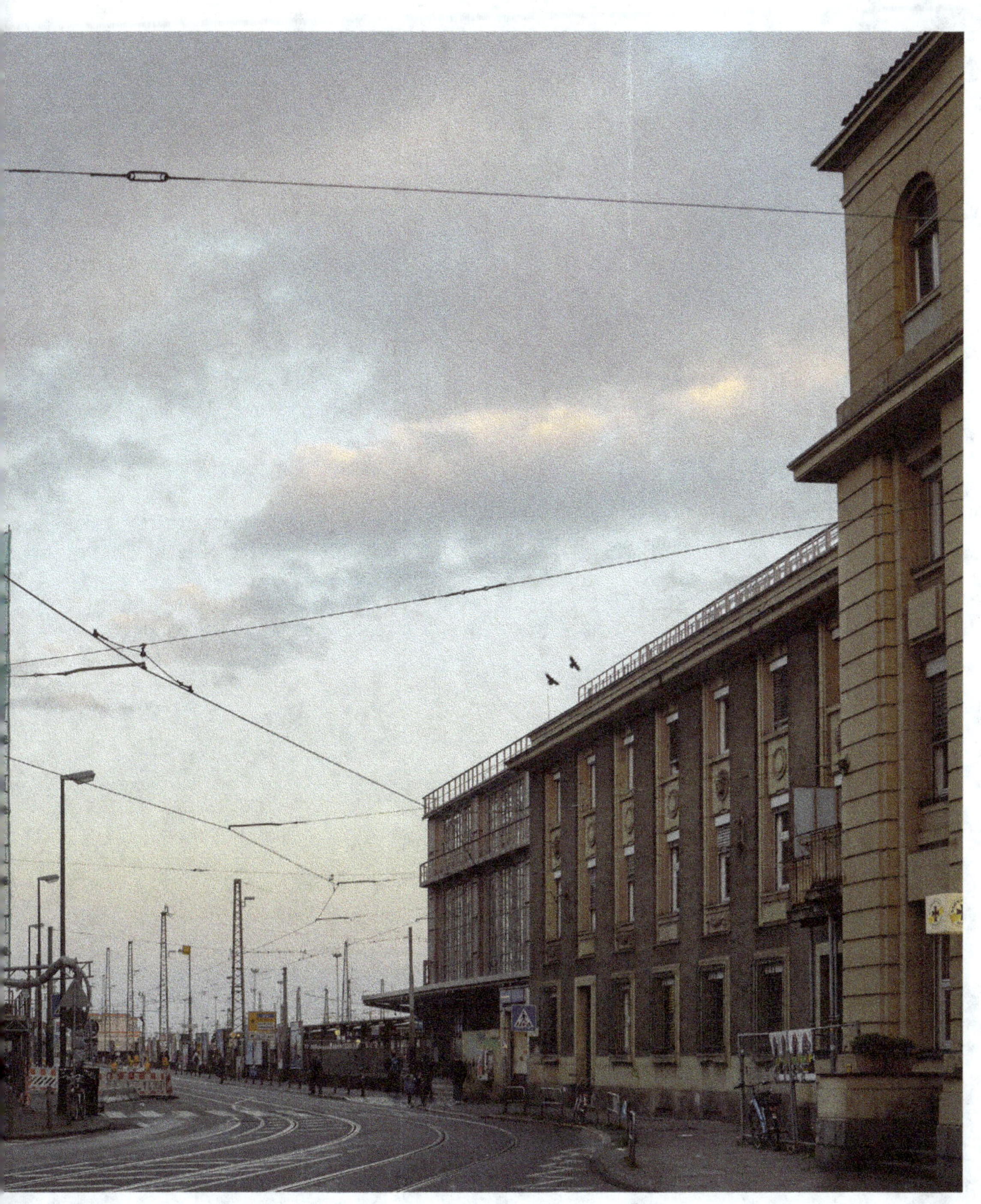

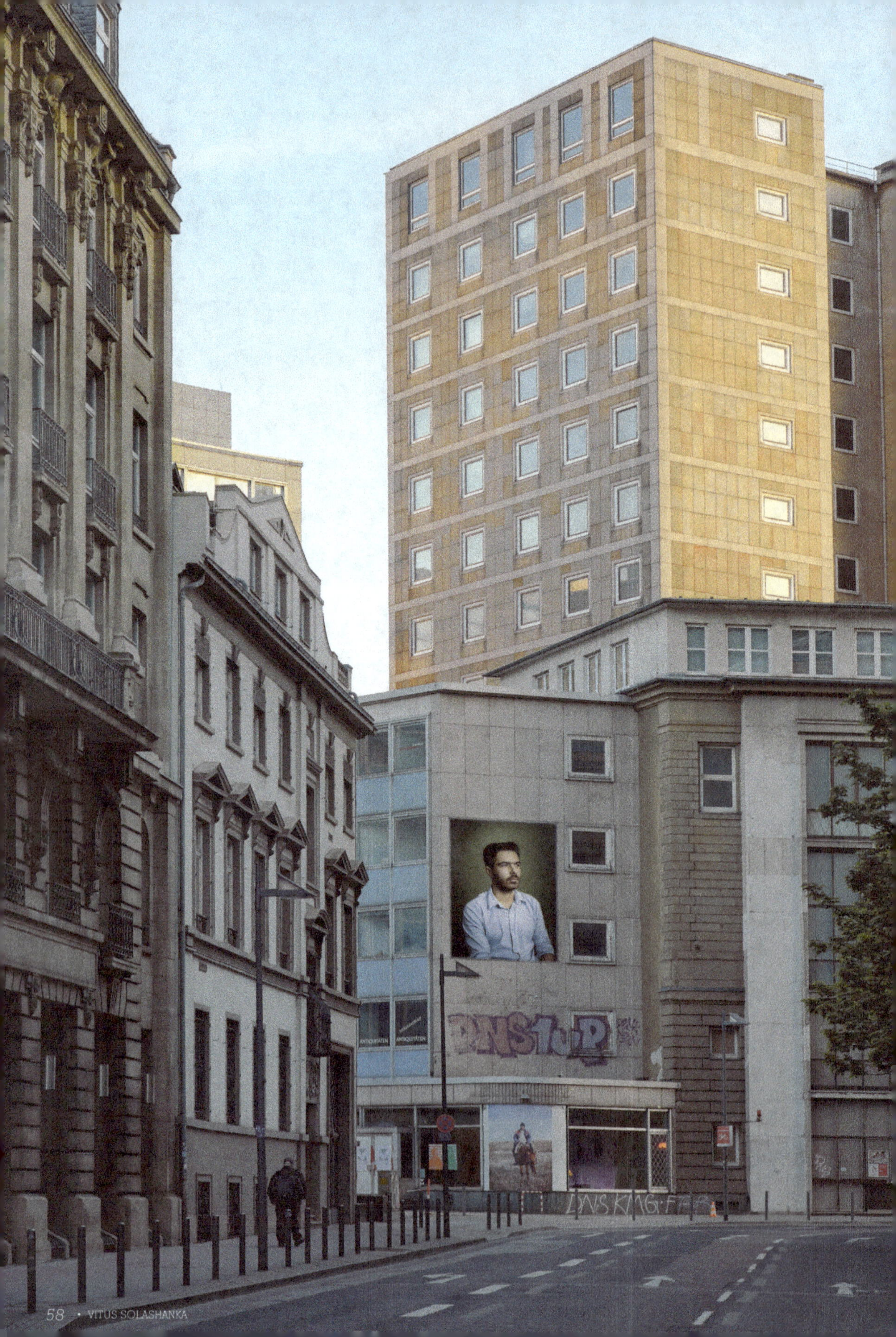

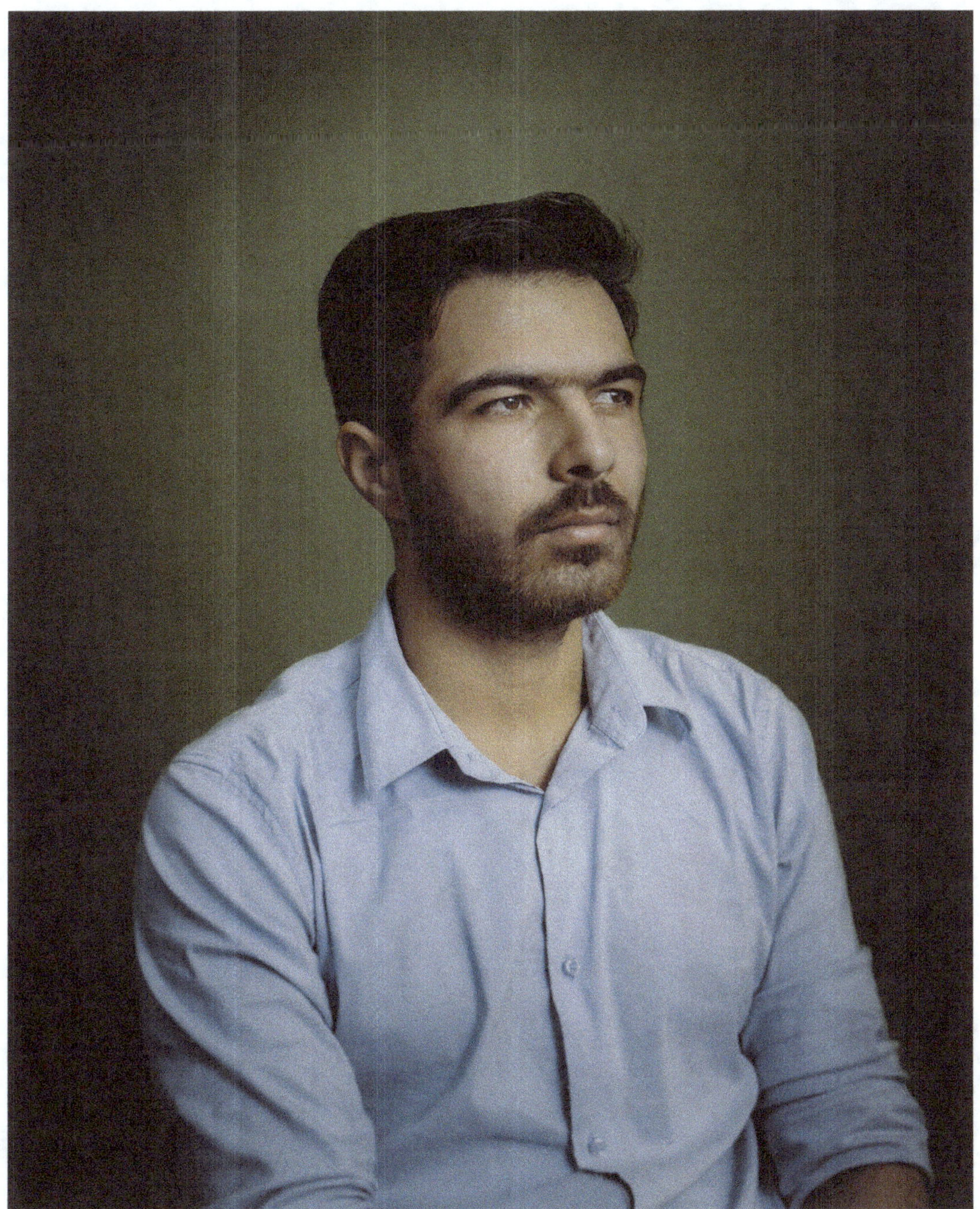

New Citizens #3, 2017

LEFT - *"Hamed" Neue*
Mainzer Str. 57,
Frankfurt

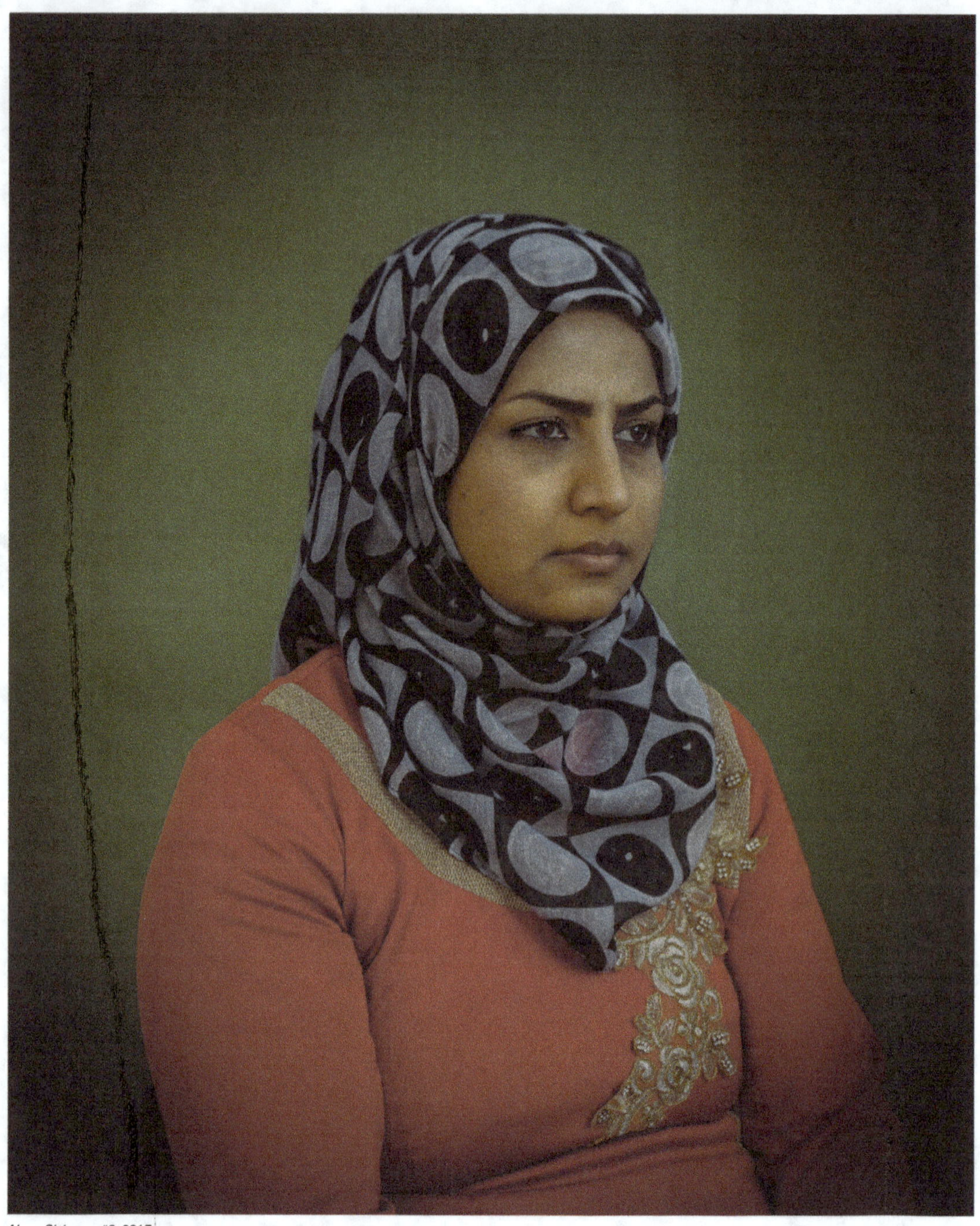

New Citizens #2, 2017

VITUS SALOSHANKA
A photographer based in Frankfurt, Germany, Vitus Saloshanka is originally from Minsk, Belarus and relocated to Germany in 2002. His photographic work focuses on built landscapes and how their populations, centers and boundaries are reworked due to political or social upheaval. Saloshanka's 2014 book, *High Hopes*, a photographic study of Sochi, Russia preceding the Winter Olympics, was shortlisted for the 2014 Rencontres d'Arles Book Awards. His current project, *New Citizens*, which features intimate portraits of refugees living at a camp near Saloshanka's home in Frankfurt, is showing as a large-scale public art project throughout Frankfurt.

NEW CITIZENS
A photographic study by Vitus Saloshanka, *New Citizens* focuses on refugees from Syria, Afghanistan, Iraq, Iran and Eritrea who are living indefinitely in a camp outside of Frankfurt, Germany, waiting for asylum. Saloshanka befriended them, taking close-up portraits that focus intimately on the individuals who lived through the tragic refugee crisis, which swept Europe beginning in 2015. A public art project also entitled *New Citizens. [Neue Bürger]* features his large-scale portraits hung from buildings across Frankfurt.

Once meant to be temporary accommodation, the camp has since become a sort of self-contained unit that coexists with the city, though starkly disparate. Solashanka lives in the surrounding neighborhood and began to notice this sharp divide between his daily life and that of those stuck inside indefinitely, hoping for the possibility of asylum. "I regard this fence as a physical as well as a symbolic boundary between societies," he tells me over email. For many months, Saloshanka watched the camp's atmosphere fluctuate as refugees, many of whom are families with children, oscillated between hope and anxiety. "There are people with whom I had great empathy," he says. "I wish their problems could be solved quickly, but it is a very long way, sometimes with very bitter experiences. Some are frustrated, some are satisfied… That inspired me to discuss this subject myself."

In his project *New Citizens*, Solashanka approached the terse realities of displacement at a more personal level—he began to visit the camp in his Frankfurt neighborhood and meet the people who lived there. "It was important to be there and talk to people without necessarily keeping a camera at hand," he says of his process. "After seven months, I could make the first recordings…. Many had simply been afraid." He began photographing those he met close-up and without context—poised, human and alone. Avoiding the "mass media image," he says, "I wanted to look at people as human beings, to present them as individuals first." With close-cropped portraits, he frees his subjects of "generalizations and victimhood."

What Saloshanka describes as the "mass media image" has intermittently commanded headlines since 2015, when Europe began to see its worst refugee crisis since World War II. Refugees were often photographed in the context of crowded, makeshift camps or braving journeys through the Mediterranean on dangerous, overloaded boats. These images and stories shocked the world, with the height of public outcry marked by the tragic, now-indelible photograph of a small boy in a red t-shirt dead on the beach. An outpouring of empathy and aid clashed with fear of terrorism and economic concerns—could Europe handle such a massive, sudden influx of people from different cultures? If so, how?

Many advocated for full assimilation of refugees, who fled a range of situations including civil wars, human rights atrocities by authoritarian leaders like Syria's Bashar al-Assad, or terrorist groups spreading across the Middle East, namely ISIS. Under Chancellor Angela Merkel, Germany offered to take in refugees with open arms, and over a million

"I WANTED TO LOOK AT PEOPLE AS HUMAN BEINGS, TO PRESENT THEM AS INDIVIDUALS FIRST."

— VITUS SALOSHANKA

asylum-seekers arrived in the country alone. With this commitment, Germany has shouldered much of the weight of the crisis with humanitarian intent and Merkel's constant refrain, "Wir schaffen das" or "We can do this." But since the initial influx, there are thousands who wait indefinitely to know what their future holds, with camps similar to that in Frankfurt still spread across Europe.

Now, nearly two years later, as countries like Germany—among others including France, Greece, the UK, Austria, Hungary, Norway, Sweden and Finland—still struggle to house and integrate refugees, many wait to overcome administrative or policy hurdles. None of it is simple; none of it without huge stakes. But Saloshanka seeks to refocus the image of the immigrants away from the tragic, recasting them as real people and, hopefully, real citizens.

Saloshanka is not a native German himself, but moved from Minsk, Belarus in 2002. As he talked

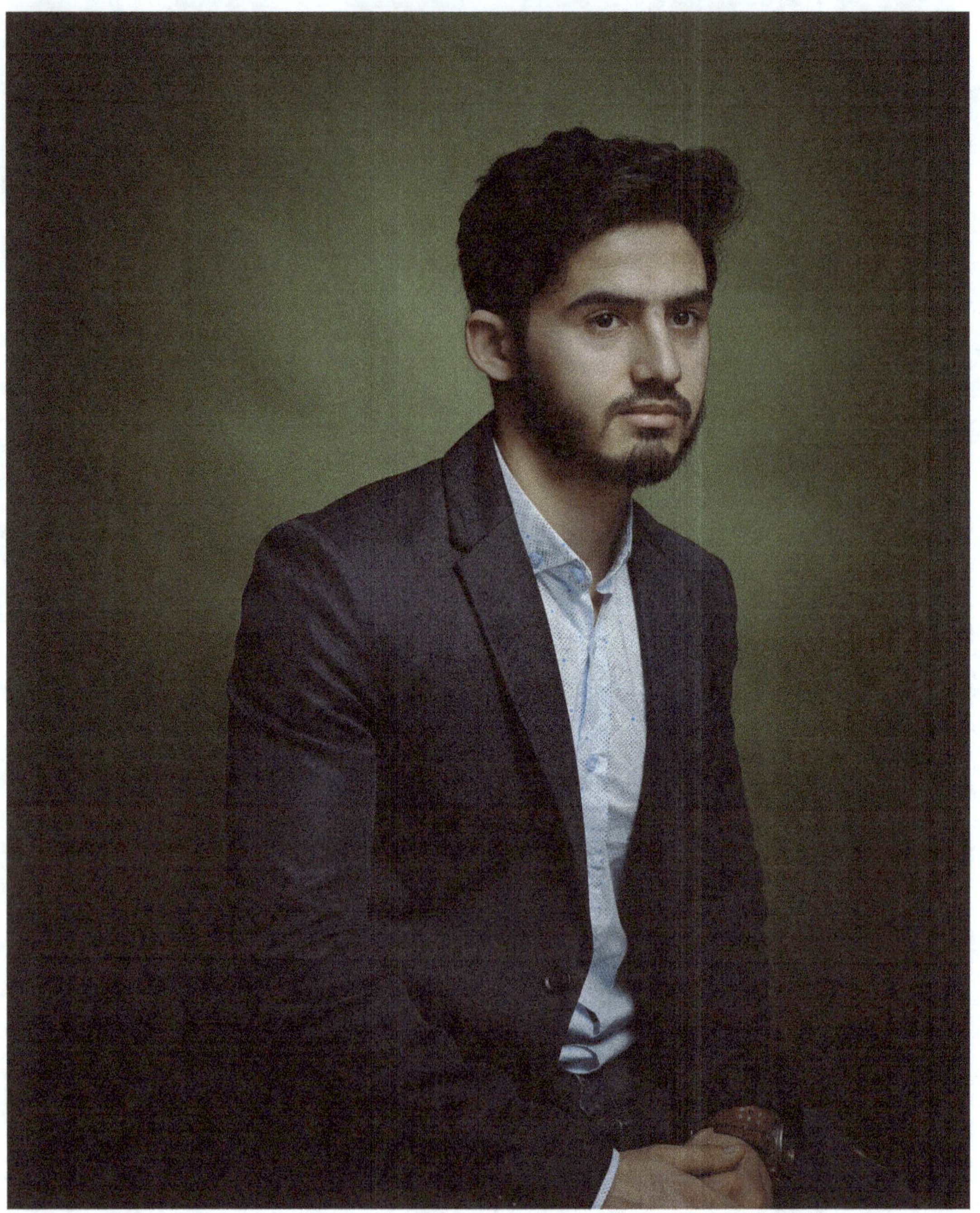

New Citizens #14, 2017

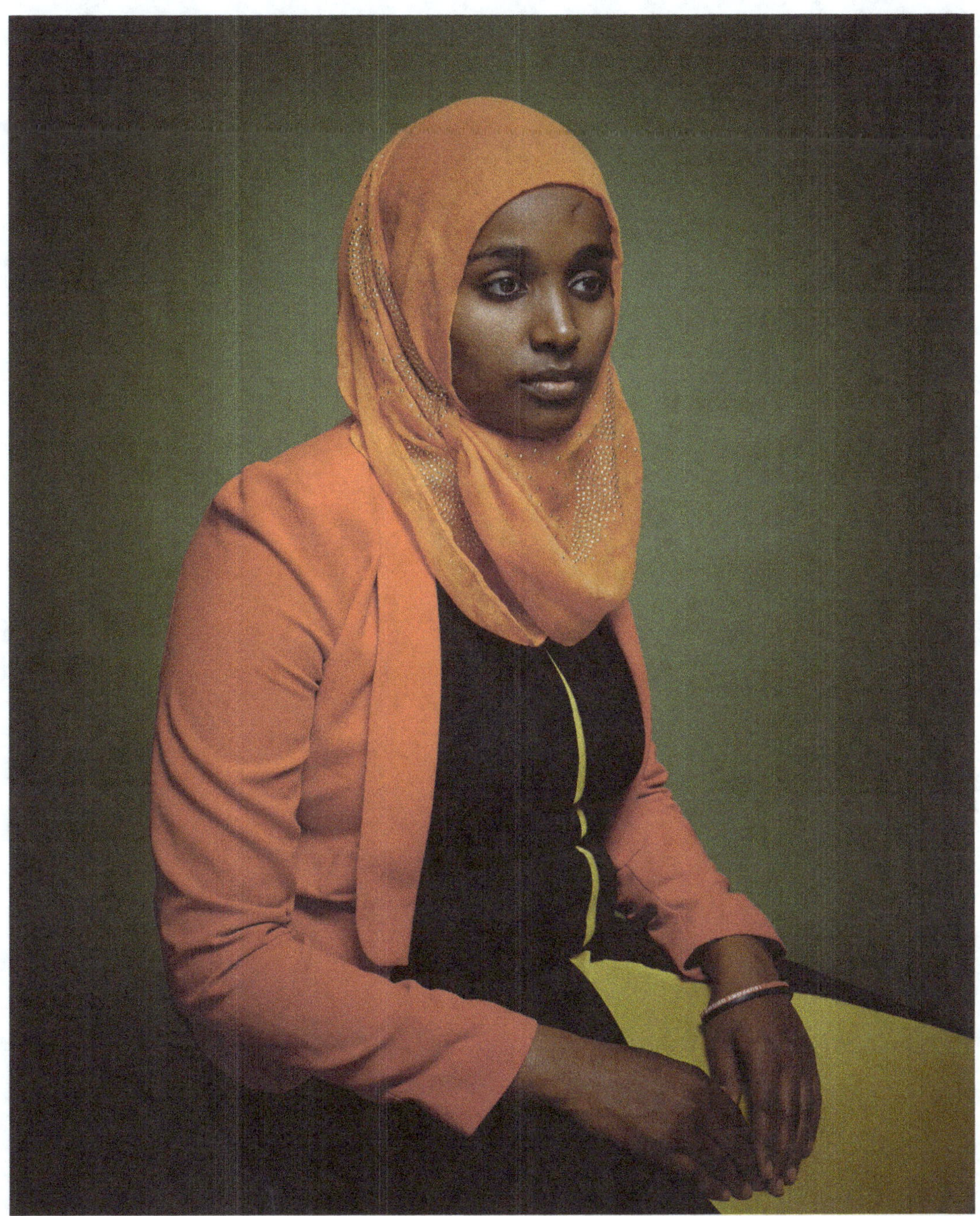

New Citizens #16, 2017

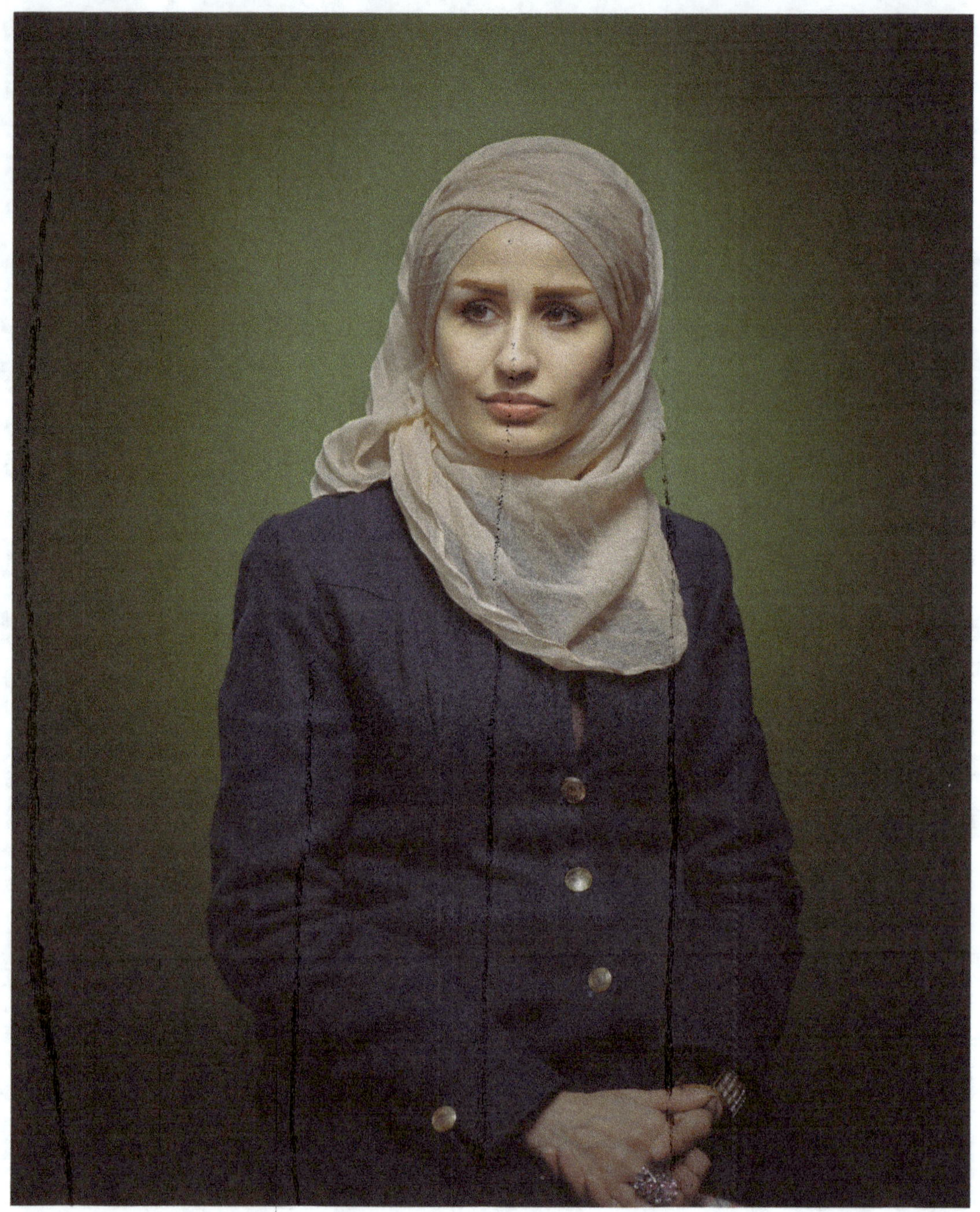

New Citizens #15, 2017

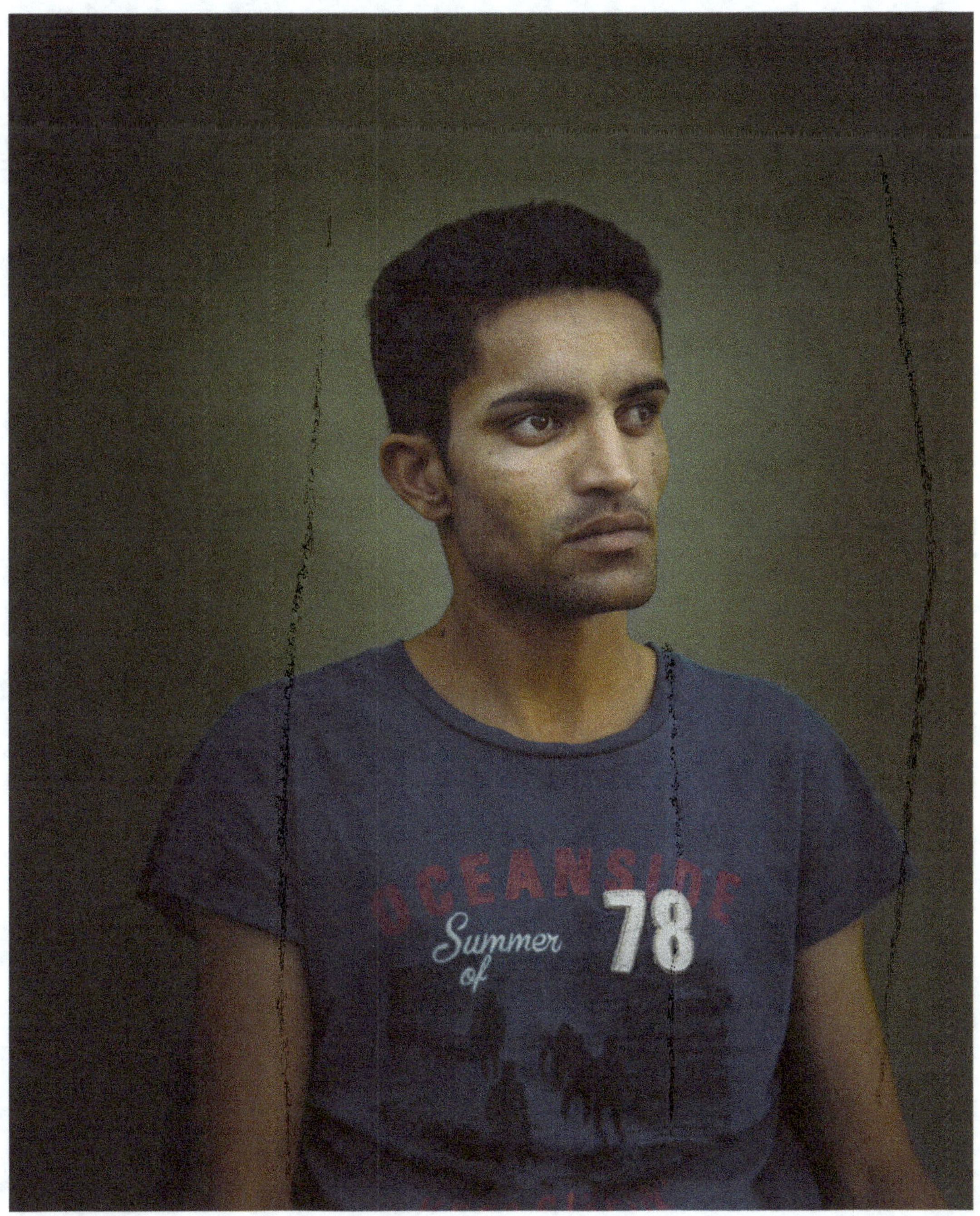

New Citizens #10, 2017

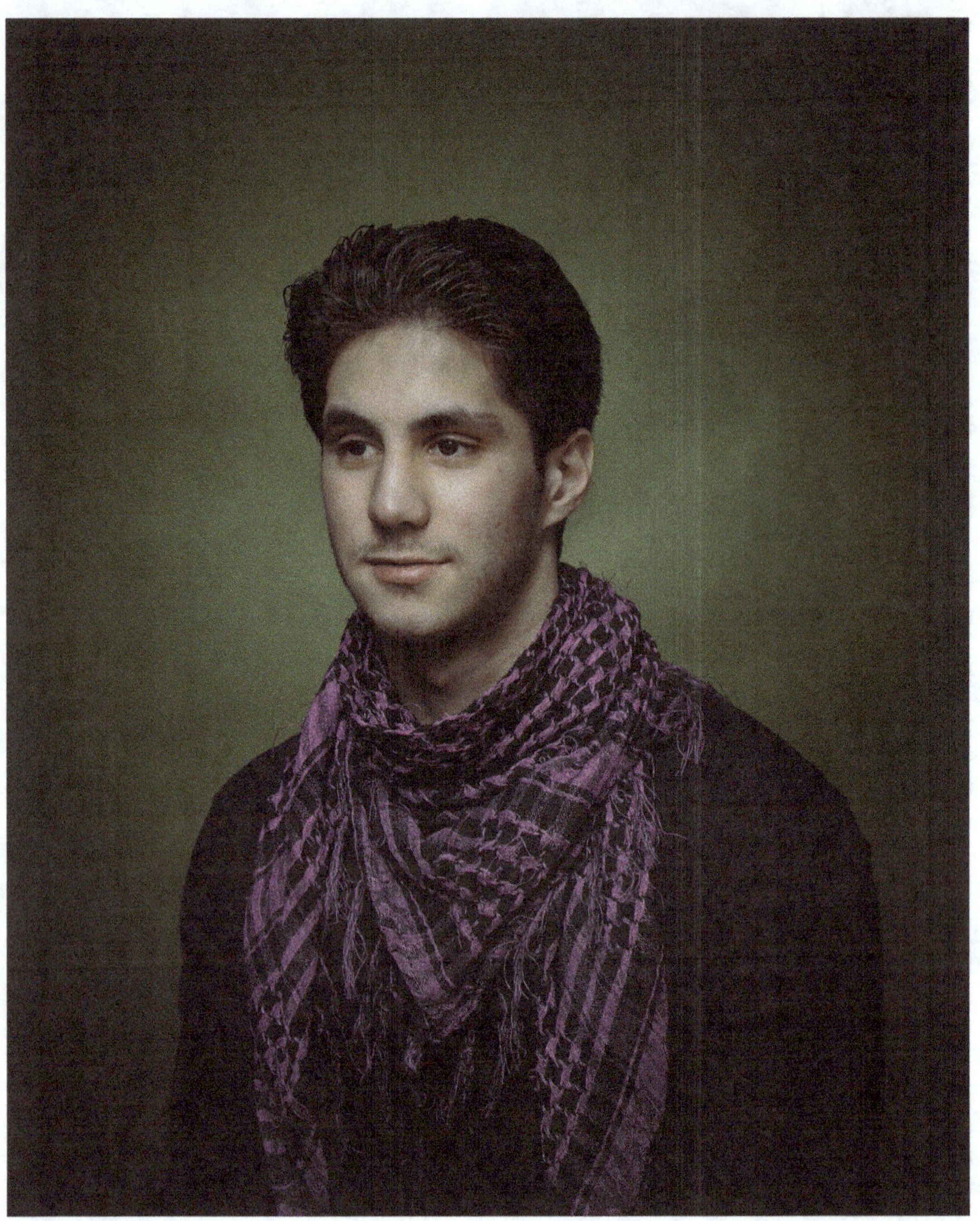

New Citizens #7, 2017

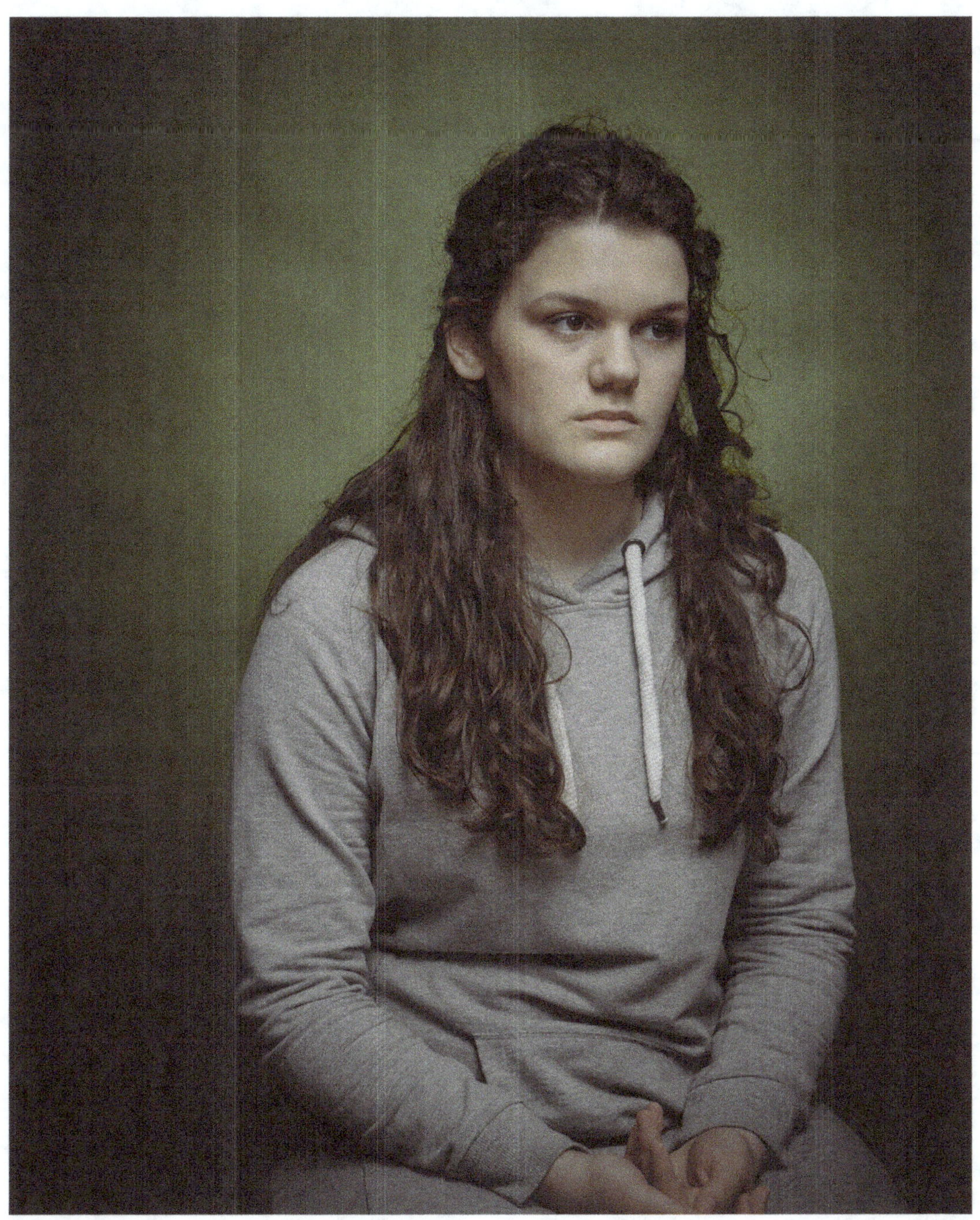

New Citizens #6, 2017

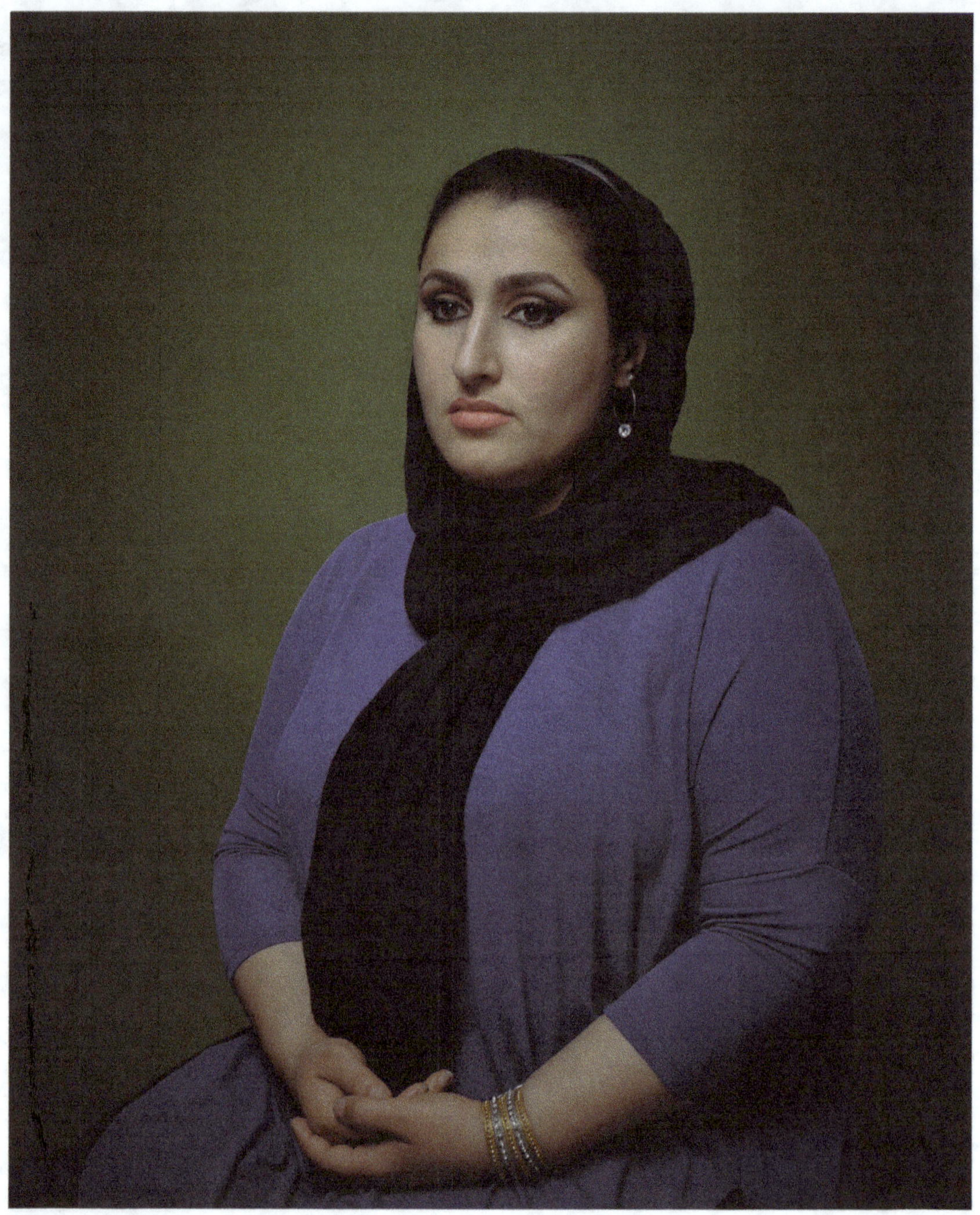

New Citizens #13, 2017

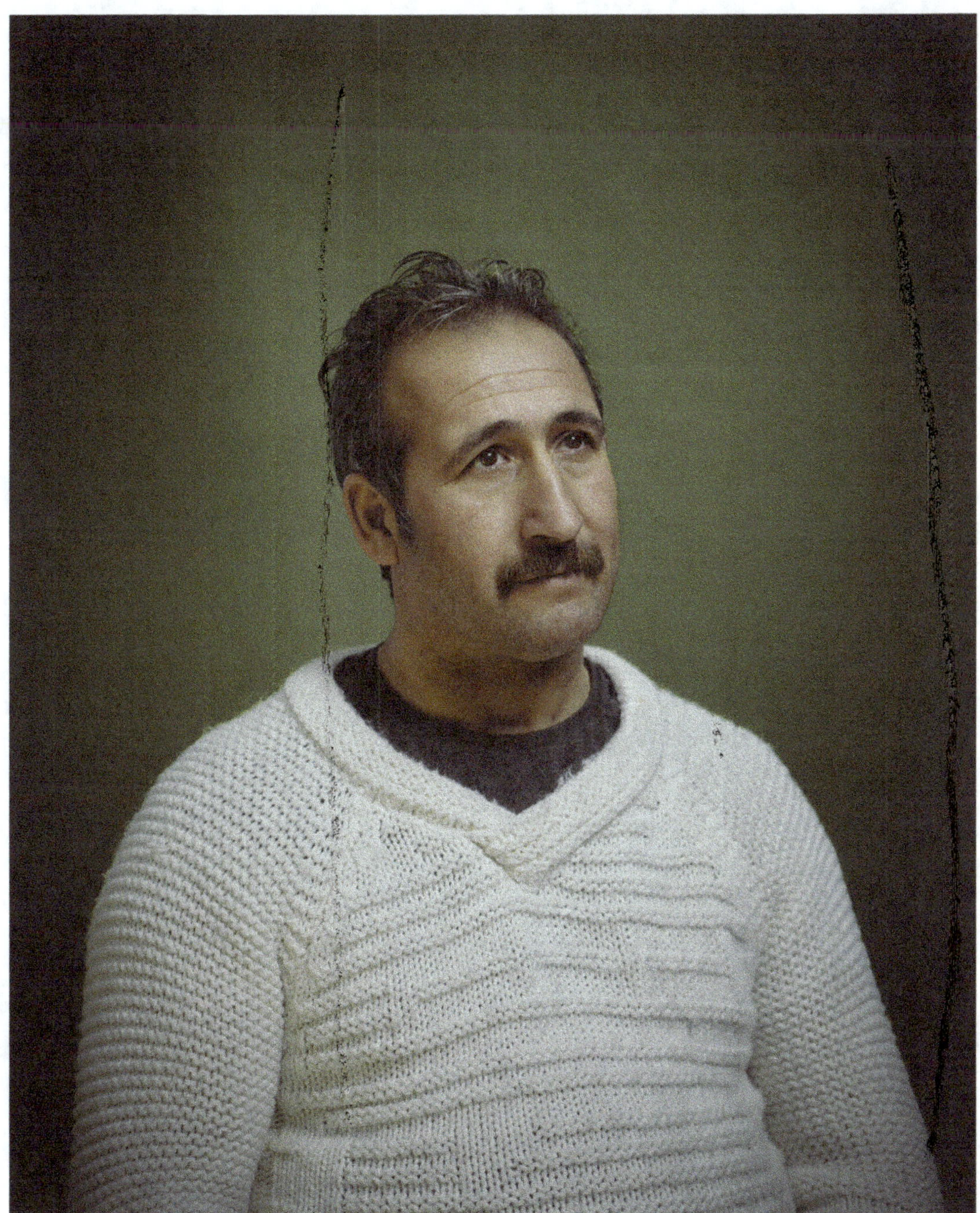

New Citizens #12, 2017

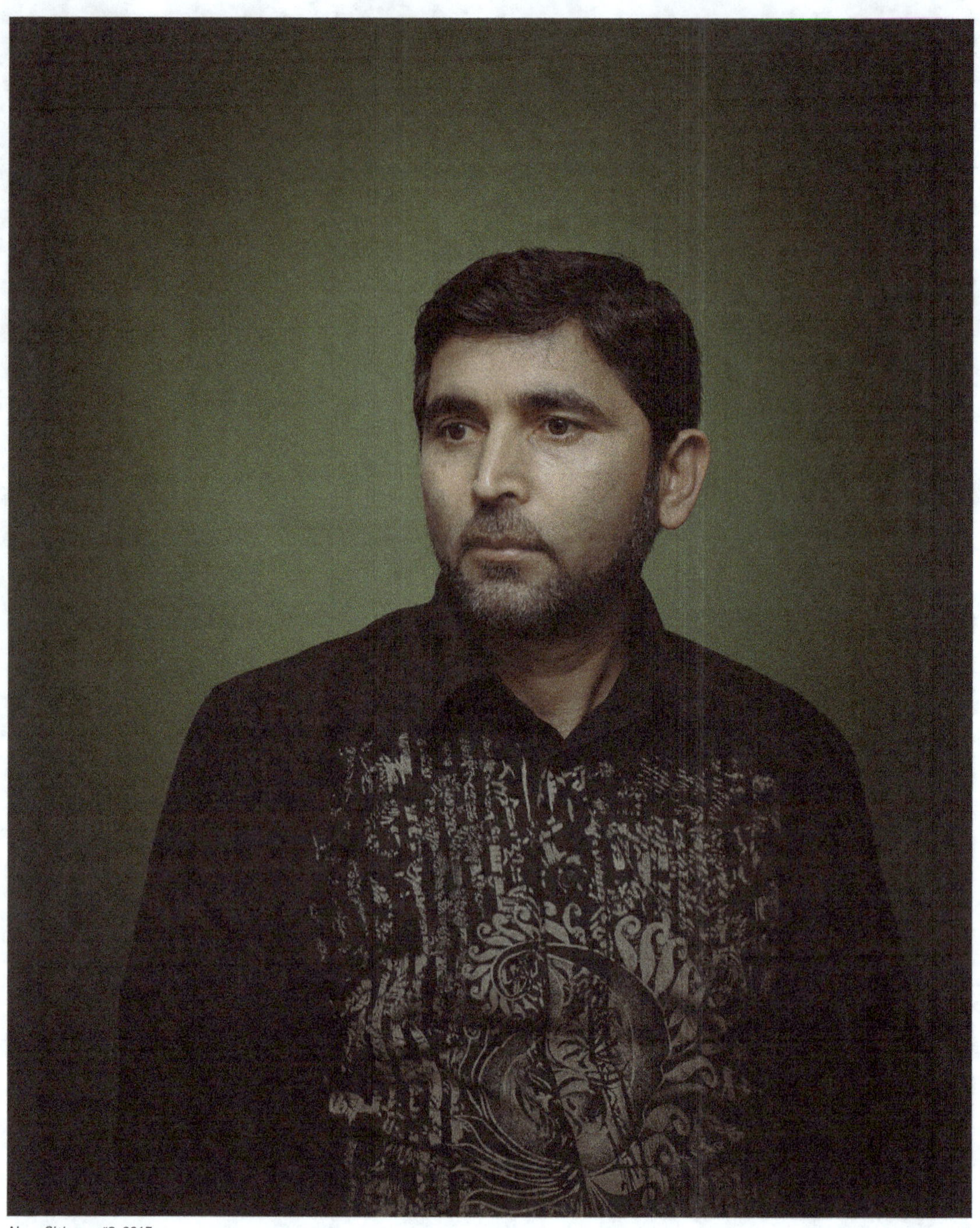

New Citizens #8, 2017

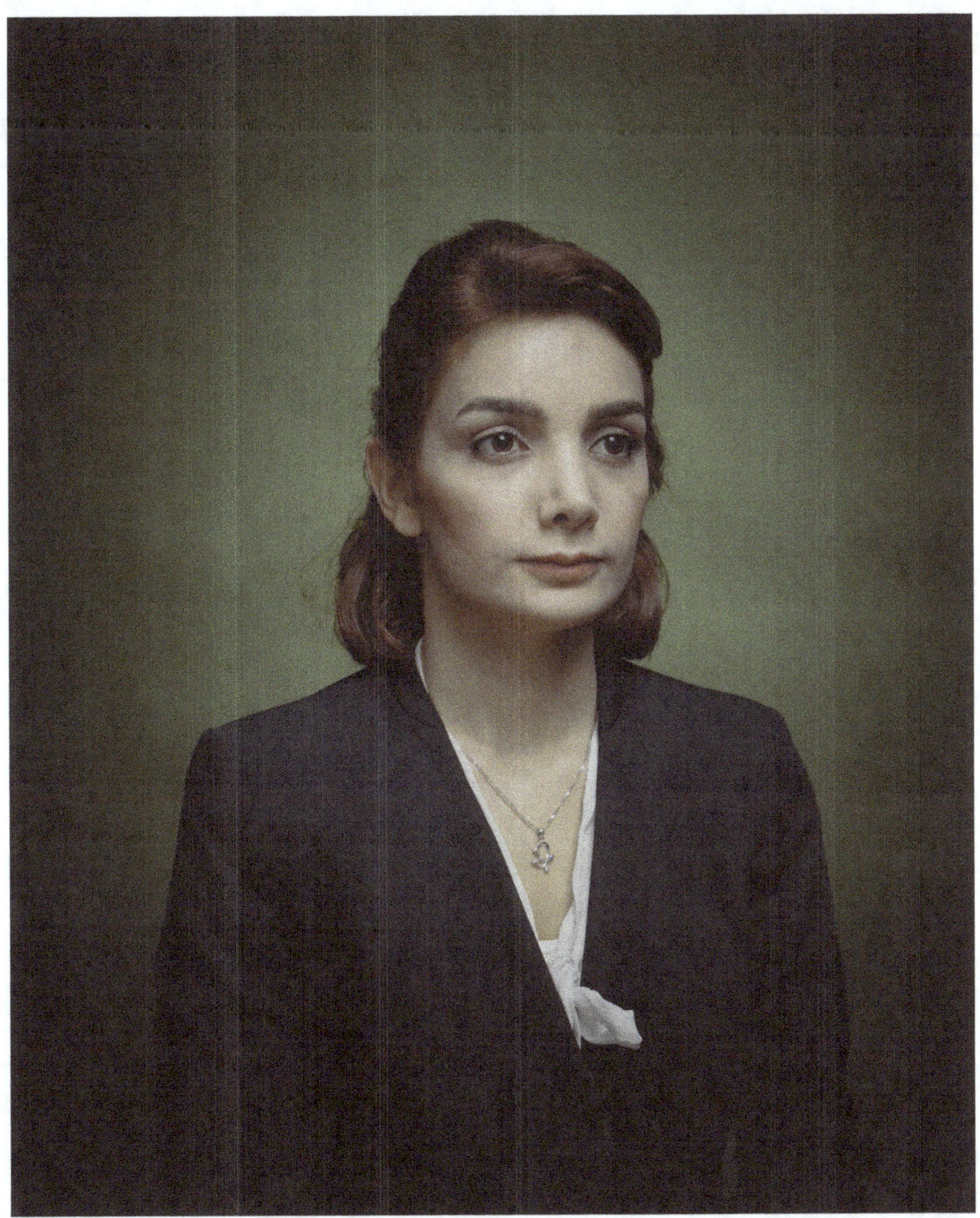

New Citizens #5, 2017

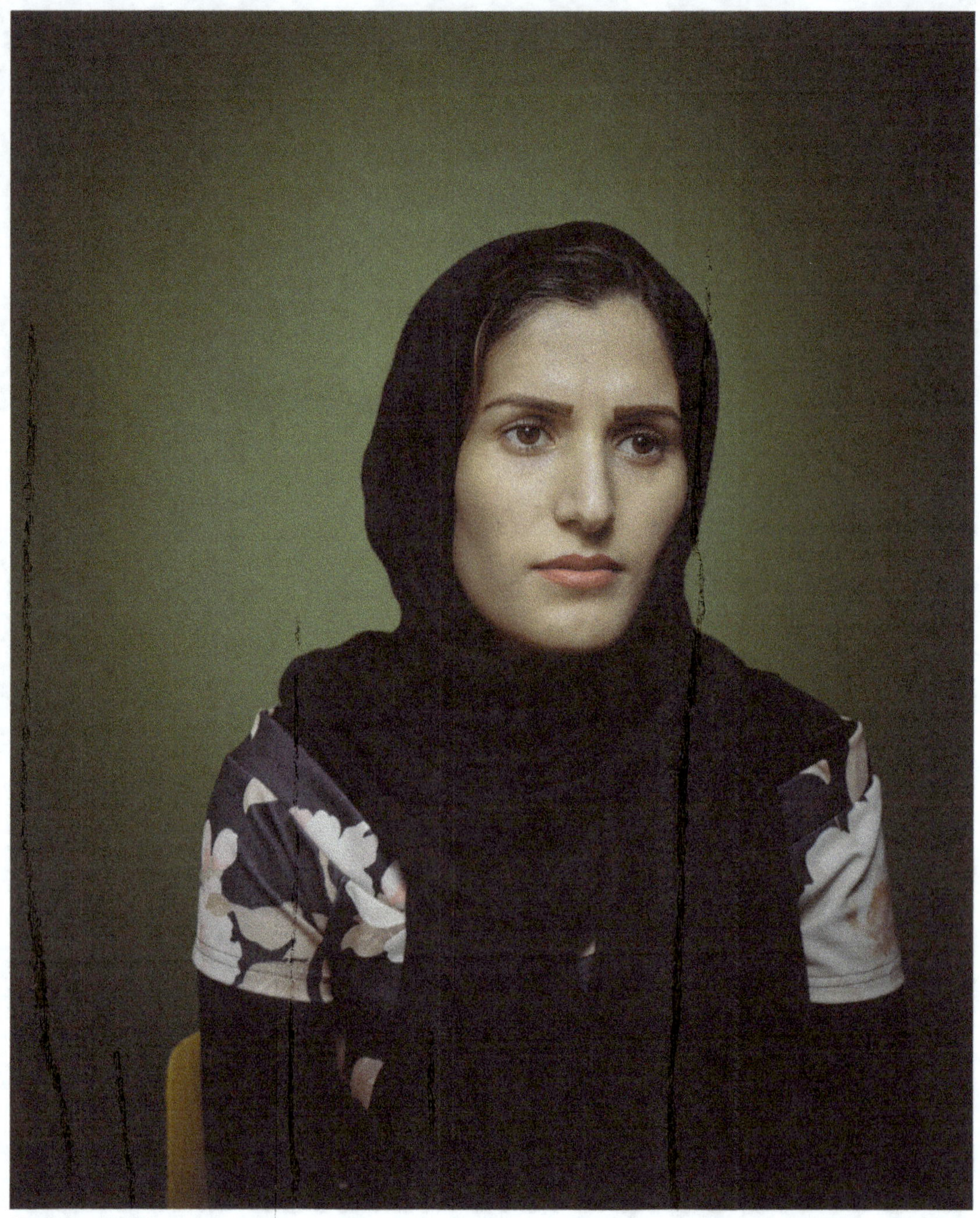

New Citizens #4, 2017

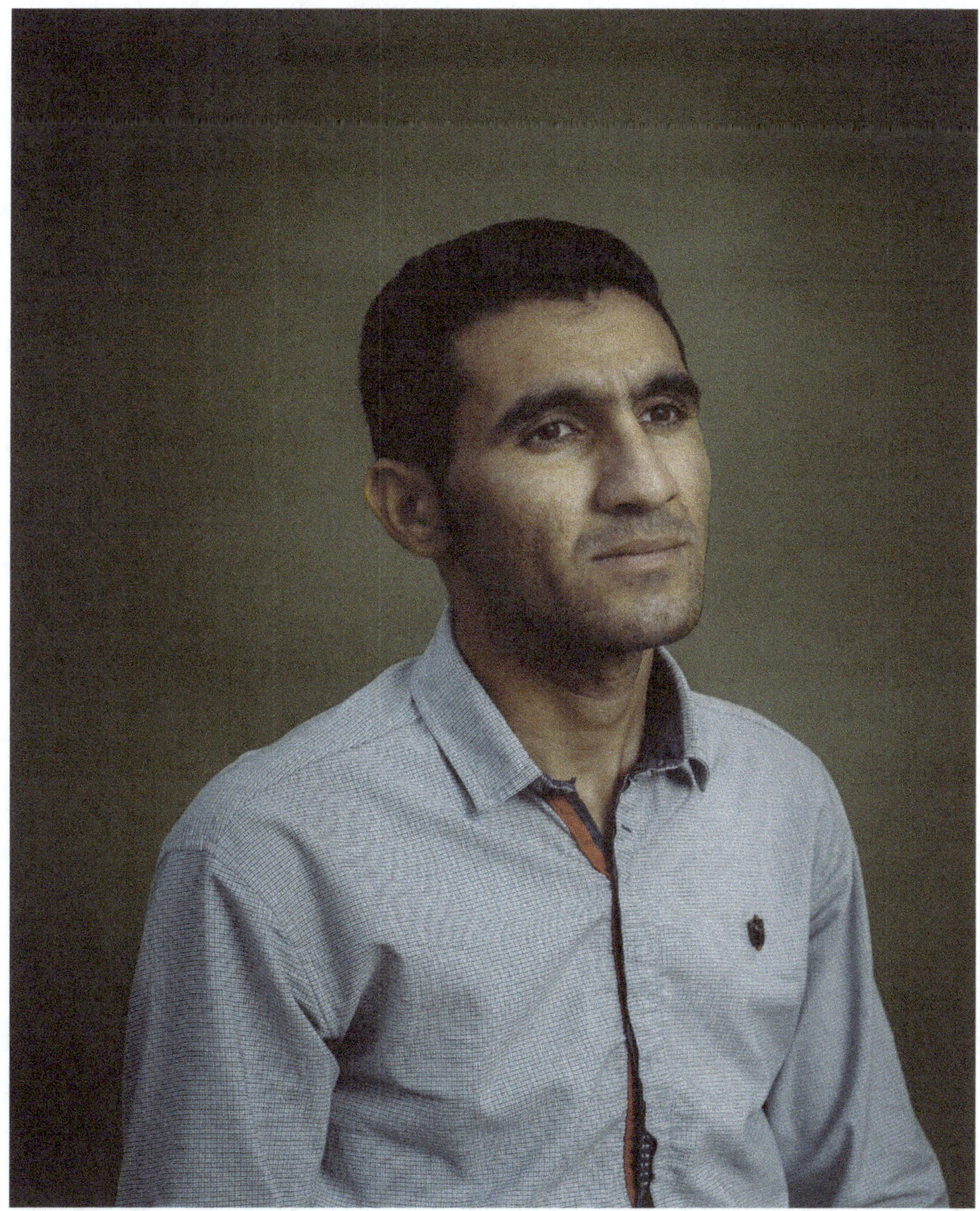

New Citizens #11, 2017

and worked with the refugees, he heard their stories and began to understand the precipice on which they stood—a break between their livelihoods, families and places of worship at home and the lives they hoped to lead in Germany. "Many tell of the war before their doorstep, but also tell of persecution, injustice, discrimination against women and no opportunities, training or jobs. Some had experienced death directly to their relatives or friends."

The public art project of *New Citizens* seeks to spread this discourse of understanding and welcoming cultural differences "to the widest possible public and continue to develop it there," Saloshanka says. His work unfurls like a new kind of flag over the facades of Frankfurt, one without a country's symbol or designation but that signifies the welcoming of new faces into the city.

is a big story" and one that he will "continue in this year."

New Citizens marks an aesthetic break from Saloshanka's previous photographic work, which focuses on the edges of built landscapes and those who live there. But thematically there is a through-line of commingling people and place and exploring how the two lend themselves to one another. His recent work includes *High Hopes*, a three-year photographic study of Sochi, Russia that documents the city and its people as they prepared to host the 2014 Winter Olympics. The series highlights the process of transformation that proceeds such a massive, global event, as well as the glimmers of change coming to a younger generation of Russians. An allusion to the grand ambitions and expectations that enraptured Sochi, *High Hopes* zooms out to capture

"IT HAS BEEN AN APPROXIMATION PROCESS FOR MYSELF. I NOW REALLY SEE THESE PEOPLE WITH OTHER EYES."

— VITUS SALOSHANKA

For Saloshanka, the series is "an attempt to lead this dialogue. I believe that art has an indirect effect on society… My idea is to play with another perception." The German title of the project, *Neue Bürger*, Saloshanka says has a "different connotation" than *New Citizens*. "It also means taking a lot of responsibility for the society, which is not the case for the immigrants. Their status has few possibilities."

The most interesting and fraught part of the process, according to Saloshanka, was photographing women "because their culture forbids this" or often men "decide whether the woman is allowed to be shown." These cultural and religious differences often surround the use of a headscarf, which one woman working on the series decided to take off for her portrait. This deeply impacted Saloshanka, who says that "the emancipation of the woman

massive overhauls and construction, juxtaposing colorful scenes of nature against built landscapes, with keen attention to those living in its midst.

Saloshanka's next project will focus "on the North-Eastern border areas of the EU." He explains, "Until recently, this area formed a cultural and political entity. I want to explore the border areas of the former Iron Curtain, visualize changes and find out what characterizes today's EU border." Examining boundary zones and the intimate human impact when borders are redrawn, Saloshanka will continue to mine changed political and social landscapes to highlight subjects caught in limbo: the displaced, the unrepresented and the resilient. Of *New Citizens*, he says, "It has been an approximation process for myself. I now really see these people with other eyes."

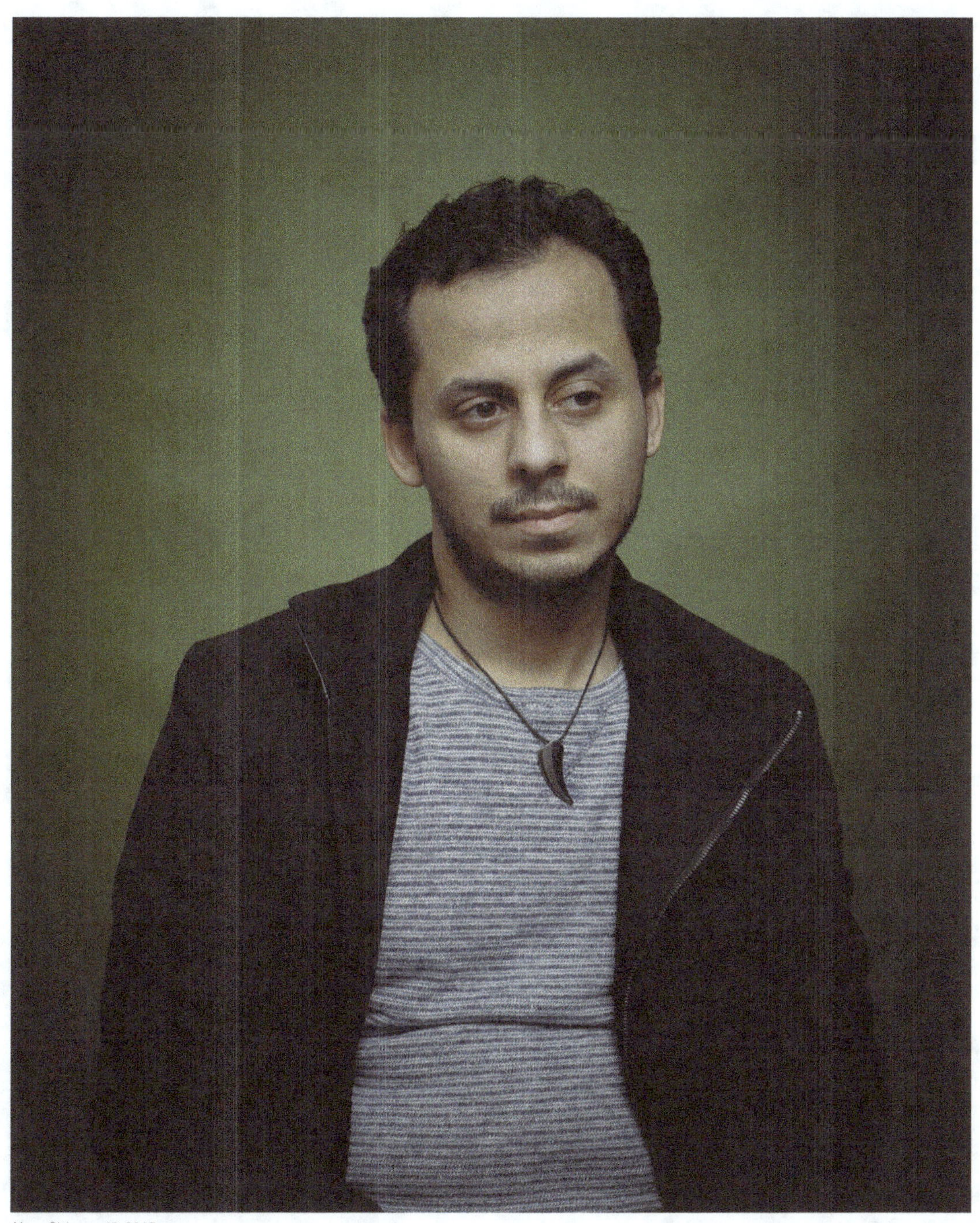

New Citizens #9, 2017

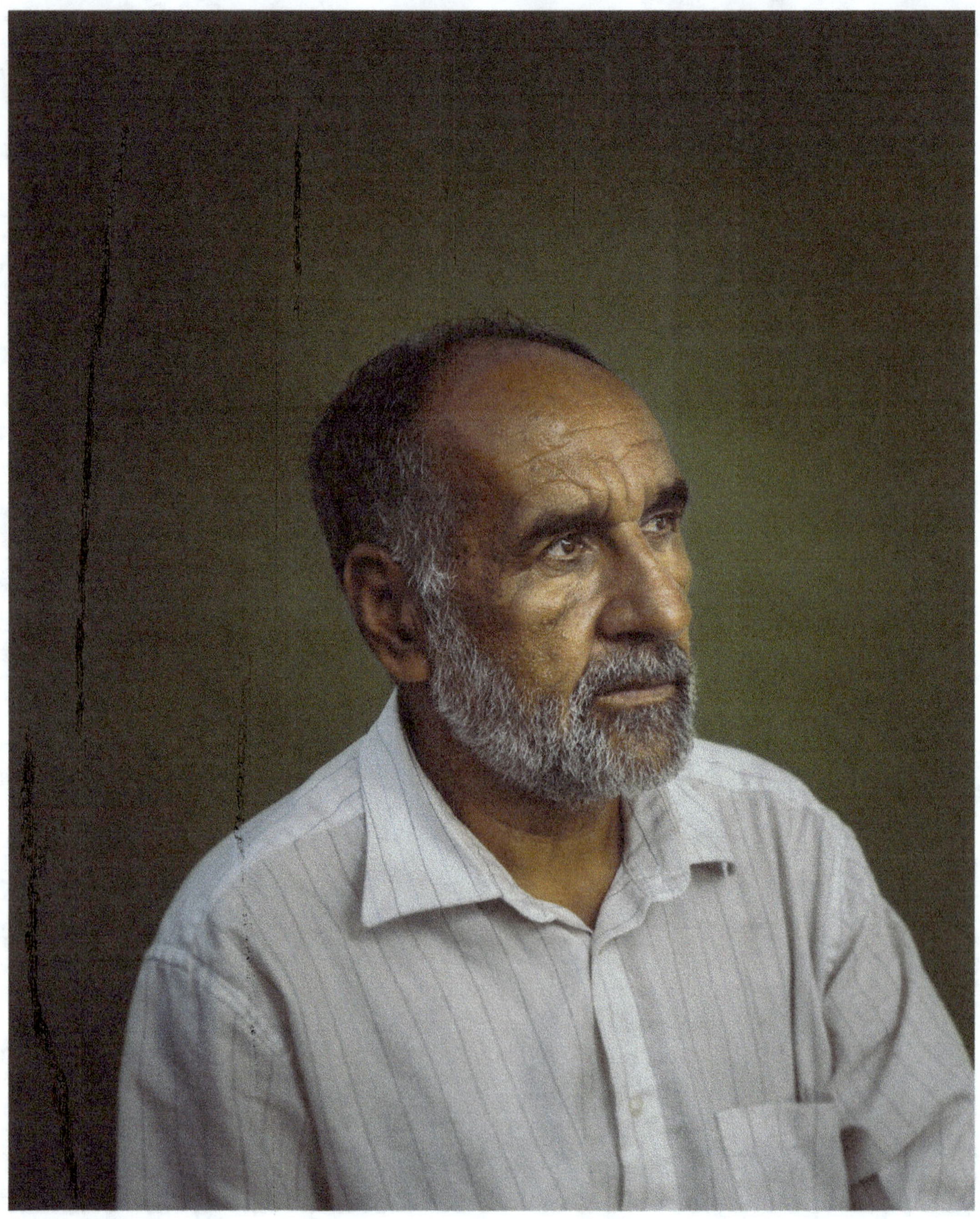

New Citizens #1, 2017

RIGHT - *"Mohammad Karim" Winx Tower, Frankfurt*

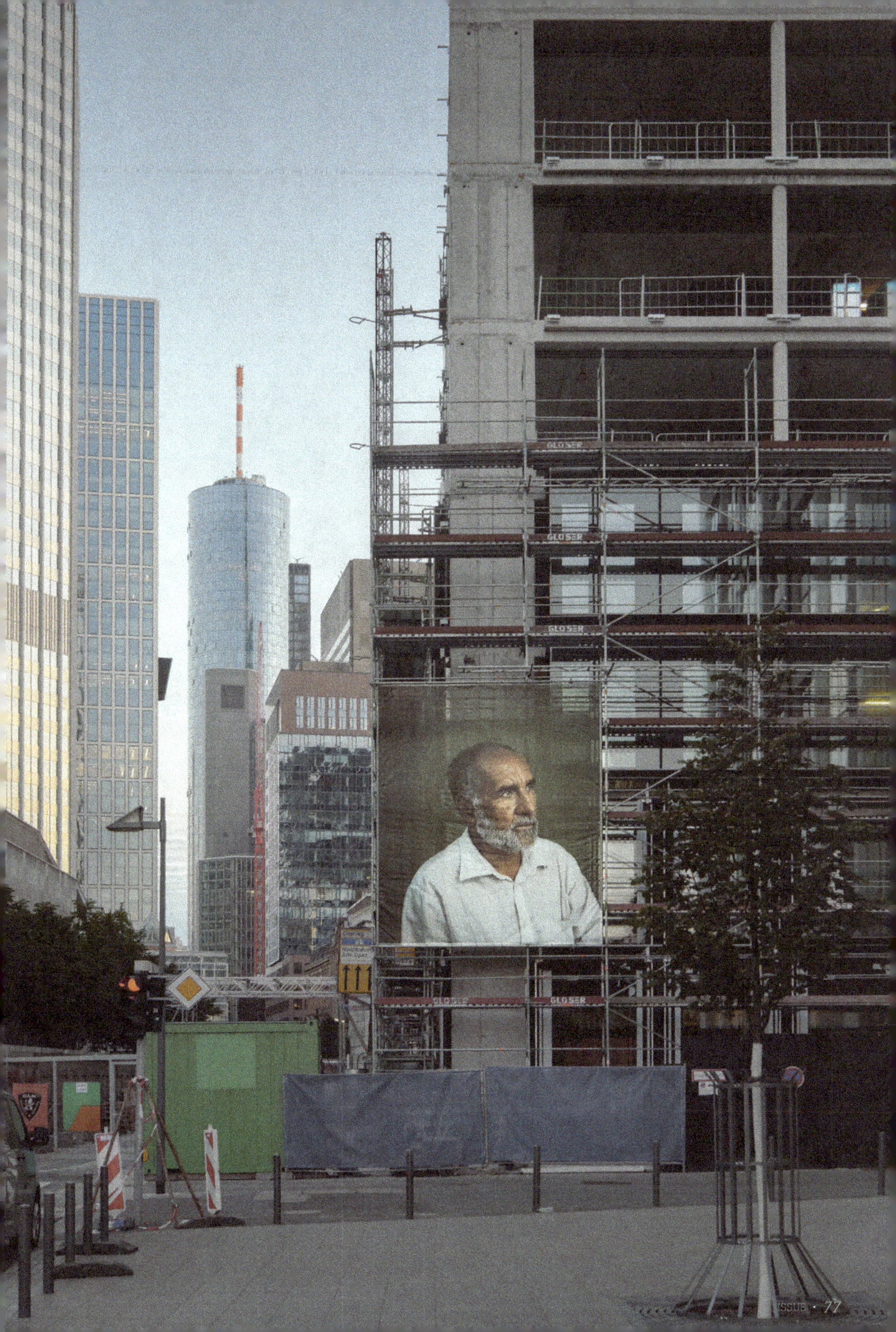

ROBERT KNEPPER

Raised in the small town of Maumee, Ohio, actor Robert Knepper recently finished a reprisal of his popular role as T-Bag in the 2017 mini-series Prison Break: Sequel. *He also appears in Showtime's* Twin Peaks: The Return, *a highly-anticipated sequel to David Lynch's '90s cult TV show.*

Birthplace: Fremont, Ohio.

Ambitions: To not lose my mind, my country, to idiots.

Favorite Food: Mexican (and don't forget the margaritas)

Favorite Band: Tom Waits

Last Book Read: *Dark Night of the Soul*

Your Idea of Heaven: More time!

Turn offs: Negative, lazy, boring complainers. Really cheap restaurants that put really stiff toilet paper in their bathroom.

Where are you from? I'm from a little town in Ohio called Maumee. It's a suburb of Toledo. Years ago I would never admit to that, and now I'm like, "You know what, I grew up there." I'm proud of it.

What was your first break? I was at Northwestern University, and I went to downtown Chicago with the advice of my professor who said, "You know, Dennis Zacek will be at the

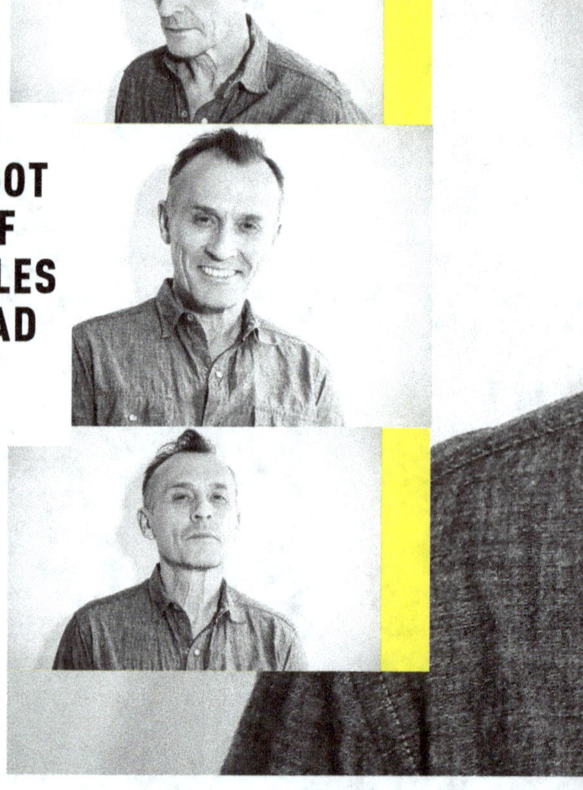

> ## "I COUNTED THEM UP—I GOT ABOUT HALF GOOD GUY ROLES AND HALF BAD GUY."
>
> — ROBERT KNEPPER

Victory Gardens Theater at this window of time. You want to get into that play? Wait there for him and ask him to audition." I waited, and he said, "Sure, come on in." I bugged him every day for a week, and when he cast me he said, "I gave you the part because you never stopped bugging me."

What have you been in? What have I not been in? Thirty-two years I've been in this business. Twenty-seven years I kicked around in a lot of things. IMDb me—you can wallpaper your wall with all the stuff I've done. Most people know me from *Prison Break, Heroes, Twin Peaks* coming up and *iZombie.* I played nine or ten characters last year. I'm on *Homeland* right now. I did a great movie called *Dating Game Killer* which comes out this spring. I counted them up, and I got about half good guy roles and half bad guy. I did a great music video with Kiefer Sutherland. It's his song

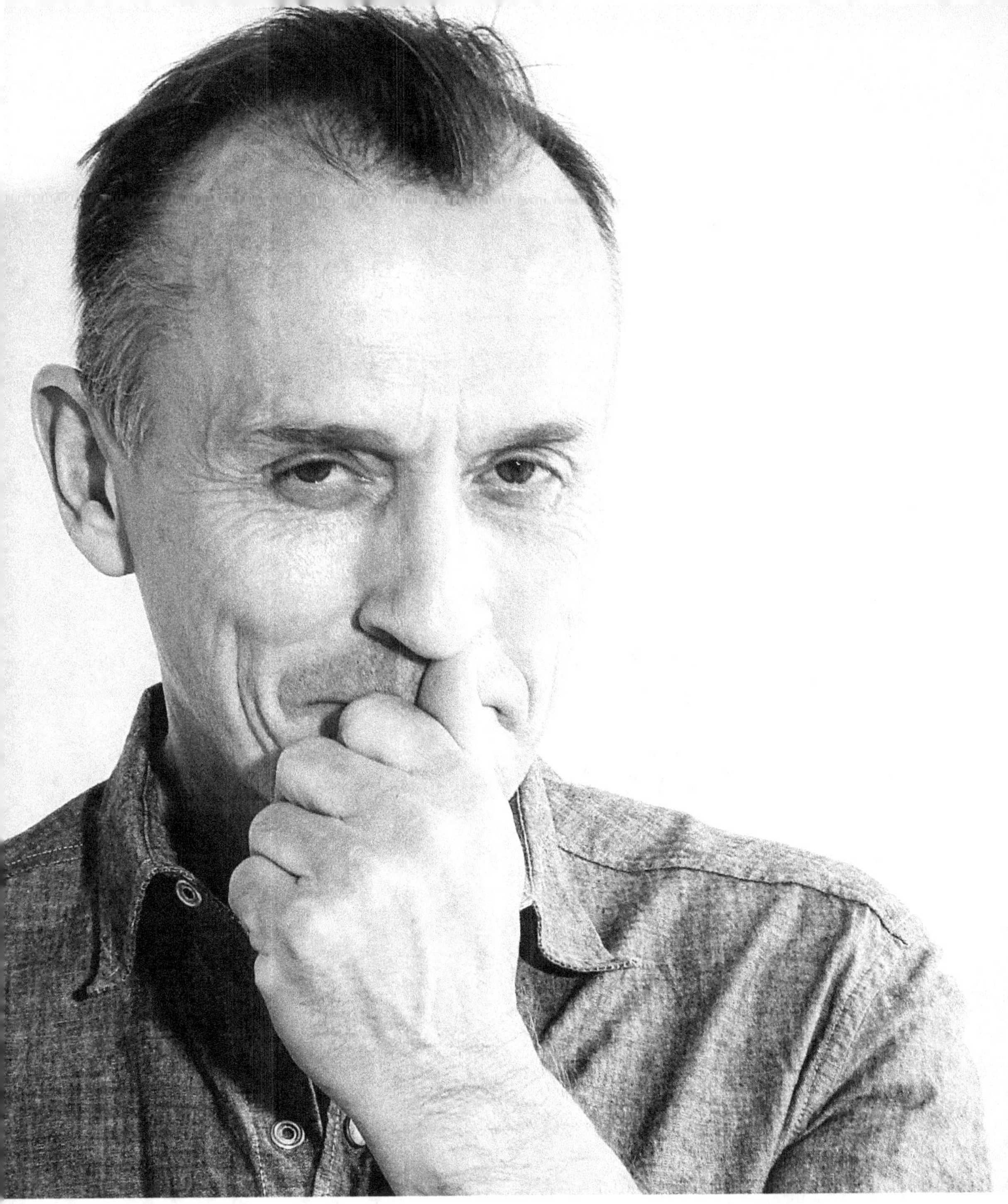

called "Shirley Jean"—a very catchy "Waltzing Matilda" kind of song. We just shot that EP. He texted me and said it looks freaking great.

How do you feel about this career? I always say I never go to work, I always go to play. I go from one job to the next, and one of these days, I'll look back on everything and go, "That was my career." But so far I have a lot of fun.

How did you decide to become an actor? I always wanted to be an actor. I'm one of those people that always knew what he wanted to do. My father's a veterinarian, and I would either have been a vet or an actor. I went to Northwestern because I could eventually segue into veterinary school if I wanted to do it that way. I was my dad's right hand man growing up. I held all the pets for him, all the dogs and cats, and I got bitten right and left. He has a tremendous patience for animals, and I probably don't because I've been bitten so much.

How would you describe your specialty or type? I'd like to think of myself as a chameleon. I originally began this business as a stage actor, and I was influenced by the British, by the Irish, by the Welsh. The American actors influenced me later. Brando and De Niro, Dean and everybody like that. Duvall especially. In my twenties I would have said I can do anything. I even played a woman, or a character that everyone thought was a woman, who was about to have a surgery to become a woman. It was one of the first transgender shows, and my agent said, "You sure you want to do this?" I said, "Yeah. I love it. I think it's a great part." You know, when you're a kid, like a lot of kids your cheeks are fuller, you look friendly, you look—most kids always look loveable—and then you get older and you start getting cheekbones or you don't. Bigger-cheeked people tend to maybe do more comedy, and bonier guys like me tend to do more drama or sometimes scary parts. So I would say if

you had to pitch it on me, which I wish you wouldn't do, you would probably go, "Oh, he's got an angular look. He's gonna go for the more dramatic guys." But I love comedy. I got to do so much comedy in *Prison Break* and call it dangerous comedy. I hope to be able

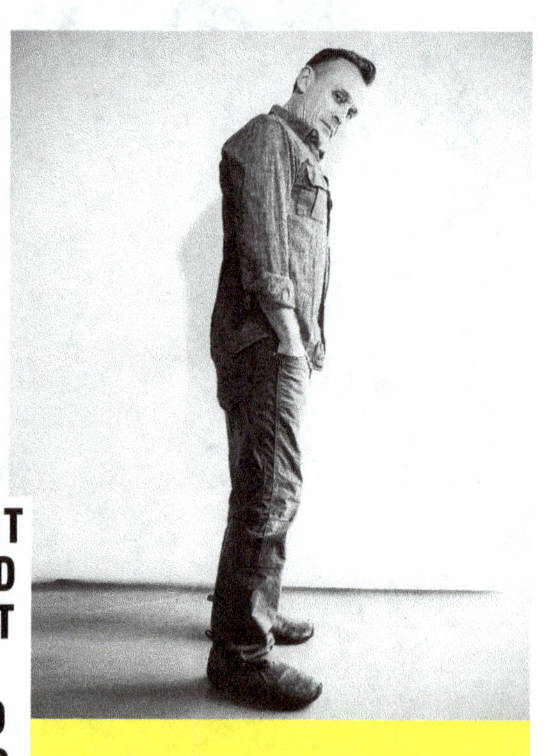

> ## "I ALWAYS WANT TO BE THAT KIND OF PERSON THAT JUST GETS REALLY TURNED ON BY WORKING WITH PEOPLE, HELPING PEOPLE, SHARING AND PLAYING BALL. THAT'S HOW I THINK OF ACTING, REALLY. IT'S LIKE A SPORT."
>
> **— ROBERT KNEPPER**

to do it all, including comedy and drama— "dramedy."

Who's your favorite actor you look up to? Anthony Hopkins. I just met him, so I'll be able to tell that story sometime soon. Hopefully I'm also going to be working with him, but I can't talk about it yet because it's not done. I also got to meet Robert

Duvall. Several years ago, I was representing *Prison Break* at the Monte Carlo TV Festival, and I was nervous as crap because we had studied the same way in New York and I just love him. I'd love to work with Cate Blanchett. I'd love to work with Meryl Streep. I like to work with anybody that's good.

What would your ideal job be? I really have it. I can't imagine people having to go to work. I'll always be a kid. I'll always explore. When I first met David Lynch for *Twin Peaks*, I was amazed at how much of a kid he was and that he really wanted me to do *Twin Peaks*. And I thought, that's a role model for me. I always want to be

<u>ROBERT KNEPPER</u> With a career spanning over 25 years, actor Robert Knepper is best known for his role as T-Bag on the Fox series *Prison Break* (2005–09), a role he reprised for the 2017 mini-series *Prison Break: Sequel*. He also stars in Showtime's *Twin Peaks: The Return* (2017) and has appeared in films such as *Jack Reacher* (2012), *Good Night, and Good Luck* (2005) and shows *Heroes* (2006–09) and *Mob City* (2013).

Images by Jan-Willem Dikkers

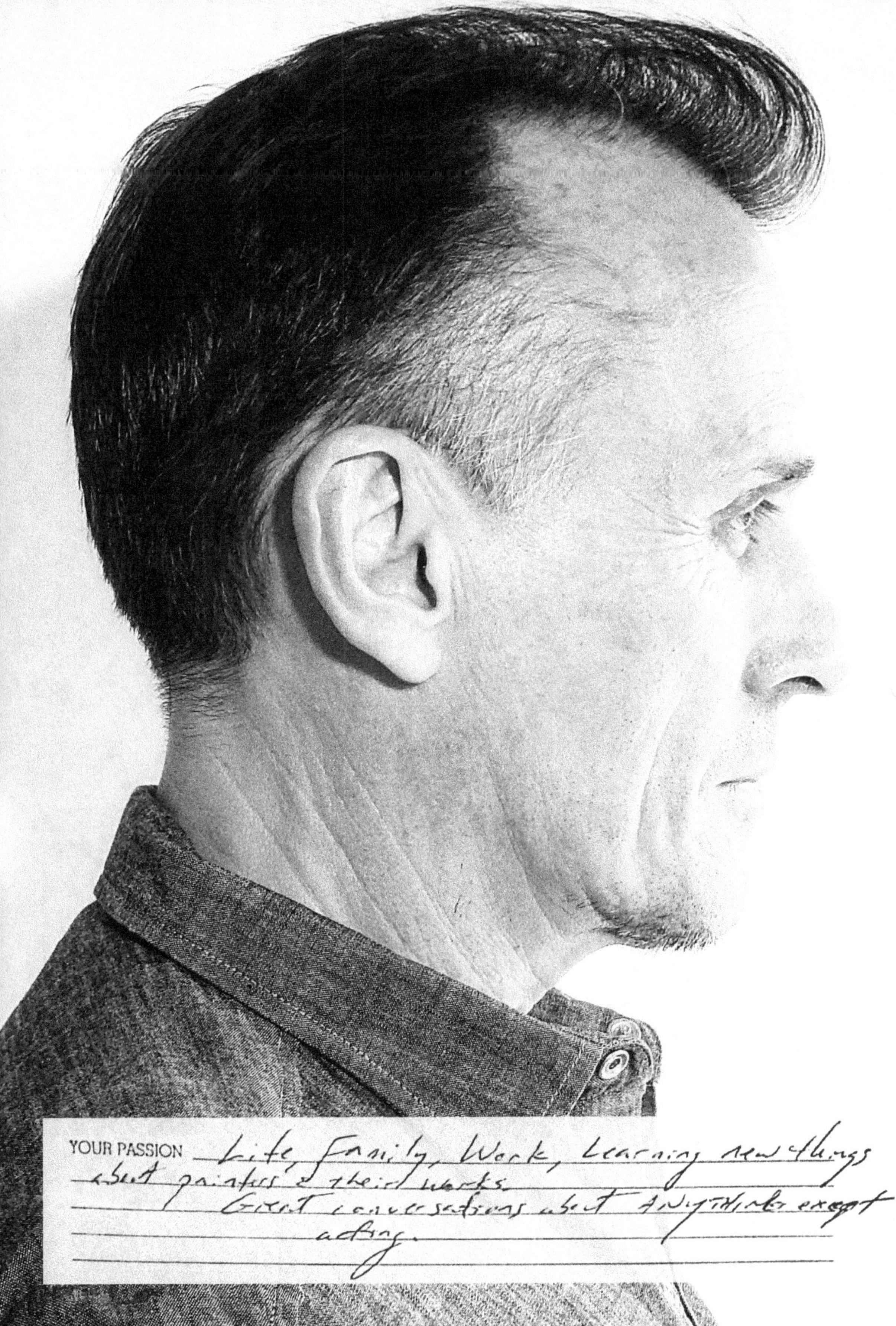

YOUR PASSION   Life, Family, Work, learning new things
about painters & their works.
Great conversations about anything else except
acting.

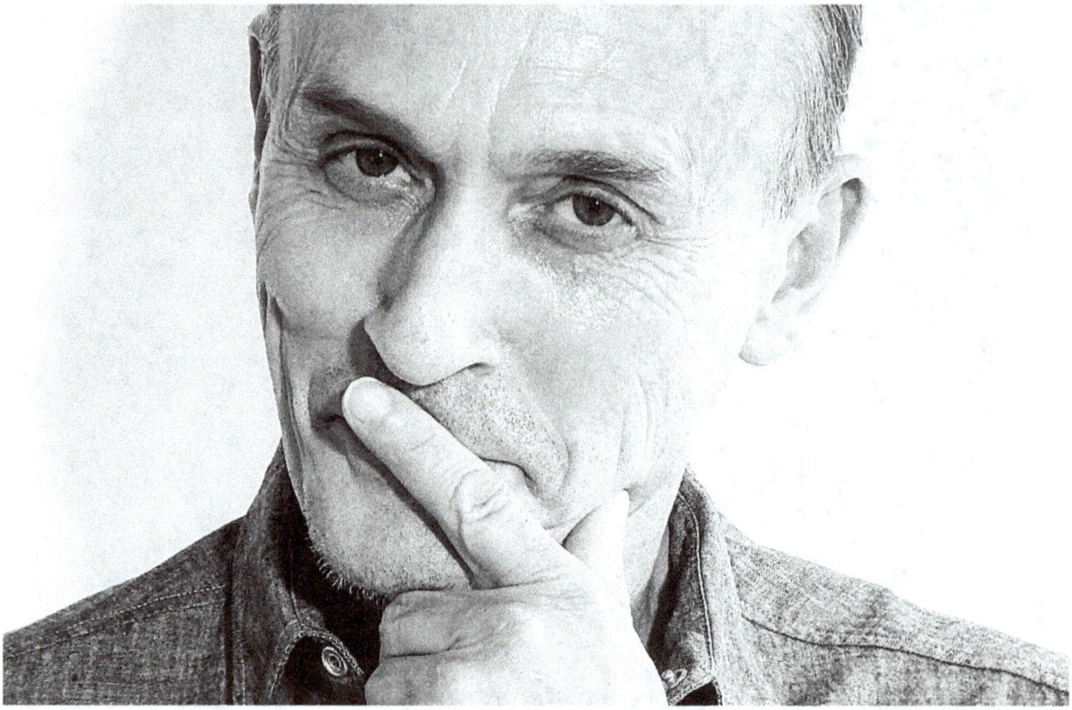

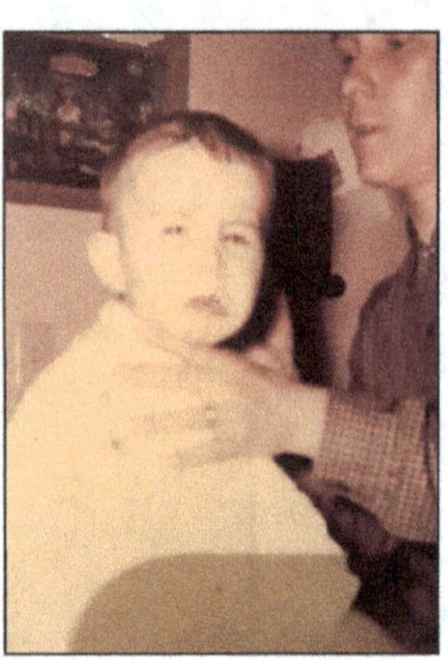

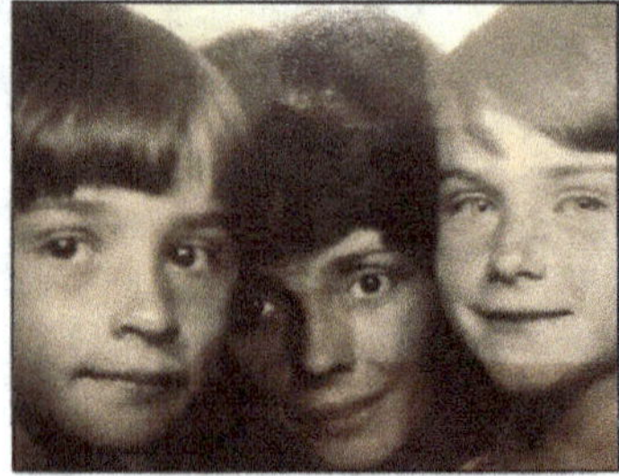

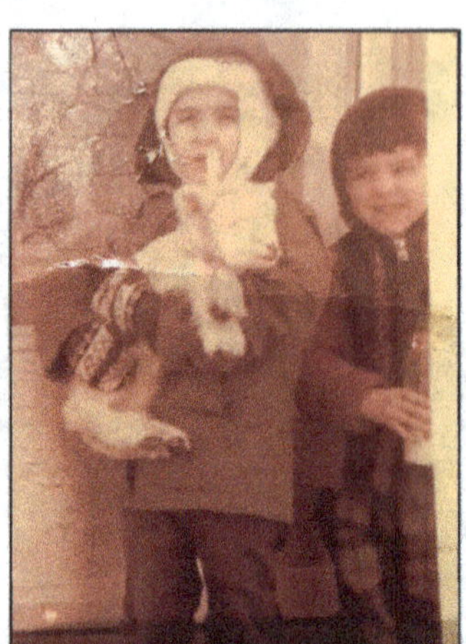

LEFT - I'm bawling during a haircut? That's my Dad, the veterinarian, giving me a "pineapple" cut with his dog clippers.
MIDDLE - I'm on the left. Mom's in the middle. And my sister Kay's on the right.
RIGHT - Me and the lamb. That's "Coco," one of hundreds of lambs my sister and I raised.

that kind of person that just gets really turned on working with people, helping people, sharing and playing ball. That's how I think of acting, really. It's like a sport.

Do you consider yourself to be lucky? Very. But I also consider that there's a lot of hard work that goes into this. I'm really, really glad that I studied acting. I am fortunate enough to have learned some life lessons and got my act together with my family. I'm there for them, and they're there for me. In that regard, I feel lucky. As far as a career, I work really hard and, damn it, I deserve it.

What advantages do you have? I would say age and experience. I think it helps bring focus, and I don't take things so seriously anymore. It's nice to be lightened up. I remember thinking when I first moved here when I was 25, "I gotta make this happen. I gotta make ends meet." I was too serious back then.

Would you rather have a car or a diploma? Can I say both? I love to drive. I grew up in Ohio. I love driving in snow, I love driving in rain. I love putting the top down. If I had a diploma, I would want it not for acting. I would love it in something that people would go, "Wow, he's like really, really brainy." Something in the sciences, discovering a cure for cancer or something like that.

How do you feel about how intercon- **nected the world is becoming?** It's crazy. I mean look at what just happened in London on Westminster Bridge. People from all over the world were involved in that attack. We feel each other's pain, and as an actor I think I feel it a little bit more. That's our job: to feel people's pains no matter if you would paint them as a bad guy or a good guy. Bad guys and good guys are both part of great storytelling, and they're necessary.

What is the future look like to you? I am so full of hope for the future right now. Not only in my life, but I feel like our consciousness as a country, all coming together. We're right at the brink of facing a lot of issues, and we have to come together and work this out. There's no separation anymore. There's no "me vs. you." There are a lot of bad guys out there, and I think those bad guys need to be erased—there's no doubt about that— but those people also need to be heard. I'm willing to be one of those people that goes, "I want to listen to you. I want to hear you," and then come back and talk to my people and see if we can work something out. I think it's a beautiful open road, and I'm just riding on it right now, with my diploma.

How do you feel about having chil- **dren?** I love my kid. I have a 14-year-old and my life is so much better because of him.

What challenges do you feel the world is facing today? Peace. Getting along. Communication. Learning how to say I'm sorry.

What are you most grateful for? I'm grateful for my family. I'm

> ## "IT'S NICE TO BE LIGHTENED UP. I REMEMBER THINKING WHEN I FIRST MOVED HERE WHEN I WAS 25, 'I GOTTA MAKE THIS HAPPEN. I GOTTA MAKE ENDS MEET.' I WAS TOO SERIOUS BACK THEN."
>
> **— ROBERT KNEPPER**

grateful for my job after job after job which we call "career." I am grateful to be alive. I'm really grateful that I didn't get killed driving to this interview.

What is your favorite way to communicate? I wish I knew sign language. I had—I think I can tell this—I had a date with Marlee Matlin years ago, who is just a beautiful woman and amazing actress. She took me to a Lakers' game, and I could not communicate with her. She could read my lips when I turned to her, but she couldn't hear me so it was a little tough. It was so frustrating to not be able to say, "You're really cute, and I like this date." I think body language is a huge way of communicating.

People can tell if you're not open to communicating with them, no matter what language you speak.

What is your favorite book, film and music right now? I really like Benjamin Booker's song "Witness." It feels like a religious choral experience. I love Rilke, an Austrian poet, and his *Letters to a Young Poet.* I love *Letters on Cézanne.* I love *Moonlight* and *La La Land.* I know it's a typical answer for an actor, but I love *The Godfather* and *Godfather Part II.* I love the old film *Tora! Tora! Tora!* And I love about every Hitchcock that's ever made. You can keep *Rope,* but the rest of my love to all. 🖌

SARAH RAMOS

Native Angelino actor Sarah Ramos recently wrote and starred in her web-series City Girl *and stars in NBC's forthcoming fantasy series* Midnight, Texas. *She is recognized for roles including Haddie in* Parenthood,

Favorite food: French fries

Favorite movie: *Citizen Ruth / Bottle Rocket / To Die For*

What was your first break? A Boeing commercial. And then I did the Universal Studios print ad with Sponge-Bob and Shrek.

the pros outweigh the cons.

How did you decide to become an actor? I heard an ad on Radio Disney advertising for child stars like, "Are you the next?" And I was like, "Yeah." Then we went and it was a scam, and they told us to pay two thousand

ideal job be? Working with Laura Dern and Mike White.

What advantages do you have? You're going to make me talk about them? Well, I have a great support system. I have a great job. I get to do what I want to do and have fun for a living.

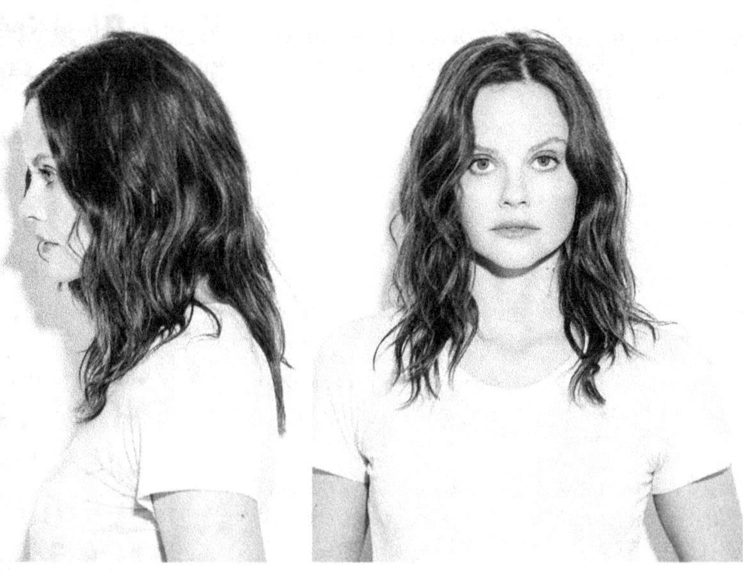

"I ALWAYS MENTION I DID AN EPISODE OF *WIZARDS OF WAVERLY PLACE* ON DISNEY CHANNEL WHERE I PLAYED A WEREWOLF."

— SARAH RAMOS

and 2017 indie film The Boy Downstairs, *and she produces the pop culture podcast* This Week Had Me Like.

———

Birthplace: Orange County, CA

Education: Columbia University, Creative Writing

What have you been in? I was on a show when I was nine called *American Dreams.* Most people know me from *Parenthood.* I was in *The Affair* recently, and I always mention I did an episode of *Wizards of Waverly Place* on Disney channel where I played a werewolf.

How do you feel about this career? I have mixed feelings about it. But, mostly

dollars. We didn't do that. But we did continue pursuing this.

How would you describe your specialty or type? I'm about to be on the show *Midnight, Texas* playing like a girl next door with an attitude. Maybe that?

Who is your favorite actor who you look up to? I love Laura Dern.

What would your

What do you think about the need for instant gratification? It's totally natural and disgusting.

How do you feel about how interconnected the world is becoming? I hope that the pros outweigh the cons.

How do you feel about having children? I'm open to it, you know. That's in the future and I haven't thought about that.

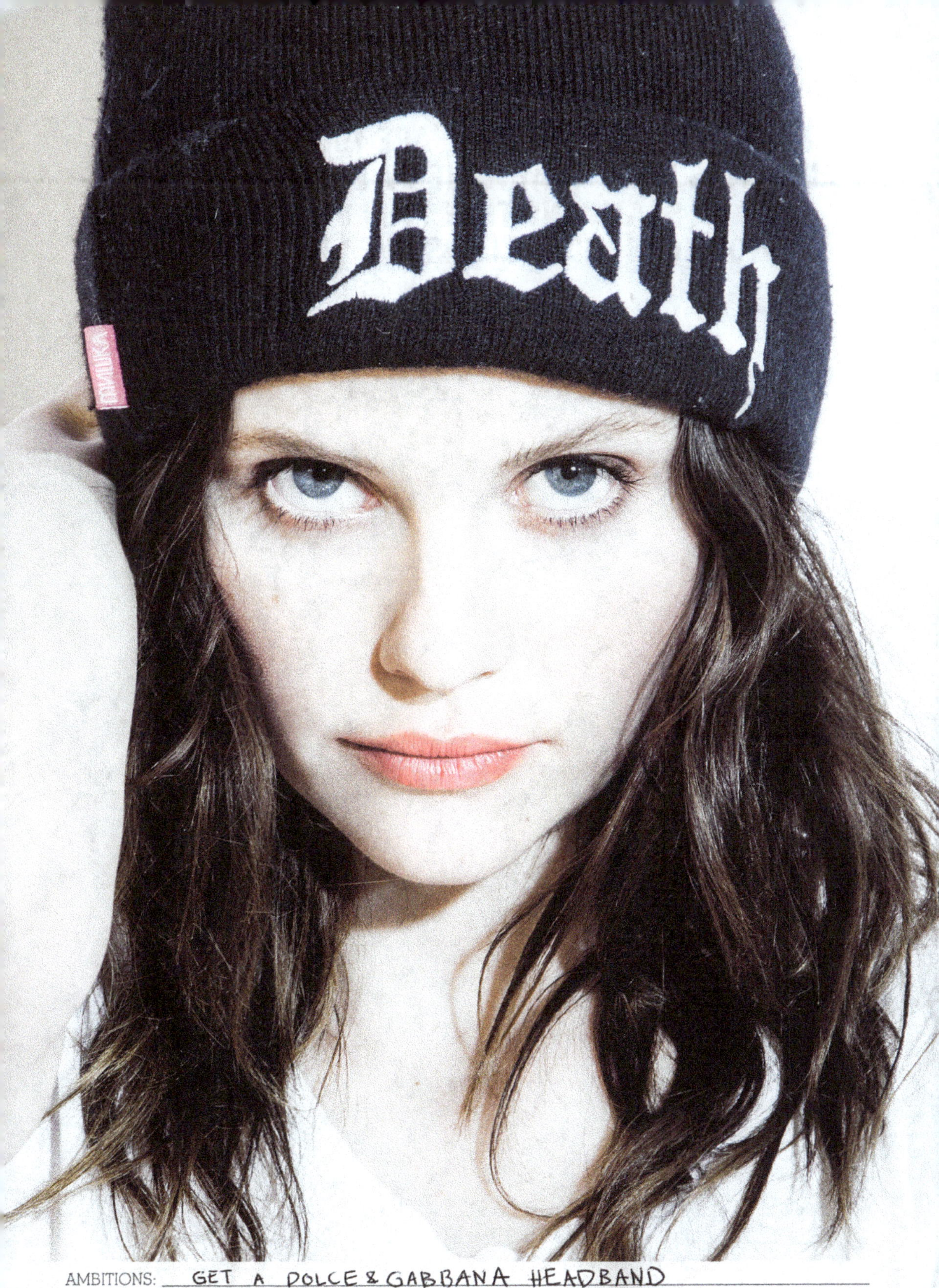

AMBITIONS: _GET A DOLCE & GABBANA HEADBAND_

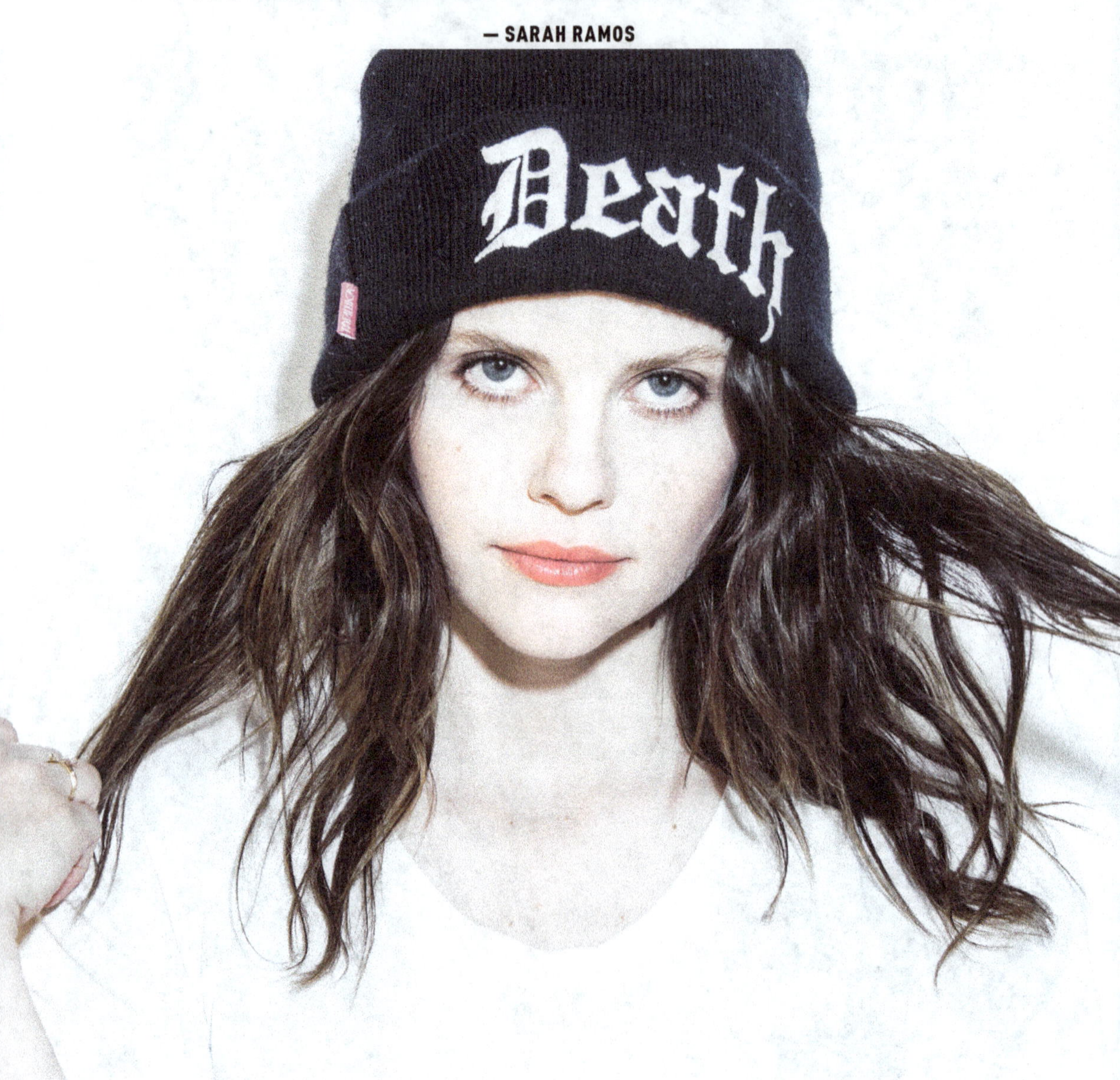

"I HEARD AN AD ON RADIO DISNEY ADVERTISING FOR CHILD STARS LIKE, 'ARE YOU THE NEXT?' AND I WAS LIKE, 'YEAH.' THEN WE WENT AND IT WAS A SCAM, AND THEY TOLD US TO PAY TWO THOUSAND DOLLARS. WE DIDN'T DO THAT."

— SARAH RAMOS

WHAT'S NEXT? TURN MY PODCAST *THIS WEEK HAD ME LIKE* HOSTED BY MY BFF CAROLINE GOLDFARB INTO A TV SHOW!!!!!

What challenges do you feel the world is facing today? Inequality, not listening to each other. We have got to do better.

What are you most grateful for? I can only think of joke answers. Like how if I'm not

Tampa by Alissa Nutting, which is a book about a 26-year-old high school teacher who is a pedophile and preys on 14-year-old boys. And movie, I'm watching *Big Little Lies*. That's a TV show, but I hope that counts. 🔸

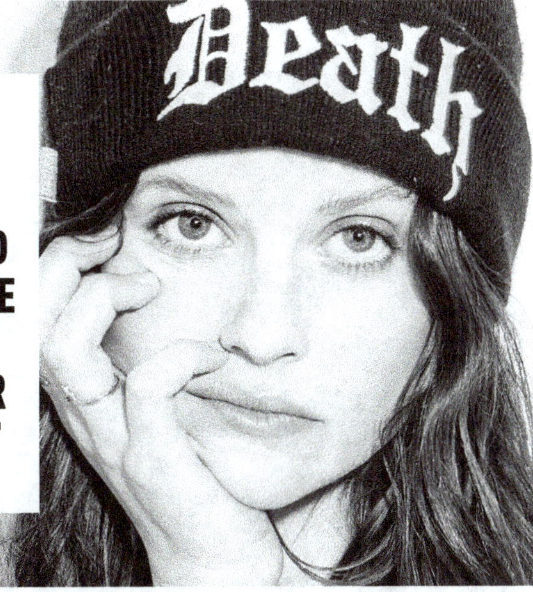

> "IF I'M NOT GRATEFUL MY FRIENDS ARE GOING TO SEND ME THIS AND BE LIKE, 'YOU'RE A LOSER. YOUR ANSWERS!'"
>
> — SARAH RAMOS

SARAH RAMOS
LA-based actor Sarah Ramos stars in the upcoming TV series *Midnight, Texas* (2017), her web-series *City Girl* (2017) and films *We Don't Belong Here* (2014) and *The Boy Downstairs* (2017). Other well-known roles include *Parenthood* (2010–15), *The Affair* (2016) and *Runaway* (2006–08).

grateful, my friends are going to send me this and be like, "You're a loser. Your answers!" I'm grateful for my friends and family.

What's your favorite way to communicate? Via text so I don't have to see them.

What is your favorite book film and music right now? That song "Issues" by Julia Michaels. I just read

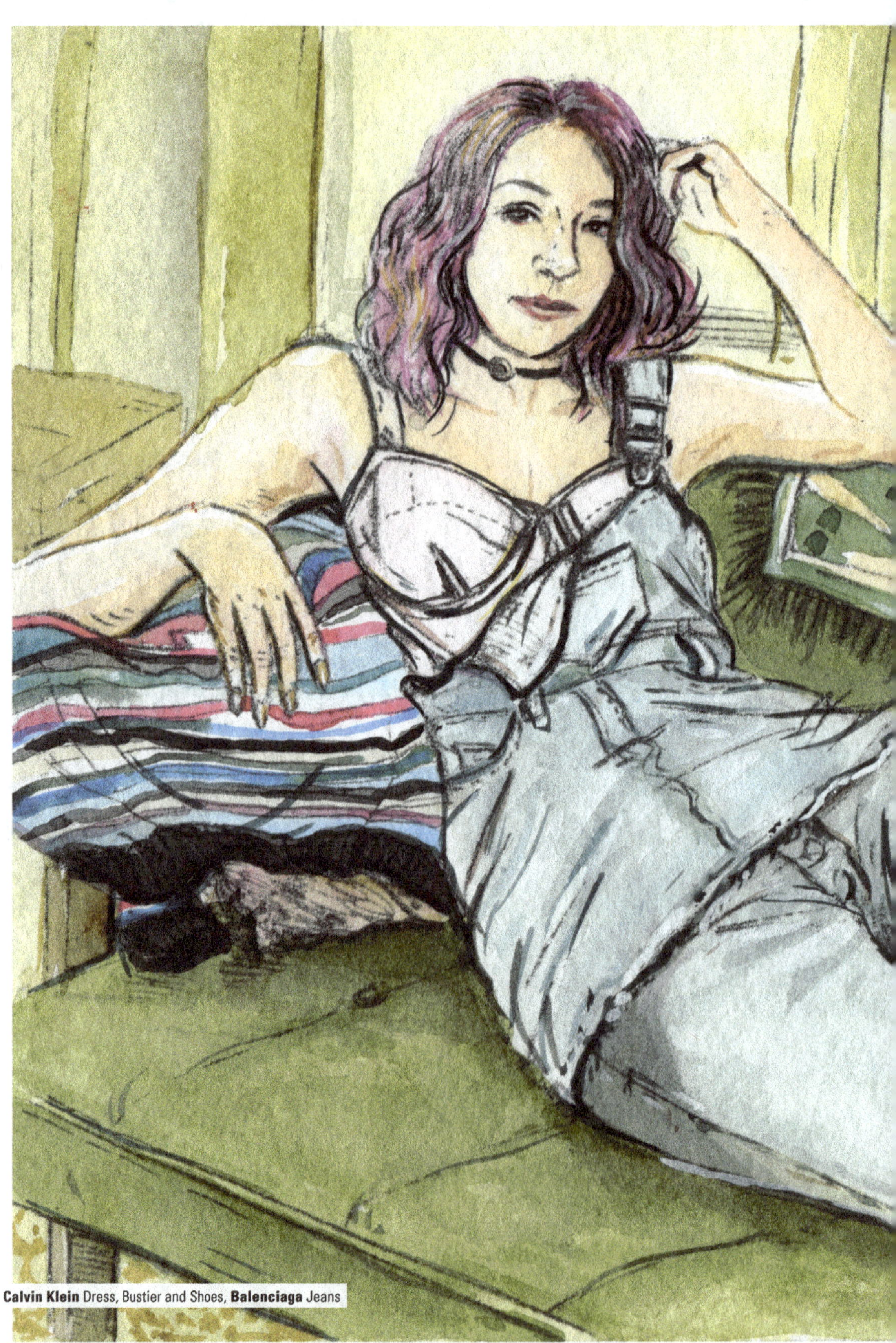

Calvin Klein Dress, Bustier and Shoes, **Balenciaga** Jeans

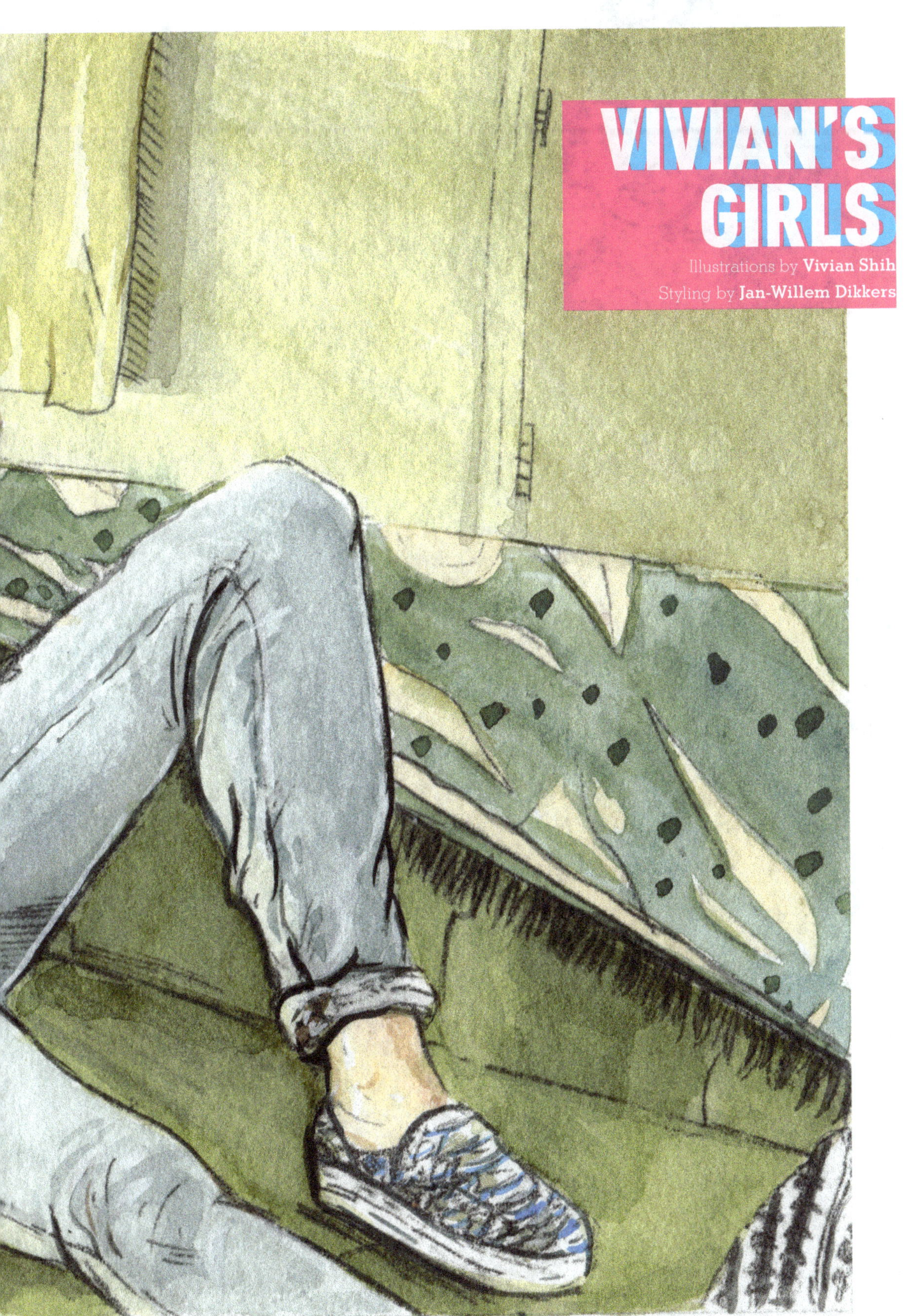

VIVIAN'S
GIRLS
Illustrations by Vivian Shih
Styling by Jan-Willem Dikkers

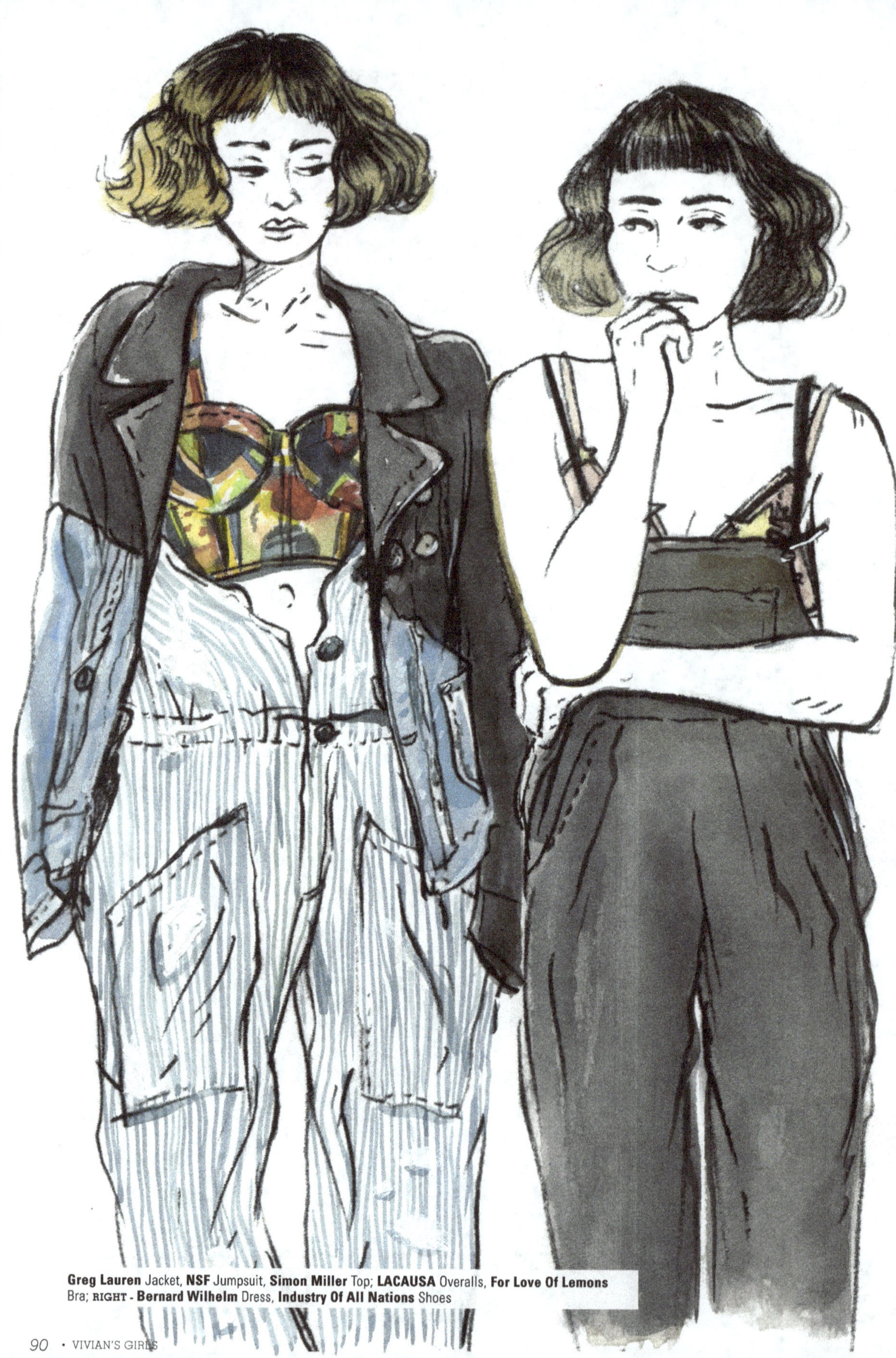

Greg Lauren Jacket, **NSF** Jumpsuit, **Simon Miller** Top; **LACAUSA** Overalls, **For Love Of Lemons** Bra; RIGHT - **Bernard Wilhelm** Dress, **Industry Of All Nations** Shoes

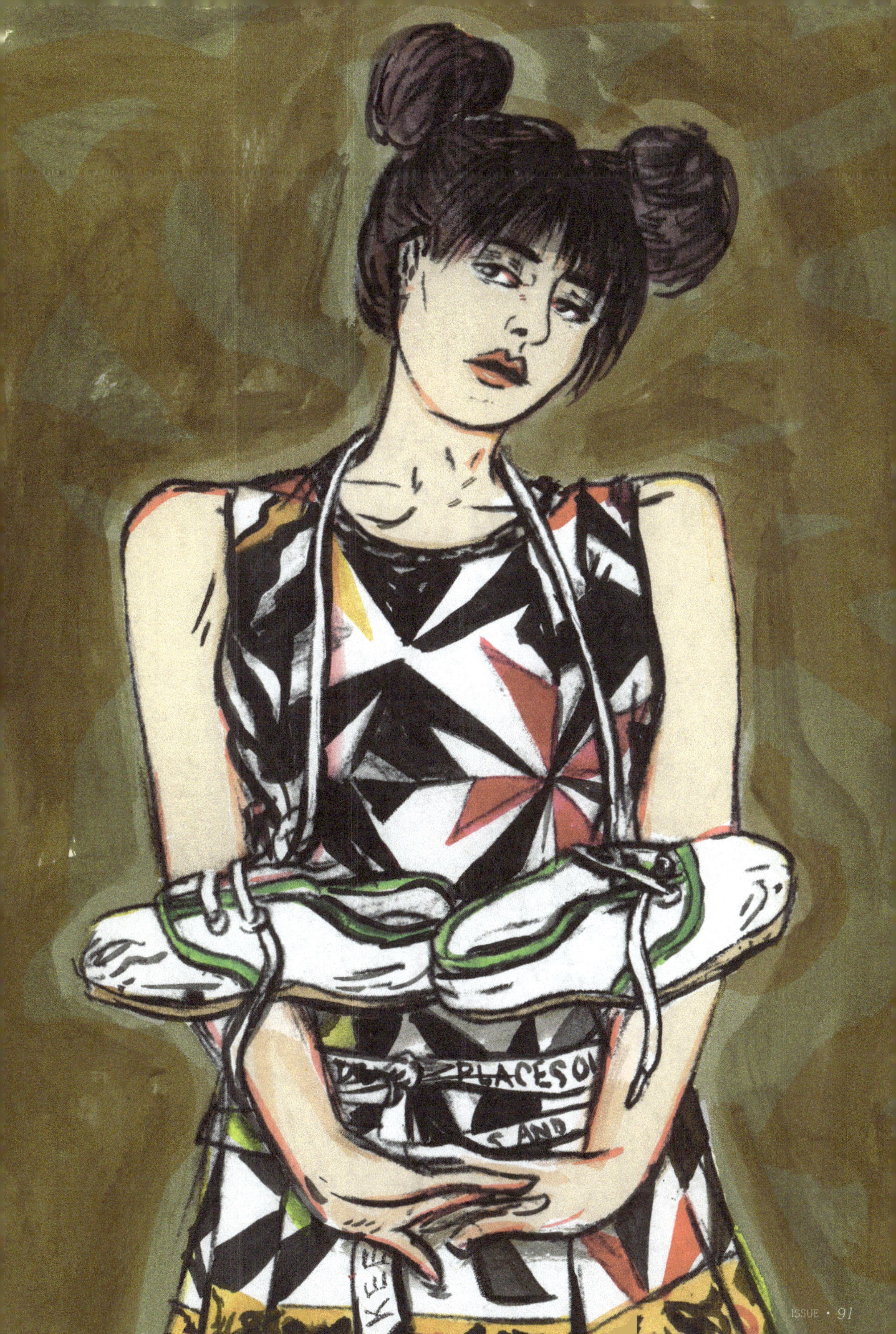
PLACES OF
S AND

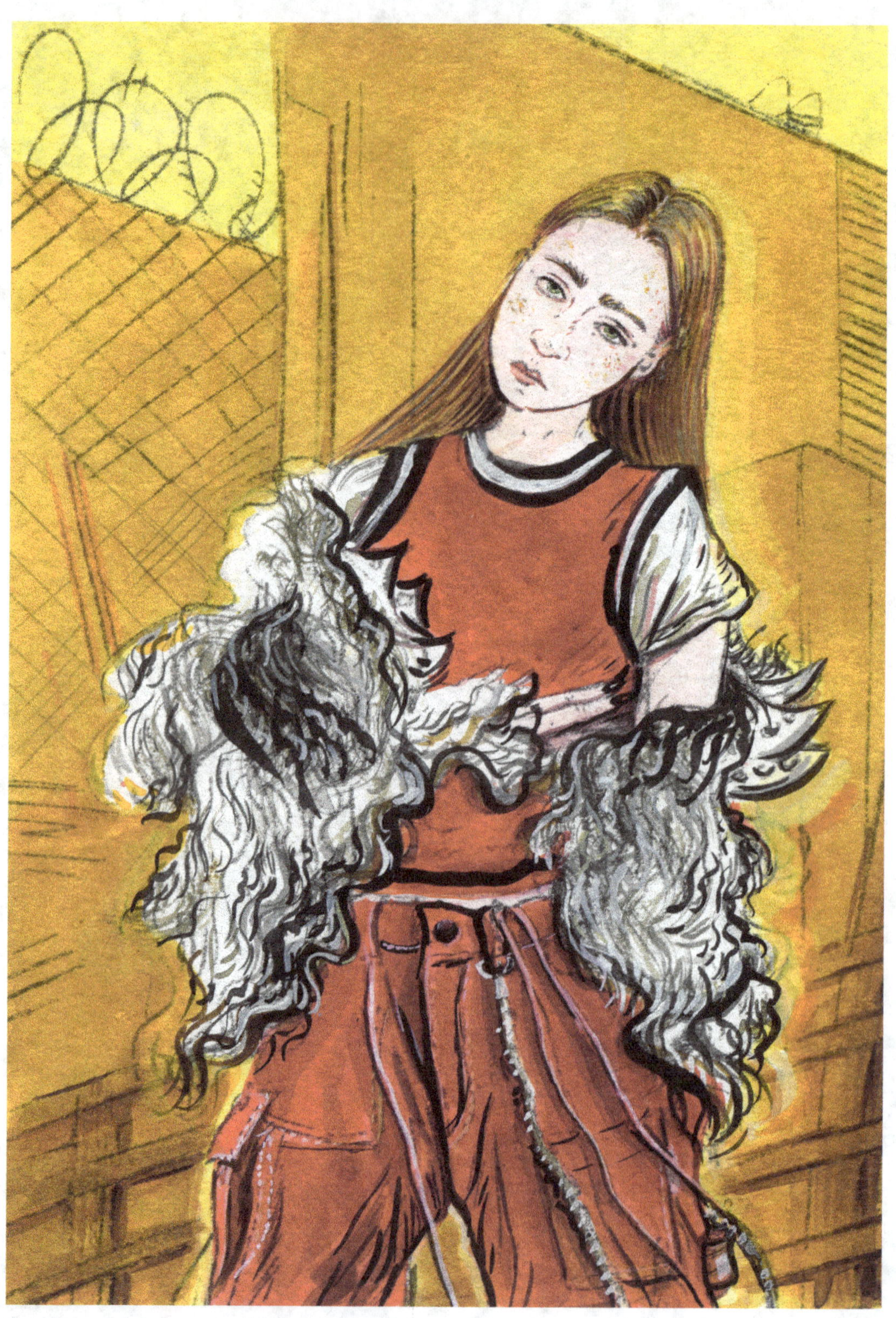

Rodarte Coat, **Prada** Sweater, **Homme Boy** Shirt and Pants;
RIGHT - **Alexander Wang** Sweatshirt, **Adidas x Stella** Shorts and Sweatpants, **Anine Bing** Boot, **Prada** Glasses

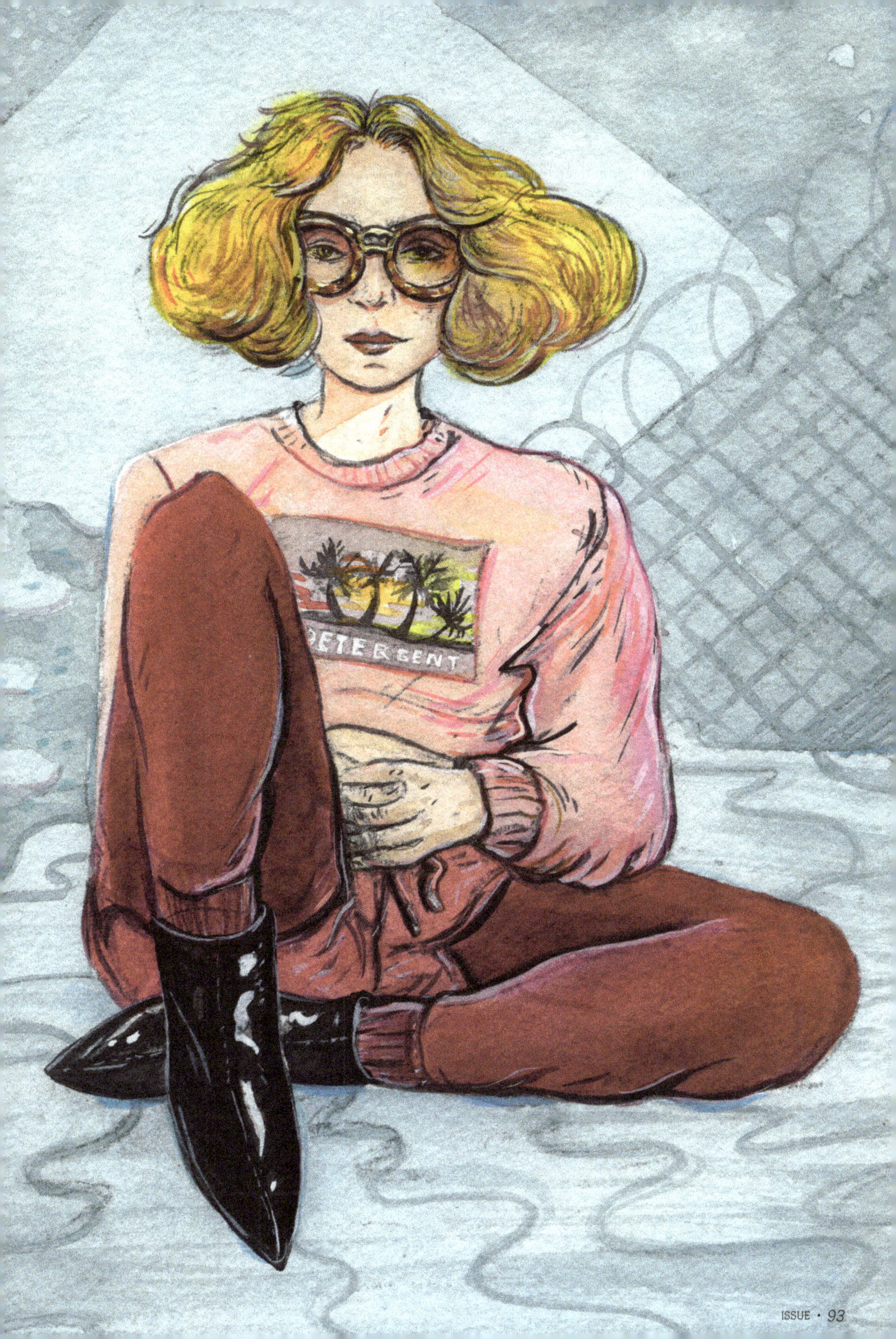
DETERGENT

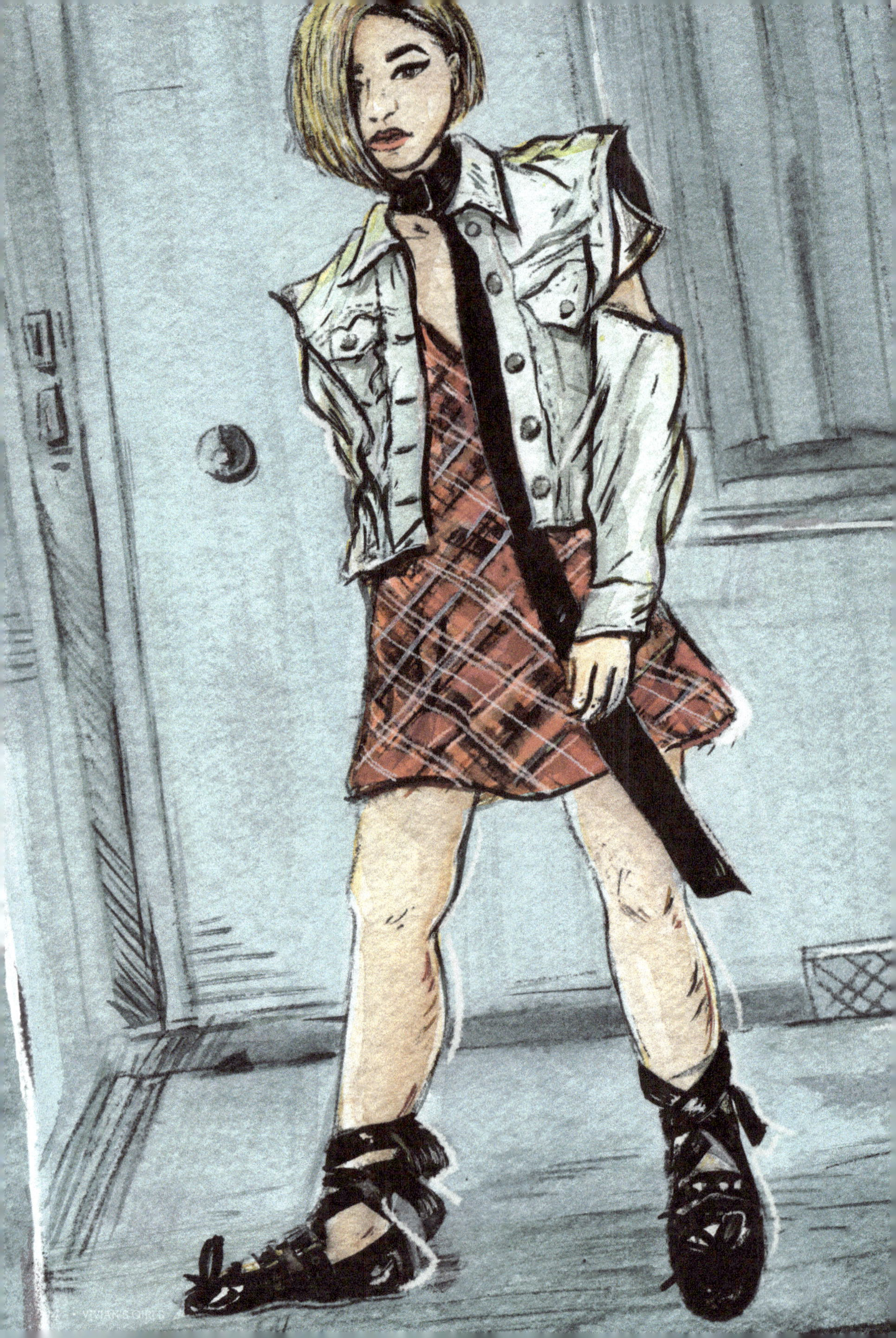

94 • VIVIAN'S GIRLS

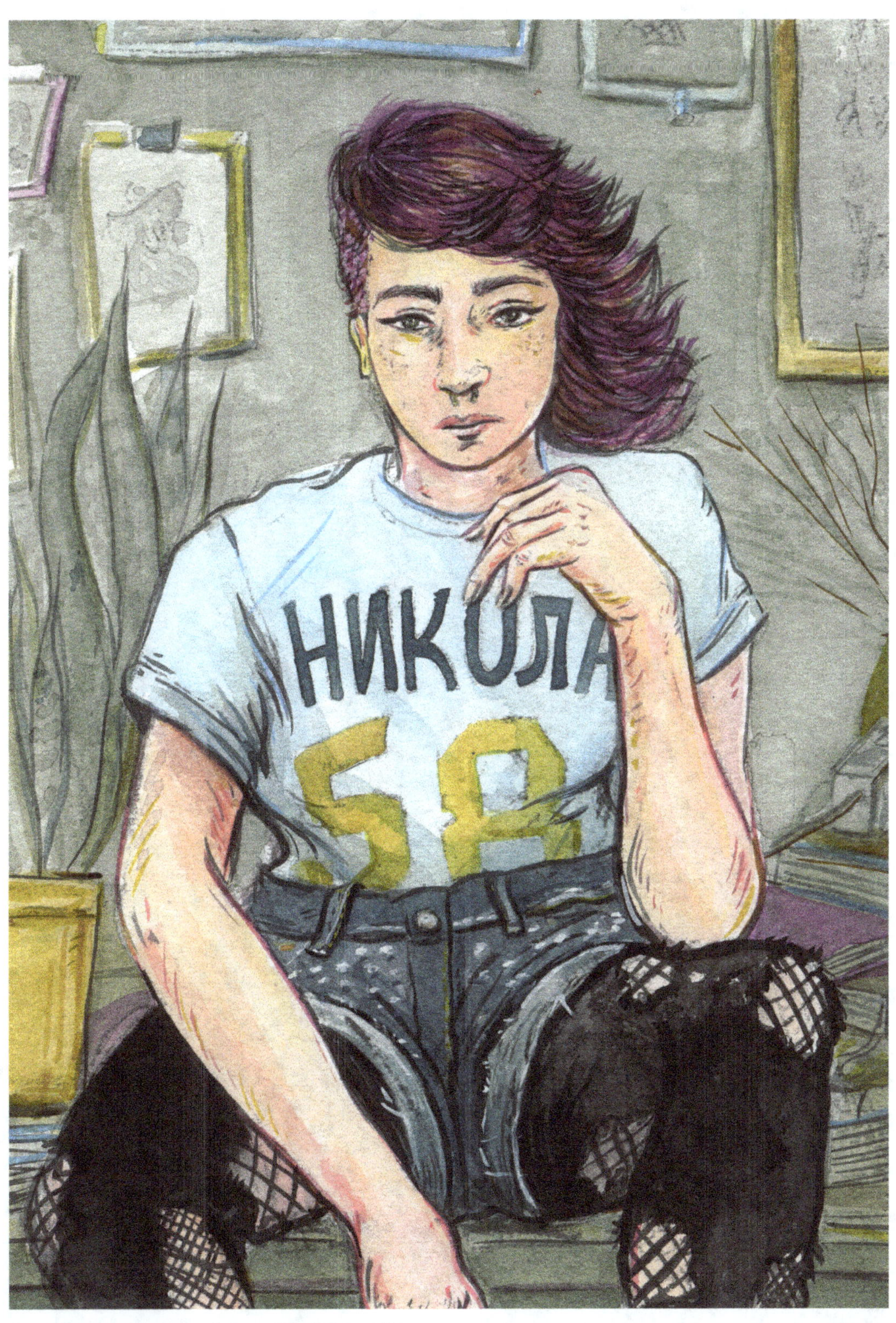

Junya Watanabe Comme Des Garçons Shirt, Shorts and Tights;
LEFT - **MM6** Jacket, **Adaptation** Dress, **Miu Miu** Shoes, **Shaina** Mote Belt

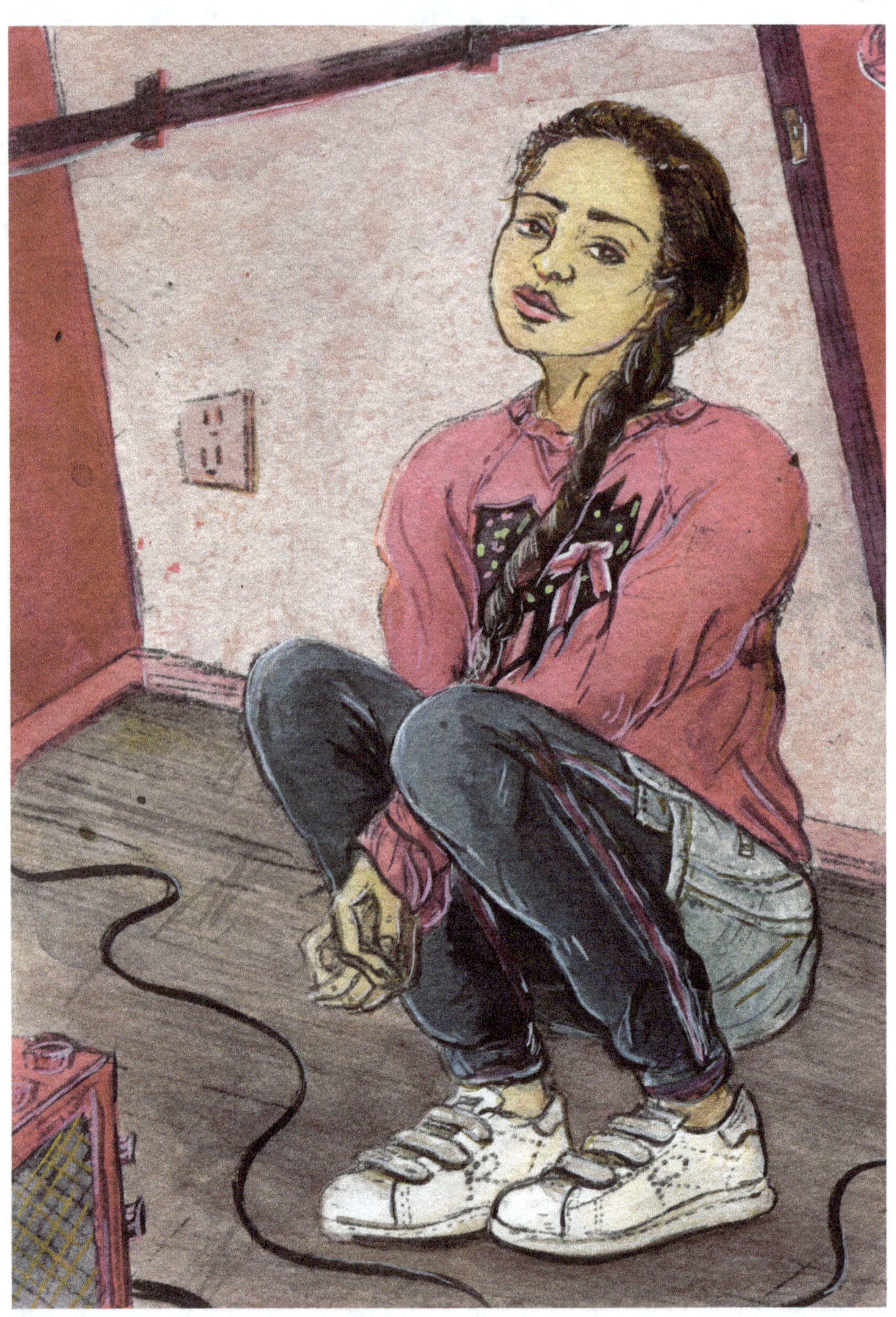

Marc Jacobs Sweatshirt, **Saint Laurent** Skirt, **Stateside** Sweatpants, **Adidas x Raf Simons** Shoes;
RIGHT - **Gucci** Sweater, Sweatpants and Bag, **Shaina Mote** Shirt

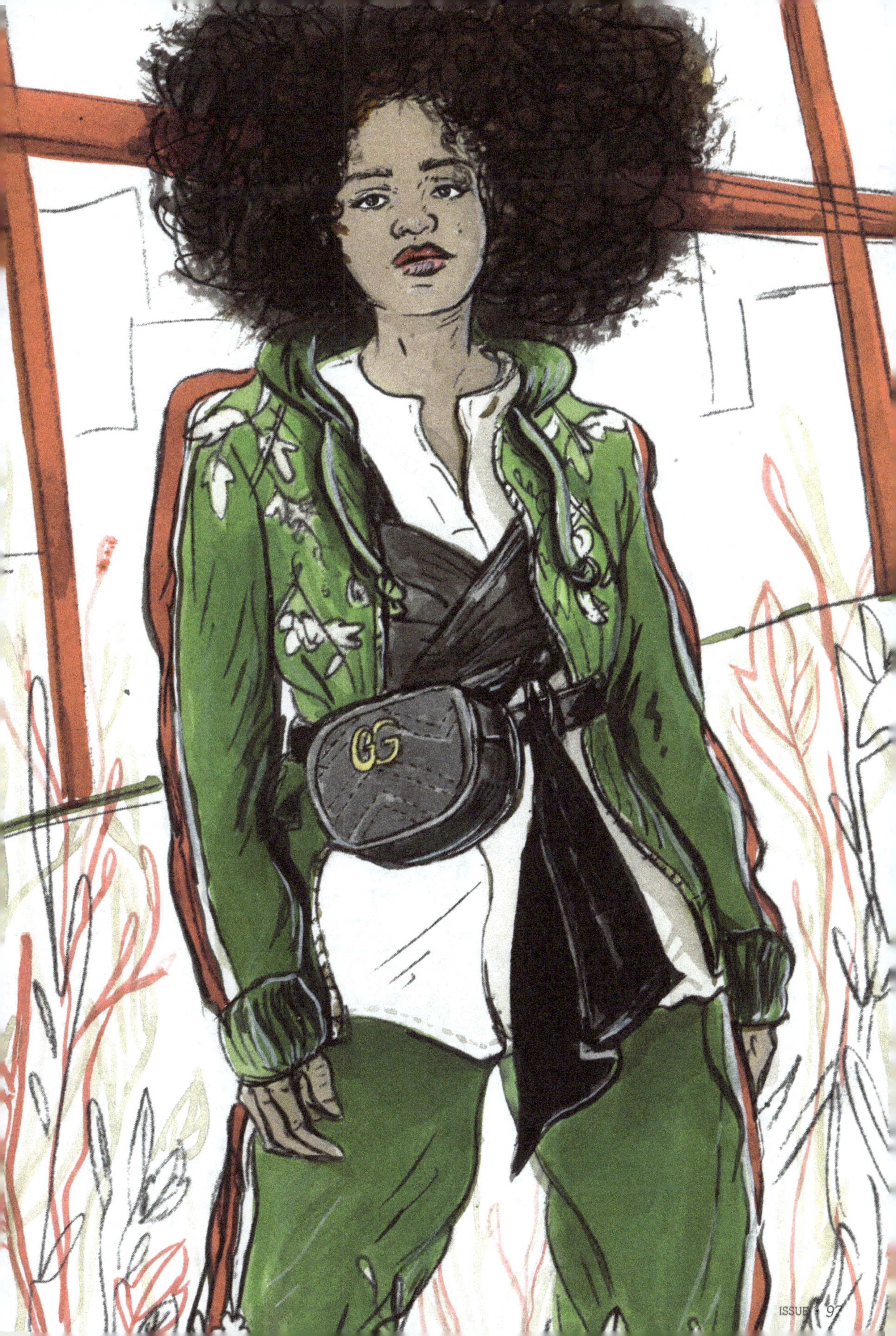

KEITH POWERS

Keith Powers found his breakout roles playing Dr. Dre's younger brother Tyree in 2015's acclaimed Straight Outta Compton *and Theo on the* drama Famous in Love.

————

> ## "HOW DO WE COME TOGETHER? I THINK THAT'S THE BIGGEST PROBLEM WE FACE TODAY, AND IT'S SIMPLY JUST PUTTING OUR PRIDE ASIDE, HONESTLY. THAT'S THE FUNNY THING: IT'S SO SIMPLE THAT IT'S DIFFICULT."
>
> **— KEITH POWERS**

MTV series Faking It. *Powers is set to star as Ronnie DeVoe in the highly anticipated BET miniseries* The New Edition Story, *which follows the rise of the R&B group in the 1980s, and he appears in the Freeform*

Birth Place: Sacramento, CA

Favorite Food: Roscoe's Chicken and Waffles

Favorite Movie: *Friday*

Favorite Band: New Edition

Last Book Read: *The Four Agreements*

Ambitions: To be an A-list actor, produce my own films and eventually do a bunch for my community.

Artist you would most like to work with? Viola Davis, Will Smith, Issa Rae.

How do you like to spend your time? Doing something that involves me laughing

Your idea of heaven: No worries, happy with my family, everyone of all races uniting, no hate.

Your influences: My hometown because it shaped me to be who I am. It's the reason why I am grounded and take my work so seriously. Also because my family is back home.

How do you feel about this career? I feel good about it. It's something that I really love. It's unpredictable. It's spontaneous. It brings out the best in you because it's such a challenge.

How did you decide to become an actor? Through modeling, actually. I was like, "Let's see what happens. I'm going to take a leap of faith." I was introduced to it in the best way possible because my first job was in South Africa, so I fell in love with a craft overseas too. I was like, "This is what I want to do for the rest of my life."

How would you describe your specialty or type? Being a down to earth person, my humility. I'm all about being authentic and real and adding to people's lives rather than taking away.

Who is your favorite

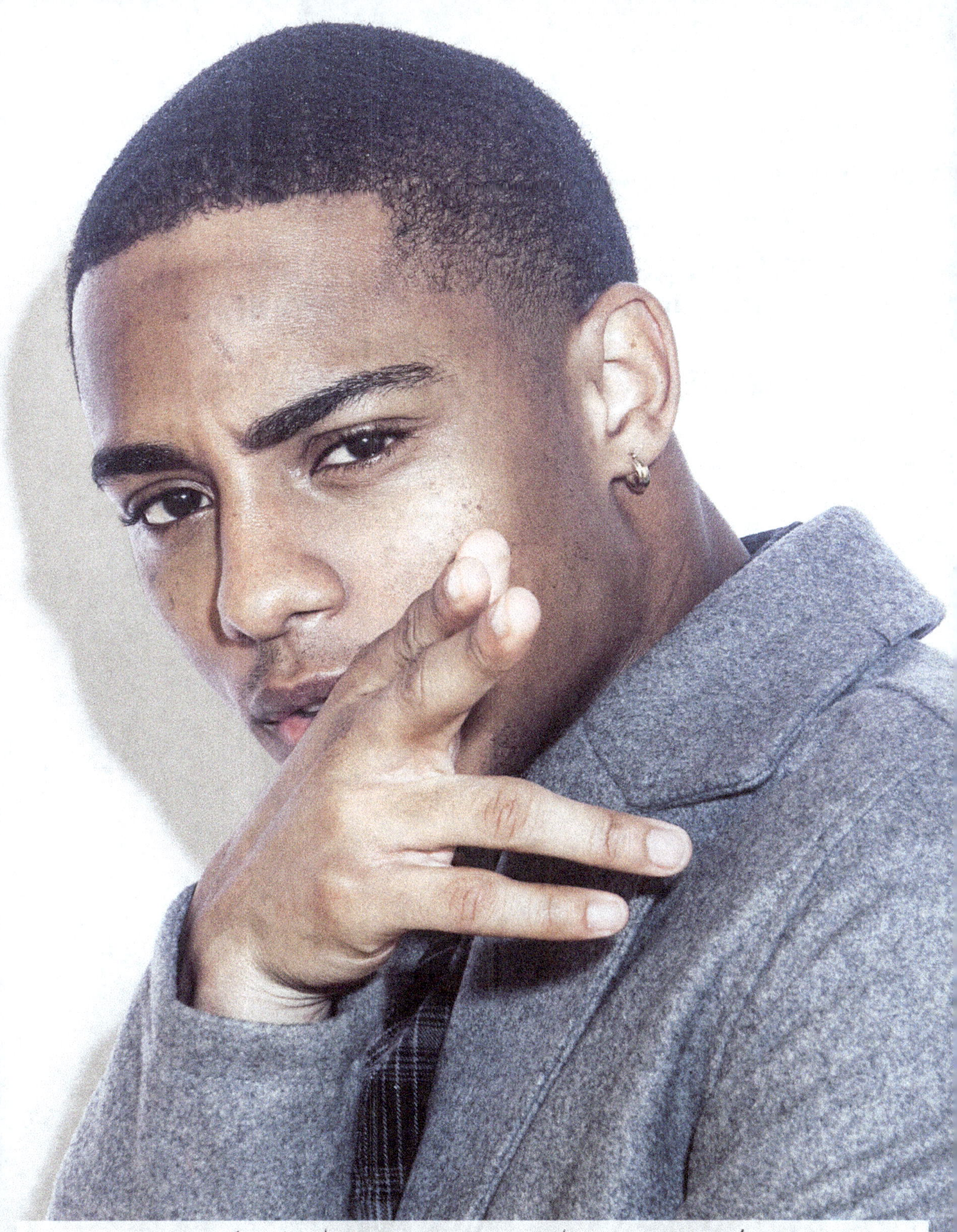

YOUR INFLUENCES: My hometown is my influence because it shaped me to be who I am today. It's the reason why I am grounded and I take my work so seriously. My family is also back home so theres another one of my influences.

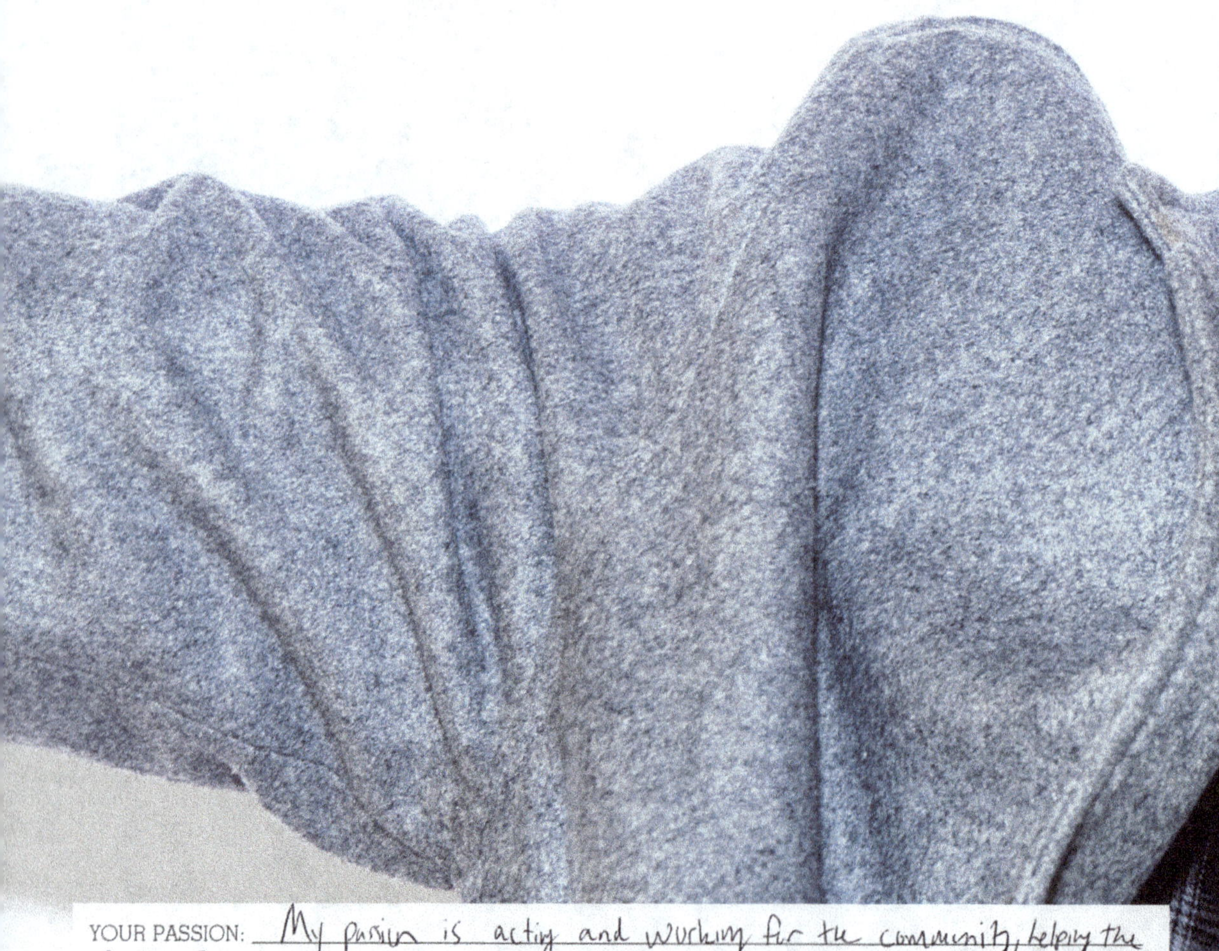

"IT'S SOMETHING THAT I REALLY LOVE TO DO.
IT'S UNPREDICTABLE. IT'S SPONTANEOUS.
IT BRINGS THE BEST OUT
IN YOU BECAUSE IT'S SUCH A CHALLENGE."

— KEITH POWERS

YOUR PASSION: My passion is acting and working for the community, helping the people. I love to inspire people and be a positive light in their life.

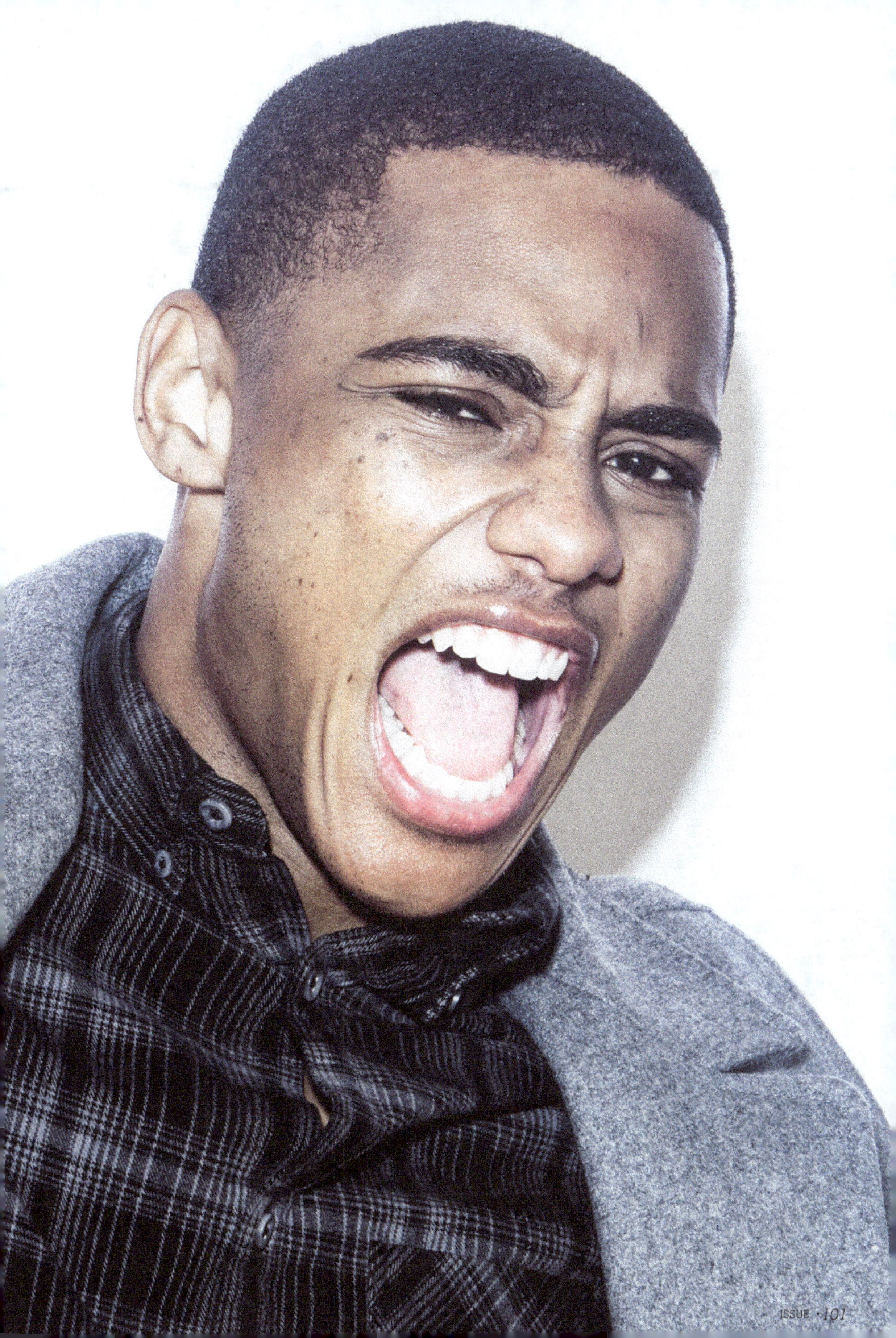

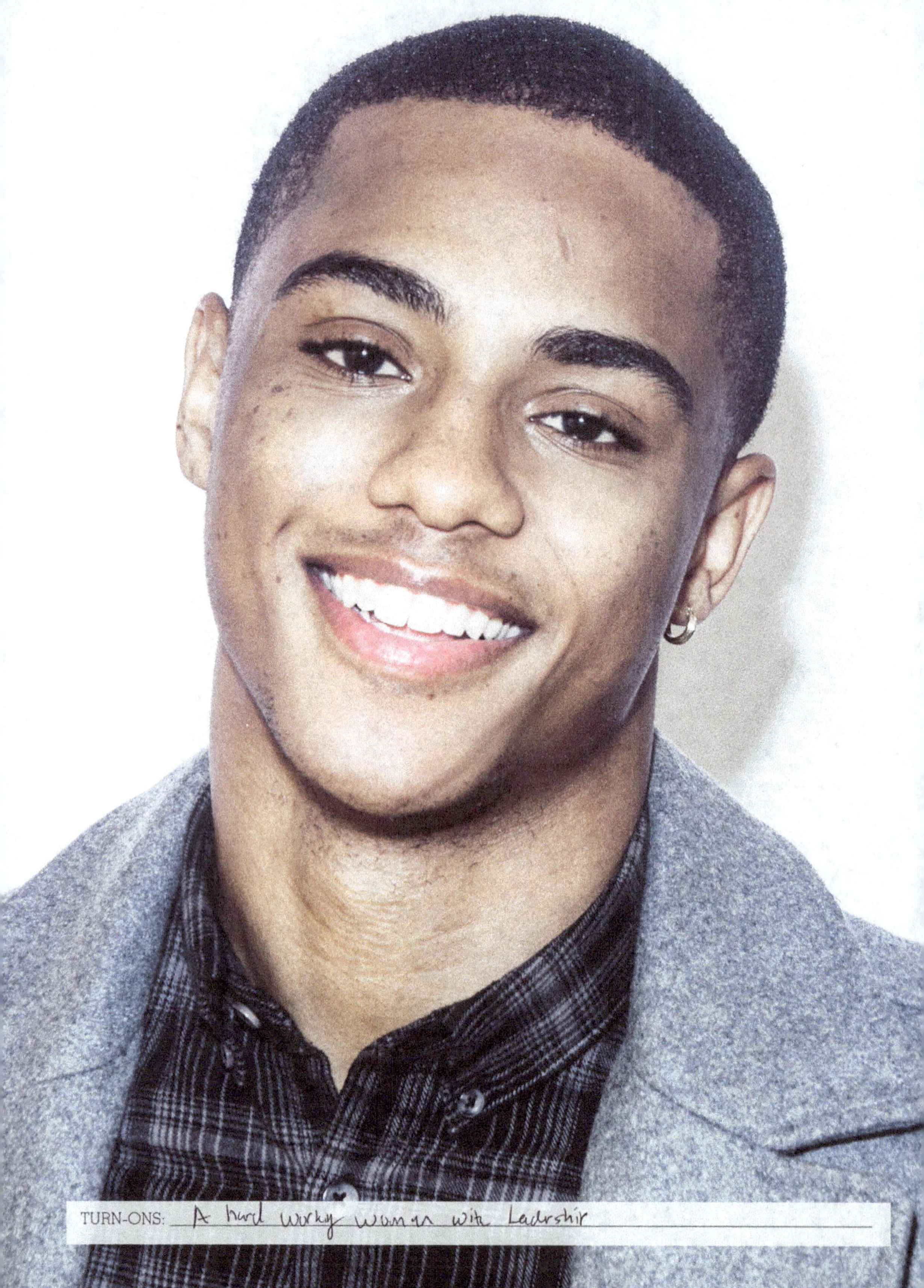

TURN-ONS: A hard workng woman with Ladrship

actor who you look up to? Will Smith. When you see him on screen you want to be his brother, or you want him to be your dad, or if you're a girl you want him to be your lover. You want to be involved with him in some way. I feel like that's because of who he is off-screen as well, and that inspires me. I watched him growing up and people like Leonardo DiCaprio, Viola Davis, Meryl Streep… I've got a couple favorites.

What would your ideal job be? My ideal job would be one that I'm writing, producing and acting. That would be my ideal job, and I think these days it could definitely happen. So many networks are looking for new talent and taking all these different projects. This is an era where we can create, and it's not too far out.

Do you consider yourself to be lucky? I consider myself blessed because I've worked so hard, but at the same time you need a little luck. You need the stars to align. But I would moreso say blessed.

What do you think about the need for instant gratification? I call it the fast food era. Anything you do you feel has to be instant. We don't bask in anything anymore. We just want something then we want the next.

I think it's bittersweet.

How do you feel about having children? In a perfect world, I want like 10 kids. I want that big house with a family like my grandparents did, but I know that's not going to happen. I would have to start now.

What challenges do you feel the world is facing today? Whether you voted for our

"IN A PERFECT WORLD, I WANT LIKE 10 KIDS. I WANT THAT BIG HOUSE WITH A FAMILY LIKE MY GRANDPARENTS DID, BUT I KNOW THAT'S NOT GOING TO HAPPEN. I WOULD HAVE TO START NOW."

— KEITH POWERS

President or not, I think he's showing us that we're not as united as we thought. The real problem is not him, it's us. It's a test. We've all got to come together. We've got social media. We see everything that's going down. How do we come together? I think the biggest problem we face is simply putting our pride aside. It's so simple that it's difficult.

What will your mom say when she sees this? That it was good, even if she really didn't see it, because she's my #1 fan!

What's next? *Famous in Love* by Freeform and *#realityhigh*, a lovely film I'm in for Netflix. 🟧

KEITH POWERS
Born in Sacramento, Keith Powers has appeared in *Straight Outta Compton* (2015), MTV's *Faking It* (2014–16) and Freeform's *Recovery Road* (2016). His upcoming projects include *The New Edition Story* (2017) on BET, *Famous in Love* (2017) on Freeform and *#realityhigh* (2017) on Netflix.

JOEY KING

Los Angeles native Joey King started acting when she was just four years-old. She stars as Michael Caine's granddaughter in Zach Braff's newest film Going in Style. *King's*

Ambitions: Be a boss, be kind to everyone, win an Academy Award

Favorite food: Ice cream and my grandma's brisket

How do you like to spend your time? Going on adventures

sounds so generic, but sometimes I look at like what I'm doing and ask, "how did I even get here?" I was in Africa for two months shooting, and I have a movie coming out now with Morgan Freeman, Michael Caine and Alan Arkin. Then

and weren't afraid to hold back, so we kind of progressed through them. Then we started doing commercials, and it just kind of progressed into guest stars on TV shows and now films.

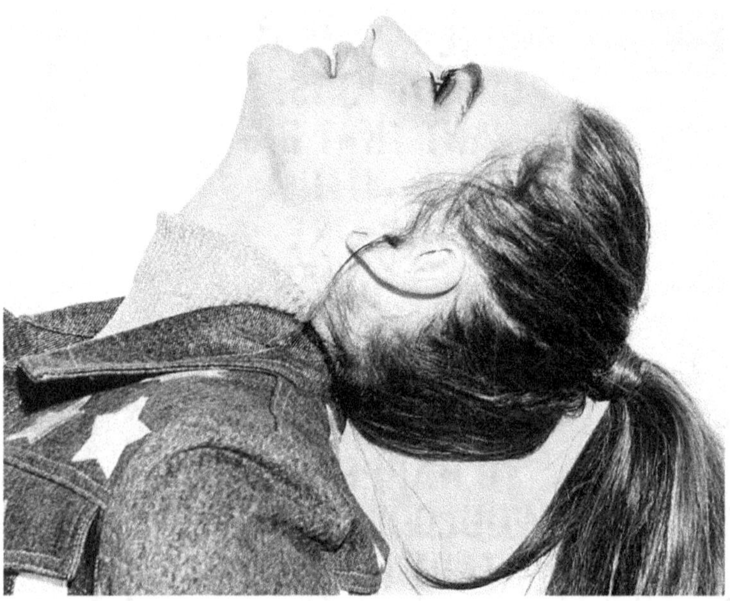

acting credits include Noah Hawley's TV series Fargo, White House Down, The Conjuring *and, of course,* Ramona and Beezus.

Birthplace: Los Angeles

in IKEA, listening to amazing music while driving, doing friends' makeup, spending time with my sisters.

Turn-ons: Will play hide'n'seek with me, up for any adventure, likes Mexican food, good taste in music.

How do you feel about this career? I honestly feel like I'm the luckiest person alive. I know that

I have two other films coming out this year. Sometimes it's like, "Why me?" Pinch me.

How did you decide to become an actor? How I really decided to become an actor was that me and my sisters were in little stage-door theater plays when we were younger, and we had so much fun together. We were all very expressive

How would you describe your specialty or type? I don't think I'm all that special, to be honest. I want to take a natural approach to everything, but I don't want to put other actors or other crew members or anyone at risk with my methods. I respect people who are method, but I love to study a character so that it becomes like second

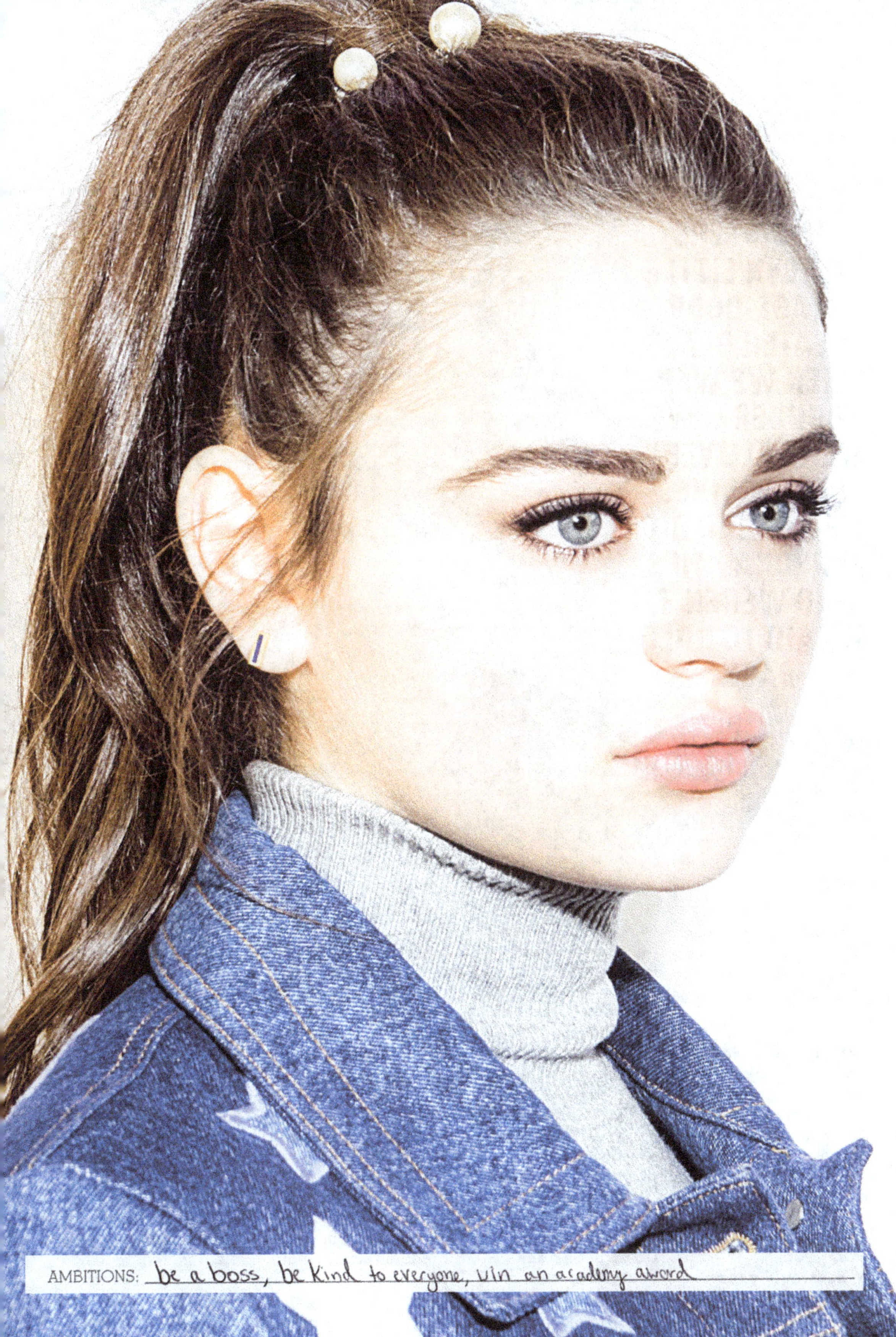

AMBITIONS: be a boss, be kind to everyone, win an academy award

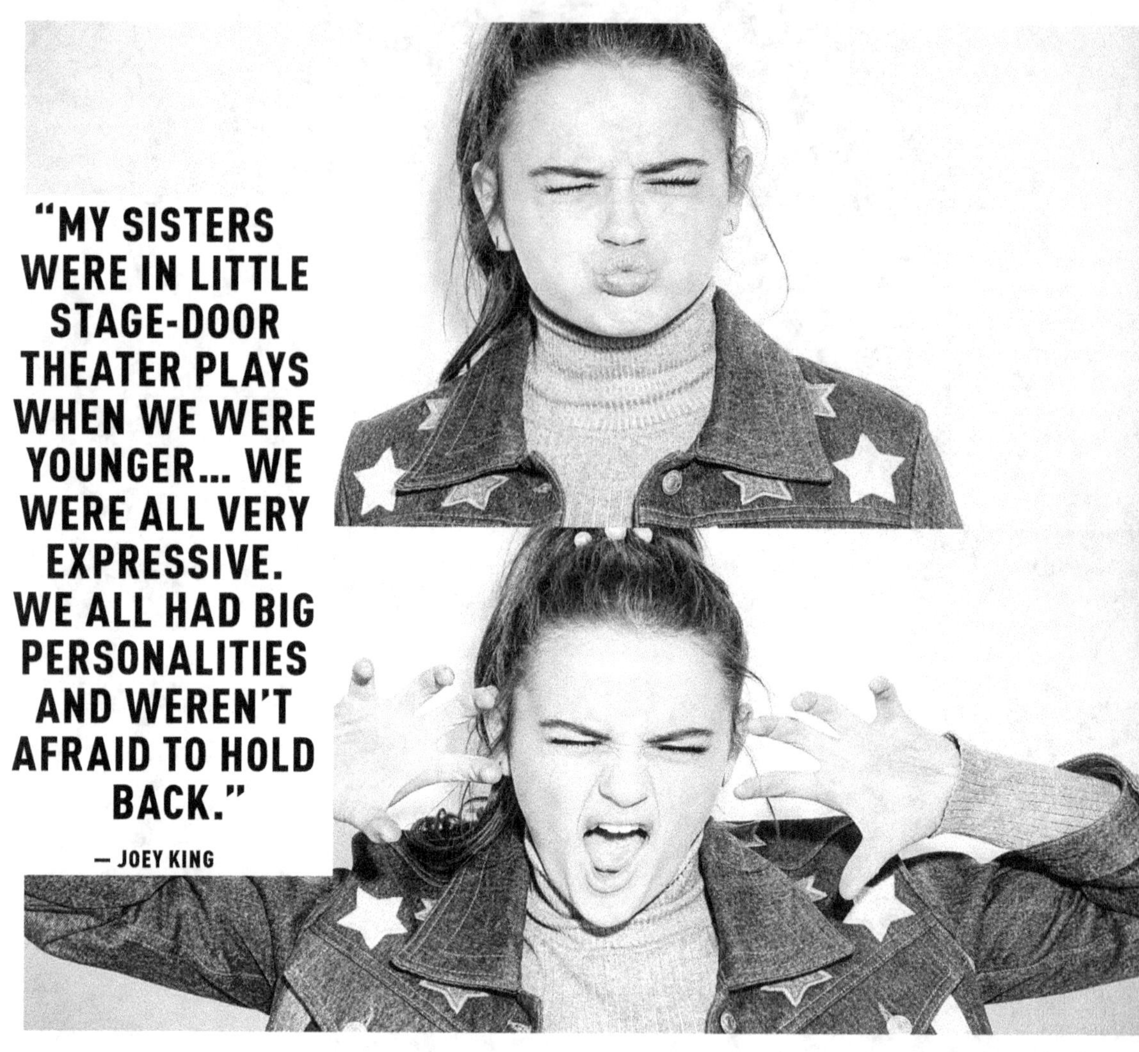

nature to me—so I can turn that character on, then once they say "cut" I can go back to myself.

Who is your favorite actor you look up to? Jessica Chastain. Her work is incomparable. She can play subtle so well. She can be expressive and very energetic. Everything that she does is so believable.

What would your ideal job be? I don't know. It's hard to say when there's so many things I want to do. My ideal job might be— maybe—to play a psychopath or a prisoner. Honestly, I might have just shot my dream job by doing a film with all these legends, with Michael Caine playing my grandfather. I have so many dream jobs planned, and hopefully every one of them comes true.

Do you consider yourself to be lucky? Absolutely. I think I am the luckiest girl in the world. I'm surrounded by an amazing family who supports what I do so well, and they're proud of me and cheer me on. They call me after an interview and say how much they loved it, and they call me after a movie. No matter how many people you have supporting you that aren't your family, sometimes it's just special to get that phone call from your grandma saying that she saw your film and couldn't be prouder.

What advantages do you have? I never knew anyone in the business when I was younger. I didn't have like a cousin who was Julia Roberts or knew a casting actor. So I kind of just grew from the bottom. I think my advantage now is that I have created such amazing friendships. That's my advantage: having memories and relationships with people from set, people who are in this industry who I will have in my life and love forever.

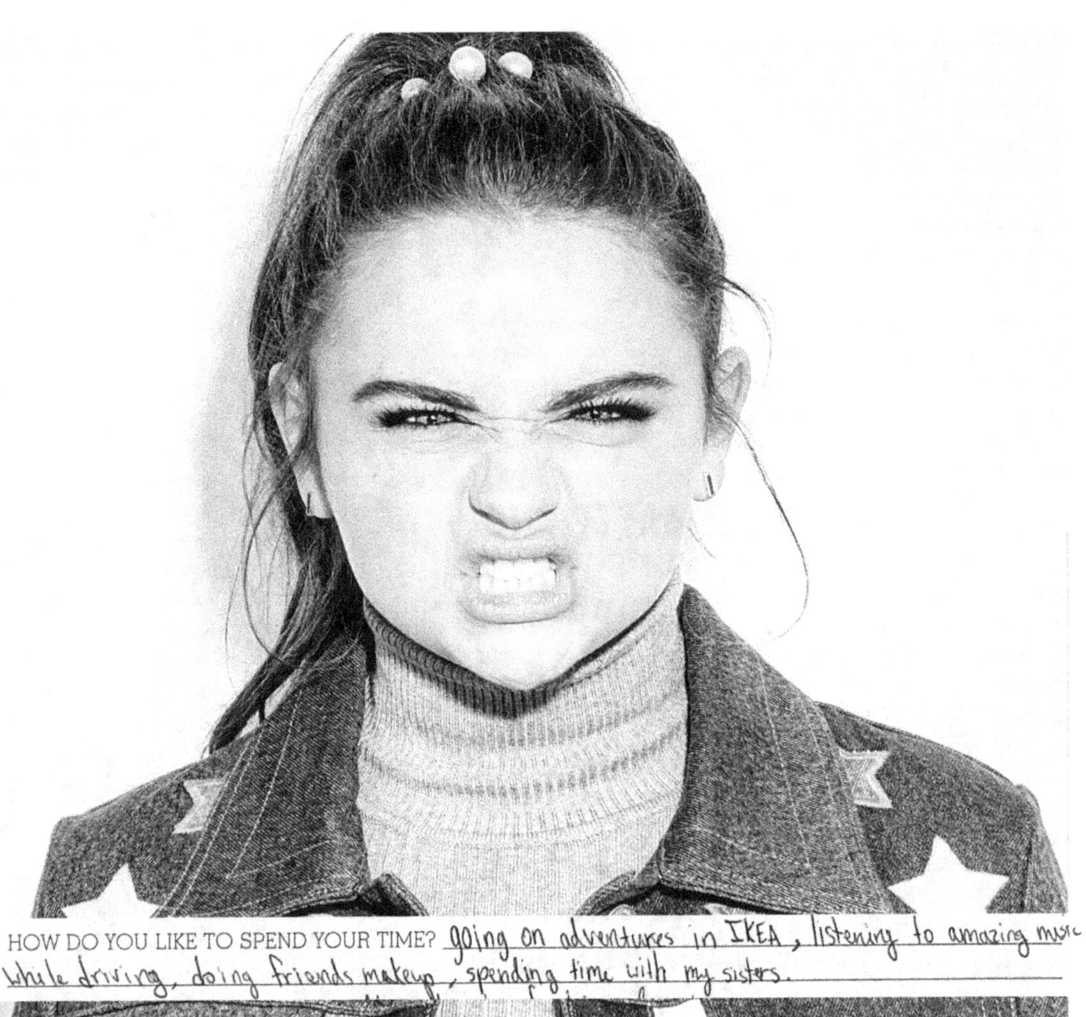

Would you rather have a car or a diploma? What's a smart answer? What kind of car? Just kidding. I think education is so so important. I do have a diploma because I graduated. Now that I have that, I would love a car.

What do you think about the need for instant gratification? I'm an actor. I'm not going to pretend like I don't like attention. It's kind of funny because a lot of actors are like "Oh, stop it, no." I'm like, "Well, you're an actor. You like attention." When someone comes up to me on the street and tells me that they love my films or they want a photo with me, it's so exciting because that means someone's watching and someone is really appreciating all the effort that I put into things.

What does the future look like to you? It looks very, very bright. I hope the same thing for the world because sometimes I get very scared and caught up when I watch the news. You start to feel like the future is not going to a bright place. But all we can do is hope, and we can't control anything. We might as well just live in the moment.

How do you feel about having children? Oh, I don't know. I'm just 17. I don't know if I want kids… Watch me have kids, and then they see this interview like, "Mom!"

What challenges do you feel the world is facing today? Well, America is facing an interesting challenge with the current president—which is ugh! And there are health care challenges, challenges with people getting along, there's protesters who are getting pepper sprayed. There are so many things that you can talk about that are challenging everyone's faith and love for each other. I hope that with all the social media that we have and all the people who are activists, including myself, we can all settle our differences and become one.

What is your favorite way to communicate? I love facetiming. You get so much done: you see the person and you get to have an actual conversation. As far as interacting with fans and stuff, I love replying to people on Twitter and reading Instagram comments. Yeah, I'd say maybe Twitter.

What is your favorite book film in music right now? My favorite book of all is *A Million Little Pieces* by James Frey. It's such a good book, and the story behind it's crazy. It was true, then it wasn't true, he went on Oprah… My favorite movie is always changing, but *Get Out* directed by Jordan Peele is definitely my favorite of 2017. Also, *Going In Style* was amazing. I just saw for the first time, and it was so funny. Kendrick Lamar just released the most fire track called "Humble." Great song, great music video, huge fan of his. And my favorite album which just continued into this year was *Birds in the Trap Sing McKnight* by Travis Scott.

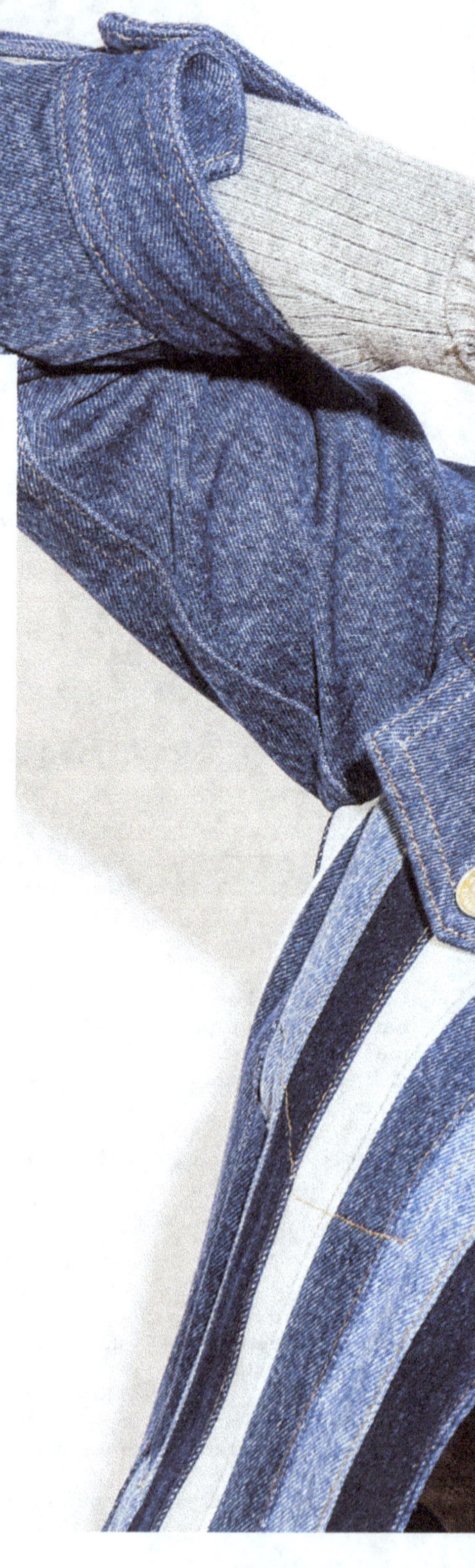

JOEY KING
Seventeen-year-old, LA-based actor Joey King has appeared in films and television such as Zach Braff's *Going in Style* (2017), *Fargo* (2014–17), *White House Down* (2013), *The Conjuring* (2013) and *Ramona and Beezus* (2010).

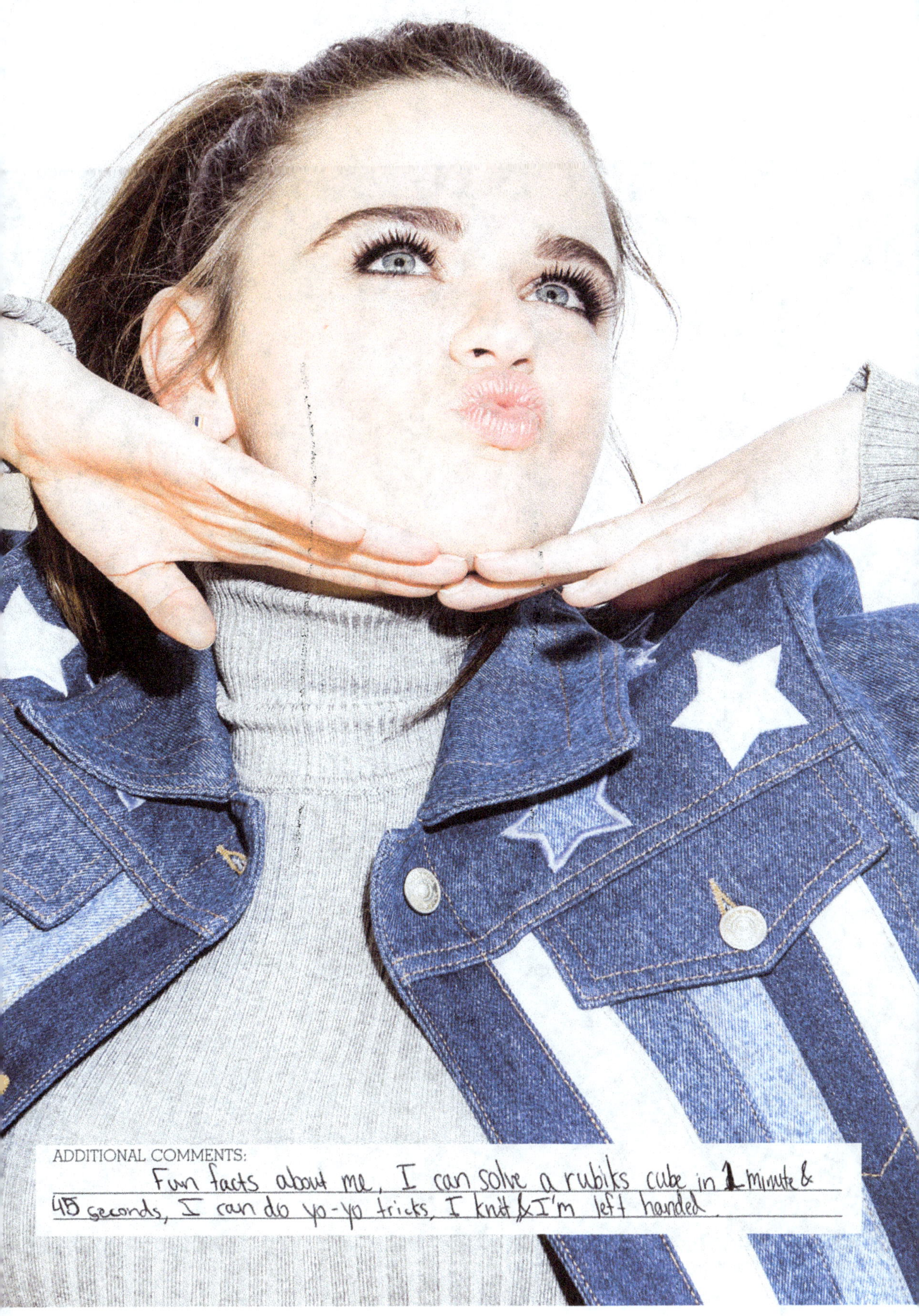

ADDITIONAL COMMENTS:
Fun facts about me, I can solve a rubiks cube in 1 minute &
45 seconds, I can do yo-yo tricks, I knit & I'm left handed

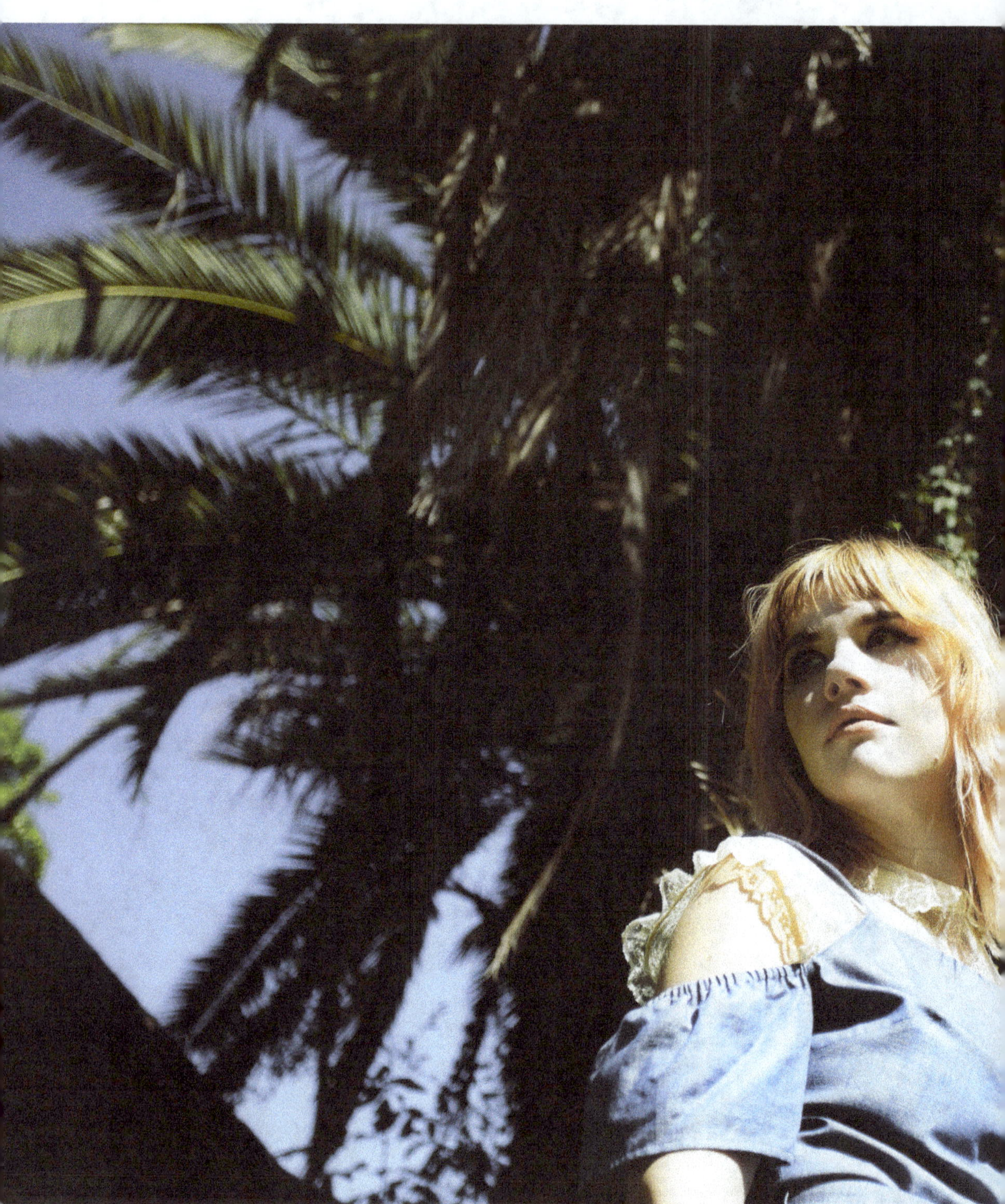

The Frilly Dress, **Ted Baker** Top

JENNIFER CLAVIN

Interview by **Cecilia Della Peruti**

Images by **Ira Chernova**
Styling by **Lera Pentelute**

Inspired by the punk shows they saw growing up in Los Angeles, Jennifer Clavin and her sister Jessica founded their first band, Mika Miko, in 2003. As the group gained popularity and played energy-infused live shows, Clavin realized that instead of interviews focused on their music, the press asked various forms of one question: "What's it like to be a girl in a band?" This treatment of gender over art indicated that being female and in a band—or worse, in an all-female band—was an act or some sort of protest instead of what it actually was: musicians making music together.

The Clavin sisters now front Bleached, which they founded in 2011, and after 14 successful years releasing albums, playing shows and making Billboard charts, they still hear variations of that same question. This year, they released their sophomore album Welcome the Worms, *which Clavin describes as her most challenging, emotionally deep record to date. If Clavin was tired of hearing these types of gender-based, beside-the-point questions, she thought her female contemporaries must be as well. She reached out to them—a prolific, powerful group of musicians including both newcomers like Julien Baker and Hinds and industry veterans like Allison Wolfe (Sex Stains, Bratmobile) and L7. Their responses are compiled in* Can You Deal?, *Clavin's recent zine which protests simplistic "girl band" journalism and speaks out against how females are treated in the music industry. Following the 2017 election, Clavin has also been active politically, releasing a set of acoustic covers for purchase via Bandcamp and donating the proceeds to Planned Parenthood. In the sort of interview she'd like to see more often, Clavin talks with her friend and fellow musician Cecilia Della Peruti of Gothic Tropic about* Can You Deal? *and shares her essay that kicked off the zine.*

———————

So, when did you start playing music and writing songs? Who inspired you to pick up an instrument? I started playing music in ninth grade, I think. My dad had guitars around the house that he made himself and my mom was a singer. We would go to these family barbecues, and they would be the band that would perform for everybody.

Our parents' generation called those "hootenannies." Oh my God, so my parents are hootenannies. So many jam sessions. I feel like I was always listening to whatever music they were doing, so when I found punk in high school, I was like, "Woah, this is so cool. My parents will not approve of this." My sister Jessie and I would go to like two shows a week or every weekend—whatever band was playing at The Showcase or The Glass House.

Did you grow up in coastal regions? No, in the valley—Northridge. But we would drive until we got to The Glass House or The Showcase in Corona. I remember

> **"WHEN I FOUND PUNK IN HIGH SCHOOL, I WAS LIKE, 'WOAH, THIS IS SO COOL. MY PARENTS WILL NOT APPROVE OF THIS."**
>
> — JENNIFER CLAVIN

BLEACHED
Bleached is a Los Angeles-based band comprised of frontwoman Jennifer Clavin and guitarist Jessica Clavin, formerly of Mika Miko, bassist Micayla Grace, formerly of Leopold & His Fiction, and drummer Nick Pillot. The group has released the studio albums *Ride Your Heart* (2013) and *Welcome the Worms* (2016) via Dead Oceans. Their EPs include *Francis, Carter* and *Searching Through the Past b/w Electric Chair.*

MIKA MIKO
Formed in Los Angeles in 2003, Mika Miko released 10 recordings, including EPs, tapes and full albums, and was known for their frenetic live shows. The band was comprised of Victor Fandgore (Jennifer Clavin), Jet Blanca (Jenna Thornhill), Michelle Suarez, Jessica Clavin and Jon Erik Edrosa. The group broke up in 2009, and the Clavin sisters went on to form Bleached in 2011.

CECILIA DELLA PERUTI
A Los Angeles-based musician, Cecilia Della Peruti fronts the band Gothic Tropic. She has released *Awesome Problems EP* (2011) and the recent full-length *Fast or Feast* (2017), recorded in LA with Devendra Banhart and Electric Guest's Todd Dahlhoff. Peruti has also toured with bands including Børns, Charlie XCX and Night Terrors of 1927.

CAN YOU DEAL?
A 2017 zine compiled by musician Jennifer Clavin of Bleached. In a series of essays, images and personal accounts, artists share their experiences of their female

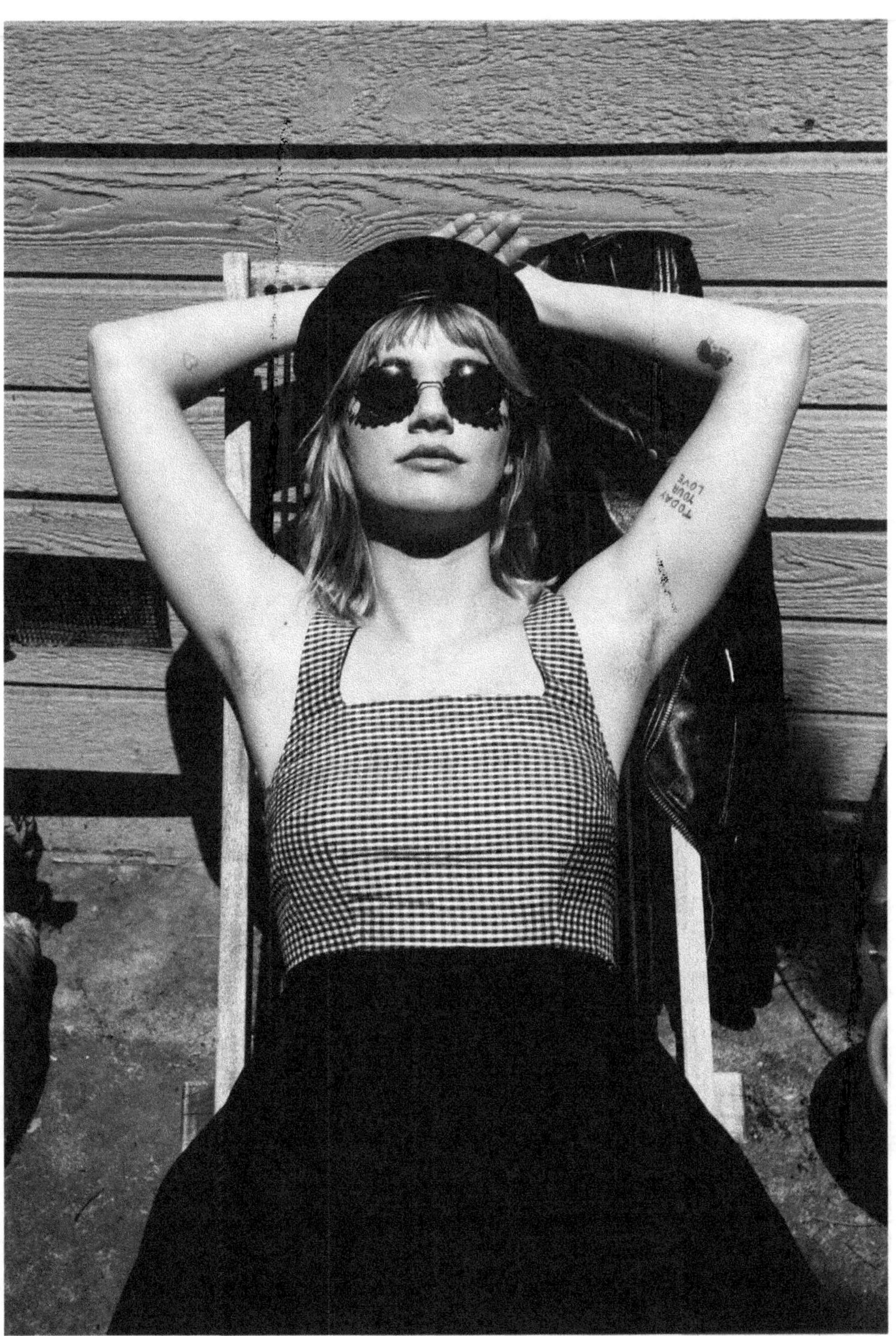

Shaina Mote Pant, **Saint Laurent** Leather Jacket, Vintage Top and Beret

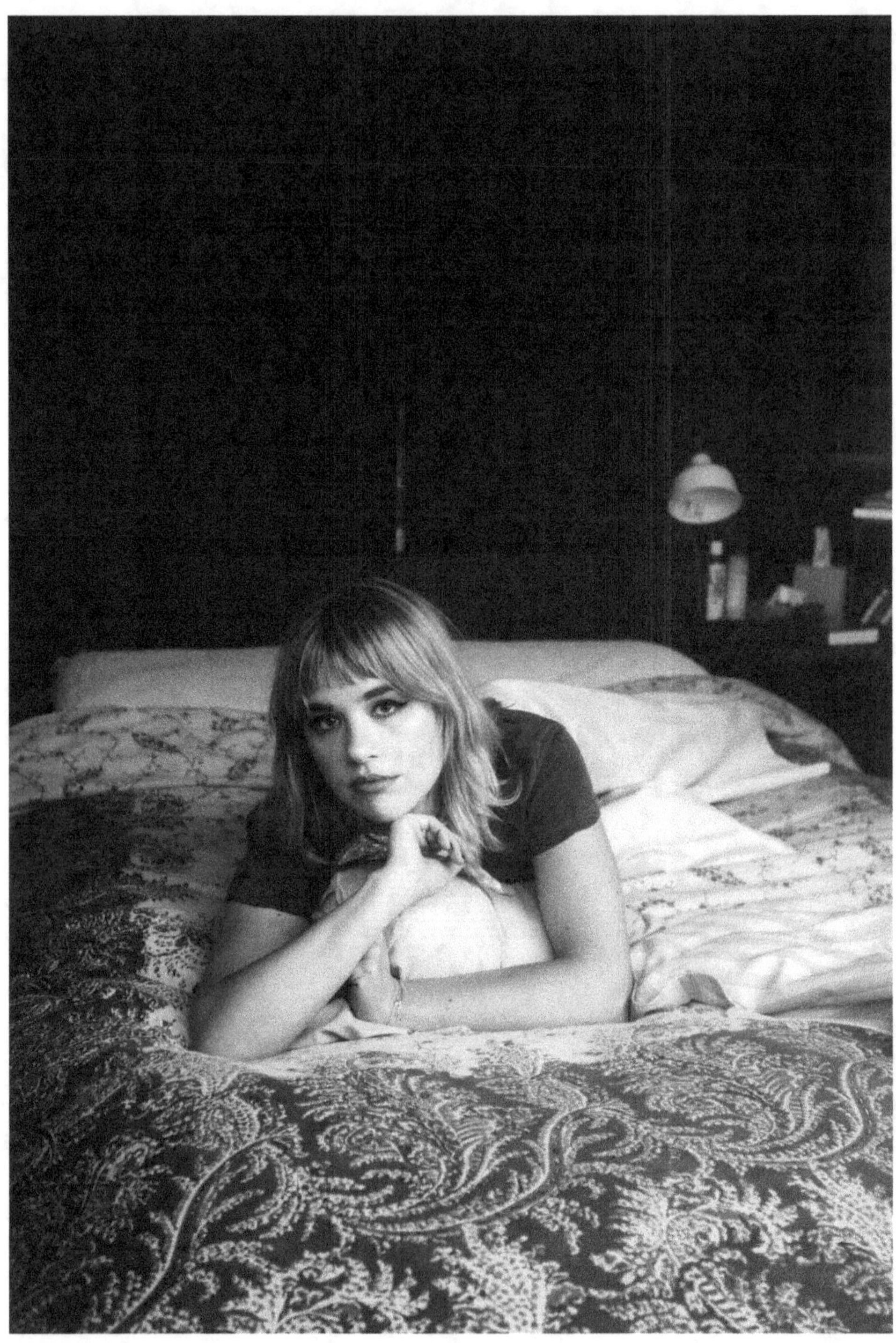

Stateside Tee, **Town Clothes** Culotte Trouser, **Echo** Scarf, Vintage **Dior** Jacket

gender defining other people's narrative of their art. www.can-youdealzine.com

F-MINUS
A hardcore punk band from Huntington Beach, California, F-Minus was formed in 1995 by Jen Johnson and Brad Logan, though the lineup changed before the band's breakup in 2004. F-Minus released four albums including *Self Titled* (1999), *Suburban Blight* (2001), *Wake Up Screaming* (2003) and *Won't Bleed Me / Failed Society* (2005), as well as six EPs.

seeing a lot of older bands like The Attics or The Rezillos or Subhumans. One time we saw this band F-Minus play. I'd been going to shows every week-end and for some reason seeing them both onstage made me think, "Wait. Why don't my sister and I have a band?" Jessie was already playing bass heavily at that point. I remember trying to play bass a little bit, and that's when I decided I should pick up a gui-tar, since they were laying around my house, and learn to play so me and Jessie could be in a band together. We had our friends singing. So basically we started playing music to be able to be in a band. It was seeing F-Minus that made me decide to pick up an instru-ment, and I always wonder that it must have been because there were women on stage.

Do you feel like seeing F-Minus and having an early real-life example of women playing instruments was an invitation to do it yourself? Yeah, totally. It seemed like something that I could actually achieve. I've never taken a class to learn an instrument, so it's weird that I got this idea like, "I think I can do that too," just by seeing a woman on stage.

So when you start-ed, did you ever recognize any sex-

> "IT WAS SEEING F-MINUS THAT MADE ME DECIDE TO PICK UP AN INSTRUMENT, AND I ALWAYS WONDER THAT IT MUST HAVE BEEN BECAUSE THERE WERE WOMEN ON STAGE."
>
> — JENNIFER CLAVIN

ism at that age and do any experiences come to mind? I think about this question a lot. I always wonder how much sexism I experienced and how much of it was me not being confident in myself. When I would go to shows like, I remember a guy grabbed me.

Did you realize at that time that it was maybe worse than you thought? Because I remem-ber brushing it off easily for no other reason than, "Oh, it's normal." Yeah, same. I feel like maybe I didn't want to make a scene. This guy's way bigger than me if I were to say something back.

Fear of being misunderstood is difficult. That scene was very emotion-ally harsh. You don't want to feel like you're lame or something. I was full of a lot of rage and anger back then, so there became a point where I was fueled by the sexism and wanted to stand up to it, for myself and for my sister. One time, I made out with a guy, and he was like, "Do you want to go to the bathroom and give me a blowjob?" I was so offended. I would never say, "Do you want to go to the bathroom and eat me out?" I was like, "Fuck you. You're gross. Never into you again." There are so many moments as we grow up that we don't understand it, and so when it happens it kind of throws us for a loop.

It's a social domino effect wherein one little girl watches another little girl stand up for herself to influence the rest of the group. Totally. I remember my best friend at the time would not take shit from anybody, so I really learned a lot from her.

I had a kind of "hurt puppy complex" growing up, so I was the underdog, with a doormat life. There was so much resentment as a result of not standing up for myself when I should have. I remember one time when I was a kid, before I started a band or even found punk, I went to New York with my mom. We were on the subway, and she lifted her arm to hold onto the pole in the fully-packed subway. It was super hairy, and I was so embarrassed like, "Oh my God, how could my mom think it's okay to put her arm up?" I always think back on that because now I have full, hairy armpits and most of my friends do.

That's the early priming that all the Disney movies try to accomplish with their standard of beauty—being clean-shaven, white, doe-eyed. It starts when you're a kid and it's so cool that people are more conscious about

— CECILIA DELLA PERUTI

that in the consumer world. Usually I hate on the Internet, but maybe that's one good thing about it: having the young girls follow your Instagram and realize, "She has hairy armpits."

So, how did the zine come to be? We had just released *Welcome The Worms* and were touring for almost a year straight, playing shows almost every day. There were so many interviews going on around me and the release of the new record, and a majority of the questions were like, "What's it like to be a girl in a band?" Or the headlines would say All-Girl Band. I've been playing music for over 10 years, and my first band, Mika Miko, used to get this question all the time. We were all girls for a while and then we had a guy drummer. It used to bother me so much because the questions always seemed like they were saying, "So you put all your girl friends together to start a band to make a statement." And at that time, I was like, "No, we are just friends. These are my friends. We all learned how to play music together, not trying to be like 'fuck the men' by starting an all-girl band." But we got asked that question so many times. We were also always labeled "riot grrrl" back then.

It just feels weird to say that a woman

playing music is an act of resistance in itself. I know, right? That has really bugged me. I feel like I just got used to all those questions. You kind of let it go in one ear and out the other. You're just like, whatever, I feel sorry for the person who's asking me this, but at the same time I just don't feel like making a big deal about it. So, this started happening again with *Welcome The Worms*. It was the first record where I went so deep inside myself and really wrote about honest stuff. It took a lot out of me. But then, once again, we're doing interviews and they were based more around my gender than what the record is about.

You had just poured your heart and soul into it and are now in a generous position to elaborate on what you are writing about. And if no one asks you what you're writing about, it just kind of feels like you put all this into it and are not given the opportunity to share the real content. If we're given such a limited time to talk, ask me stuff that matters.

board and play music.

My best friend and I would dress up like boys and go to the local backyard punk shows in either east LA or the valley. I had cut off all my hair at that point. We would put on baseball hats, tape our boobs down and just hang out. When

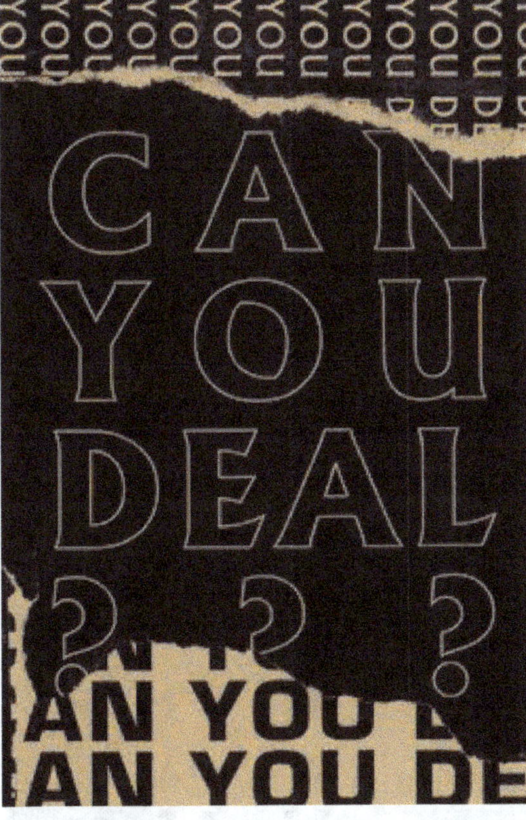

"IF WE'RE GIVEN SUCH A LIMITED TIME TO TALK, ASK ME STUFF THAT MATTERS."

— JENNIFER CLAVIN

to be a woman. I was finally comfortable expressing my femininity and confident enough to brush off the sexist remarks, inappropriate slurs, uninvited advances or misconduct I would encounter: a back and forth of acceptance in itself.

Eventually one of my first bands, Mika Miko, got some recognition. Interviewers would constantly ask "What is it like to be a girl in a band?" or "Did you purposely construct your band with all girls to make a statement?" I was thrown off by these questions. Mika Miko was my best friends and my sister, not a carefully constructed statement. I wasn't aware that females starting a band together was anything more than us making music. Now I was rebelling? Over the years we all learned to ignore the question, be polite about it and move on. What would you like me to say? Even one interviewer was shocked when I listed my favorite bands at the time… She couldn't believe I didn't list one band with a female singer. I wasn't thinking about gender, I was thinking about the music that makes me fucking feel something!

Last year my band Bleached released a full length album titled *Welcome The Worms*. This record was very personal to me. I wrote about being in

Jennifer Clavin (Bleached):
Growing up I didn't feel comfortable with society's standards of being a "girl". Not that I wanted to be a boy, I just wasn't interested in wearing makeup, the color pink or talking about boys. I wanted to learn how to skate-

I would get mistaken as a boy I felt so accomplished. I wanted my name to be Victor no matter what I looked like and to be honest, I still love that name.

Later, I began to embrace the feminine side in me. Wearing dresses and embracing my curves. I eventually felt excited

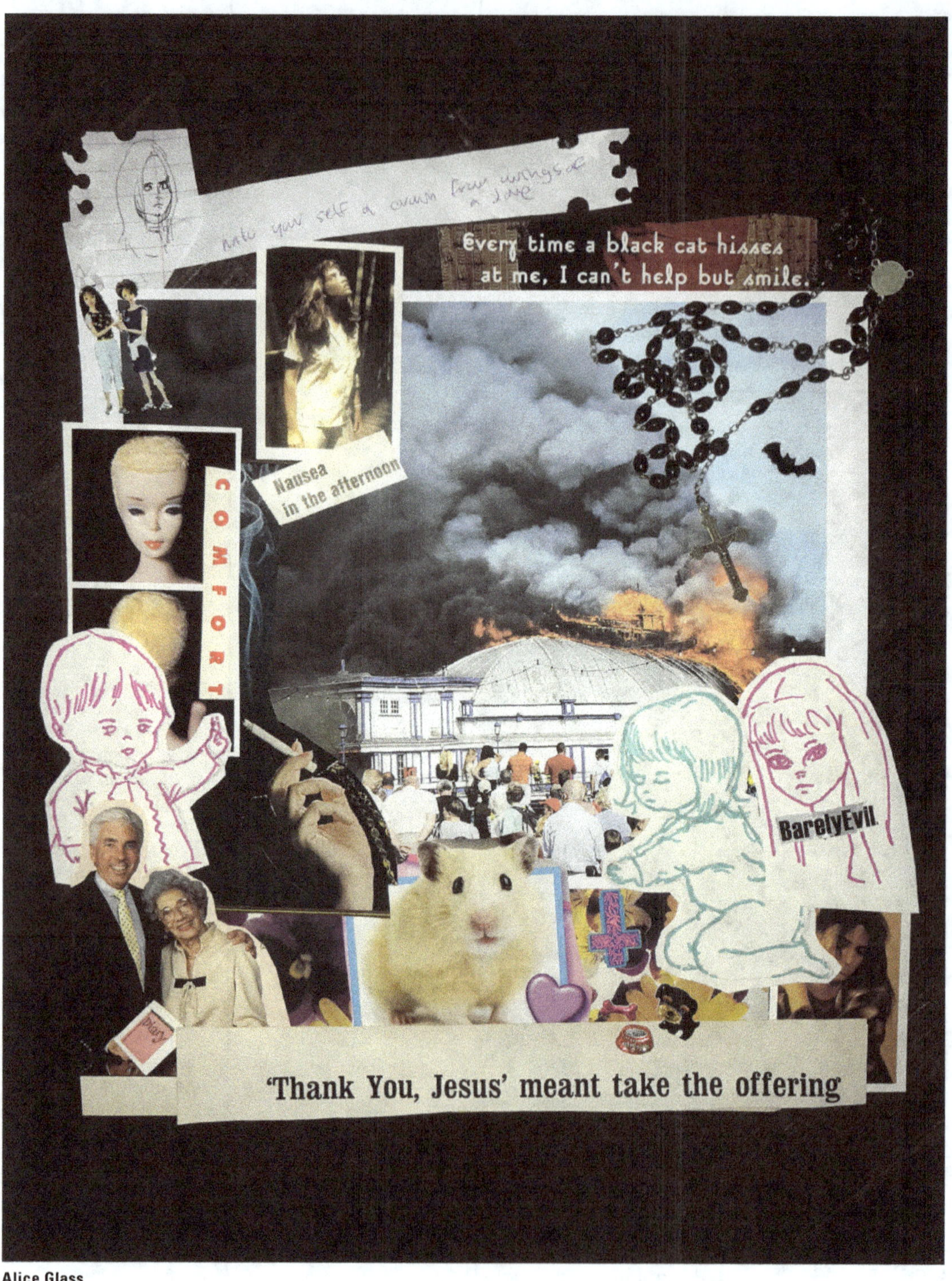

Every time a black cat hisses
at me, I can't help but smile.
Nausea in the afternoon
COMFORT
BarelyEvil
'Thank You, Jesus' meant take the offering

Alice Glass

ALICE GLASS
Alice Glass is the co-founder and former frontperson of electronic band Crystal Castles. The third single from *Crystal Castles (II)* (2010), "Not in Love," which featured Robert Smith from The Cure, became the band's highest charting single to date. In October 2014, Glass announced her departure from the band to pursue a solo career.

and getting out of an emotionally abusive relationship. It was a record about getting spun out on drugs and alcohol. It was a record about totally losing myself in order to find myself. It was also our most ambitious body of work yet, containing the guitar work and production we had only dreamed of until then. To this day I am still fielding interview questions that have more to do with my gender than with the art I am creating. Somehow, the conversation still derails into some variation of: "What is it like to be a girl in a rock band?" People act surprised that women can play well, play loud, make records and tour as if it has not been happening for years. I'm done with this novelty they've turned me into: a girl playing guitar. I am a musician.

So, here is my answer to your question. Being a girl in a band is no different than being a girl in any field. We have people consistently pointing out our gender as if it relates to our ability. Our gender is pointed out in nearly everything as if it was integral to understanding our band. Labeling me as a woman puts me in a box and forces me to conform to gender roles. This ignores everything else I am. I want to be seen beyond gender and not what the medical stamp says on my birth certificate.

> "BEING A GIRL IN A BAND IS NO DIFFERENT THAN BEING A GIRL IN ANY FIELD. WE HAVE PEOPLE CONSISTENTLY POINTING OUT OUR GENDER AS IF IT RELATES TO OUR ABILITY… THIS IGNORES EVERYTHING ELSE I AM."
>
> —JENNIFER CLAVIN

When does the novelty wear off? Labeling me is reductive. I create music and art because I need to. To express, to bond, to reconcile, and to connect and to use my voice. It is insulting to have my art received with such a generic filter. The title track to Bleached's new EP, "Can You Deal?" is about my experience with this. "You know that it's me, Who Else Could I Be? Don't You See?"

I feel the need to create a space for females to share their experiences. The first step towards change is awareness.

Can You Deal? is for every girl out there who is sick of every male sound engineer telling them what they think is right for their guitar set up. *Can You Deal?* is for every girl who has been told that "girl bands are in right now" by an A&R guy. *Can You Deal?* is for any girl mulling over press photos, knowing their band will be picked apart for looks and not the actual music. *Can You Deal?* is for everyone who can please stop referring to my band as "female fronted" or "all girl band". It is for everyone who can stop feigning surprise every time a woman plugs in and plays well, gets behind the drums or has the sickest bass style. It is 2017.

CAN YOU DEAL YET?

Mish Way (White Lung): Being a woman plays a role in my communication with the world, but not my capabilities when it comes to the music itself. Gender does and does not matter. And for now, that discrepancy somehow is keeping me sane.

Patty Schemel (Upset, Hole): Drumming is a bloodsport, like boxing. It's not for wimps. Part of developing the necessary stamina is to teach yourself to play through pain, something that women do particularly well. We labor and give birth… Some people tape their fingers and ice their knuckles, but I prefer to let it bleed.

Allison Wolfe (Sex Stains, Bratmobile): We live in a sexist society that is highly gendered, and my way of dealing with and confronting that reality has been to highlight my experiences specifically as a woman in music—to own it and embrace it.

…

I think it's more radical to not try to be "one of the guys," but to set our own standards and uplift our own teen girl bedroom scenes, for example. Instead of breaking into the all-boy clubhouse, I'd rather invite the girls over for kool-aid at my house.

…

"Riot grrrl" and "girl band" are not musical genres. Many '90s female musicians who didn't identify as riot grrrls got lumped into that label by lazy, unimaginative journalists… The media was happy to tokenize female musicians and pit our bands against each other, acting like there wasn't enough room for all of us in our variety.

> "MANY '90S FEMALE MUSICIANS WHO DIDN'T IDENTIFY AS RIOT GRRRLS GOT LUMPED INTO THAT LABEL BY LAZY, UNIMAGINATIVE JOURNALISTS… THE MEDIA WAS HAPPY TO TOKENIZE FEMALE MUSICIANS AND PIT OUR BANDS AGAINST EACH OTHER, ACTING LIKE THERE WASN'T ENOUGH ROOM FOR ALL OF US IN OUR VARIETY."
>
> —ALLISON WOLFE

Micayla Grace (Bleached): I love the saying "feminism is the radical notion that women are people."… I don't want to focus on the oppression so many women have suffered through the ages and the sexism we still encounter as an incurable disease; I see it as a guitar we are still tuning. So yeah, I'm optimistic, but it's gonna take a lot more work and the best way to honor this legacy of women being considered equals is by being an example.

Marisa Prietto (Wax Idols): "The thing is, Marisa, you're going to have to play harder and be better, and it's because you're a girl, I'm sorry."

Tegan Quin (Tegan and Sara): With more success came more respect. Sort of. Rarely do we see anything quite so blatantly sexist as calling us "Tampon Rock" (Pitchfork) or disturbingly homophobic as "pretty good even if they do hate cock" (NME). But it happens

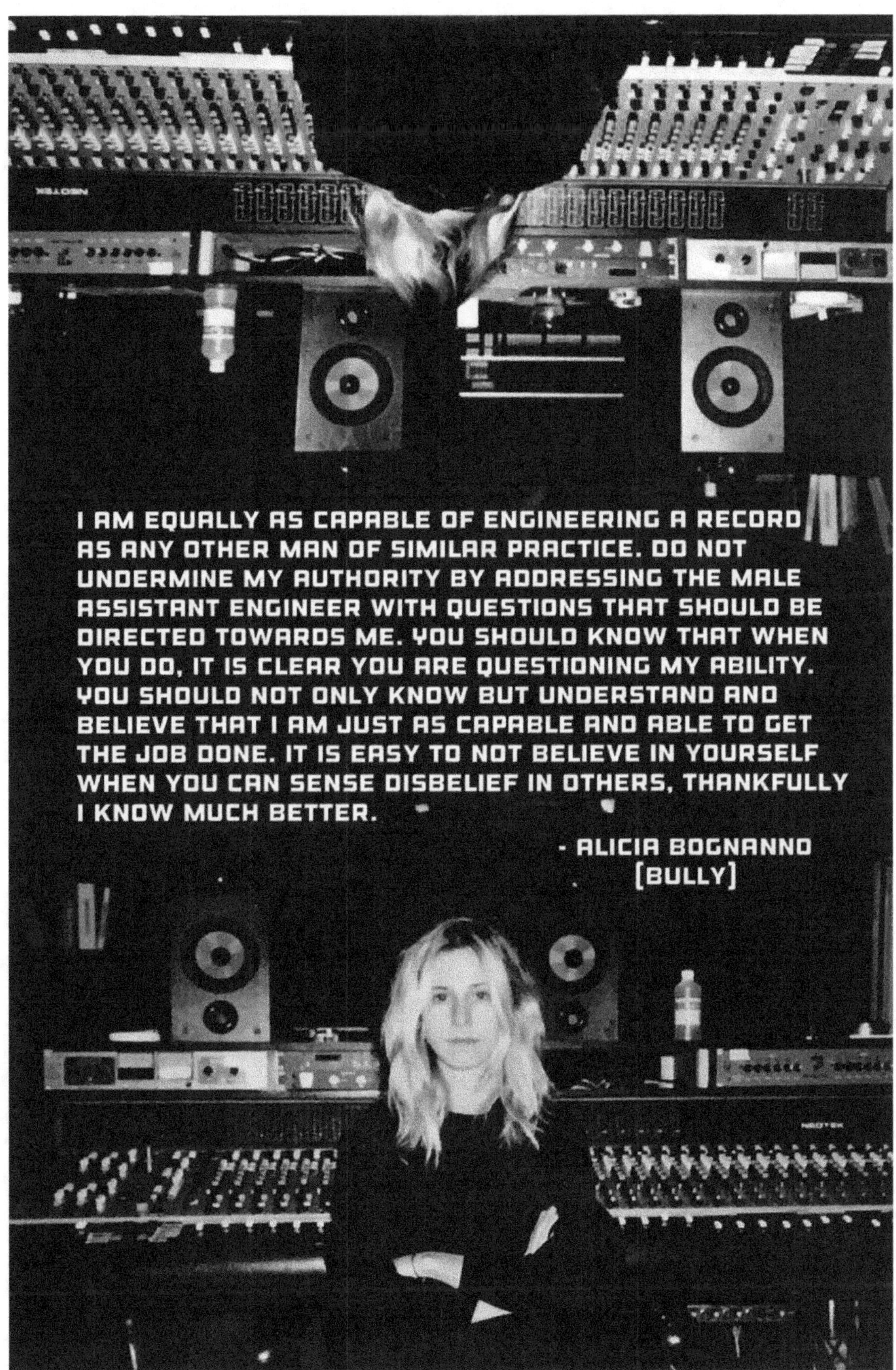

Alicia Bognanno (Bully)

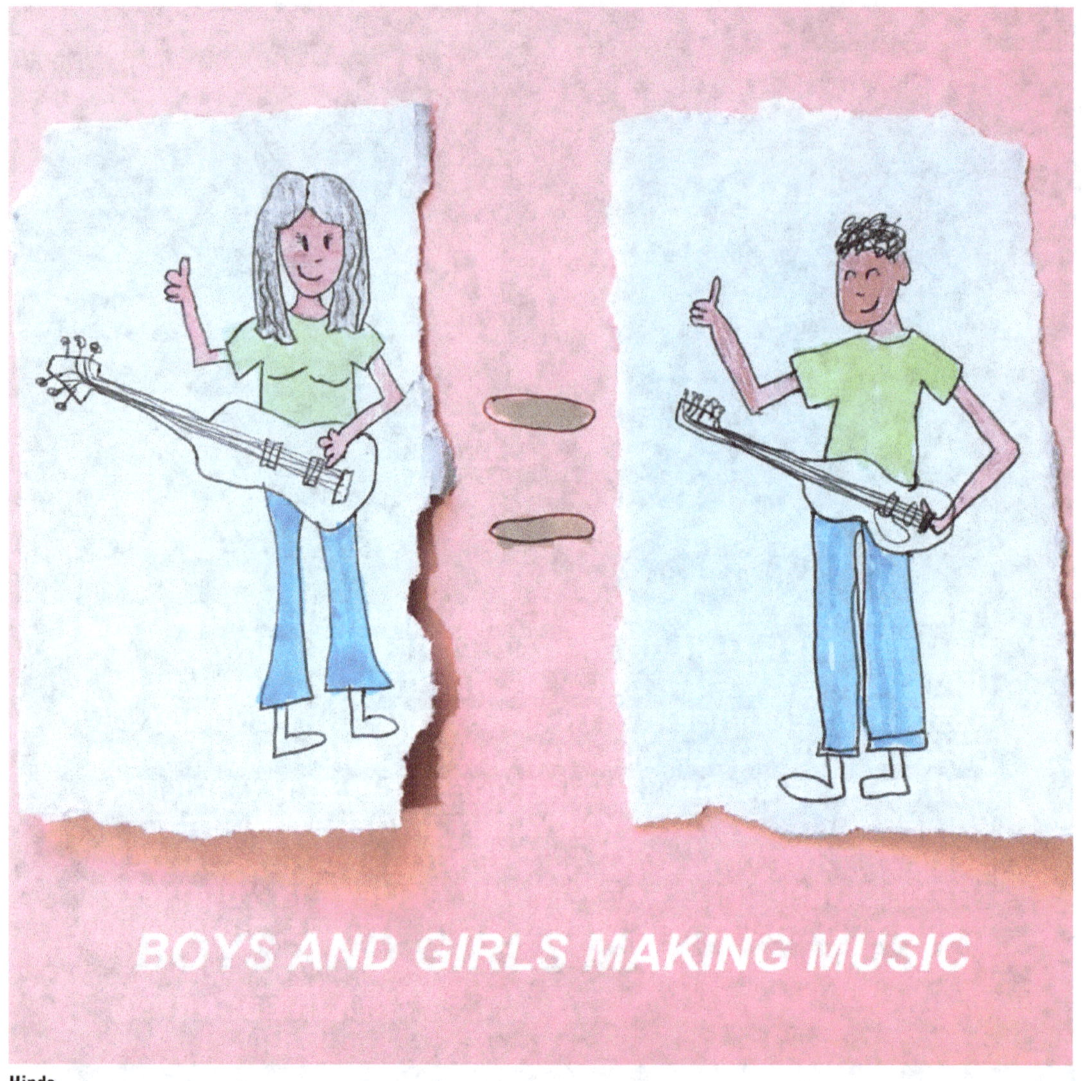

Hinds

from time to time in print, and everyday on social media.

...

As women in music it seems we HAVE to be categorized in the headline. Even now. Our gender, our sexuality, our looks — all of it has to be defined, indexed, reduced, and brought to attention before the music is ever even mentioned. If it's mentioned at all.

Liz Phair: "Little girls should be seen and not heard." I remember someone telling me this dictum at my uncle's holiday party when I was four or five years old...I didn't know what was so objectionable about a little girl's voice, but it was clearly a powerful, disruptive weapon that I was in possession of.

...

There's a reason I wrote my first songs quietly, in my bedroom. Seen and not heard is still the most popular role for a woman to play.

For a woman to lead, for her to speak her mind loudly, in front of people, is still radical. STILL?? Yes, still, in 2017. Probably until 2185. So settle in and lend a shoulder because this boulder we're pushing uphill is fucking heavy.

Lizzo:
Q: "WHAT'S IT LIKE BEING A WOMAN IN THE MUSIC INDUS-TRY?"
A: I DON'T HAVE A DICK.

Laena Geronimo (FEELS): Girl band. "Girl" to modify the definition of "band." What is a girl band anyways? I realize that most people don't consider what they are saying when it just rolls off the tongue in such a familiar way. Aside from the click provoking efforts or maybe just sheer laziness of

<u>TEGAN QUIN:</u>
Multi-instrumentalist and songwriter Tegan Quin is one half of Tegan and Sara, a Canadian indie pop band, with her identical twin sister Sara Quin. Both sisters are openly gay and active members of the LGBT community. The duo have released eight studio albums and numerous EPs.

<u>ALICIA BOGNANNO</u>
Before starting her own project, Alicia Bognanno interned at Steve Albini's Electrical Audio studios in Chicago. She recorded demos of her own material there before relocating to Nashville, Tennessee, where she formed Bully. The band's debut album, *Feels Like* (2015), was recorded live in only a handful of takes.

<u>HINDS</u>
Formerly known as Deers, Madrid indie rock band Hinds formed in 2011, and consists of Carlotta Cosials (vocals, guitar), Ana Perrote (vocals, guitar), Ade Martin (bass, backing vocals) and Amber Grimbergen (drums). They have released one album, one compilation LP and four singles.

<u>LIZ PHAIR</u>
Liz Phair is an American singer, songwriter and guitarist. Her 1993 debut studio album *Exile in Guyville* was released to acclaim, it has ranked by Rolling Stone as one of the 500 Greatest Albums of All Time.

<u>LIZZO</u>
Melissa Jefferson, better known as Lizzo, is an alternative hip-hop artist who founded the indie hip-hop groups The Chalice, Grrrl Prty, The Clerb, Ellypseas and Absynthe. *Time* included her in their list of 14 music artists to watch in 2014. *Coconut Oil* (2016)

many music journalists, I hear people whom I respect say it all the time.

People say it to me, often sandwiched into something intended to be a compliment, without blinking an eye. I cringe every time. Sometimes I ask who their favorite "boy band" is, if I'm in the mood to risk pissing someone off… it's funny when you flip the table, it sounds so ridiculous. That's because it is.

I make music. I don't make girl music. FEELS is not a girl band. We are a band. Gender plays absolutely zero role in a person's ability to play any instrument, write songs, freak out on stage, or any other aspect of being in a band. I personally feel that art itself is beyond gender or race or sexual orientation or any other physical/social identity. It is fluid, limitless and free roaming, without walls, ceilings or floors. It is a shape shifting mirror, for everyone to relate to in their own personal way.

There is literally nothing especially amazing about girls, or women, being passionate about making art. There is no inherent physical handicap being overcome, no gender-centric obstacle conquered which deserves special recognition…I refuse to participate in the special Olympics of music, in a sub-category small

> **"THERE'S A REASON I WROTE MY FIRST SONGS QUIETLY, IN MY BEDROOM. SEEN AND NOT HEARD IS STILL THE MOST POPULAR ROLE FOR A WOMAN TO PLAY… FOR A WOMAN TO LEAD, FOR HER TO SPEAK HER MIND LOUDLY, IN FRONT OF PEOPLE, IS STILL RADICAL."**
>
> —LIZ PHAIR

pool where the rules are different and the bar standard has been adjusted to be easier to surmount, in order to compensate for some imaginary affliction that I and all other women uniquely share.

Hayley Williams (Paramore): When the band started touring, I was embarrassed that every review we got back only had to do with me. Fleeting moments of acceptance were quickly followed by bigger waves of shame. Why couldn't people just forget I was a girl? Why did it matter if I was? I didn't feel particularly female, nor male, when I was on stage. Deep down, I think I was beginning to realize something profound about music, which is still the truth today: Music is bigger (and better) than gender.

It took me a while to realize that my microphone was powerful. It took me even longer to realize that in my own femininity, there was also power. Never did it occur to me that seeing a female behind a microphone could be seen as a threat. The funniest part of all of it was that on the outside I had that power but on the inside, I was still figuring out how to use it… and not always gracefully.

What I wish I had known back then was how little it all had to do with me.

Any sexist article or misogynistic remark thrown at me from a crowd—none of it was because of me. There was a social myopia plaguing our music scene. My problem was the way I was internalizing it as truth.

At some point, I realized that whether or not I could change the whole game, I had to change the way that I existed within it. So, I stopped apologizing for being female and started accepting all the power and responsibility that comes along with it.

Bethany Cosentino (Best Coast): Yes I AM a woman! and I have a lot to say... "What is it like to be a woman in a band?" How do I even answer that? "Being a woman in a band is just like being a man in a band except you have to explain that you're a woman in a band every single day."

Kate Nash: I have been called an angry lesbian, a diva and a psycho bitch. I've been told to go stick a bomb up my cunt and explode, I've been assaulted at shows, I've been mocked for writing like a teenage girl writing in her diary, I've had rape and death threats online, I've been called "everything that's wrong with music distilled into one slag," I've been told "we've come a long way," I've been told to

stop playing instruments, to stop doing that "screamy thing where you sound like a little girl," I've been asked "have you been a naughty girl?" I've been told not to be so angry.

Cecilia Della Peruti (Gothic Tropic): If you're in a band and you happen to be a girl, you're often going to hear the phrase "girl band", and there seems to be an obvious sense that "girl band" is a marginalized gender-based idea. Compliments might also be accompanied by the shocking revelation that women can actually play their instruments! The world wants to define you, and to be fair, allowing the public to describe you is integral. Accurately describing a band's sound is an underrated talent, so I've just tried to brush them off as an earnest attempt. But a part of me wants to ask, "why was my gender a point of focus?" This caricature of the "femme-fronted bad ass chick" makes it easy for uninterested people to digest your work in this age of rapid consumption. The obsession with packaging is also what inspires the idea that bands that have "girl" or "vagina" in the name have negative meanings. The only reason people feel a need to bundle and brand female musicians by gender, is because the col-

was her first EP off the major label Atlantic Records.

<u>LAENA GERONIMO</u>
LA-based band FEELS was started by Laena Geronimo, born out of her previous project, Raw Geronimo. Their self-titled debut LP (2016) was produced by Ty Segall and showcases the band's raw, frenetic punk energy.

<u>HAYLEY WILLIAMS</u>
Hayley Williams is the lead vocalist and primary songwriter of Paramore. The band's second album, *Riot!* (2007), was a mainstream success and certified Platinum in the US, with hit singles including "Misery Business," "Crushcrushcrush," and "That's What You Get." Paramore received a Best New Artist nomination at the 2008 Grammy Awards.

<u>BETHANY COSENTINO</u>
Bethany Cosentino is the singer, songwriter and guitarist of Best Coast, which she formed in Los Angeles in 2009 with Bobb Bruno. The band's debut LP, *Crazy for You* (2010), was described as "striking the perfect balance between reverb-drenched vocals and classic California pop hooks."

<u>KATE NASH</u>
English-born singer, songwriter Kate Nash's debut album, *Made of Bricks* (2007), peaked at number one in the UK. In April 2011, Nash announced the launch of her own record label, Have 10p Records. Nash appears in the new Netflix series *GLOW*.

<u>KIM SCHIFINO</u>
Matt & Kim are an indie electronic duo from Brooklyn, New York. The group formed in 2004 and consists of Matt Johnson (vocals and keyboards) and Kim

> "I HAVE BEEN CALLED AN ANGRY LESBIAN, A DIVA AND A PSYCHO BITCH. I'VE BEEN TOLD TO GO STICK A BOMB UP MY CUNT AND EXPLODE."
> —KATE NASH

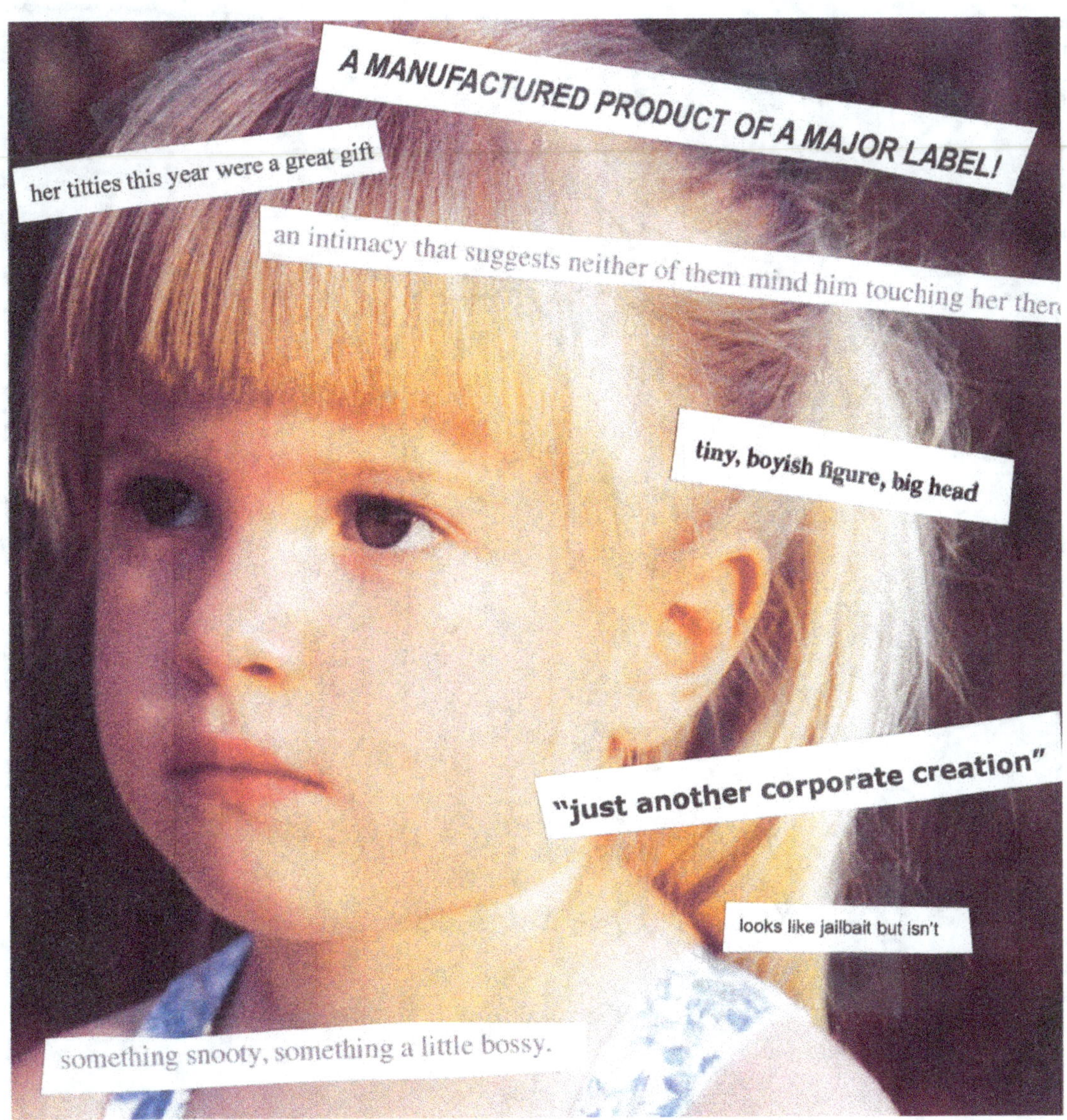

Hayley Williams (Paramore)

"I WAS BEGINNING TO REALIZE SOMETHING PROFOUND ABOUT MUSIC, WHICH IS STILL THE TRUTH TODAY: MUSIC IS BIGGER (AND BETTER) THAN GENDER."
—HAYLEY WILLIAMS

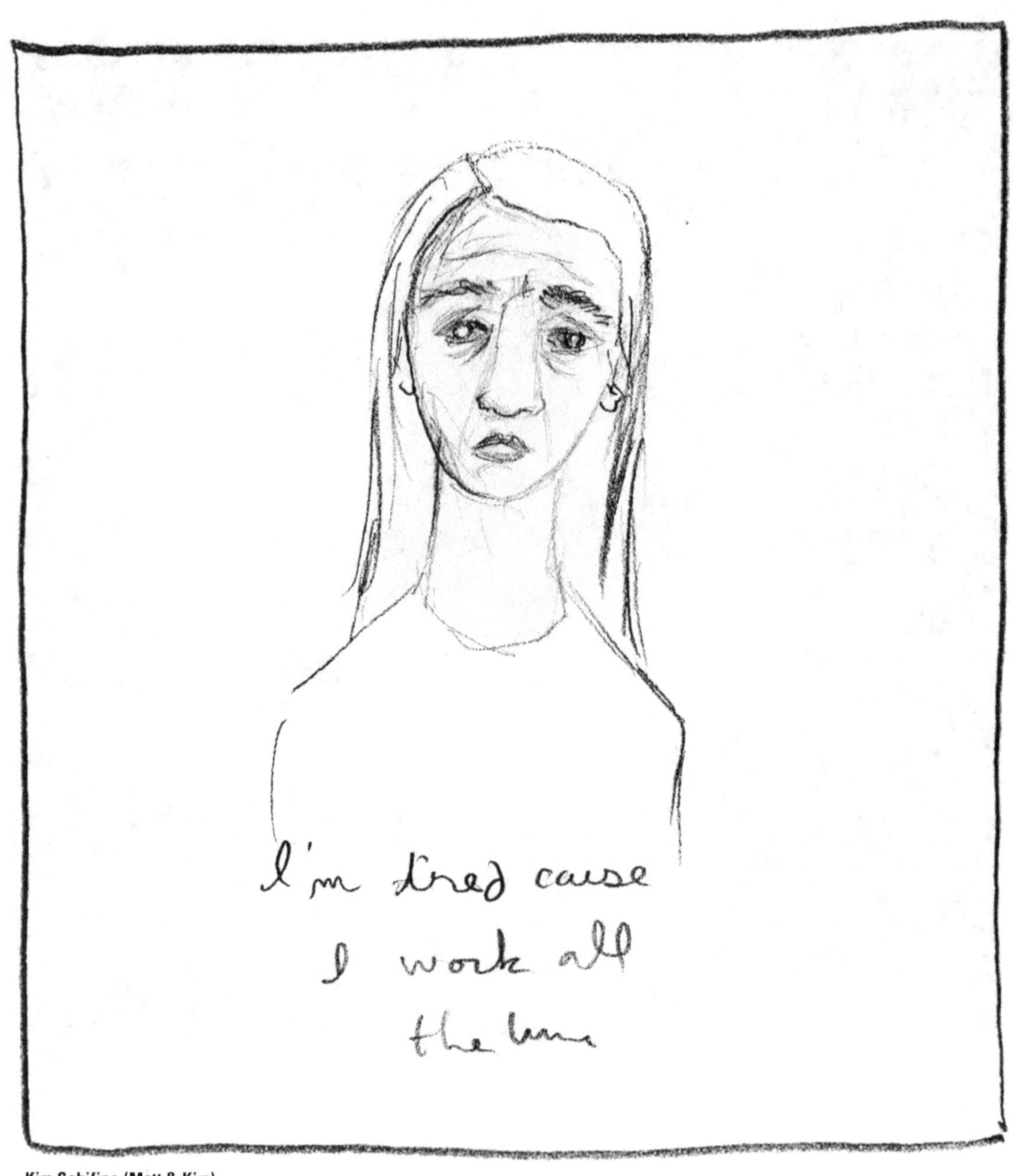

Kim Schifino (Matt & Kim)

"YOUR FREEDOM TO CREATE IS WORTH FIGHTING FOR.
YOUR BODY IS YOUR ALLY, NOT YOUR ENEMY.
BE FIERCELY AND RELENTLESSLY LOVING."
— ALI KOEHLER

Schifino (drums). The duo is known for its up-beat dance music and energetic live shows. Since they started performing together in 2004, they have released five studio albums.

MELISSA BROOKS
California-based band The Aquadolls were founded by lead vocalist Melissa Brooks in 2012. The band is comprised of Brooks, Ryan Frailich, Jacob Brown and Bella Devroede. Their debut album *Stoked on You* (2014) was released by Burger Records.

JD SAMSON
JD Samson is a musician, producer, songwriter and DJ best known as a member of the bands Le Tigre and MEN, which Samson started as a queer art collective. She also co-founded the performance art group Dykes Can Dance. Samson joined Le Tigre in 2000 and recorded and released *Feminist Sweepstakes* with the band.

ALI KOEHLER
After playing drums for both Best Coast and Vivian Girls, Ali Koehler went on to form the band Upset. The lineup consists of Ali Koehler (guitar, lead vocals), Patty Schemel (drums), Lauren Freeman (lead guitar) and Rachel Gagliardi (bass, vocals). Their debut album *She's Gone* (2013) was released on Don Giovanni Records.

JULIEN BAKER
Julien Baker is a musician and guitarist from Memphis, Tennessee. She is a member of the alternative rock band Forrister. Her debut solo album *Sprained Ankle* (2015) was met with critical and commercial acclaim, and in 2017 she signed to Matador Records.

lective mental default setting for "band" is male. The language is proof that gender double standards exist. "What's it like to be a guy in a band?" I think not.

Honoring the artist means giving uninterrupted freedom to create. Artists don't need permission, there's no assembly line of ap-

proval an idea needs to pass through to get to the other side. Artists are the gift givers, and they're often everyone's source of joy.

Melissa Brooks (The Aquadolls): My gender does not define the art I make.

My breasts do not make me different. My art is me, not he or she. It's my representation of personal freedom.

Ali Koehler (Upset, Vivian Girls): THE FACT I EVEN STILL BOTHER DOING THIS IS AN ACT OF RESISTANCE. I REFUSE TO LET SOME

TOXIC IDEAS KEEP ME FROM DOING SOMETHING THAT ULTIMATELY BRINGS ME JOY, AND I THINK THIS IS A BATTLE THAT SO MANY YOUNG WOMEN ARE FIGHTING. IF YOU'RE LISTENING, KNOW THIS: YOUR FREEDOM TO CREATE IS WORTH

FIGHTING FOR. YOUR BODY IS YOUR ALLY, NOT YOUR ENEMY. BE FIERCELY AND RELENTLESSLY LOVING.

Julien Baker: The fact that gender discrimination still exists in music demands that it be addressed, yet media's focus on the novelty of female experience in music perpetuates a stereotype of female musicians. Press that praises women who participate in a male-dominated field as something revolutionary because of its unusualness admits the reality of the issue, but also risks tokenizing female musicians and preventing women's presence in music from being normalized…. Normalizing female presence in music begins when we stop feeling compelled to legitimize art made by women for any other reason than that it is art.

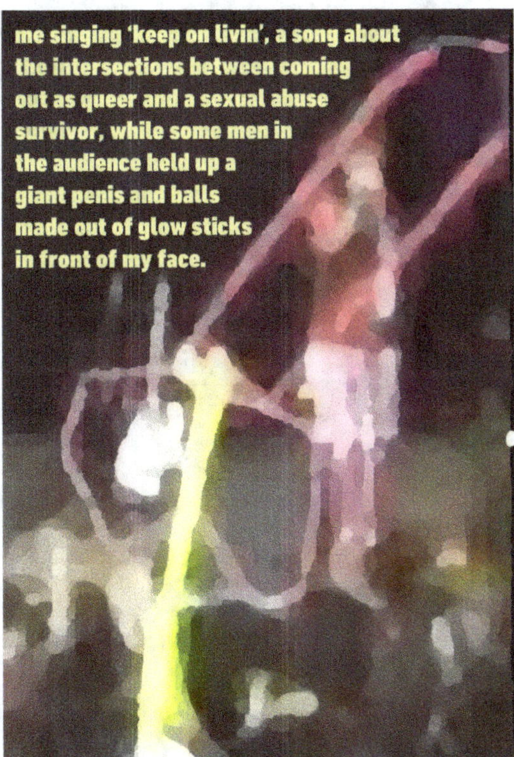

JD Samson

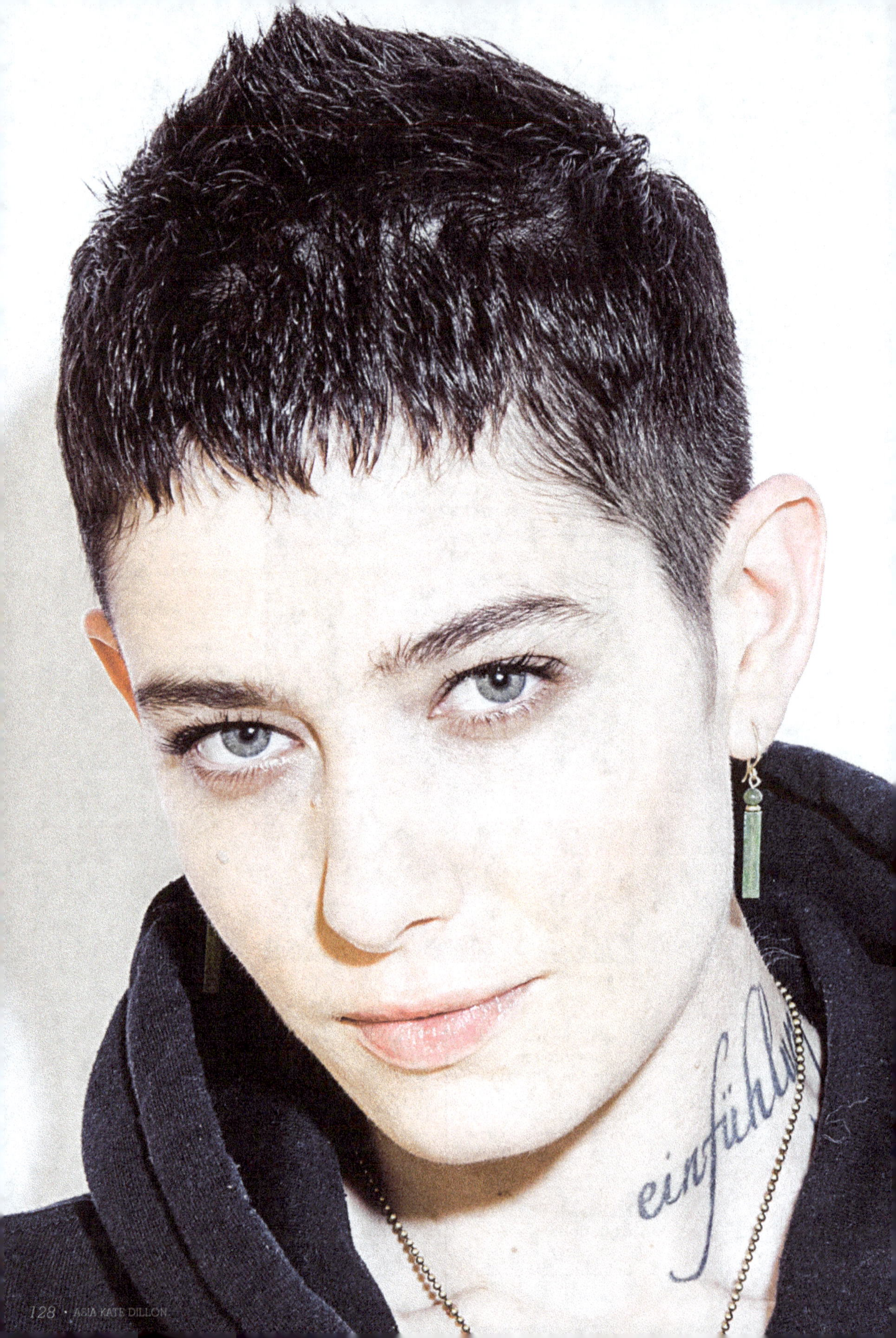

ASIA KATE DILLON

Actor Asia Kate Dillon currently stars on Showtime's Billions *in a groundbreaking role as Taylor Mason, a brilliant, gender non-binary finance intern. Dillon likewise identifies as non-binary and was recently nominated for an Emmy for Best Actor (a category Dillon chose for its gender neutrality) for their portrayal on* Billions. *Dillon first gained attention last year for their role on Netflix' hit series* Orange is the New Black.

Birthplace: Ithaca, NY

Education: Actor's Workshop of Ithaca + AMDA

Ambitions: To connect. To tell the truth. (Ongoing.)

Favorite Food: BBQ Potato Chips

Favorite Movie: *American Beauty* and *American History X*

Favorite Musician: Michael Jackson

Last Book Read: *Between the World and Me*

Turn-ons: Honesty

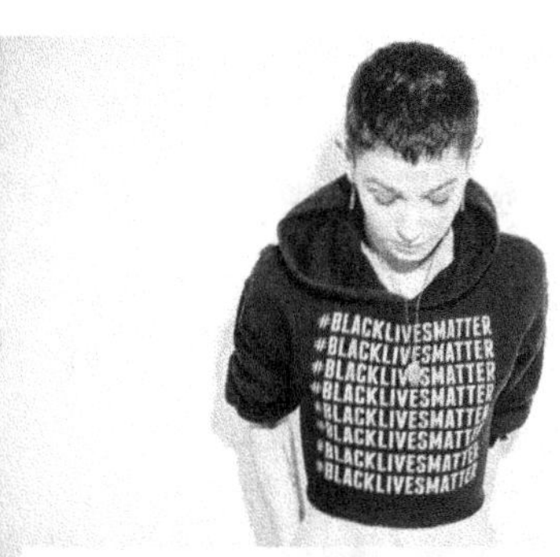

"I ALWAYS WANT THE WORK THAT I'M DOING, WHETHER IT'S ACTING OR MY OWN WORK, TO BE UPLIFTING AND SUPPORTING HISTORICALLY MARGINALIZED AND HISTORICALLY DISENFRANCHISED PEOPLE. SO AS LONG AS I'M STAYING TRUE TO THAT I FEEL GOOD."

— ASIA KATE DILLON

Turn-offs: Disloyalty

What was your first break? *Billions* would be considered my first break, but when I moved back to the city to audition for The Fleet Theater Company and booked a role in a show there, that felt to me like the beginning of my big break.

Can you tell us what else you've been in? Before *Billions* I was working on *Orange Is the New Black*. I did a couple of one-liners on *Younger* and *Master of None* sprinkled here and there, with some theater as well. I have an extensive theater background prior to that.

How would you describe your specialty or your type? Generally, when I walk into a room, I'm the first person that looks like me and has my vibe. That can be really exciting for me and for other people as well.

Would you rather have a car or a diploma? I don't have a diploma, and I am still standing here today, and I am hoping to get some kind of car very soon.

What do you think your ideal job would be, if you're not already in it? I'm in my ideal job. I will say that I always want the work that I'm doing to be uplifting and supporting historically marginalized and historically disenfranchised people. So long as I'm staying true to that I feel good.

What advantages do you have? As someone who is assigned female at birth, I think I have advantages because of that because I can pass as a woman—whatever that means, right? And also I'm light skinned, or as we say "white," and so that has certainly given me advantages that I am conscious of, but also I'm sure advantages that I'm not aware of.

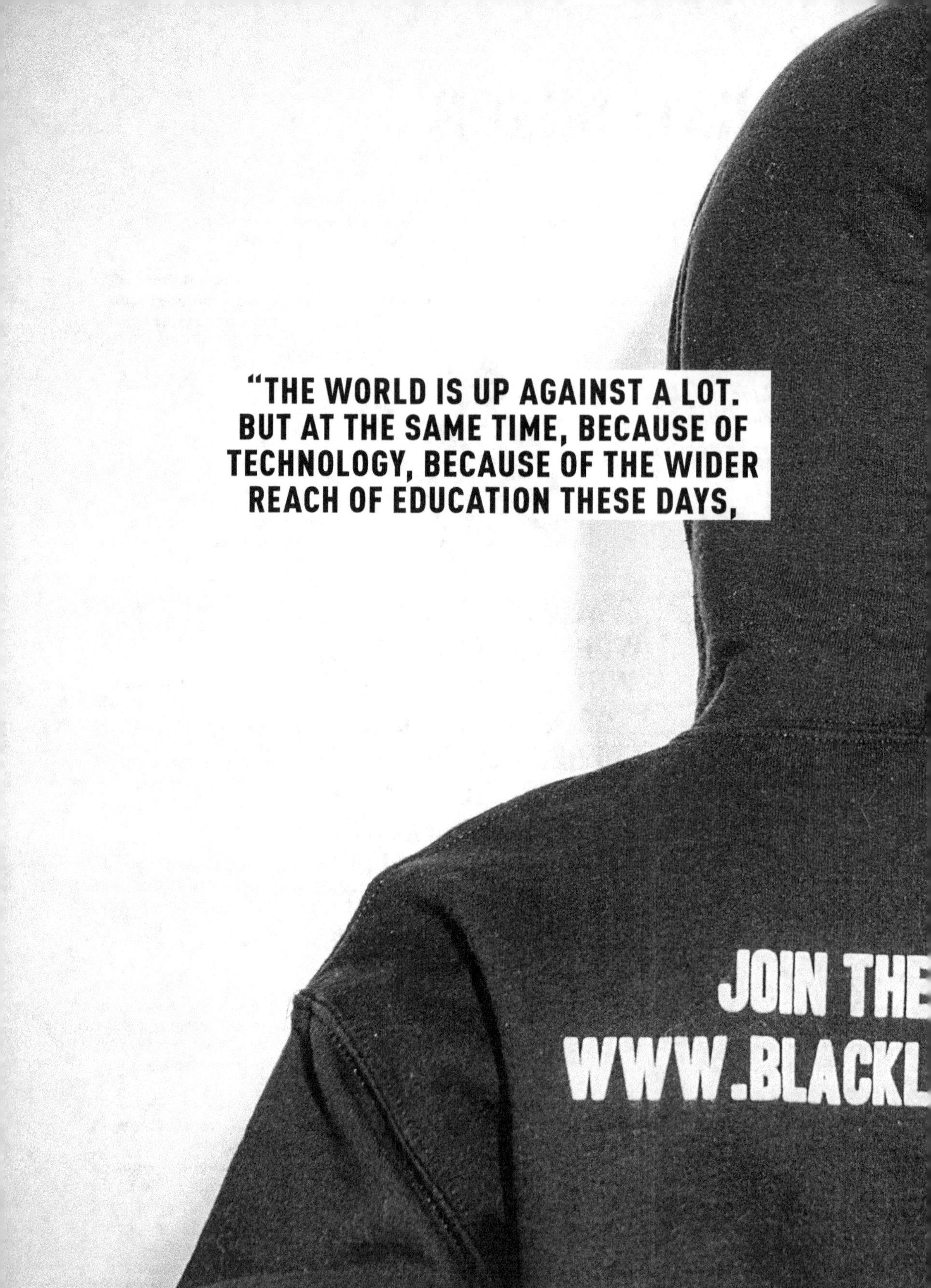

"THE WORLD IS UP AGAINST A LOT.
BUT AT THE SAME TIME, BECAUSE OF
TECHNOLOGY, BECAUSE OF THE WIDER
REACH OF EDUCATION THESE DAYS,

JOIN THE
WWW.BLACKL

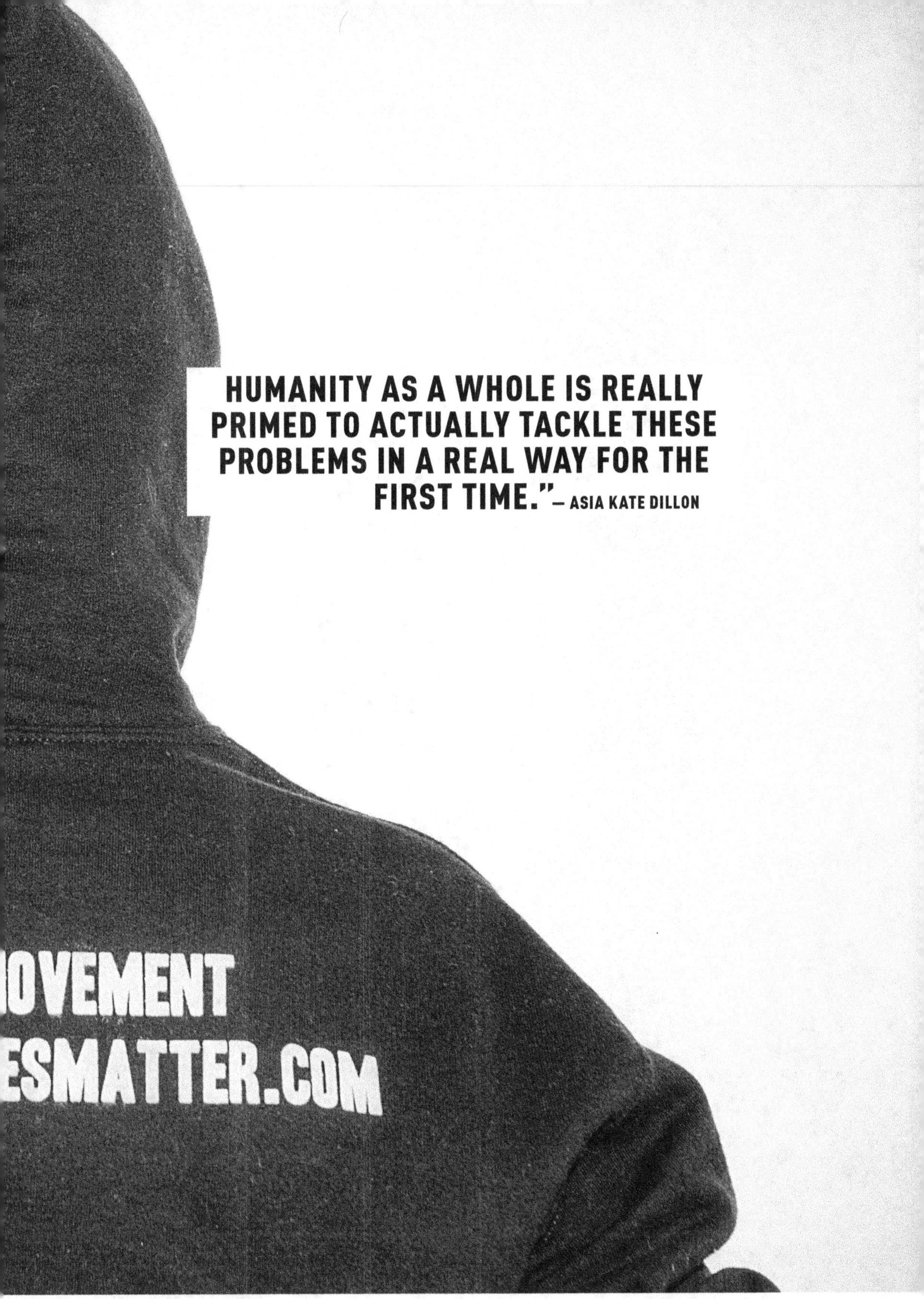

HUMANITY AS A WHOLE IS REALLY
PRIMED TO ACTUALLY TACKLE THESE
PROBLEMS IN A REAL WAY FOR THE
FIRST TIME." — ASIA KATE DILLON

OVEMENT
ESMATTER.COM

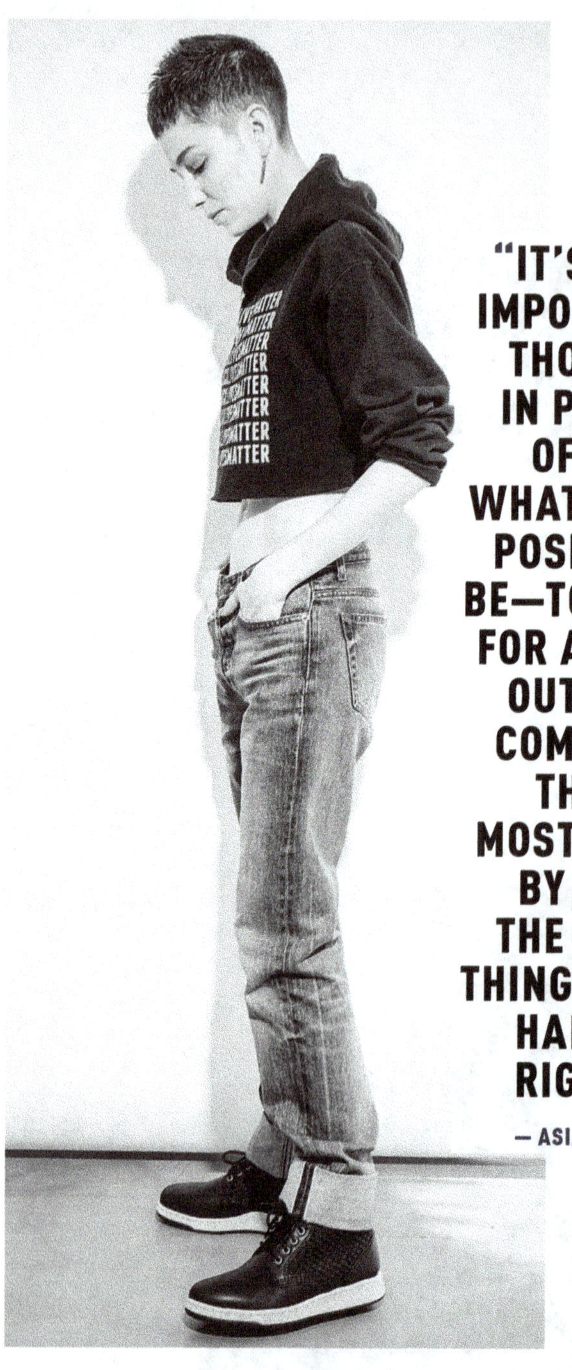

What does the future look like to you? The future to me looks exciting. It looks more inclusive. I feel there's a lot of love and a lot of understanding. The people who have historically faced disenfranchisement and violence are things that are happening right now.

What challenges do you feel the world is facing today? There are a lot of things coming to the surface, what I like to call "the great uncovering of things," like systemic racism and how that relates to the prison industrial complex and things like poverty and global warming. The world is up against a lot. But at the same time, because of technology, because of the wider reach of education these days, humanity as a whole is really primed to actually tackle these problems in a real way for the first time.

"IT'S REALLY IMPORTANT FOR THOSE OF US IN POSITIONS OF POWER—WHATEVER THAT POSITION MAY BE—TO STAND UP FOR AND SPEAK OUT FOR THE COMMUNITIES THAT ARE MOST AFFECTED BY SORT OF THE TERRIBLE THINGS THAT ARE HAPPENING RIGHT NOW."

— ASIA KATE DILLON

going to continue to do so, and so it's really important for those of us in positions of power—whatever that position may be—to stand up for and speak out for the communities that are the most affected by sort of the terrible

ASIA KATE DILLON
Born in Ithaca, NY, Asia Kate Dillon is known for their roles on *Billions* (2016–) and *Orange is the New Black* (2013–). Dillon became the first non-binary gender identifying actor to be cast on a major television series for *Billions* and is forwarding the conversation on what it means to be gender-nonconforming.

Images by Jan-Willem Dikkers

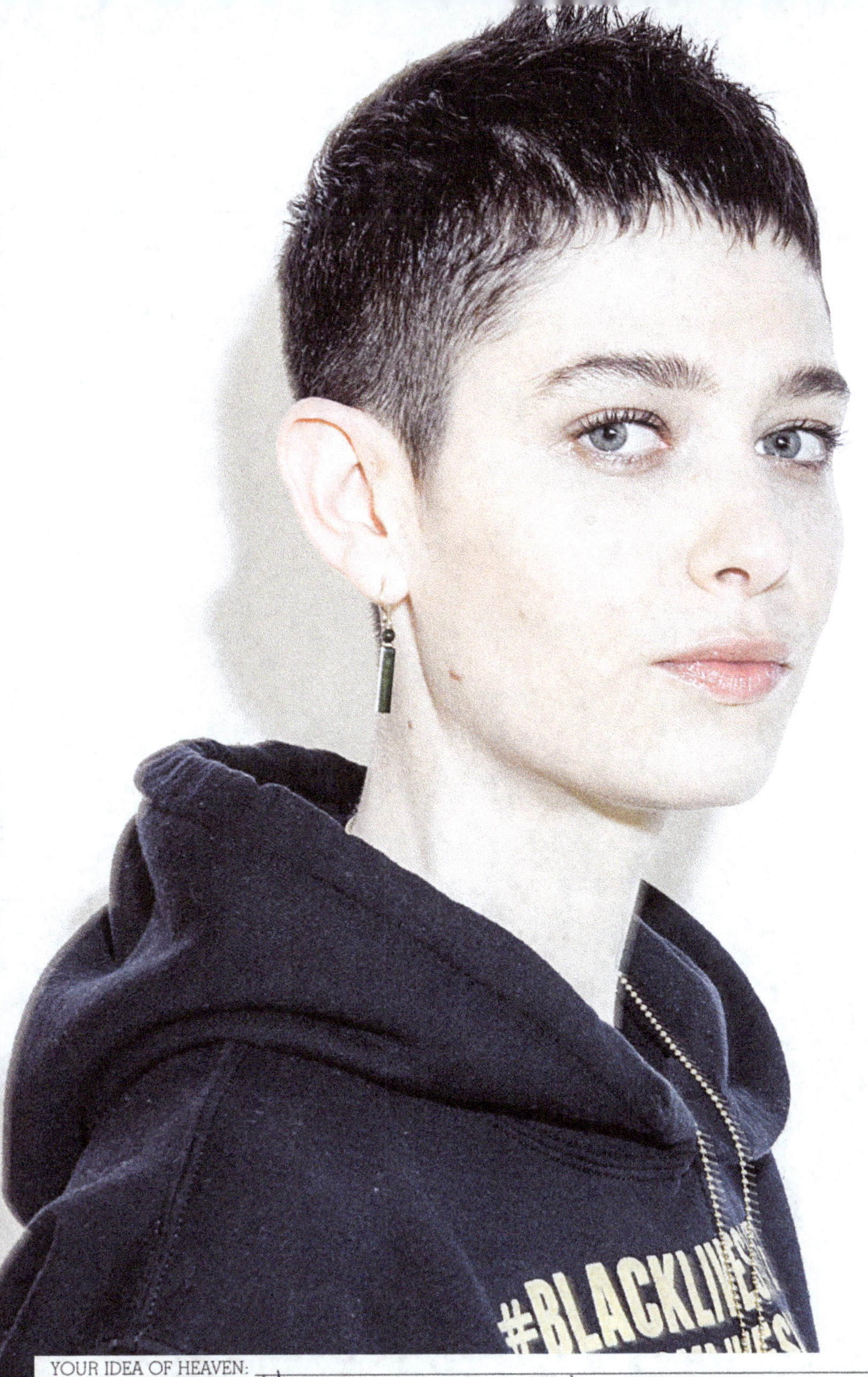

YOUR IDEA OF HEAVEN: Heaven is right here, right now.

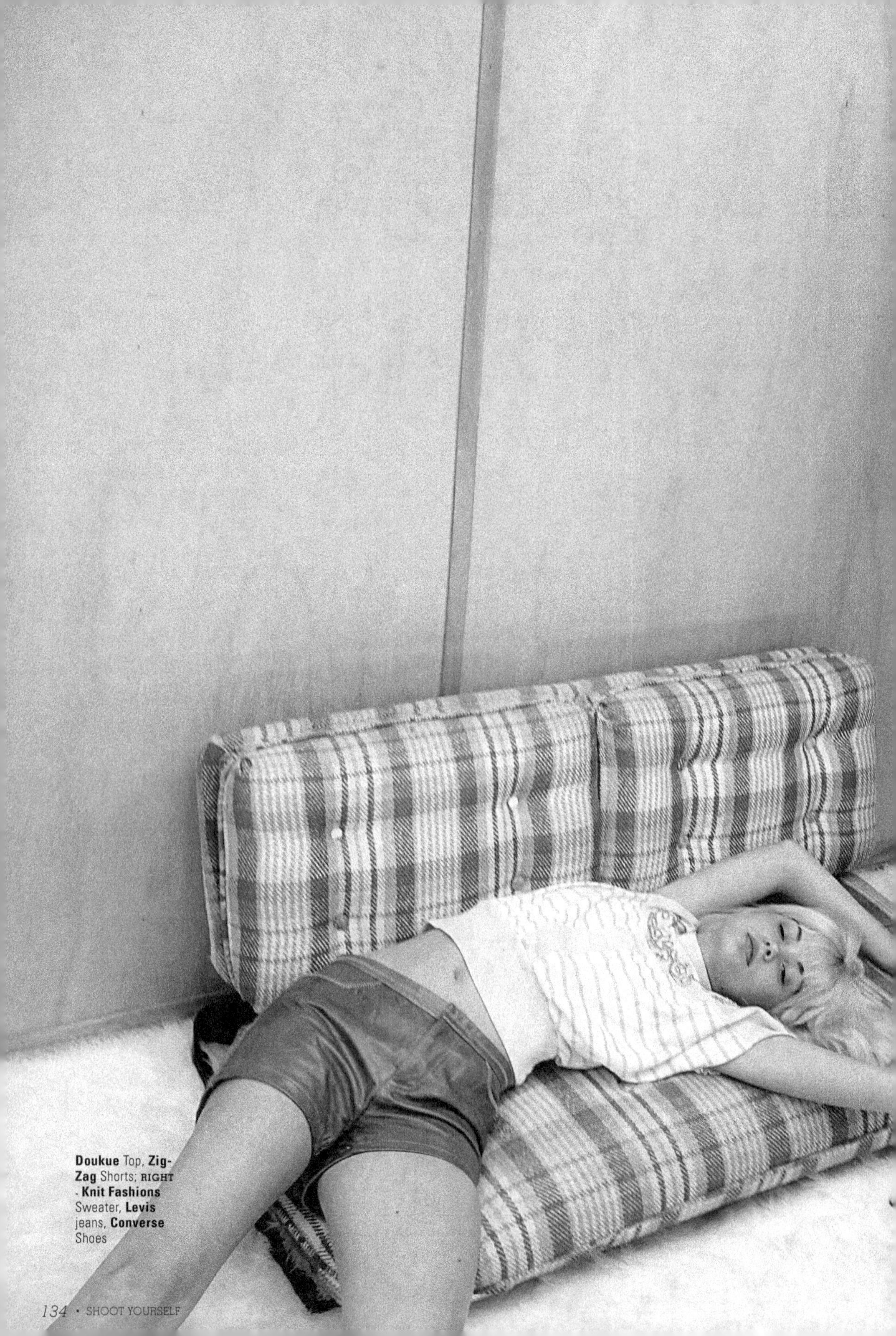

Doukue Top, **Zig-Zag** Shorts; RIGHT
- **Knit Fashions**
Sweater, **Levis**
jeans, **Converse**
Shoes

SHOOT YOURSELF

#VINTAGE

IMAGES Jan-Willem Dikkers + MODEL / PHOTOGRAPHERS
Destiny Anderson (Ford); Kenzie Kersen,
Paige Rivas, Terra Jo Wallace (Vision)
STYLING Cynda McElvana

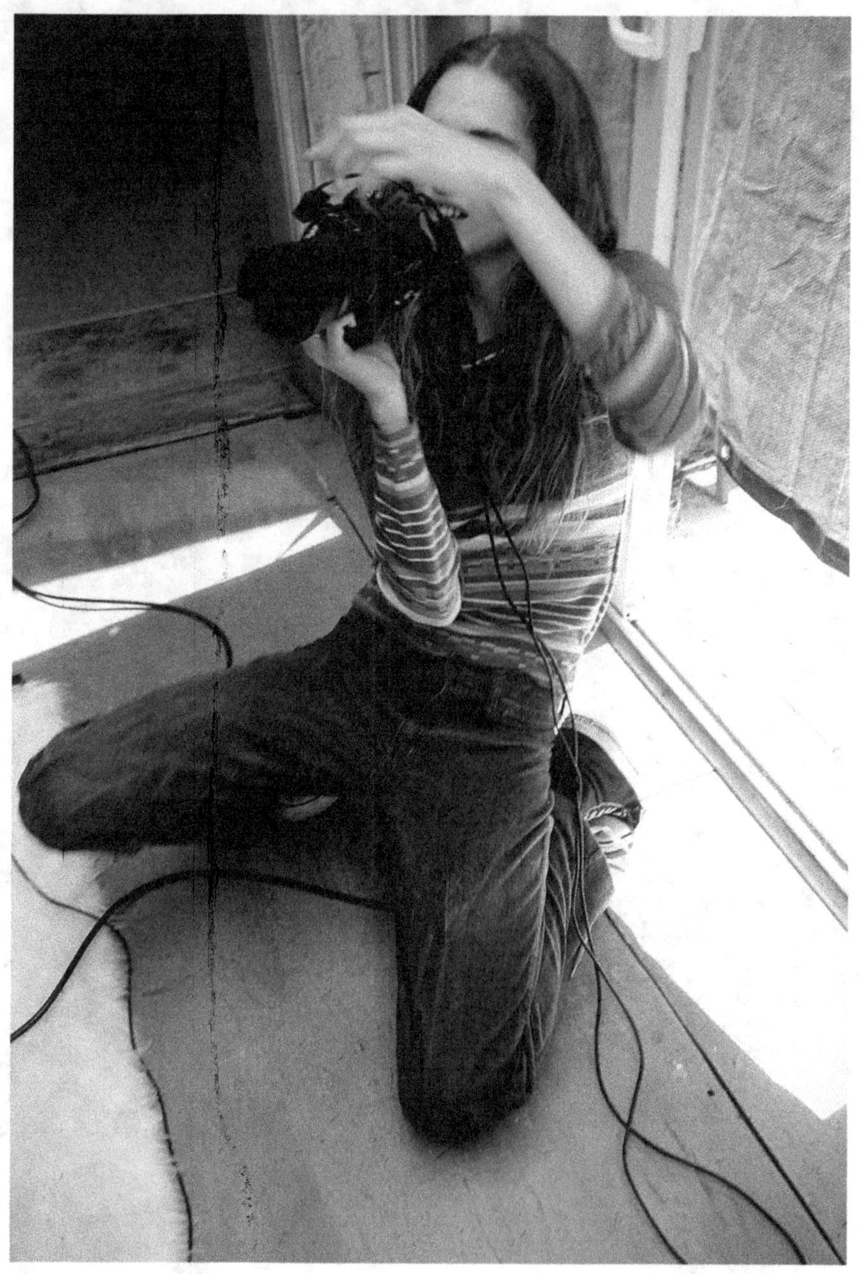

Knit Fashions
Sweater, **Levis**
jeans, **Converse**
Shoes; RIGHT -
Doukue Top,
Zig-Zag Shorts,
Converse Shoes

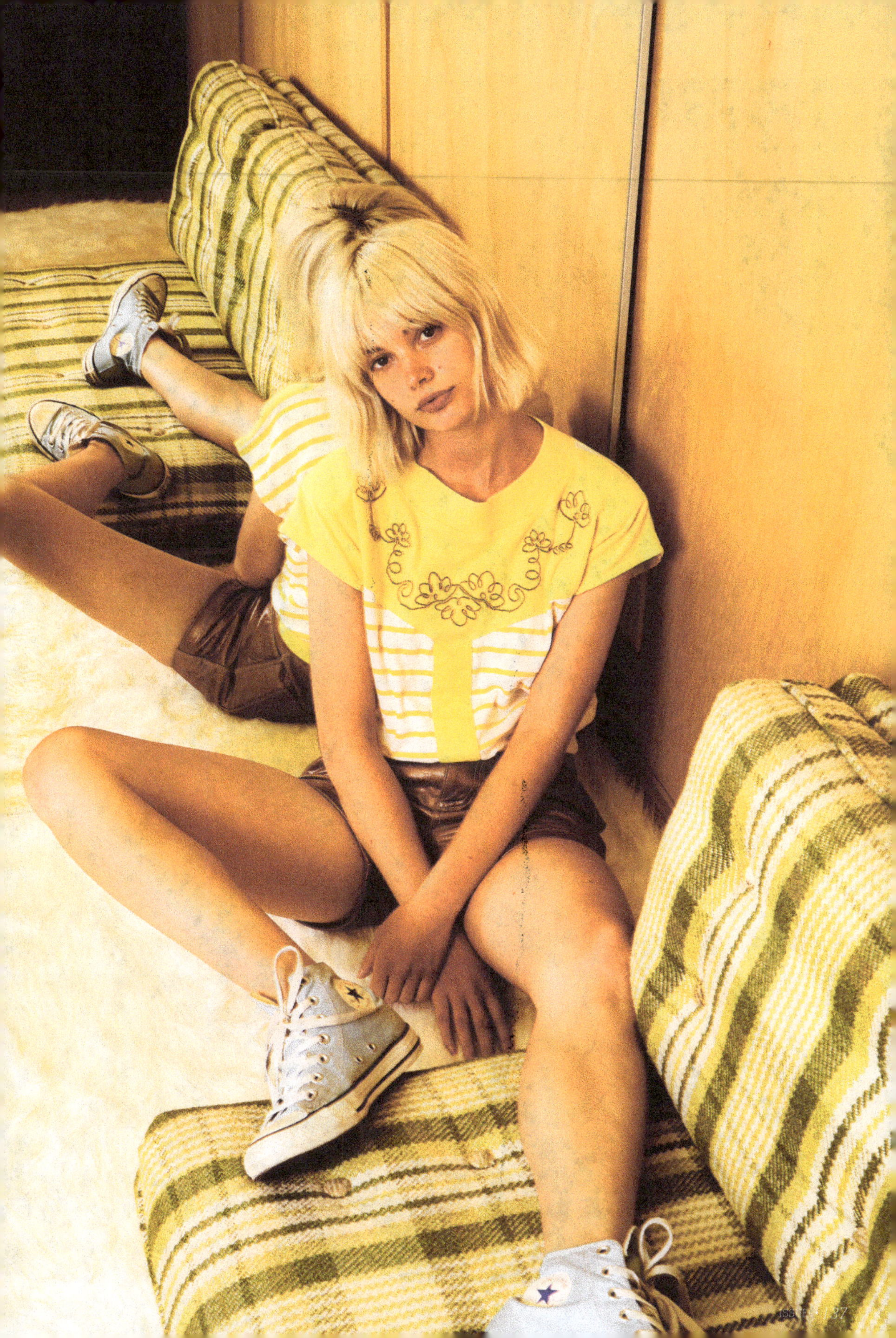

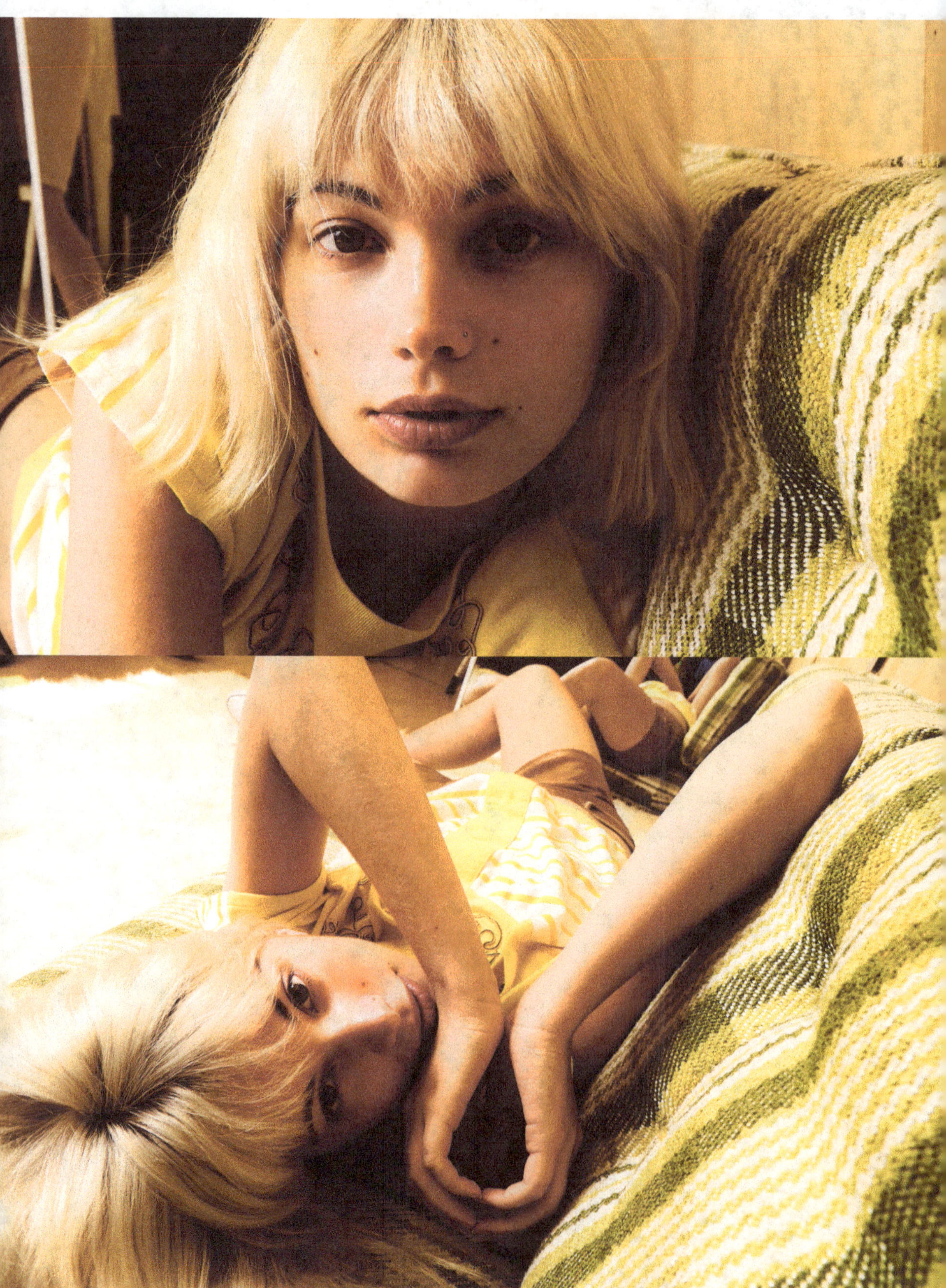

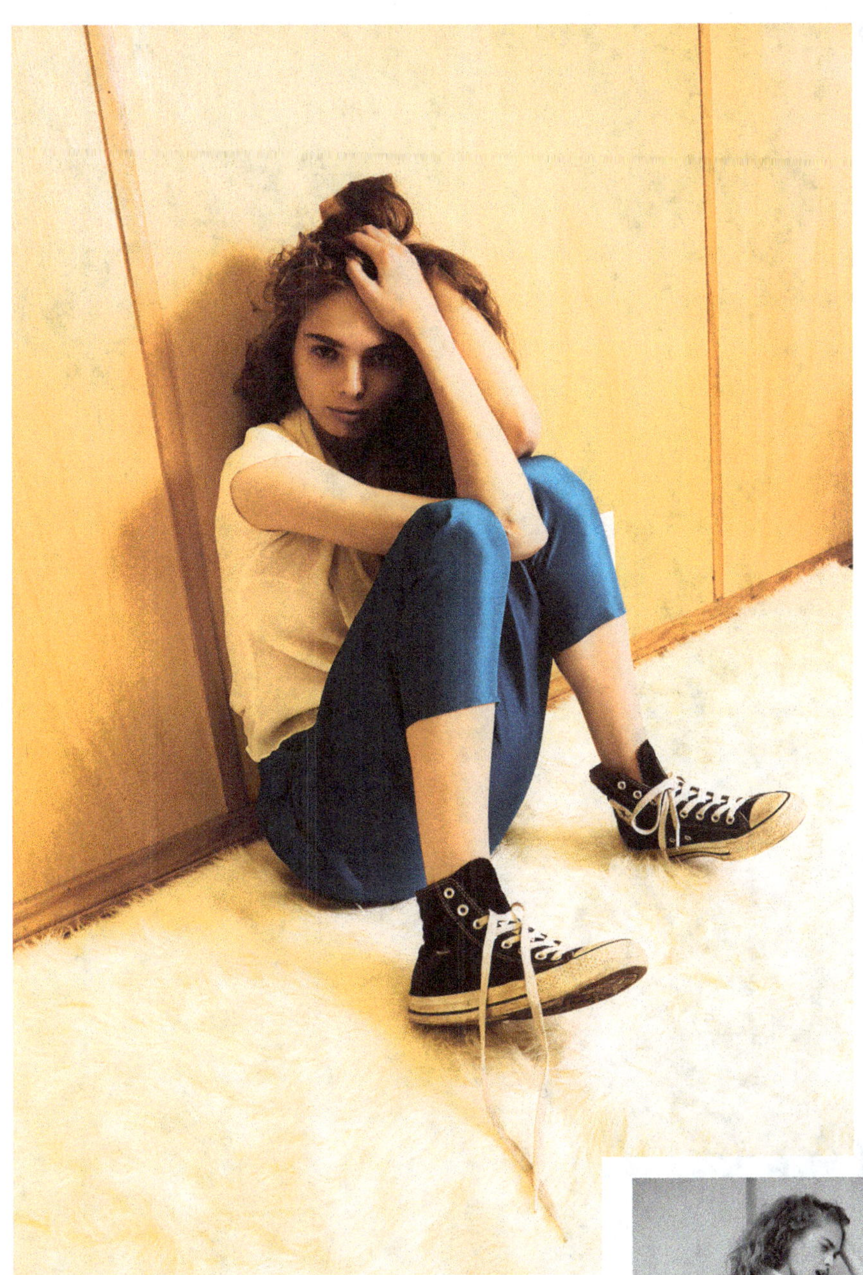

Ossie Clark
Blouse, **Restless
Clothiers** Pants,
Converse Shoes;
LEFT - **Doukue** Top,
Zig-Zag Shorts

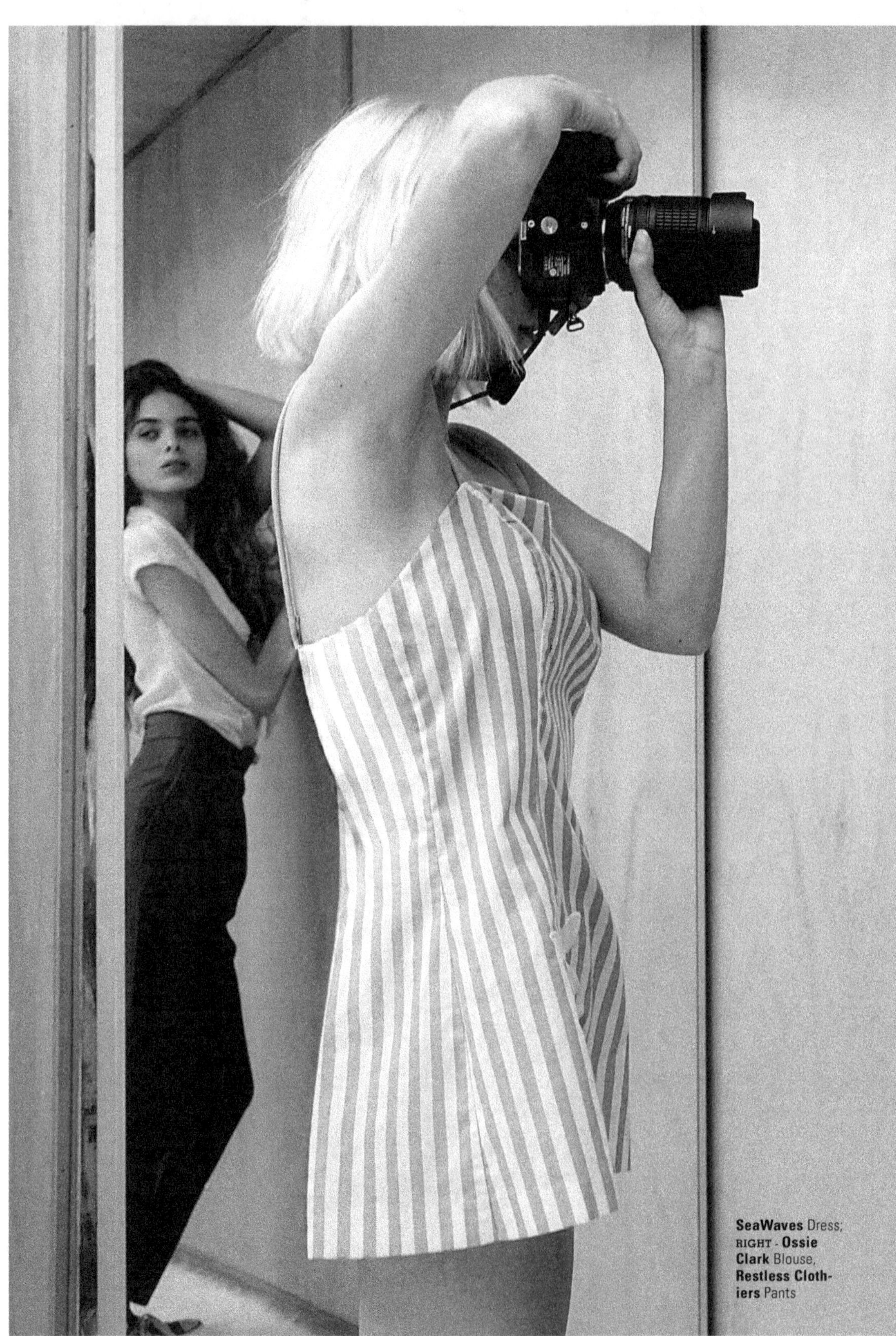

SeaWaves Dress;
RIGHT - **Ossie Clark** Blouse, **Restless Cloth- iers** Pants

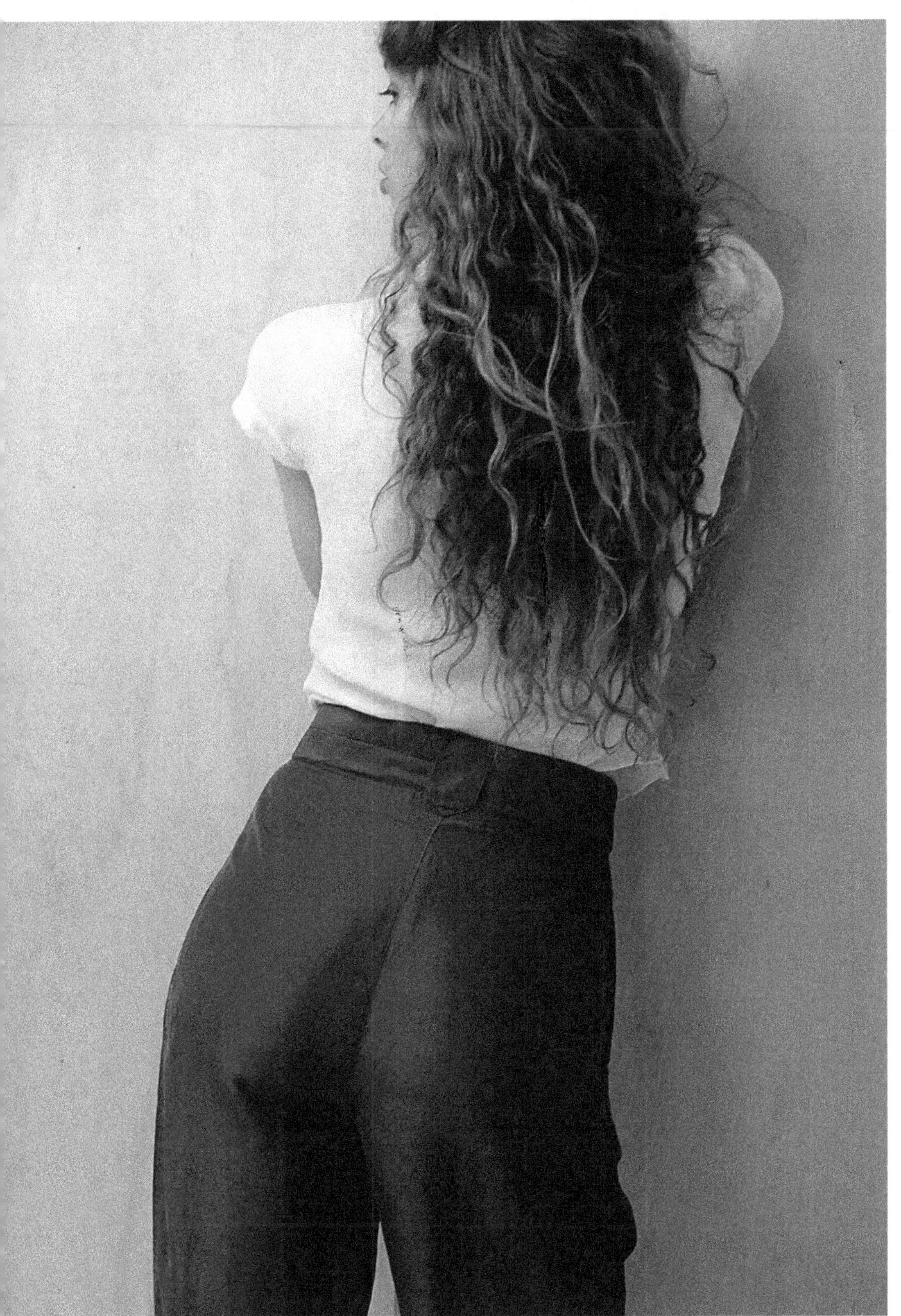

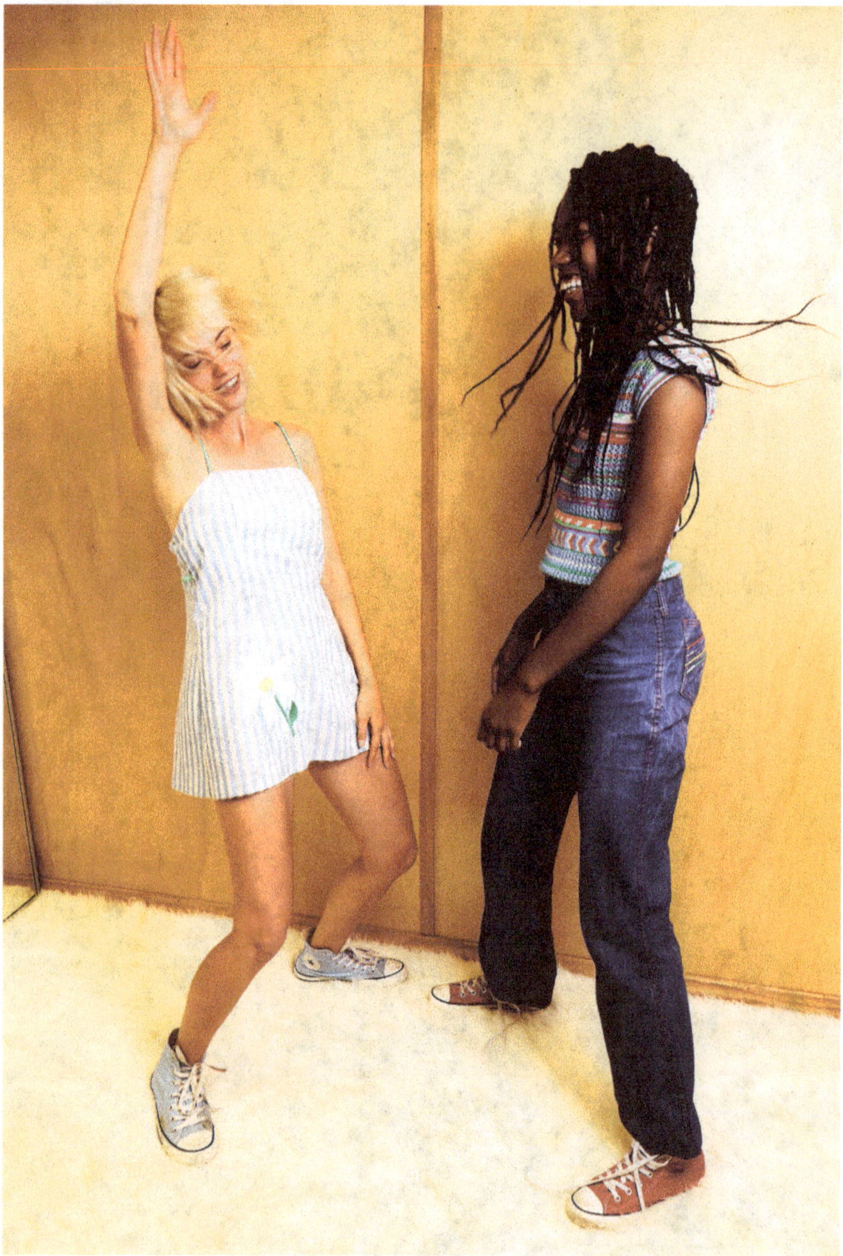

LEFT - **SeaWaves**
Dress, **Converse**
Shoes; RIGHT -
Pandora Top,
Levis Jeans,
Converse Shoes

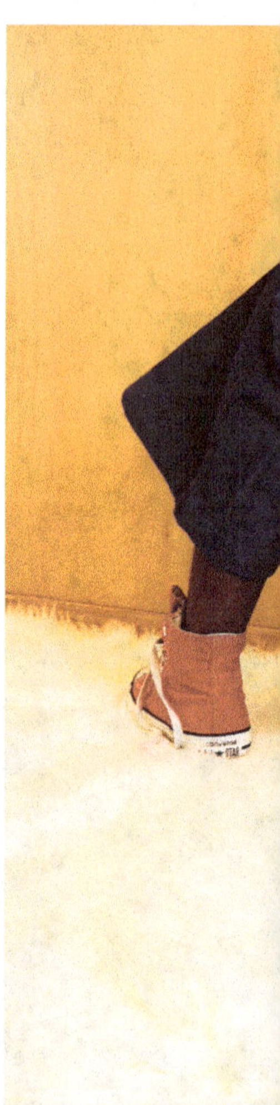

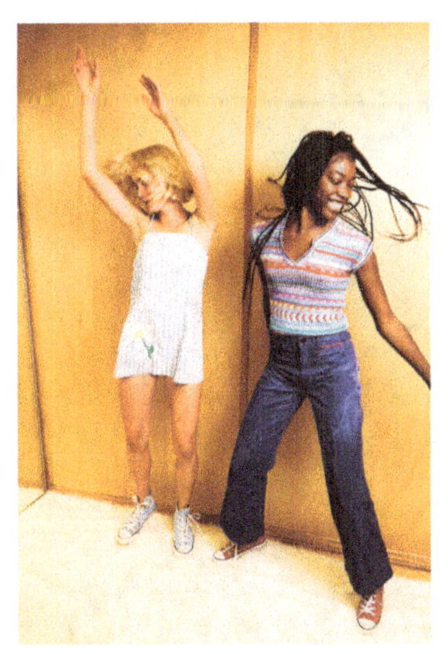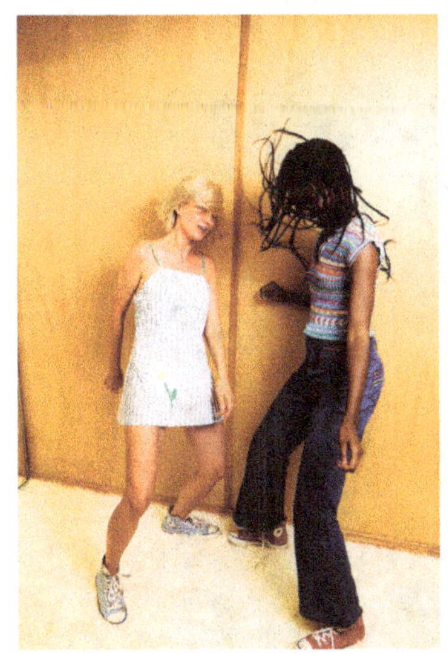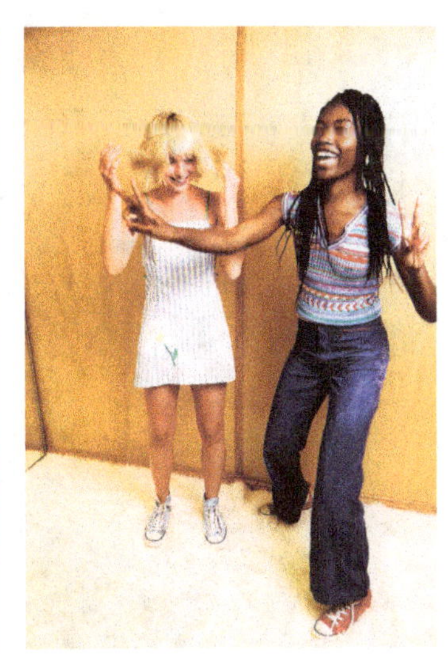

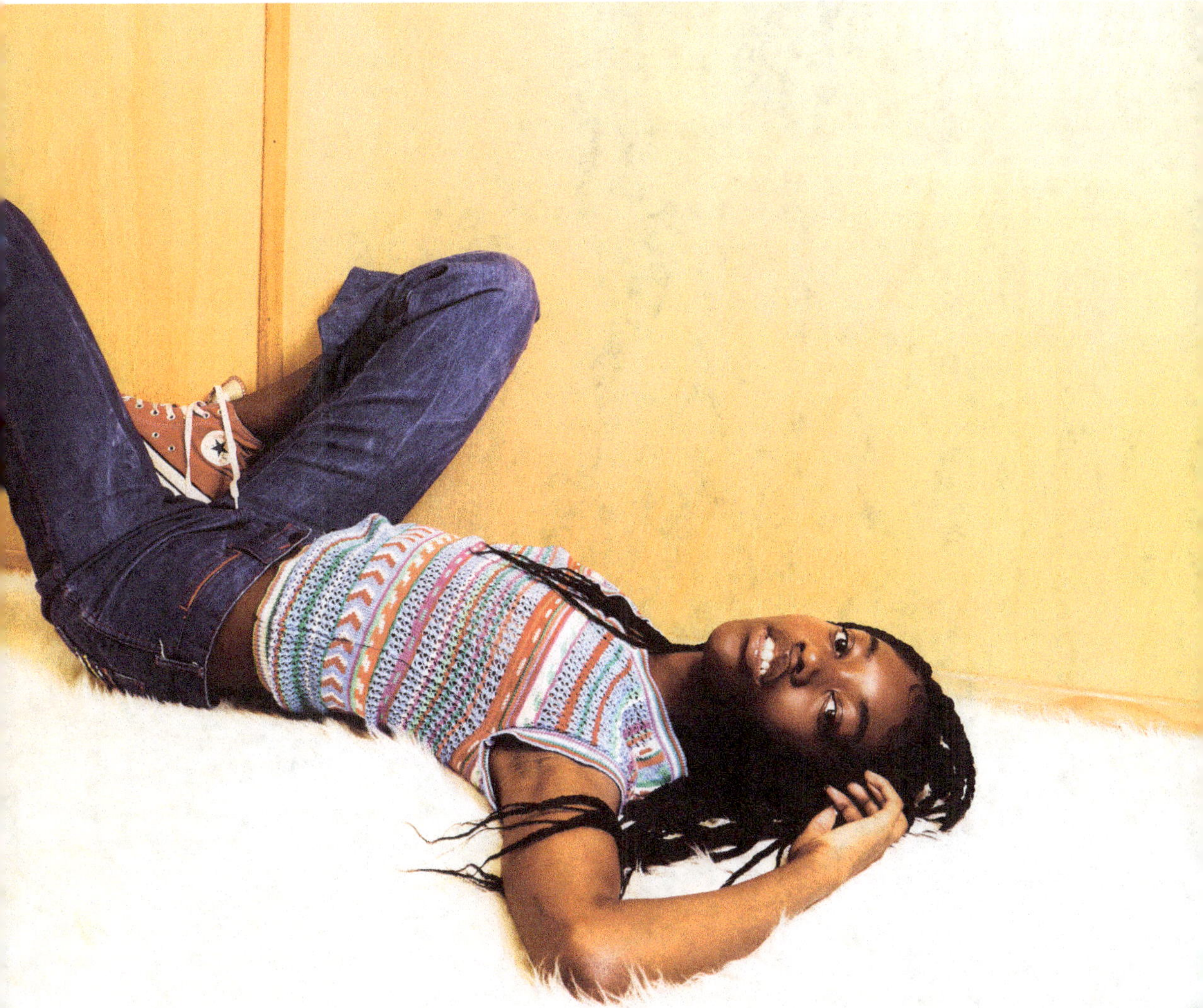

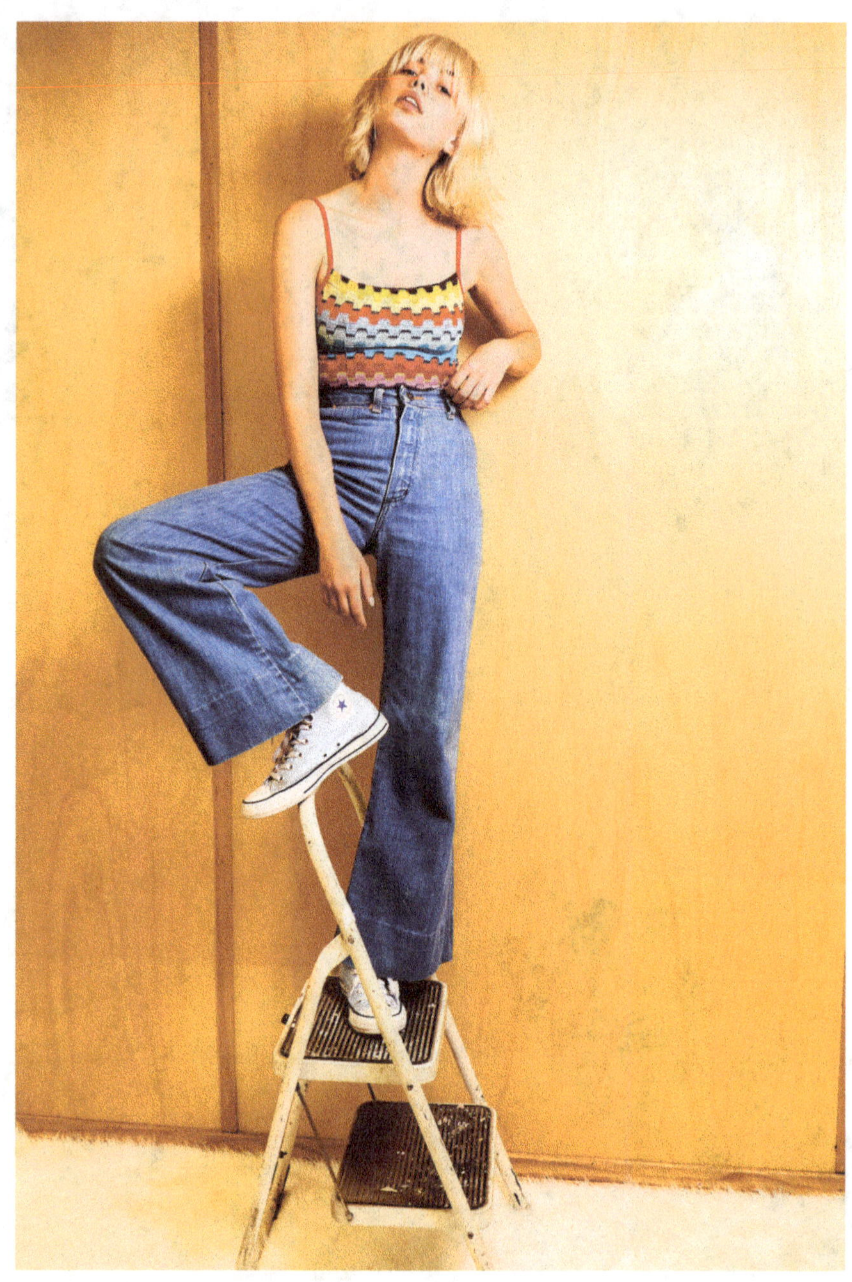

LEFT - **Be Cool** Top,
Wrangler Jeans,
Converse Shoes;
RIGHT - **Sherri** Top,
Wrangler Jeans

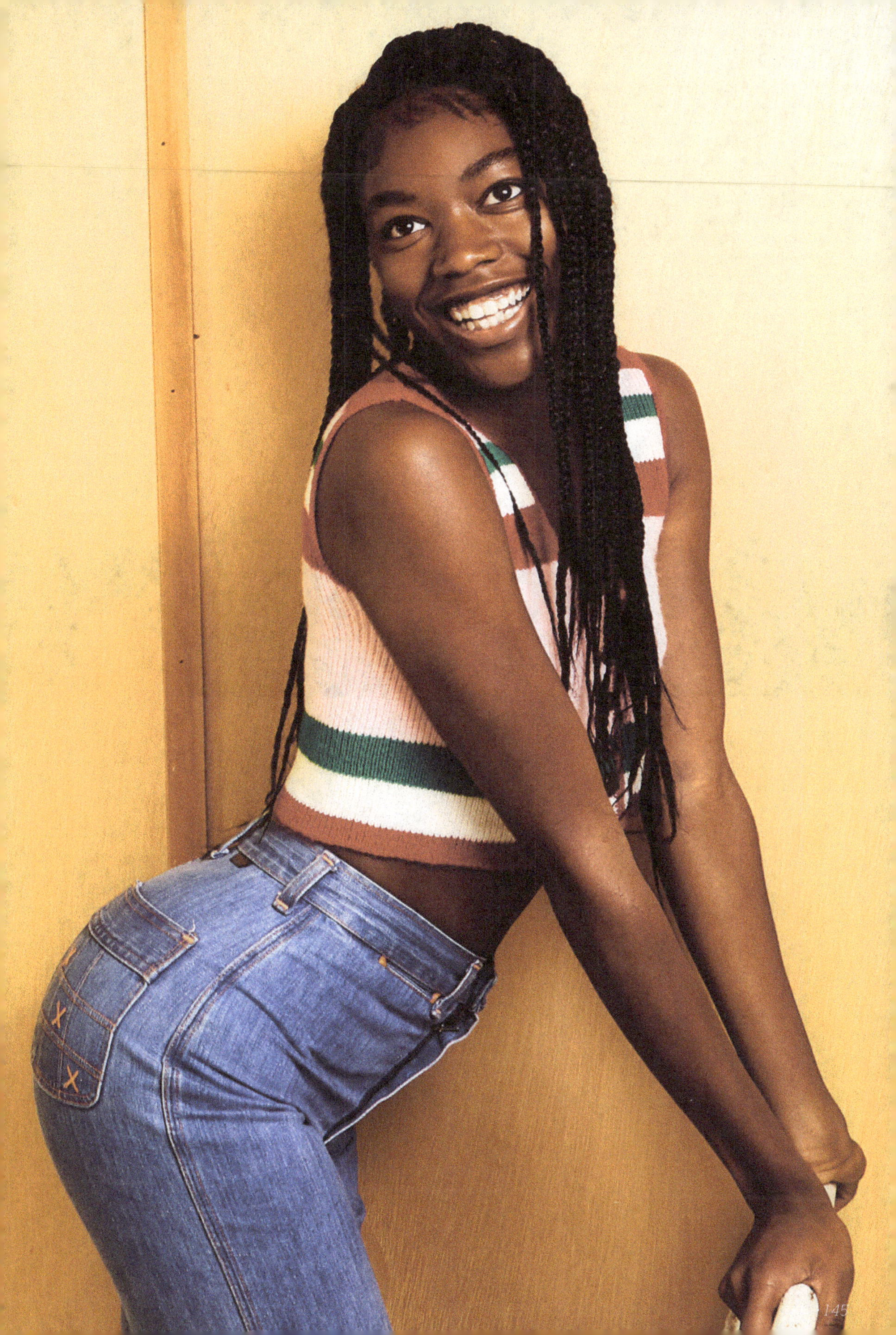

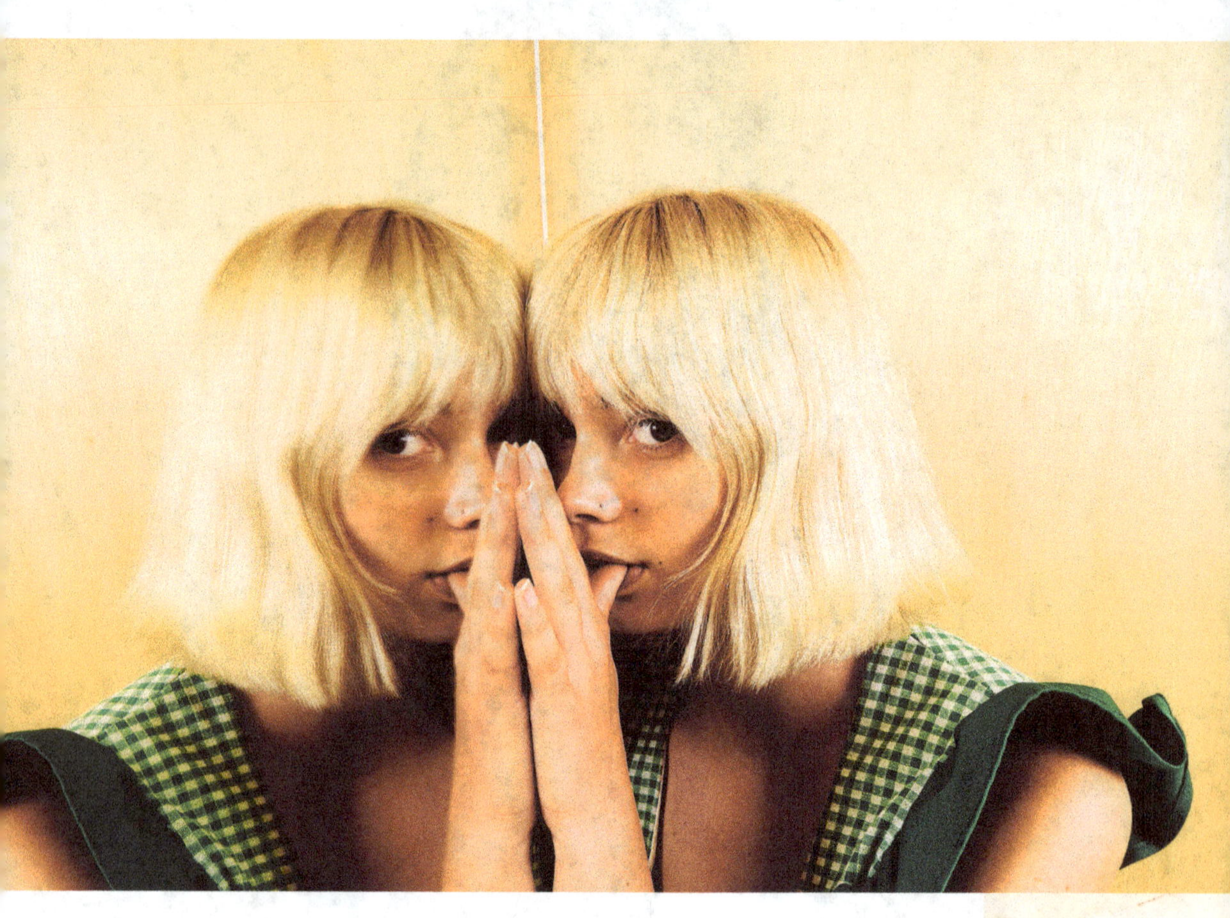

ABOVE- **Mary Quant** Top;
RIGHT - **Lee** Jeans,
Donnkenny Shirt,
Converse Shoes

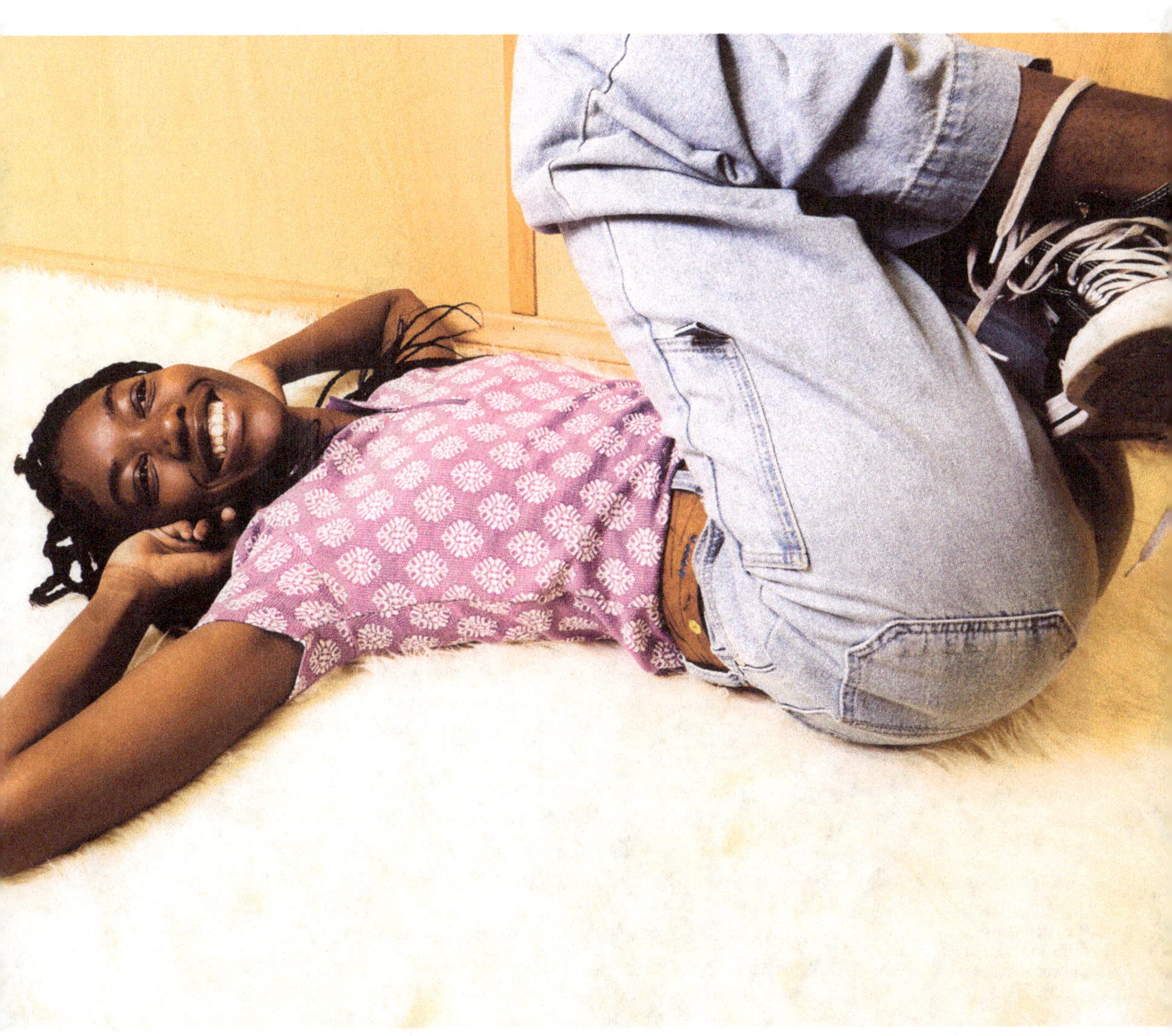

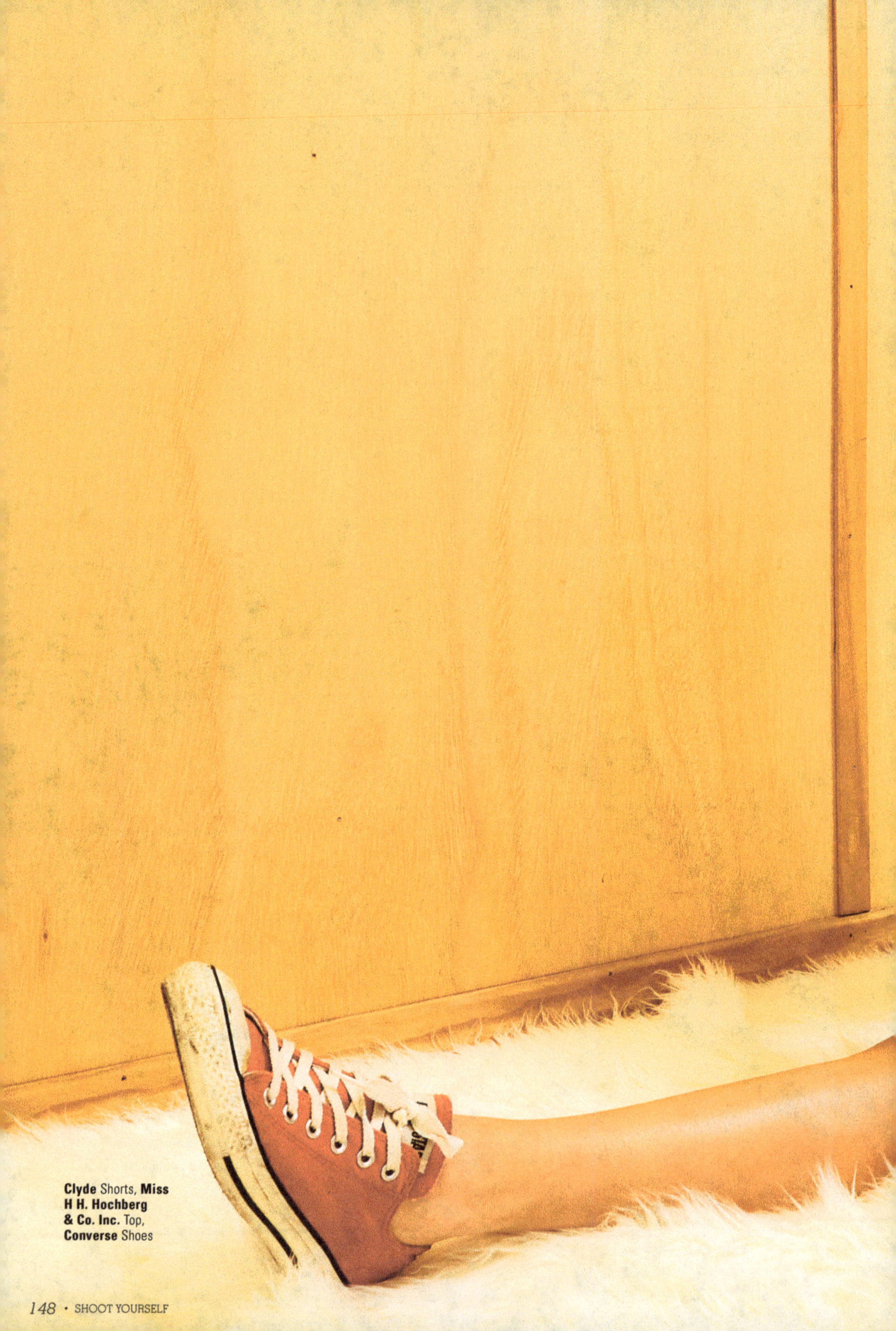

Clyde Shorts, Miss
H H. Hochberg
& Co. Inc. Top,
Converse Shoes

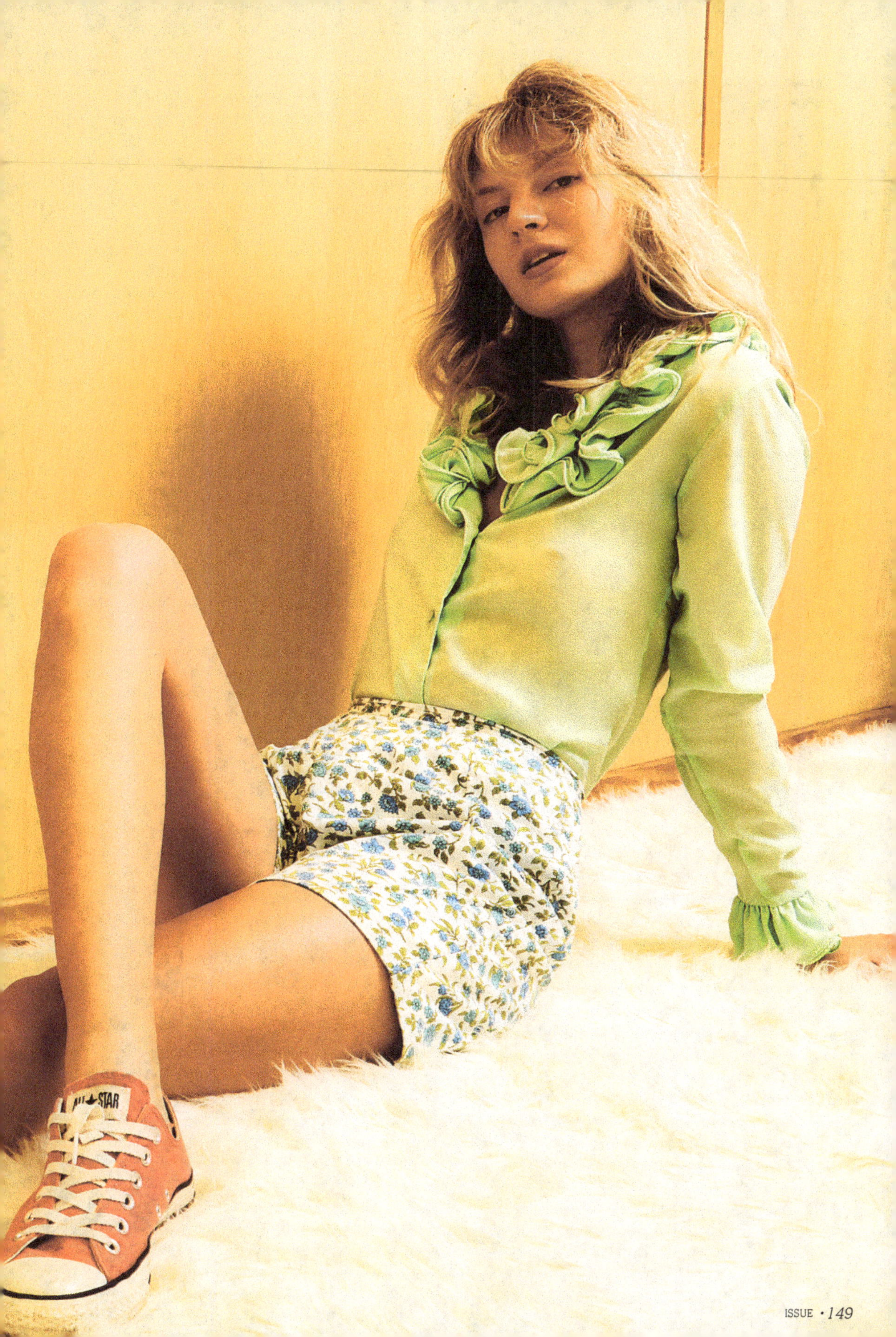

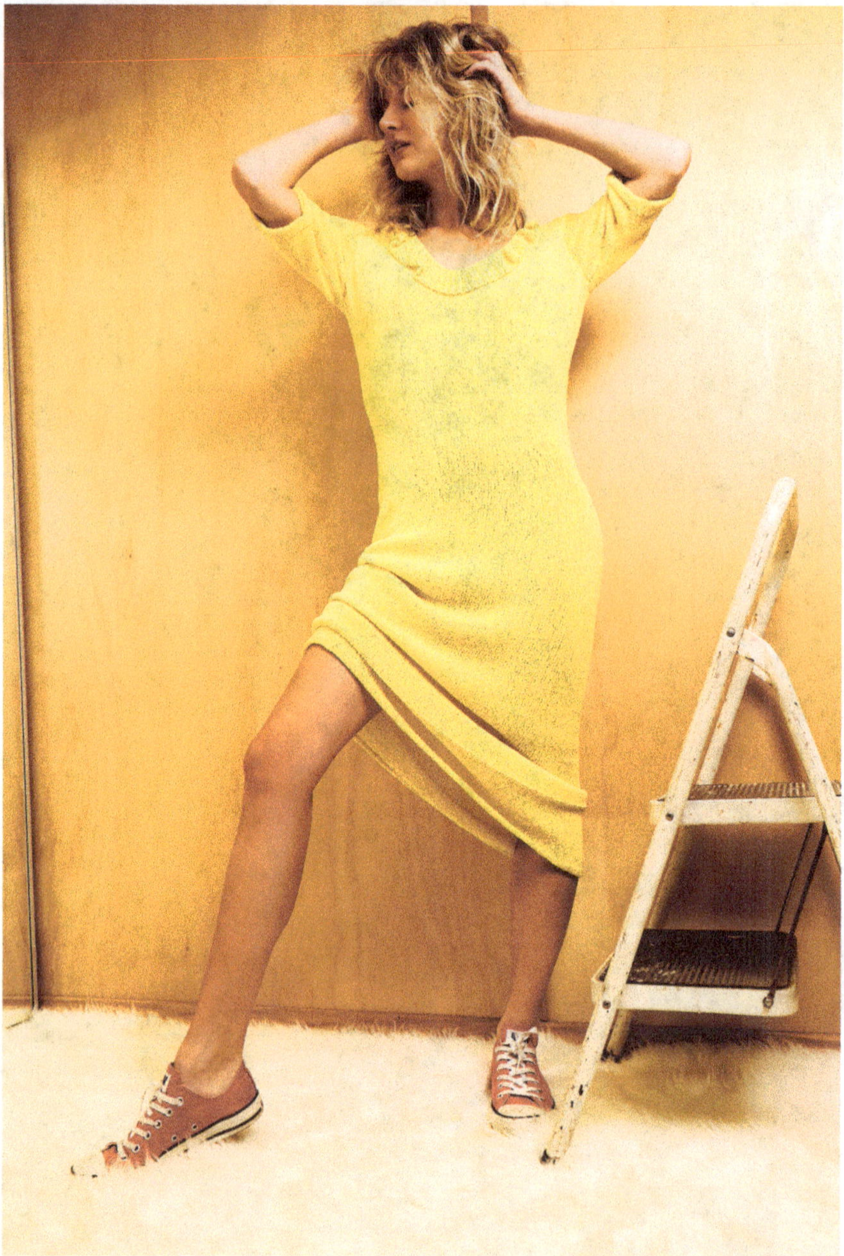

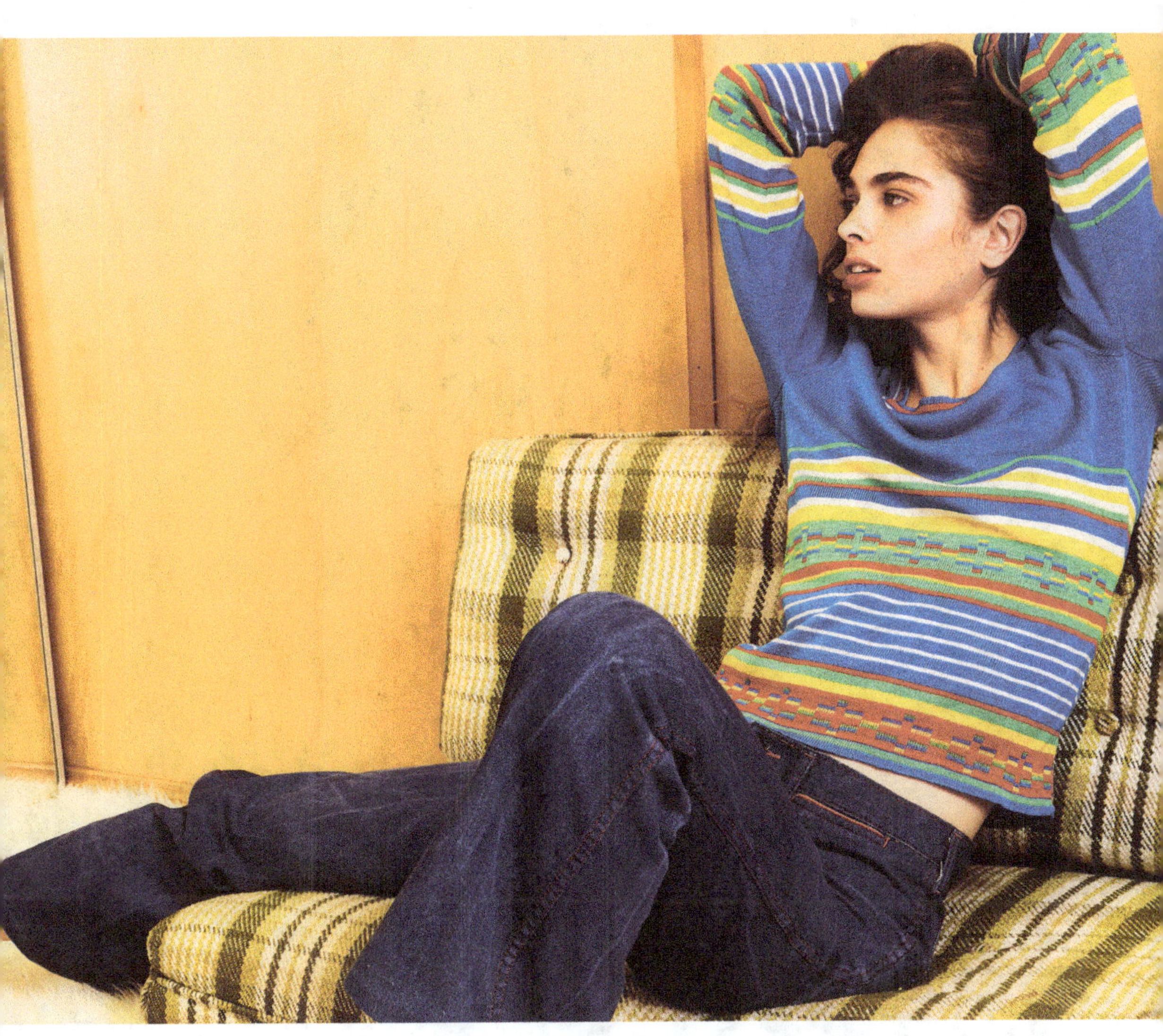

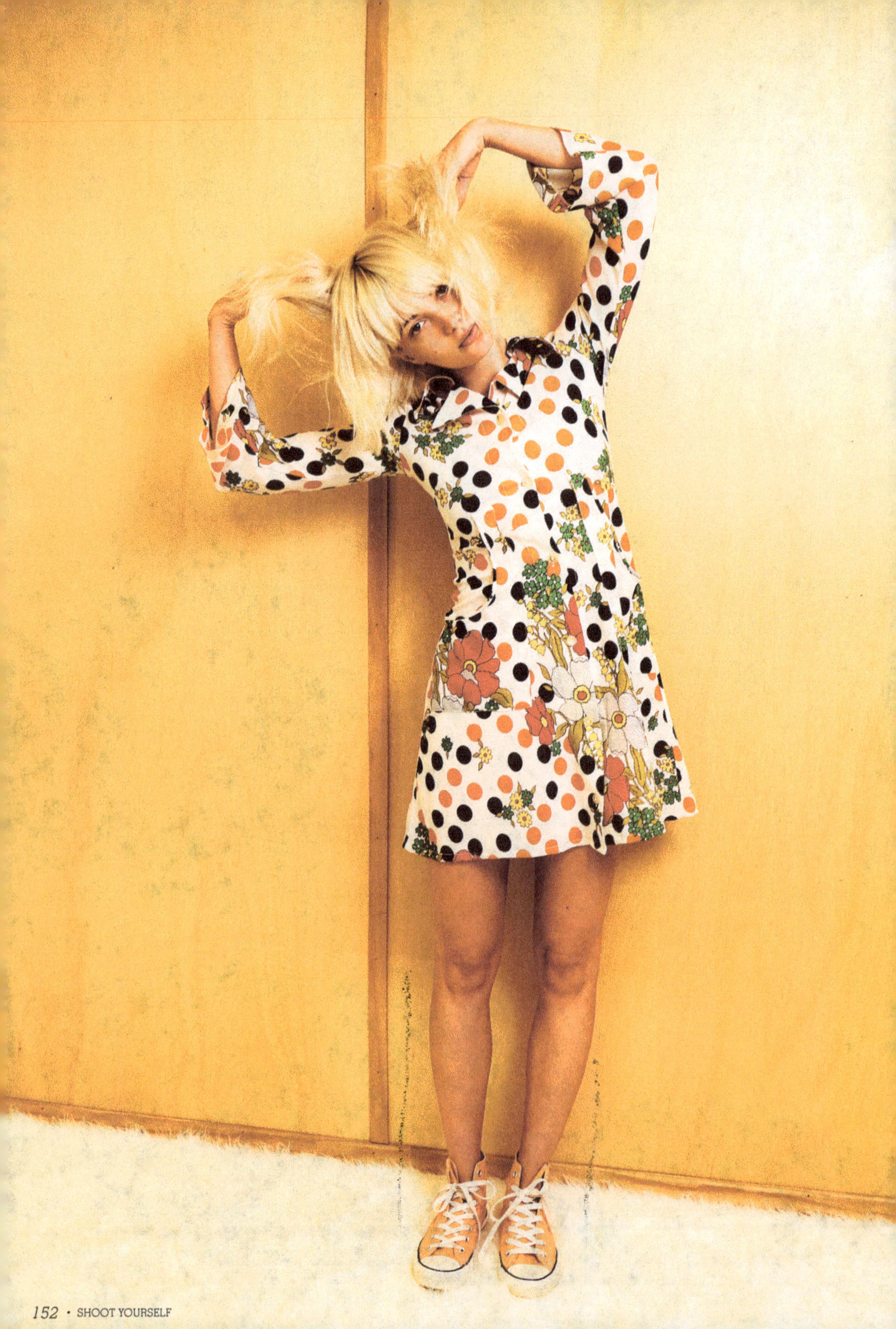

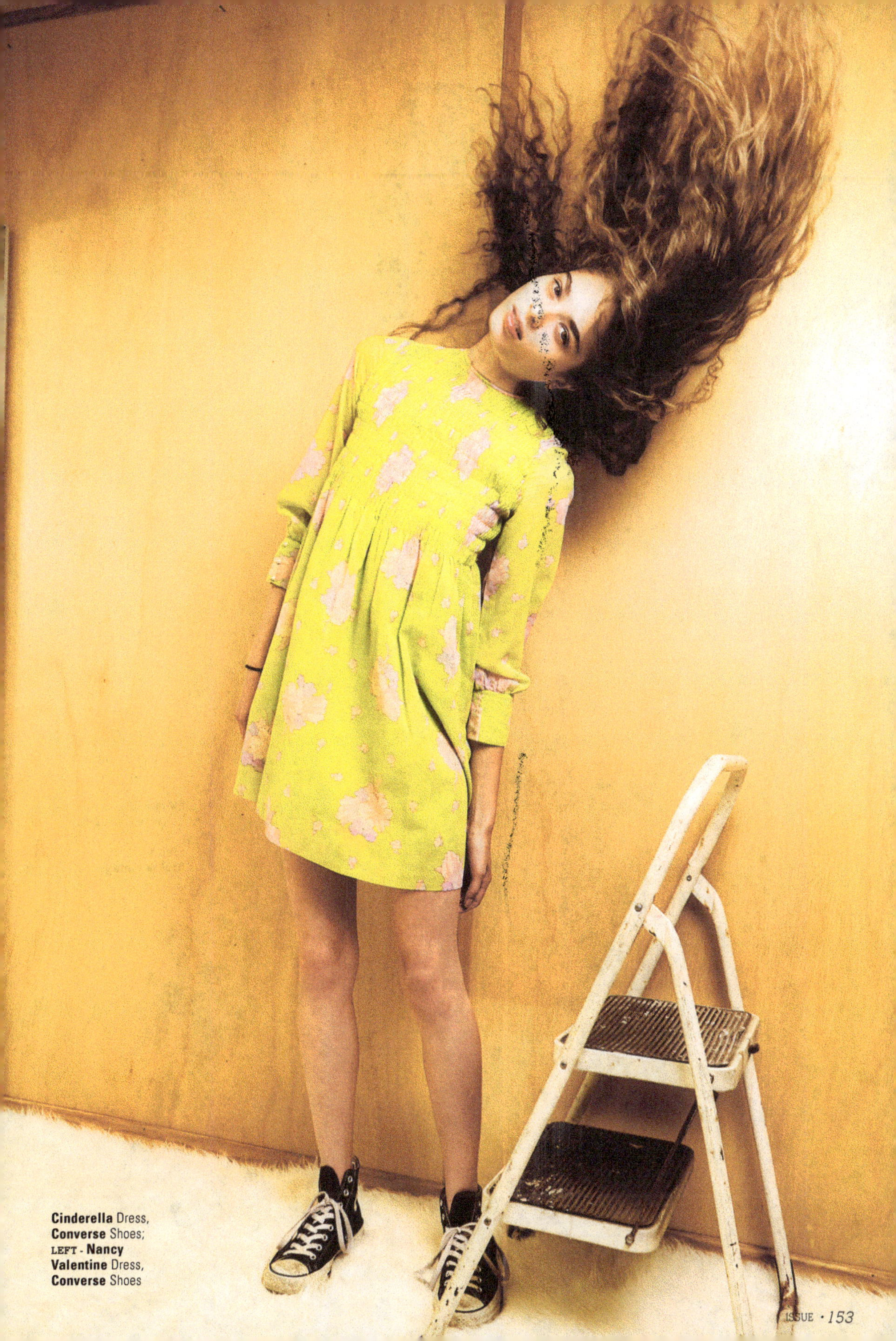

Cinderella Dress,
Converse Shoes;
LEFT - **Nancy
Valentine** Dress,
Converse Shoes

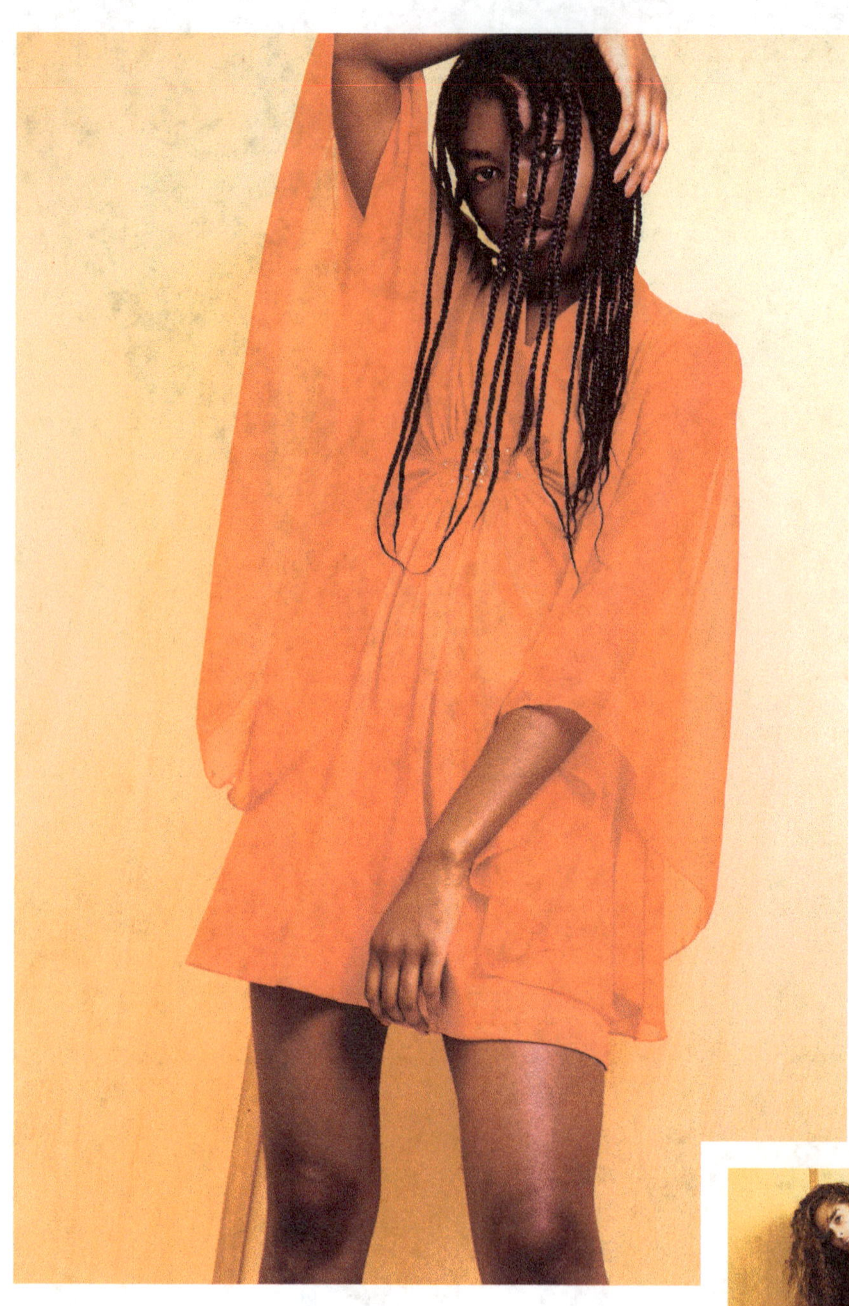

LEFT - **Daymor**
Dress; BELOW LEFT
TO RIGHT - **Ladies
Garment Union**
Dress, **Converse**
Shoes; **Sears JR.
Bagaan** Dress,
Converse Shoes

Special thanks to
Aralda Vintage

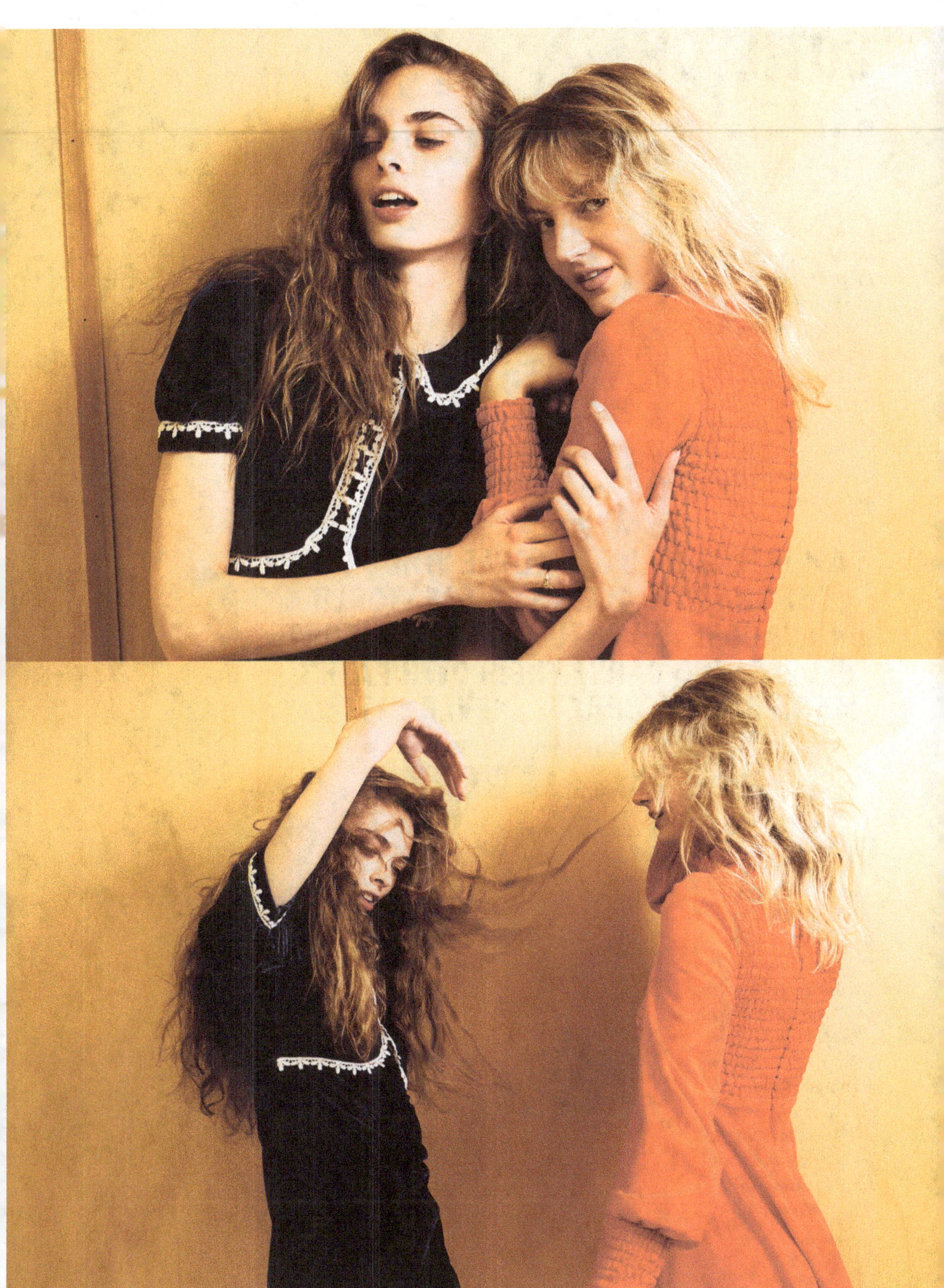

COTILLON

Introduction by
Brian Lee Hughes

I was once in a big, dumb pool with a lot of dumb, mean people. It was at night in the desert and the pool was illuminated, but the people in it and the creepy silhouettes surrounding it, were more comfort- able with the dark

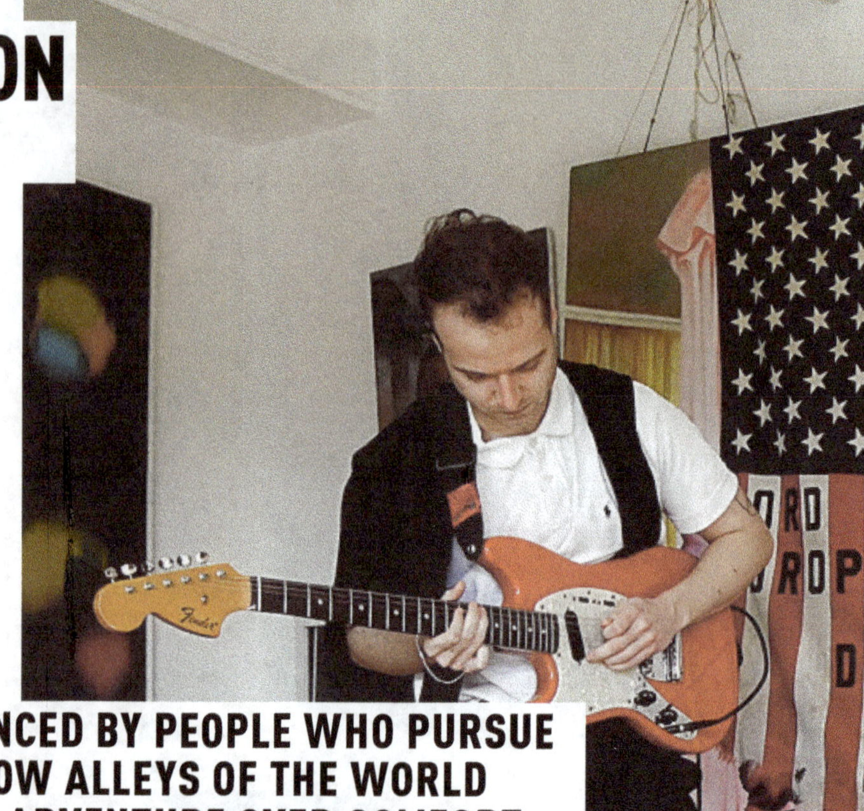

> ## "I AM INFLUENCED BY PEOPLE WHO PURSUE THE SHADOW ALLEYS OF THE WORLD AND CHOOSE ADVENTURE OVER COMFORT. PEOPLE WHO CARVE THEIR OWN PATHS, MASTER THEIR CRAFTS, NEVER SETTLE."
>
> — COTILLON

vibes than I was. As I suspiciously side-eyed them and side-creeped away, I made it to the furthest edge of the pool. There, I encountered a man who shared my state of aversion to the others. This person happened to be Jor- dan Corso, singer of the band Cotillon Flowers, which in time became the band named Co- tillon.

Assuming he shared my social anxieties, I mum- bled a rhetorical offering as a test, "This is a weird party." To which he nodded, "The weirdest party in the world." As per American conver- sational norms, there was a name exchange and then a, "So, what do you do?" He shyly, dryly replied "Musician." I asked which genre and he shrugged. I asked if he liked what he was mak-

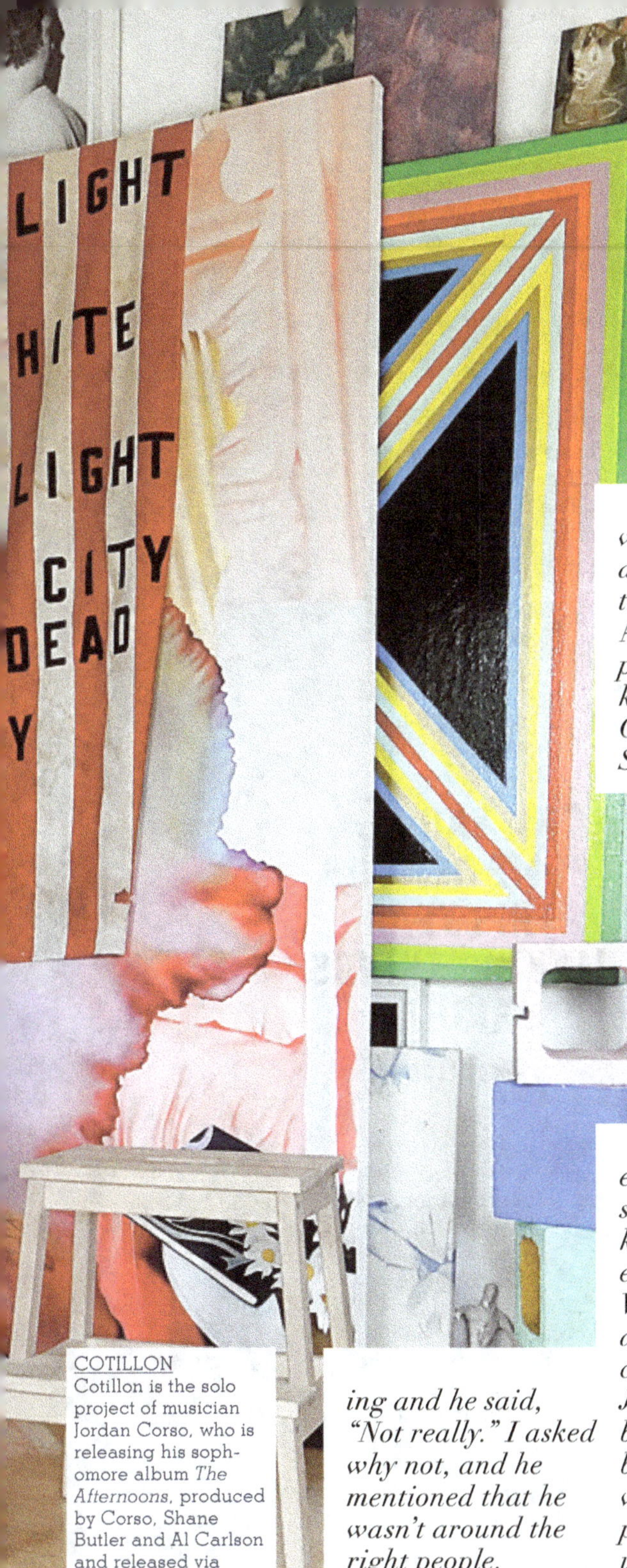

with, "The first album from Girls, the album called **Album**," I felt weaponized. I actually knew the boys of Girls from my own SF days and direct-

ed a video for their song "Laura." I knew Girls' producer and bassist JR White well enough, and I offered up connecting the two. Jordan was probably dubious of me, but nonetheless he wondered, "Is that possible?" I offered up my hunch: "All of your heroes share your own self-doubt and would love to hear that anyone wanted to make music with them."

ing and he said, "Not really." I asked why not, and he mentioned that he wasn't around the right people.

I asked what I hoped would trigger a positive turn, "What's your favorite record?" When he replied

Turns out it was truer than I knew.

A year or so later, I was in SF and Jordan invited me over to his Precita Park apartment. It wasn't just any Precita Park apartment, though: Jordan was living in Chris Owen's former bedroom and was indeed JR's roommate in the very home where Girls made their musical magic. Jordan shared with me some of the truly transcendent Cotillon tracks that made it onto his first record, released by Burger Records.

What started there has only sharpened and progressed. His new Cotillon record, **The Afternoons**, is a deeper dive into intelligent innocence in a corrupt world. Poetically, he's an elegant fighter for his own subset of like-mind-

ed people. Melodically, he's an expert at exploring the interesting wrinkles on the edges of previous masterpieces. I can say with full confidence that he will be sought after for advice by seekers like his former self.

———

Growing up, my parents were so generous and confident, and I'm so grateful to inherit their approach to life. Today, I am influenced by people who pursue the shadow alleys of the world and choose adventure over comfort. People like yourself, who carve their own paths, master their crafts, never settle.

How would you describe your music? Pop music mixed with

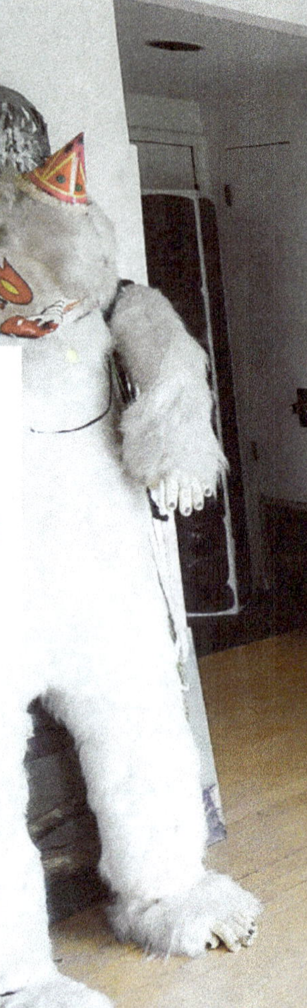

Where are you from? I was raised in south Orange County and have lived as an adult/perma-teen in Los Angeles, San Francisco and New York City.

When did you start playing music? I started playing music in high school after my dad forced me to take music as an elective.

Who influenced you growing up and who influences you today? I played in shoegaze, bubblegum, power, grit and glitter, made by someone who doesn't overthink it.

How and when did you decide that this is what you were going to do? There was never a decision. It's a natural way for me to communicate my thoughts and emotions. Never a decision.

What's your story of getting started as a musician? I played in other people's bands and felt like I could write better songs by myself. I had a lot of fun performing and writing and got addicted to the lifestyle. Not sure what else I would do without this outlet—probably be so bored.

How does it feel to have finished your album? Feels great. It came together so naturally and wonderfully. I love it.

What was the process like? I had the most intelligent people in a room with me for the span

> ## "I'M FACING SOME DEMONS THIS YEAR, MAKING THINGS RIGHT."
> — COTILLON

of a summer, with the fanciest gear, best beer and the love and support of the best people and pets ever outside of the studio. I cannot say enough about these people and how much they elevated my work: Shane Butler, Jon Nellen, Al Carlson. Straight-up geniuses with the best taste. A totally surreal time.

Who would you most like to collaborate with and why? With Hua Dong in re-TROS, a seminal krautrock band from Beijing that kills. I'm into China right now—I'm actually doing this interview from a dark bathroom in Beijing as we speak. Also you, Brian, and this other wonderful human Amber Carew—people who understand me or make a real effort to.

What are you working on now? I'm working on being a good person to those around me, supporting other people's art and visions. Trying not to only focus on myself—it's one of life's great challenges, but makes me feel the best. I'm facing some demons this year, making things right. I want people to

an incredibly tasteful
human turned me onto
recently. They remind
me of my fancy Orange
County childhood in
a good way. I've been
thinking a lot about the
film *Days of Being Wild*
by Wong Kar-Wai. I feel
like I can relate to York's
character lately.

York, Eleanor Petry. We
all just had the best
time playing in Seattle
on Saturday night, and
drinking tequila and
eating tortas.

**What are your inter-
ests and passions
outside of music?**
Pickling vegetables,

What's next for you?
I'm living in like three
different places and
am single and feel like
10 years have passed
since the start of the
year. I've been around
the world twice, got
lost on an island in
Vietnam, fought a
snake, barbequed a

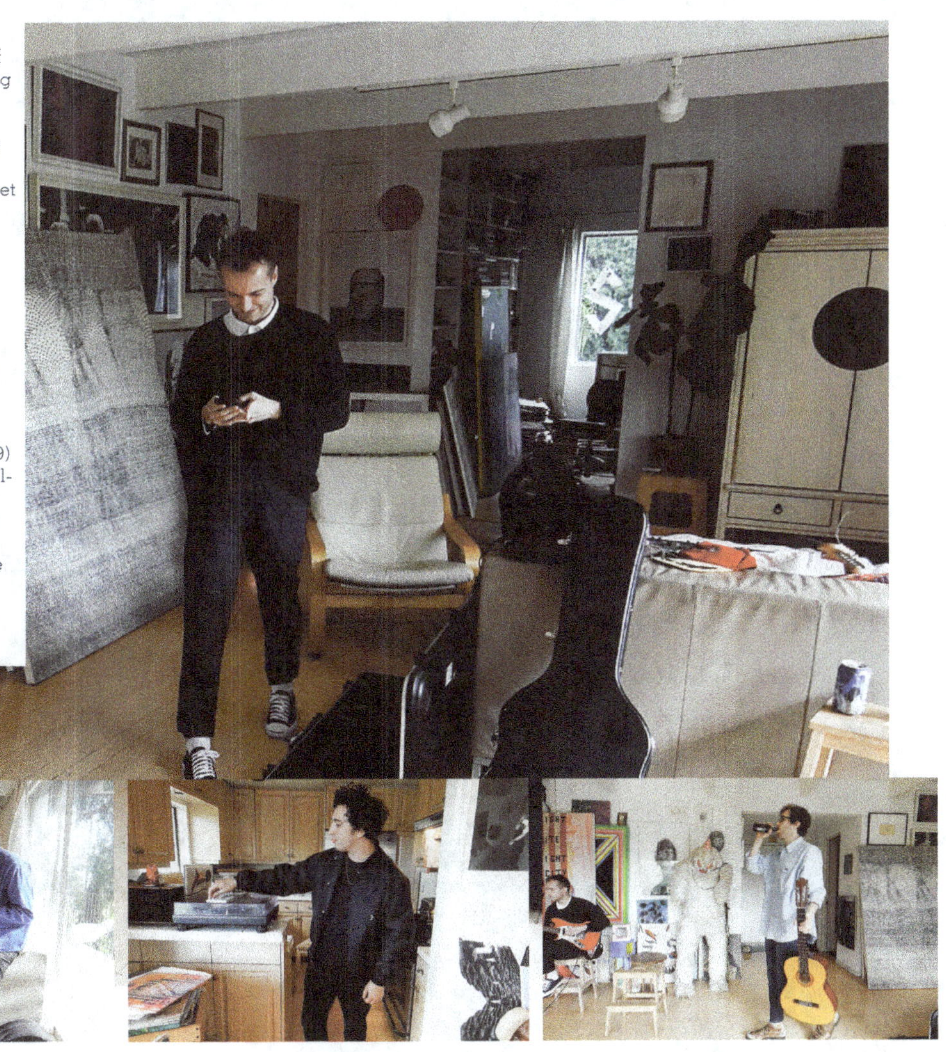

come to my funeral and
miss me when I'm gone.
Ya know?

**What's your favorite
book, film, and music
right now?** I'm into
these swanky plays by
Richard Greenberg that

I'm mostly listen-
ing to Chinese bands
right now: re-TROS,
New Pants, Queen Sea
Big Shark. But also
love these people in
Seattle that make the
best music: Chastity
Belt, So Pitted, Dude

making curries, Chi-
nese food, growing
cilantro, minimalism,
hanging out at your
house with Damiana
and mezcal guy, eating
tacos with mint in them,
making new friends,
being out there.

crocodile, got robbed
and kidnapped by a
taxi driver, jumped off
a moped. I'm touring
behind a new record
right now in China. I'll
make a new record this
summer and keep this
thing rolling. ↯

ALEX LAHEY

On her debut EP, B-Grade University, Melbourne's Alex Lahey takes on her post-grad life in all its mundanity and confusion after dropping

> ## "I DISCOVERED THAT I ENJOYED TEACHING MYSELF GUITAR AND WRITING SONGS WAY MORE THAN PLAYING SCALES IN A PRACTICE ROOM."
>
> **— ALEX LAHEY**

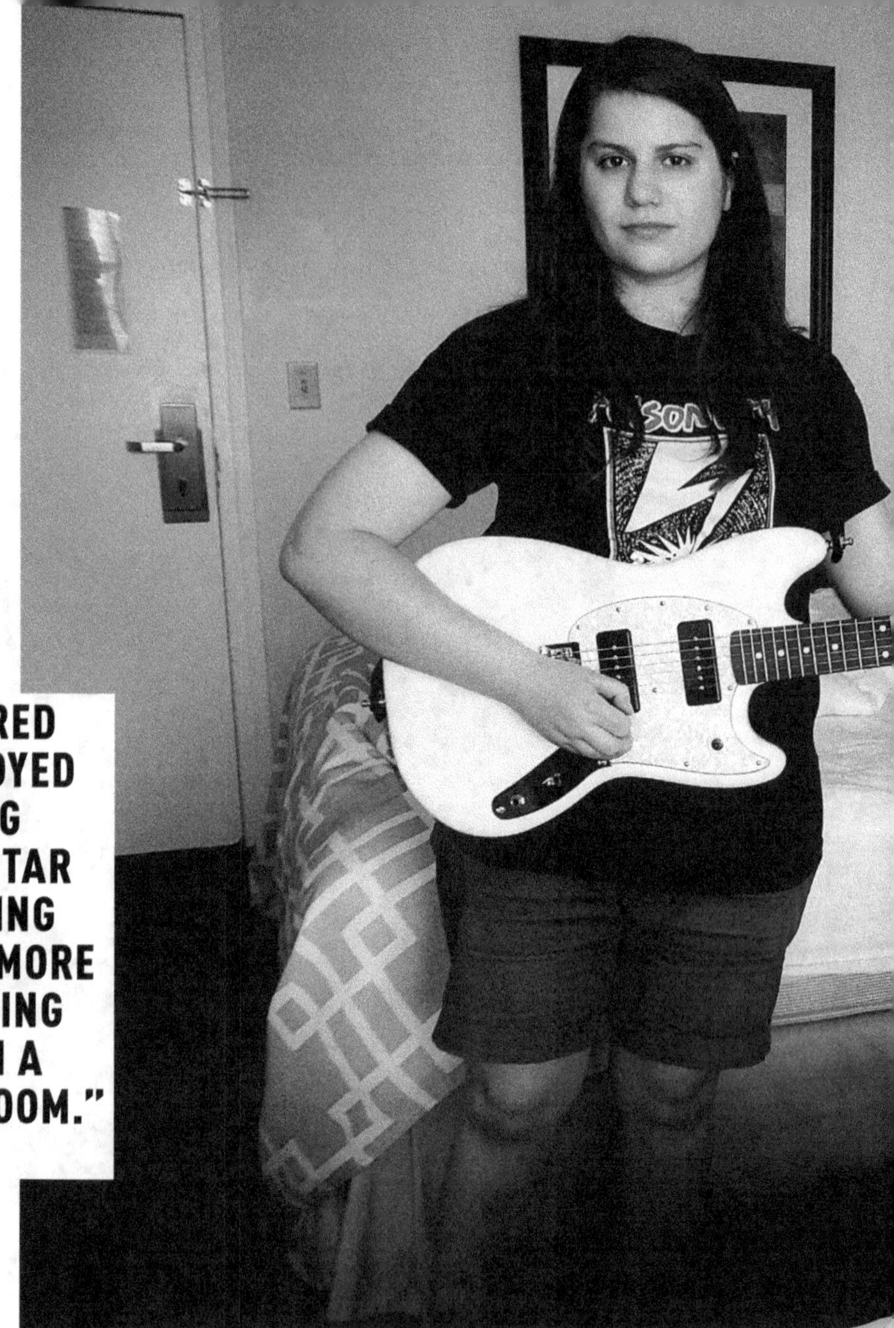

out of college to pursue her own music. Its lead track, "Ivy League", opens with the question: "If I was an ivy league kind of girl, do you think that they would give me more shifts at work?" Lahey's lyrics are imbued with this same casual, raw honesty and anxiety about life choices,

layered over fuzzy guitar and lively rhythms. The result is an optimism and infectious excitement, despite the situation, even emboldened by it. This is what makes Lahey's music so relatable and what garnered

her so much attention since she self-released the EP in summer of 2016. Lahey has since signed to Dead Oceans, and B-Grade University is now receiving its official US release.

When did you start making music? I've been playing music my entire life, but picked up the guitar and started writing songs when I was about 13 years old.

Who did you listen to growing up and who is your music influ-

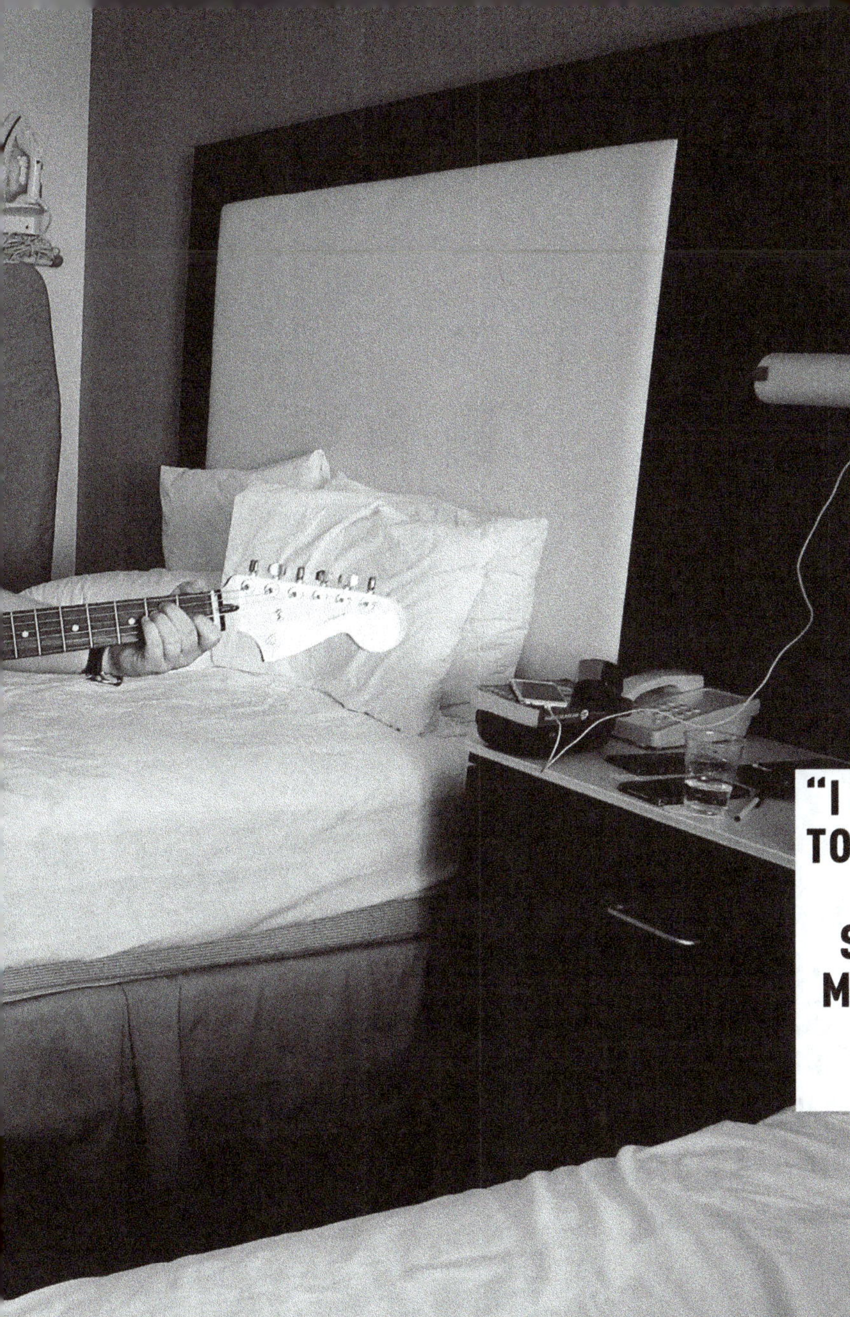

recording of the EP was a relatively relaxed process that took place in my producer's little studio in Abbotsford, Melbourne. I'm really proud of it.

What are your interests and passions outside of music? My cats, eating good food and copious cups of tea.

What are you working on now? Although I'm touring a lot at the moment, I'm currently working on my debut album, which is due out at the end of the year.

"I LEARNED HOW TO PLAY IN BANDS BY PLAYING SAXOPHONE IN MY HIGH SCHOOL BIG BAND."

— ALEX LAHEY

ALEX LAHEY
Alex Lahey is a musician from Melbourne, Australia. She released her debut EP *B-Grade University* in July 2016 on her own label, Nicky Boy Records, in conjunction with Caroline Australia. The EP has received critical acclaim, and Alex Lahey has toured internationally, including a debut at SXSW in 2017. Lahey recently signed to Dead Oceans, and *B-Grade University* is receiving a US release through the label

enced by today? Growing up, I taught myself how to play guitar by learning songs by artists like Tegan and Sara, Michelle Branch, The Beatles and Missy Higgins. These days, I'm influenced by a lot of my friends and peers like Eilish Gilligan, Bec Sandridge, Julien Baker and Julia Jacklin.

What's your story of getting started as a musician? I learned how to play in bands by playing saxophone in my high school big band. During this time, I was also writing songs but just thought of it as a hobby of sorts. As I went to study jazz at university, I discovered that, in fact, I enjoyed teaching myself guitar and writing songs way more than playing scales in a practice room.

How does it feel to have finished your first EP? What was the process like? Although the EP has been finished for a while, it feels awesome to finally have it out in the US. The

MIDDLE KIDS

Sydney's Middle Kids released their first single, "Edge of Town" in May 2016 and immediately garnered international traction with extensive radio play and fans the likes of Elton John. Lead singer Hannah Joy and guitarist Tim Fitz formed the band almost accidentally when the two began collaborating and ended up merging their respective solo projects. Later joined by drummer Harry Day, the trio has since signed to Domino and recently released their self-titled EP to the same wide acclaim. Middle Kids' layered sound centers around Joy's deep, belting voice, bolstered by Day's driving rhythms and Fitz's slide guitar, and skillfully emerges both joyful and melancholic. Joy talks with us about the origins of Middle Kids EP *and the band plays* "Your Love" *exclusively for Issue in a House Arrest.*

When did you start making music?
When I was three, I figured out how to play Pachelbel's Canon on the piano after my dad played it, so they pretty quickly enrolled me in piano lessons.

Who did you listen to growing up and who is your music influenced by today?
My dad and older brother fed me a lot of music: classical but also bands and artists like Pink Floyd, Neil Young, Radiohead, Sigur Ros and The National. I still listen to a lot of the same stuff but am particularly influenced by some of the big voices like Neil Finn and Janis Joplin.

How would you describe your musical genre/style?
I think the Middle Kids sound sits somewhere loosely in the indie rock and pop world. One of our main focuses is creating full-bodied, melodic songs that you can really sing.

How does it feel to have finished your first EP? What was the process like?
It feels great and strange, like I've grown a new limb. The process was very cool and natural. Tim and I came together a couple of years ago, and he produced "Fire in Your Eyes." We ditched our solo projects and started working together (not knowing we were making an EP, just making songs at the time). The songs slowly formed and we realised, kind of in retrospect, that we had made a cool EP!

What are you working on now?

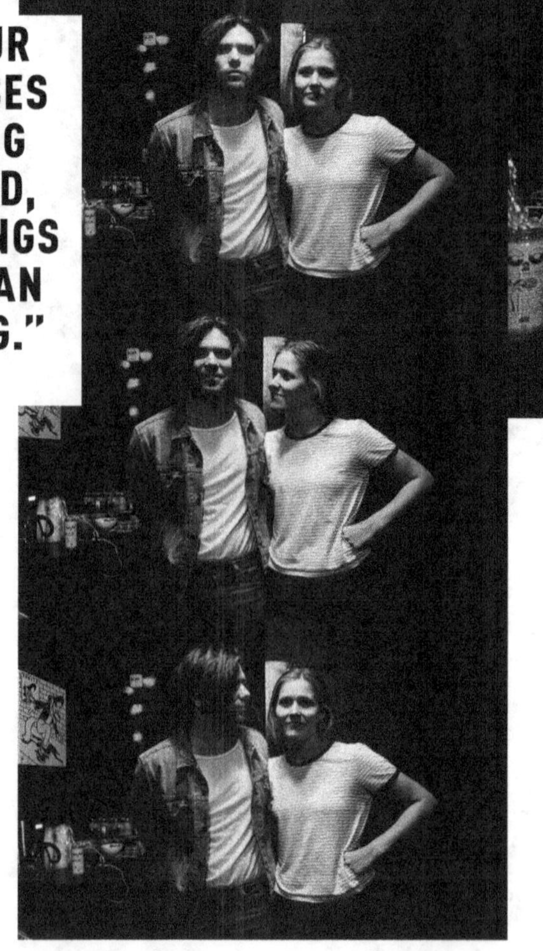

Images by Jan-Willem Dikkers

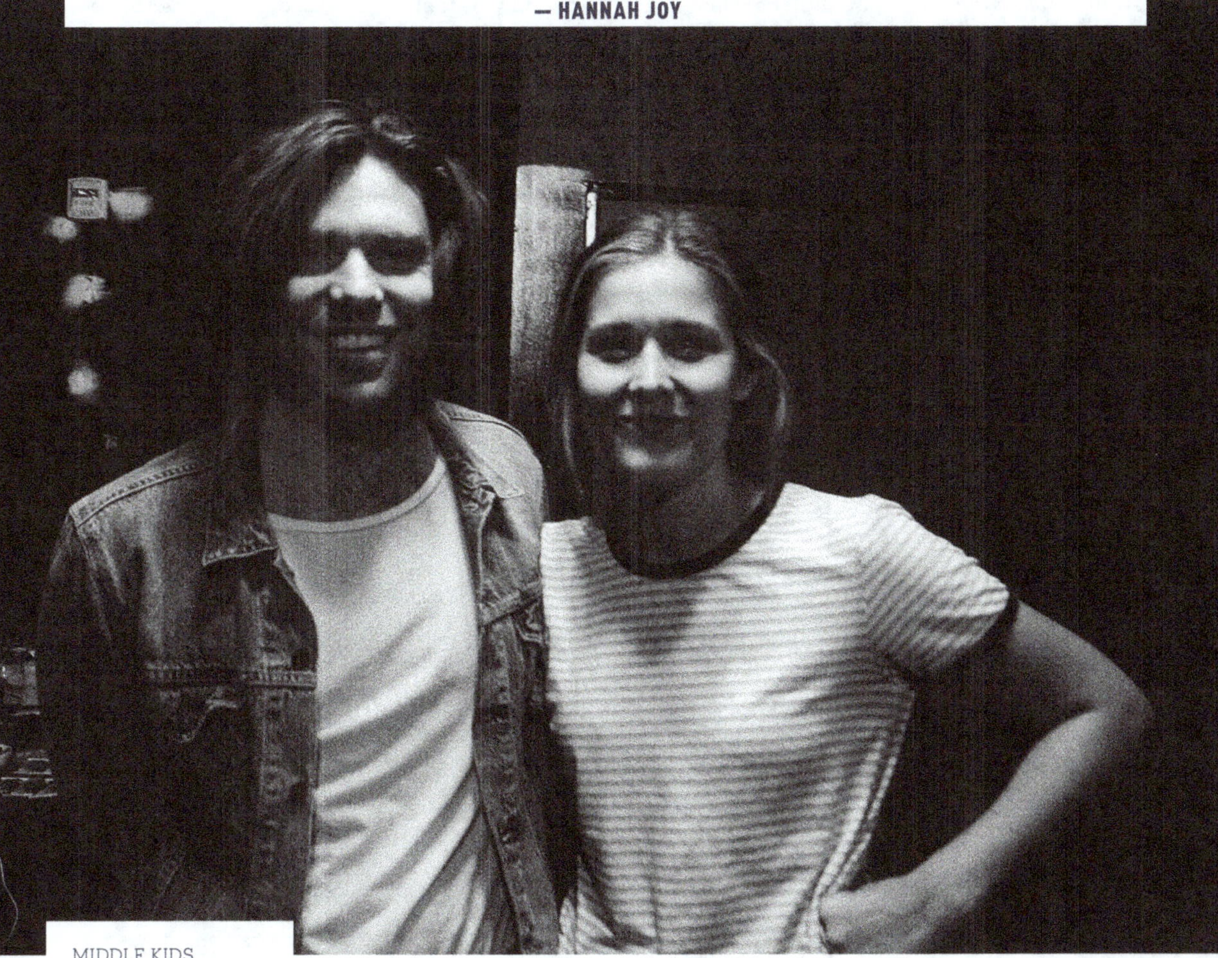

<u>MIDDLE KIDS</u>
Based in Sydney, Australia, Middle Kids is the project of lead singer Hannah Joy, guitarist Tim Fitz and drummer Harry Day. The trio released the singles "Edge of Town" and "Your Love" in 2016, followed by their self-titled EP in February 2017. Before forming Middle Kids, both Fitz and Joy had released music under self-titled solo projects. Middle Kids are currently touring internationally and working on their forthcoming debut album.

We have been making demos for the album. There's been a lot of creative energy flowing since the release of the EP, so it feels good to be looking to making the next thing. I'm also slowly working on a symphony, which I hope to have finished by the time I'm 60.

What are your interests and passions outside of music?

I love to garden, however that passion is literally wilting in light of being on tour a lot of the time. I am obsessed with the ocean and getting in it. And I feel very passionate about chicken burgers (I think Americans call them chicken sandwiches).

THEO ROSSI

New York-born actor Theo Rossi is best known for playing Juan Carlos "Juice" Ortiz in the acclaimed FX series Sons of Anarchy *(2008-14), and Marvel fans recognize him from him as the supervillain*

> ## "I LOOK AT THINGS IN AN EXTREMELY RATIONAL, BLUE COLLAR WAY. I HAVE NO DELUSIONS OF WHAT THINGS ARE."
>
> **— THEO ROSSI**

'Shades' in the Netflix series Luke Cage *(2016-17). Rossi also starred alongside Eva Longoria in the recent film* Lowriders *(2016), centering on East LA lowrider car culture.*

Birthplace: New York City

First Break: I would have to say the first thing that kind of made a big difference was *Sons of Anarchy*. That changed the game for me.

Favorite Food: Almond butter.

Favorite Artist: Edith Piaf.

Turn-offs: Small talk.

What have you been in? *Sons of Anarchy*, a show called Luke Cage now, *Lowriders* comes out this Friday, and a lot of other things. I've been doing this a long time it feels like.

How do you feel about this career? It's afforded me the right to do a lot of things that I love to do.

How did you decide to become an actor? I didn't. It was a happy accident. A complete and utter accident, and it's been happening ever since.

How would you describe your specialty or type? There is no type. People can't seem to put me in a box. They have no idea, and I have no interest in going inside the box. So no type, no box, no nothing.

Who is your favorite actor you look up to? Acting-wise, favorite actor of all time: Bette Davis… I admire a lot of people's careers based on the way they navigate the business. Paul Newman, people like Jimmy Smits, Demián Bichir. People now who are low-key and killing the game. Javier Bardem.

What would your ideal job be? My ideal job would probably be full-time. Anything to do with animals, any voiceless creature— anything voiceless.

Do your consider yourself to be lucky? No, I don't believe in luck. I believe in preparation meets opportunity, but I think that I've had a extremely navigated, looked-over life.

What advantages do you have? I look at things in an extremely rational, blue collar way. I have no delusions of what things are. I try to see things from every single perspective, not just my own.

What did you do before? *Criminal Minds, Blue Collar.* I've been working since I was 9-years-old—delivering papers, working in poor stores. Any way I had to make a dollar. I've always been hustling. Hustle life my whole life.

Would you rather have a car or a

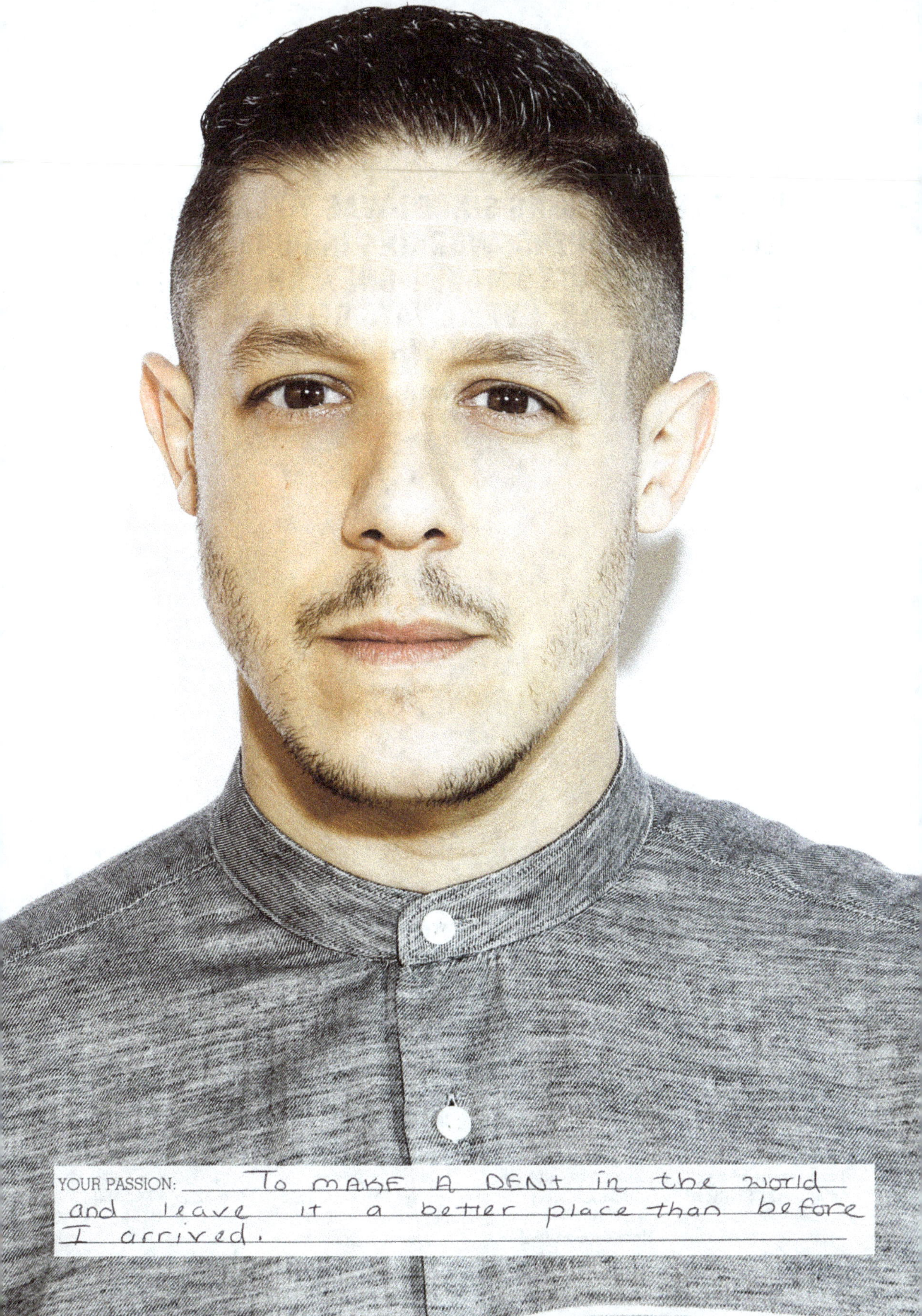

YOUR PASSION: To MAKE A DENt in the world and leave it a better place than before I arrived.

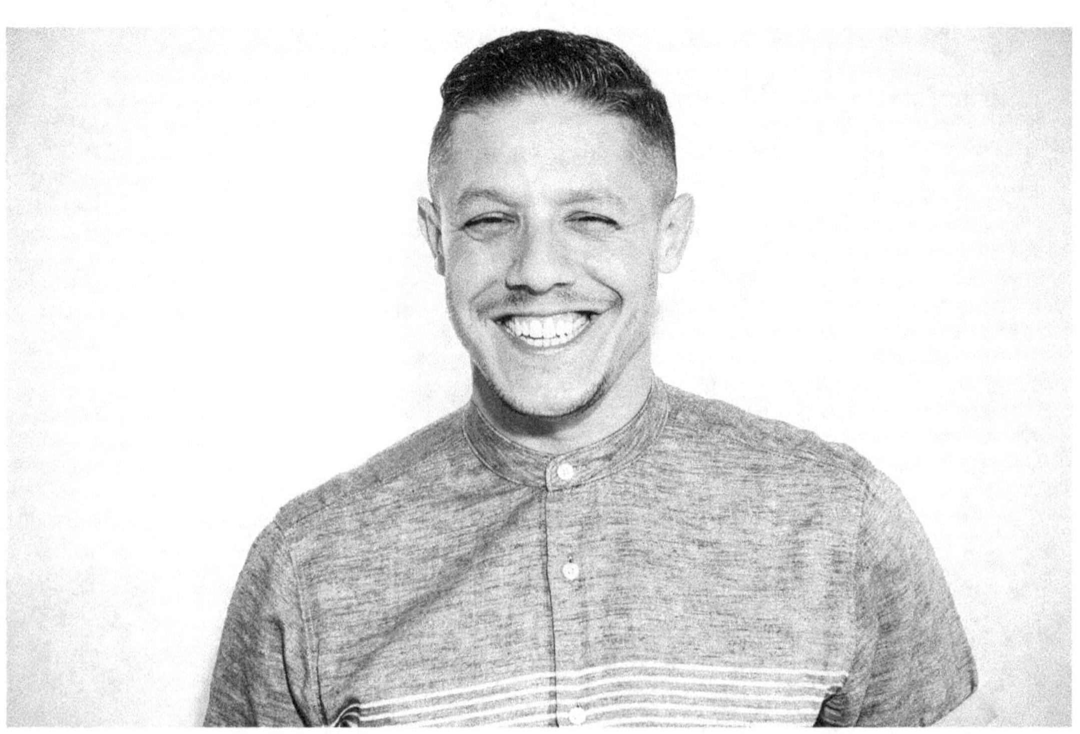

HOW DO YOU LIKE TO SPEND YOUR TIME? _moving_

diploma? Education, diploma.

What do you think about the need for instant gratification? The need for instant gratification does not give people time to reflect and think about anything in the headline society that we live in. I think instant gratification has stopped us from truly thinking about things and processing them.

How do you feel about how interconnected the world is becoming? Utterly fascinating. It's given us the awareness of other people, other cultures, other heritages, things that are going on. It's given us the ability to organize, set up revolutions. It's given more people a chance to experience other people's lives, quicker.

What does the future look like to you? Watching my kids grow all the time. And looking up at them when I take my last breath.

How do you feel about having children? It's what I was

meant to do. It feels like the reason that I was put here.

What challenges do you feel the world is facing today? The biggest challenge that the world is facing today I think is self-centeredness. We're becoming a "me" society, and that's all out of fear. Fear has overridden everything. It is the basis of most of the things going on right now, and that fear has led us to make decisions in almost all cases. Whether it's being braggadocious or wanting to live a certain life—just fear. Ultimately, people are scared. They don't know what's going to happen next, they don't know what their next job's going to be, they don't know if their next meal is gonna come, they don't know how anything is going to happen. Being so unsure has made people make some really bad decisions.

What are you most grateful for? My life. The fact that I am actually standing here, because this was not even a remote possibility. The fact that I am able to do what I love, that I am able to pursue a million other things because of this and that I am able to show my kids that they can absolutely do anything—I am extremely grateful for every day.

What is your favorite way to communicate? Conversation. Looking someone directly in the eyes and having a personal conversation. No lies, no bullshit. Just honesty.

What is your favorite book, film and music right now? Music right now: I've consistently come back to Edith Piaf. My son is obsessed with her song "No Regrets" right now. Films: I'm trying to watch more new films especially since I've been flying all over, and I've been utterly blown away by one of my friend's films *Moonlight*. I thought it was absolutely incredible. I always sound like a pretentious actor, but I'm an old film guy. I watch a lot of old films repeatedly from *All About Eve* to *Godfather* to Kubrick films. I'm talking like *Armageddon* and *The Rock*, *Con Air*, anything with Nicolas Cage. Books: I'm reading a motivational Tim Ferriss book that's kind of cool, *A People's History of the United States* and a lot of scripts. 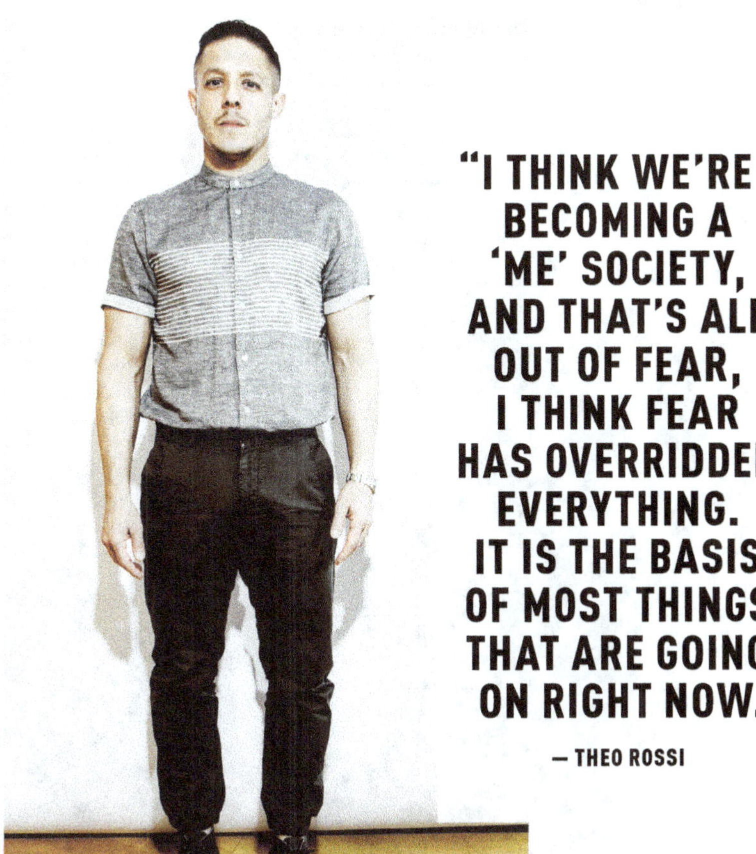

THEO ROSSI
Actor Theo Rossi recently starred alongside Eva Longoria in the film *Lowriders* (2016) about East LA's car subculture. He is best known for his roles as Juan Carlos "Juice" Ortiz on FX's series *Sons of Anarchy* (2008–14) and as Shades on Netflix's ongoing series *Luke Cage* (2016–).

KATIE ASELTON

From the small town of Ellsworth, Maine, actor Katie Aselton stars in Fargo *creator Noah Hawley's new FX marvel series* Legion, *fea-*

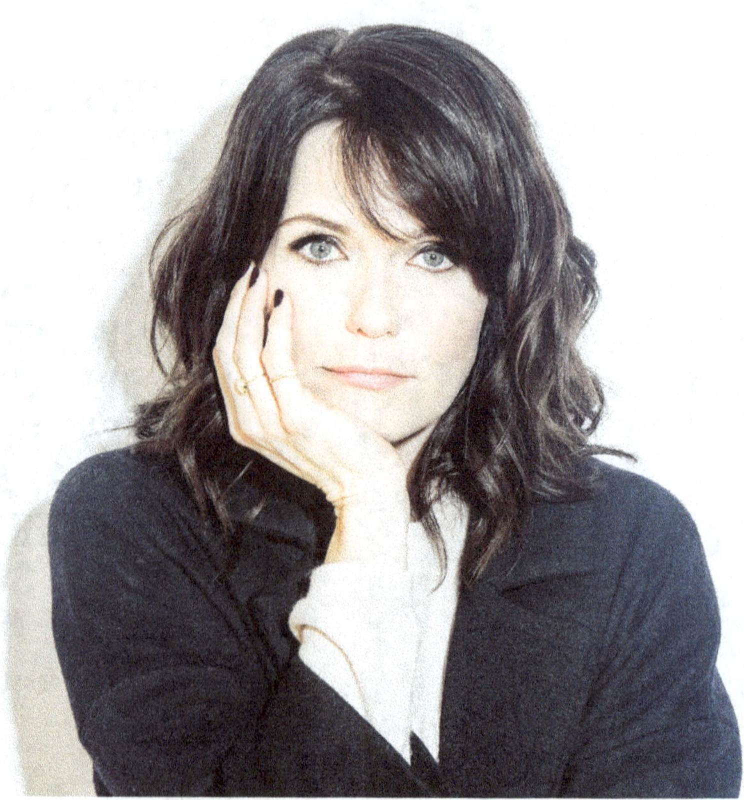

turing Dan Stevens and Aubrey Plaza, and in the Hulu TV series Casual. *She is also well-known for her TV roles as Jenny on* The League *and Amy in* Togetherness.

———

Birthplace: Ellsworth, Maine

Favorite actor: Meryl Streep

How did you get involved in this line of work? I used the secret.

Ambitions: To climb the mountain and turn around…

Passions: Good food, travel, good movies, bad TV, hearing other people's passions, connecting, cooking, great design, kid laughter, spontaneous dance parties, and doing what I do.

What was your first break? My first job was an episode of *Spin City* that I was cut out of, but I would say probably my first break was *The Puffy Chair.*

What have you been in? Notably I was in *The Office* and *The League.* Those are the two things people are like, "You're that girlfriend!"

How do you feel about this career? It's great. I feel like I am living the dream. I said that sarcastically, but I don't mean it sarcastically. I mean it genuinely.

How did you decide to become an actor? I'm the youngest by far of four kids, and I think that just happens to us sometimes. They'd all be talking politics over my head at dinner, so I would take the napkins and wrap them around my head and make babushkas and create these weird characters to entertain myself.

How would you describe your specialty or type? I don't know if I have one. I think I'm probably like the approachable girl who's cute but not too pretty.

Would you rather have a car, or a diploma? I'm gonna give a controversial answer and say "car" because I believe that I can read all the books in the world and educate myself in that way, but diplomas are sort of test-based and not as important. But I need a car to get to my library.

How do you feel about how interconnected the world is becoming? It's a double-edged sword. In a lot of ways it's amazing that we can just press a button and know what's happening on the other side of the world. The flip side is that it can give people extreme anxiety.

How do you feel about having children? I feel like I have two of them. I feel like it's my reality. It's overwhelming and inspiring.

"I GET TO MAKE DUMB JOKES FOR A LIVING AND PLAY DRESS-UP ALL THE TIME, AND MY PARENTS TELL ME THAT THEY'RE PROUD OF ME."

— KATIE ASELTON

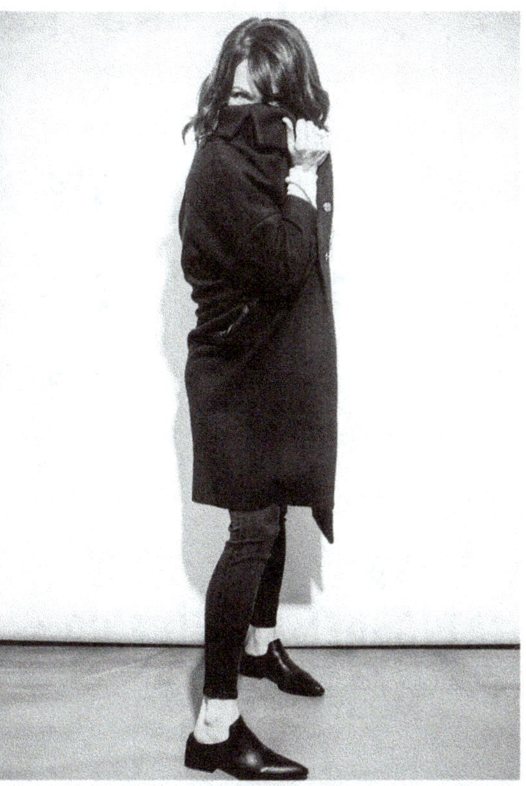

What are you most grateful for? So much. Health, my family's health, my friends, that I get to do what I do, where we get to do it, that I get to walk down the street and not feel like my liberties are threatened. I get to make dumb jokes for a living and play dress-up all the time, and my parents tell me that they're proud of me.

What is your favorite way to communicate? I prefer talking over a bottle of wine. Just how we should have done this interview.

What is your favorite book, film and music right now? My favorite book right now is *Fates and Furies*. And my favorite movie is probably always *Tootsie*. And my favorite music… I'm digging back into Chet Baker and enjoying it.

KATIE ASELTON
Katie Aselton currently stars in the new FX Marvel series *Legion*, from Fargo creator Noah Hawley and in

YOUR IDEA OF HEAVEN: *A beach, no phone w/ all my favorite people (and a personal chef)*

What challenges do you feel the world is facing today? Division, anger, lack of understanding, lack of empathy. I think everyone's having a hard time hearing people, a hard time listening.

"I THINK EVERYONE'S HAVING A HARD TIME HEARING PEOPLE, A HARD TIME LISTENING."

— KATIE ASELTON

Hulu's *Casual*. She is best known for her work in television including Jenny on *The League* (2009–15), Amy on *Togetherness* (2016) and her first appearances in shows such as *The Office* (2005–13) and the Duplass Brothers' film *The Puffy Chair* (2005).

PAST ISSUES

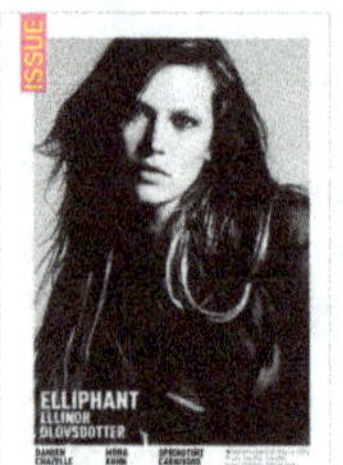

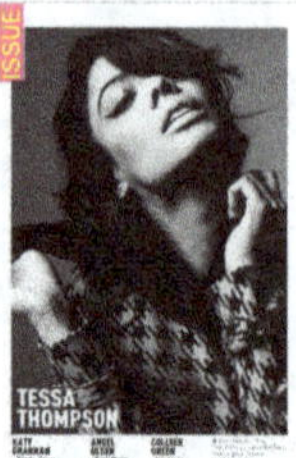

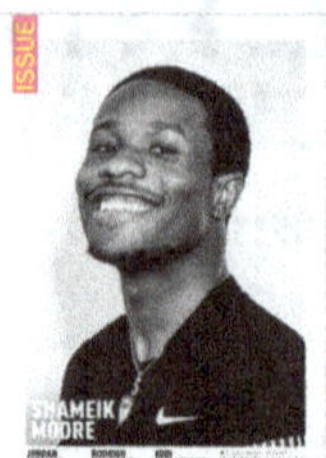

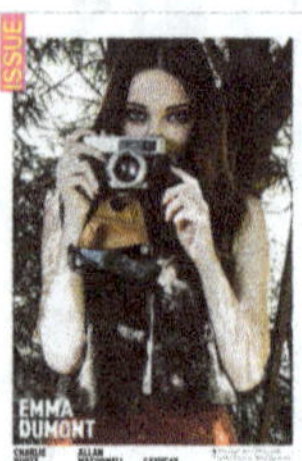

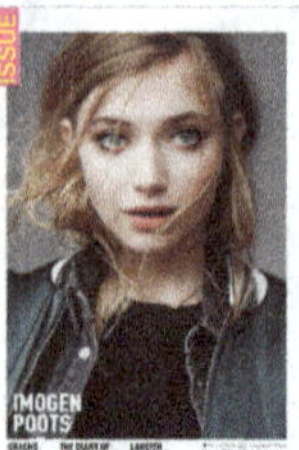

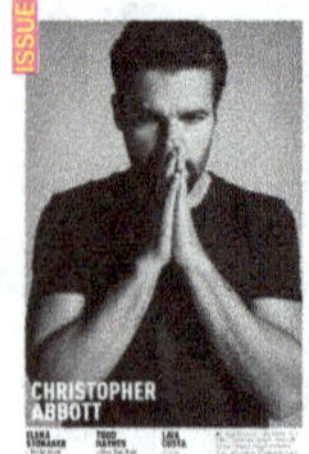

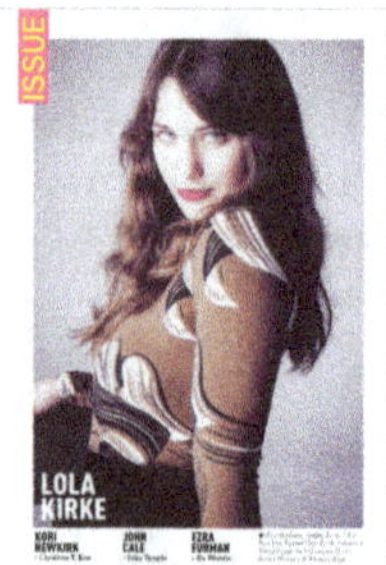

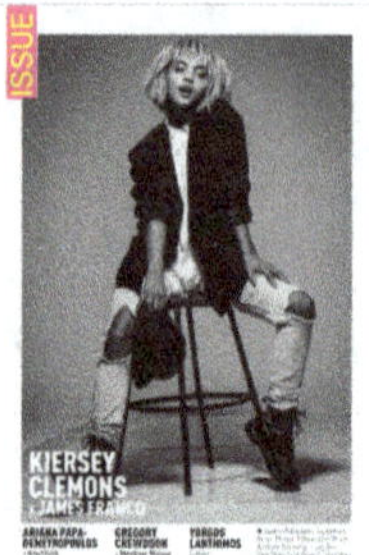

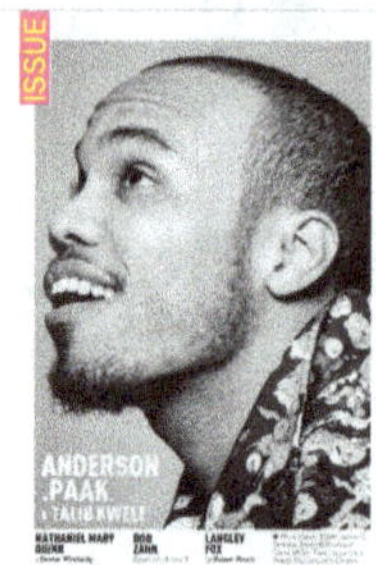

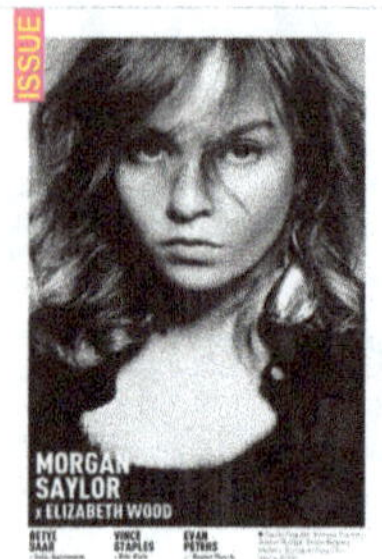

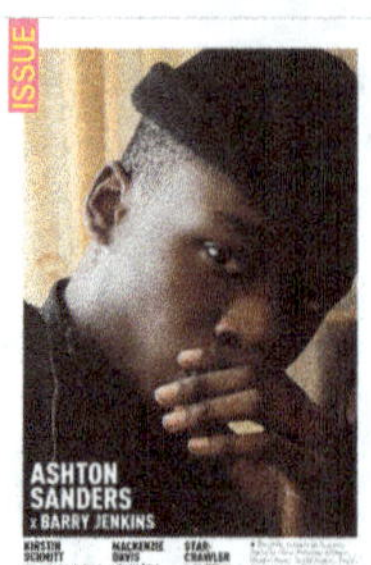

AVAILABLE ONLINE
AT ISSUEMAGAZINE.COM

FOUNDER & EDITORIAL / CREATIVE DIRECTOR Jan-Willem Dikkers **SENIOR EDITOR** Clare Shearer
COPY / EDITOR Alyson Luthi **EDITORS** Veronica Deeds, Emma Estrada
CONTRIBUTORS Destiny Anderson, Ira Chernova, Gillian Deeds, Jan-Willem Dikkers,
Kenzie Kersen, Cynda Mcelvana, Lera Pentelute, Cecilia Della Peruti, Paige Rivas,
Clare Shearer, Vivian Shih, Terra Jo Wallace

THE LATEST AND LEGENDARY IN ART, FILM, AND MUSIC

MADE IN LOS ANGELES